In Care of the State

In Care of the State

Health Care, Education and Welfare in Europe
and the USA in the Modern Era

Abram de Swaan

Oxford University Press · New York

1988

Oxford University Press

Oxford New York Toronto
Delhi Bombay Calcutta Madras Karachi
Petaling Jaya Singapore Hong Kong Tokyo
Nairobi Dar es Salaam Cape Town
Melbourne Auckland
and associated companies in
Berlin Ibadan

First published 1988 in Great Britain
by Polity Press in association with Basil Blackwell

First published 1988 in North America
by Oxford University Press, Inc.,
200 Madison Avenue, New York, New York 10016

Library of Congress Cataloging in Publication Data

Swaan, A. de.
  In care of the state.
  Bibliography: p.
  Includes index.
  1. Europe—Social policy. 2. United States—
Social policy. 3. Human services—Europe—History.
4. Human services—United States—History. 5. Welfare
state—History. I. Title.
HN373.5.S88   1988
361.6′1′094   88–19535

ISBN 0–19–520703–3 (alk. paper)

Typeset in Ehrhardt 10½ on 12 pt
by Hope Services, Abingdon
Printed in Great Britain
by T. J. Press (Padstow) Ltd.,
Padstow, Cornwall

Contents

Contents

Preface

Science begins with imagination. Academics customarily devote the first pages of their books to a wholly fictitious account of their intellectual circle and their family life. They repay their social debts with the paper currency of prefatory acknowledgments. However, the caring colleagues who in other prefaces encourage disinterestedly, scrutinize closely, criticize assiduously and contribute selflessly, in my case were mostly occupied with their own work. But when I asked some of them to read a chapter, they did, coming up with suggestions which I found as often irrelevant as useful. Quite often, someone would mention a reference – a poisoned gift which I swallowed dutifully – another article or book to search, read and abstract, one moreover which I had not come across myself, signifying that I still had no complete grasp of the literature. Since I had decided to cast my net wide and far, to cover the development of a broad range of institutions in five countries in the course of half a millennium, I had to impose limitations on the material to be used. I stayed far from the archives, concentrating instead on secondary sources and – when available – on the tertiary writings by historians and social scientists who had already imposed some degree of sociological order on the mass of monographic material. This is, therefore, a 'quaternary' work. With these restrictions my net still remains wide-mesh, but it is firmly tied. Each strand connects this work with that of other scholars, some of them dead, others alive, some of them far, others near.

Most of all, I am indebted to Norbert Elias, who in his ninety-first year is still the example of scholarship to me. My closest colleague, Johan Goudsblom, read most of the manuscript in early versions and his high standards I set myself. My colleagues of the Research Group on the

Sociogenesis of the Welfare State discussed early drafts of some chapters and helped me find the tone for the book. Sir Arthur Knight, formerly of the London School of Economics, Robert Pinker, also of the LSE, Maarten Brands, Derek Phillips and Piet de Rooy, of the University of Amsterdam, Willem Frijhoff of the Erasmus University Rotterdam all read separate chapters and provided their criticisms and comments. In the final phase, Joel Krieger greatly encouraged me and the editors at Polity Press supported me throughout the final rounds.

Of course, the remaining errors are mine, the minor ones. The major mistakes may well turn out one day to be those now shared by the paradigm community of scholars involved in debating the issues of state formation and the collectivization of care.

I have no typist or secretary to appease; technical innovation has eliminated clerical drudgery as a separate task in the division of academic labor, and has freed young women, we hope, for more gratifying tasks. But I am indebted to Marijke Jalink for her assistance.

Family life in the world of prefaces is also exemplary. The author presumes that when at work, he is sorely missed by his next of kin, and at the same time feels obliged to acknowledge their patience with him when off duty. My wife Ellen Ombre while working on her own writings, helped to protect me from other engagements for the sake of writing this work. But much of the time spent in writing was time withheld from my son Meik. He and I gave up something, and therefore it is to him that I dedicate this book.

1

Introduction

In modern societies the treatment of the sick, the teaching of the ignorant and the maintenance of the indigent have become a collective concern: the province of bureaucratic management under the control of the national state. This book deals with the collectivizing process in health care, education and welfare, but from an uncommon perspective and with an unusual scope. The perspective is that of comparative historical sociology and the theory of collective action; the discussion ranges from the dawn of modernity to the present, covering developments in Britain, France, Germany, the Netherlands and the United States.

The production of collective goods is the subject of welfare economics, where it is generally treated irrespective of its historical context. Here, the focus is on the collectivizing process as it occurred in the history of the societies studied. Historians and sociologists have studied health care, education and poor relief in their social and temporal setting, but without much regard for the dynamics of collectivization involved in the emergence of the present welfare state. This study presents a historical account, at times with some detail, but throughout in terms of a specific theoretical model of collective action.

A book like the present one relies very much on the findings of others. Its strength is not in the discovery of new data, but in the confrontation of developments in succeeding periods, various fields and different countries from which connections and similarities emerge which may have eluded more specialized authors. In the choice of countries for comparison, the availability of an adequate body of literature on the subject has been the first concern. This explains the choice of Britain, France, Germany and the United States. The Netherlands have been included because the relatively little-known literature on this country is especially accessible to this Dutchman. In the research for this book, the guiding rule has been never to investigate primary sources, to avoid monographs, to rely mostly on studies that reviewed at least one institutional field in one country over an extended period of time, to consult, whenever possible, comparative studies across fields or across countries and always to seek for the social historical or sociological perspective.

The question this study sets out to answer is: *How and why did people come to develop collective, nation-wide and compulsory arrangements to cope with deficiencies and adversities that appeared to affect them separately and to call for individual remedies?*

Two strands, each belonging to a different intellectual tradition, together lead to the answer. One relates to the concept of 'external effects', as it is used in welfare economics. In the context of the present study, the term refers to the indirect consequences of one person's deficiency or adversity for others not immediately afflicted themselves. This concept provides the link with a more formal mode of analysis of diverging, but interdependent, group interests in society. The other line of argument is connected to the historical sociology of Norbert Elias and his classical predecessors: it refers to the extension and intensification of the 'chains of human interdependence' in the course of time; the concept of 'human figurations' is central to this approach. A 'figuration' is a structured and changing pattern of interdependent human beings. This somewhat unfamiliar term is used here as a sensitizing concept, conveying both interdependence and process, referring to individual human beings and to the social entities they make up together.[1] The idea of the 'generalization of interdependency' helps to explain changing standards of behavior and modes of experience in terms of major, long-term social transformations. In this study the changing attitudes among the established in society towards the poor are explained by shifts in the balance of mutual dependency which are the result of the emergence of nation states and the rise of capitalism. In other words, welfare economics is used to analyze complex constellations of interdependency, and historical sociology to identify the operation of external effects in the actual development of societies.

State formation, the development of capitalism and the processes of urbanization and secularization which went with them, form the explanatory historical background in this study. In mutual competition, states established bureaucratic networks linking people together as taxpayers, recruits, students, patients, claimants, voters, thus shaping

2

them into citizens in the modern sense. Equally competitive, capitalist entrepreneurs organized manufacture and constituted markets which connected people in networks of production and exchange as workers and consumers. All this meant increasing interdependency and new, further-reaching external effects of one person's deficiencies and adversities upon others. The resulting conflicts inspired different group loyalties and a new awareness of the ways in which changing group interests affected one another.

The interdependence between the rich and the poor, or between the strong and the powerless, is central to the collectivizing process. In feudal times, the poor represented both danger and opportunity to the established in society: the threat of violent attack on the person and property of the rich and, at the same time, the opportunity to use the 'sturdy poor' as workers and soldiers in the power struggles among competing elites. In later phases of state formation and capitalist development, the poor were seen as a threat to public order, to labor harmony and also to public health, while at the same time they constituted a reserve of potential laborers, recruits, consumers and political supporters.

But on their own, those established in society could not ward off the threat that emanated from the poor, nor could they individually exploit the opportunities that the presence of the poor also afforded them. The external effects of poverty and its potential benefits collectively affected the established in society. And this created a dilemma familiar from welfare economics: any joint effort on the part of the rich to control the 'externalities' or to exploit the opportunities the poor offered, might also benefit those among the established ranks who had not contributed to it.[2] Thus, as the indirect consequences of poverty increasingly affected those established in society, they also intensified interdependence among the rich themselves. To the established in society, the problem of poverty represents a problem of collective action. The dynamics of the collectivizing process in poor relief, health care and education stems largely from the conflicts among the elites over the creation of collective goods and the distribution of costs among them.

The example of cholera in nineteenth-century cities may illustrate this: the outbursts of mass epidemics were soon recognized as the consequence of living conditions among the urban poor. The better-off citizens could individually decide to move to healthier quarters, which they did in great numbers. As a – largely unintended – aggregate result of individual moves, urban space was partitioned into socially more homogeneous neighborhoods, ranging from residential areas to slums. But if the well-to-do wished to prevent epidemics from spreading

3

beyond the poverty areas and paralyzing the city in its entirety, a collective effort at sanitation was still indispensable.

By the middle of the nineteenth century a consensus on the necessary measures was emerging among experts. Fresh-water supply and sewage removal were to be the remedies. But they required an immense effort and considerable rate increases, taxing the limits of existing administrative capacity and of the citizens' willingness to pay. This led to intense conflict among the urban elites.

In the newly settled, richer neighborhoods, fresh water and sewerage connections were provided to paying subscribers, a common but privately divisible good. It was not until after mainpipes had been constructed throughout the city and urban space was almost saturated by sanitation networks, that the remaining slum areas were connected, most often compulsorily and at public expense. Only then did sanitation networks become a true public good. (This is the subject of ch. 4.)

The present study attempts to synthesize historical sociology and welfare economics, but it is not eclectic. The theory of collective action is reformulated in terms of the sociogenesis of collective entities. The dilemmas of collective action are shown to be mostly of the theorists' own making. The weakness of welfare theory is not predominantly its reduction of social processes to individual choices, as its critics often contend. On the contrary, formal game models are well suited to demonstrating the interplay between social structure and individual choices. In addition, the concept of the 'unintended aggregate results' of individual actions in formal 'decisionist' theory closely corresponds to the idea of 'blind process' in historical sociology.[3] The main fault of formal theory as it stands is its inability to deal with processes – with changes over time. This reduction from dynamics to statics may be overcome in a sociogenetic approach. The logical paradox disappears in sociological analysis: a paradigm shift.[4]

Welfare economics takes for granted both the collective nature of such goods as defense – or public sanitation for that matter – and the existence of a collectivity, such as the nation or the city, which may or may not provide these goods. In the sociogenetic view, the dilemmas of collective action are a transitory phenomenon: one which belongs to an intermediate stage, when agents are already interdependent and aware of this interdependence without their actions being coordinated, yet at a higher level of integration, that of the collectivity. In the course of the collectivizing process, collective action produces both a collectivity capable of coordinating the actions of its members effectively and a collective good which corresponds to this level of integration, but can not exist apart from it.

Domestic and internal security are the textbook examples of collective goods, their defining characteristic being that no member of the collectivity can be excluded from their use. (This may tempt some to benefit without contributing, hence the necessity of compulsory taxation.) Indeed, it is natural to think of violent attacks as a threat to the entire community, to be dealt with collectively, by the police or, if they come from abroad, by the army.

Yet the notion of a collective good presupposes a collectivity to which such a good is collective. In the case of defense, the existence of a nation state which can deal more or less effectively with threats to security is taken for granted. But in fact, defense unities have emerged in the course of violent conflict, as each of the sides has forced the other to close and strengthen its ranks, in the process transforming themselves into larger and more coherent entities. Previously a threat to one family, or a single village might have been considered an adversity which concerned only that unit and hardly affected the ones not threatened at the time. As defense units grew in size and cohesion, an attack on any part of them came to be regarded as an attack on the whole, which had to be countered accordingly. This again changed the nature of violent confrontations until they assumed the character of contemporary warfare between nations, and even 'superpowers'. As the idea of a nation, one and indivisible, holds such sway over contemporary minds, it appears to be inherent in the nature of defense arrangements to be collective on a national scale. But just as there is no intrinsic collective essence in defense – after all individual human beings are maimed and killed, or inflict the damage – other provisions, such as health, education or welfare, are not in essence individual or collective.

The collectivization of defense has long since been taken for granted, because nation states have been in existence as collective-defense units for centuries. The large-scale collectivization of caring for the sick, of teaching the ignorant and of assistance in times of need, on the contrary, is a more recent development, spanning not much more than a lifetime. As a result, the collective character of health care, education and income maintenance is more controversial.

The collectivizing process may proceed by errors and illusions, as it often does, or by the intervention of a 'large actor', either a foreign usurper or a domestic initiator. But it may also come about by the gradual increase of informal control among participants, by gossip, ostracism and other forms of increasing social cohesion within groups. Effective collectivity is therefore an emergent property of social aggregates. But the process is reversible throughout, until the collectivization has proceeded to the point where all defectors may be adequately punished and even then it may dissolve again.

This may best be elucidated with the example of medieval poor relief at the parish level. The sturdy poor, who could walk, and therefore also work and fight, were feared as bandits and sometimes needed as farmhands. Moreover, they could move from one farm to another, from one hamlet to the next. Miserly farmers risked their wrath, but more generous homes were soon swamped by beggars. Their need for security and for a labor reserve prompted the rich to provide for at least some of the dispossessed. In this figuration, Christian teachings of charity functioned as a script everyone assumed to be familiar to others. Priests operated as charitable entrepreneurs, suggesting – often falsely – that one farmer's generosity would be matched by his neighbor and that avarice would be punished by damnation in the hereafter and by social disapproval in the meantime.

Sometimes a charitable equilibrium emerged: farmers could trust their peers to give in equal amounts and that together they could ostracize the miserly. Almsgiving became a highly visible and ceremonial occasion, one of the major collective events in the social life of the emerging parish community. In other words, the parish did not exist prior to, and independently of, the collective charitable fund; it was shaped in large part by the collective efforts to maintain the poor. And only as the charitable equilibrium emerged did avarice become a sin, not so much against the poor as against the parish community, and punished accordingly by peer and priestly disapproval. (This is the subject of the opening sections of ch. 2.)

Charity could persist only if one could trust one's peers to be equally charitable: that one would not remain alone – ineffective *and* destitute in the end – but that others would join in the effort. And this they might do, if only they could in turn trust their peers to do likewise. Even then, the general charity might tempt some to evade their Christian duty. Charity, too, was caught in the dilemmas of collective action: each person's virtue presupposed the virtuousness of others. Charity, therefore, is not just a personal sentiment or an individual disposition, but an expectation of similar inclinations among one's fellows.

The dilemmas of charity and relief repeated themselves once a higher level of integration was achieved.

Local voluntary charitable equilibria were essentially unstable, even at the local level. They were also continually threatened by upheavals within the larger, regional figuration, such as wars, famines and epidemics, which caused the poor to roam the countryside and threaten the food supplies of the towns. Local communities were confronted with a familiar dilemma: either feeding the poor and risking an invasion of beggars, or chasing them away and exposing the harvests in the region to plundering bands.

In the absence of an effective central coordinating agency, the dilemma was overcome through an illusion: the mistaken notion that the vagrant poor could be locked up in poorhouses and made to work for their upkeep, so that each community might admit its share of vagrants and solve the dilemma with an individual strategy, which was optimal, no matter what other towns did.

The effect of this illusion was an unstable regional near-equilibrium of local poorhouses. Large towns often took upon themselves a disproportionate share of poor relief so as to secure their supply-lines. The weak central governments tried to maintain the equilibrium by imposing distribution rules for taking in the indigent or by providing grants to the local authorities who admitted vagrants. (This is the subject matter of the later sections of ch. 2.)

The collectivization of care arrangements proceeds along three dimensions. In the course of the process, the *scale* of coping arrangements came to encompass entire nations and to include all citizens, or formally designated categories among them. The arrangements became more *collective* as their benefits to individual users became more independent of their contribution and came to depend increasingly on their condition as assessed in terms of some scheme of provisions. Finally, the arrangements were increasingly carried by the *state* or some *public* body, thus providing them with the authority necessary to exact compliance and the bureaucratic apparatus needed for their implementation.

These large-scale, collective and compulsory arrangements as remedies for deficiency and adversity developed more readily to the extent that certain conditions applied. First, *uncertainty* as to the *moment* and the *magnitude* of adversity. Second, *uncertainty* as to the *efficacy* of remedies against adversity or deficiency. This uncertainty of effect might be greater when measures had to be taken a very long time ahead, or required a sizable outlay, as for example in the case of education and pension provisions. And, third, the extent and reach of the *external effects* of adversity and deficiency upon others not directly afflicted themselves.

Uncertainty of moment and magnitude and uncertainty of effect may be managed more effectively in large-scale, collective entities. The larger and the more heterogeneous the membership becomes, the greater the chances that risks will be spread evenly and that at any moment the good fortune of many may make up for the hardship of some. But precisely these conditions, of increasing number and variety, tend to sharpen the

7

dilemmas of collective action as they impede mutual control and diminish common solidarity.

But even if uncertainty brings individuals together in a collective arrangement, this need not be compulsory. They might, for example, seek coverage against risk by means of large-scale and collective, yet voluntary, commercial insurance. But external effects are more difficult to deal with in markets or voluntary arrangements, as they are – by definition – consequences that affect others than the parties directly afflicted themselves.[5]

The intensity and scope of external effects depend on the density and extension of the social network: as the social figuration comes to include more people and their interdependence increases, the consequences of the adversity and deficiency of some of them upon others, not directly afflicted themselves, tend to increase. But this does not necessarily imply that the persons involved indeed will understand the extent and impact of these externalities. The awareness of such external effects is again a function of the social figuration in which they occur and which may be so structured as to hamper or to facilitate insight.

Although uncertainties and externalities may be managed more effectively in large-scale, collective bodies, such entities will encounter dilemmas of collective action which may only be solved by either mutual trust or compulsion. As the scope and impact of external effects expanded, the bonds of confidence had to stretch accordingly, or the agencies of compulsion had to extend their reach – and often, as more people came to trust each other, the coercion of deviants was facilitated, while such coercion in turn might ease mutual suspicion.

It is the emergent aspect of collectivities and collective goods, their historical character, that has been ignored by most formal theorists. The few formalizing scholars who have sought a confrontation with history limit themselves to a critical discussion of the grand masters of historical sociology, Marx, Weber or Elias, and do not embark upon a reading of the contemporary historical literature itself. Even Jon Elster[6] in his encounter with Marxism has stopped short of historicizing his decisionist premises.

But this book does not explicitly address theories or theorists, and it hardly contains polemics. The debate is mostly implicit, the positions adopted are justified by the plausibility of the historical interpretations based upon them.

This also applies to the debate on the role of ideas and of great men in the history of poor relief or education. The charitable teachings and saintly models of Christianity were known throughout Europe for a thousand years or more, but this does not explain why, for example, workhouses emerged in early modernity, or why elementary education began to spread among the masses from the seventeenth century onward. Religious teachings (or ideological tenets for that matter) are being revised all the time and a fully developed doctrine is rich and complex enough to justify wholly contradictory policies and actions. It is therefore inadequate to explain why one rather than another course of action was in fact adopted at a given moment. On the contrary, the sociological question should be why certain ideas gained currency in one period, while others were quietly abandoned, or stubbornly defended by dissident groups.

The established churches in France and England, for example, staunchly resisted the establishment of elementary schools by the central state with a full panoply of theological arguments. 'Metropolitan' elites, oriented toward the national state and the national market, promoted public elementary education with equal religious zeal. But then, they stood to gain from immediate access to the rural population as potential workers, consumers and taxpayers. The vested local elites held a monopoly in mediation between their traditional clientele and the political and economic center. This monopoly was also very much a matter of translating between regional and national speech, and of mediating between an illiterate clientele and a national network of communication in written messages. The battle was fought over religious and traditional values, but it also involved the opposing interests of elites within the overall communication network. Mass elementary education entailed the initiation of the rural and urban masses into the codes of national communication: the standard language, literacy, numeracy and 'the country's history' or 'national geography'. Nations and national states have never existed separately from this effort at mass education in the national codes of communication – they were in great part constituted by it. (This is the subject matter of ch. 3.)

It was only in the course of the nineteenth century that the state apparatus evolved to the stage where its own internal dynamics became a decisive element in the collectivizing process. Social security was not the achievement of the organized working classes, nor the result of a capitalist conspiracy to pacify them. As in previous episodes, a class struggle was involved, but the familiar alliances were reversed.

The initiative for compulsory, nationwide and collective arrangements to insure workers against income loss came from reformist politicians and administrators in charge of state bureaucracies. Such activist regimes needed support either from large employers or from reformist union leaders. And everywhere they had to overcome opposition from middle-class entrepreneurs who resisted big business, big government and big unions and who relied on private accumulation as the means to provide against adversity or for old age. Social security, on the other hand, is based upon the collective and compulsory accumulation of transfer capital. It entails guaranteed benefits to all wage-earners: a series of legally enforceable claims to income transfers, which themselves are not transferable, but which may be assessed at their expected and capitalized value as a kind of property – 'transfer property'.

The accumulation of transfer capital represents a collectivized alternative to the providential functions of private savings. This is what made it so hard to accept for the independent, propertied middle classes and so suitable a program for a coalition of an activist regime with large employers or unions or with both. (This is the subject of ch. 6.)

In the course of several centuries, the collectivization of health care, education and income maintenance has transformed the relations between people and thus changed their modes of interaction and experience. Where no compulsory and collective arrangements existed, a stranger's adversity and deficiency held an immediate appeal to the beholder's pity and generosity, which he might then heed or reject. But in the course of the collectivization of care, such misery was felt to appeal less to personal intervention and was increasingly considered as a matter to be left to specific institutions, which then deserved support. In recent times a 'social consciousness' came to prevail: an awareness of the generalization of interdependence which links all members within a national collectivity, coupled with an abstract sense of responsibility which does not impel to personal action, but requires the needy in general to be taken care of by the state and out of public tax funds.

The collectivizing process of care arrangements has also levelled out the rare peaks of affluence and the many abysses of misery in most individual lives. It has also made people a little more equal to one another in material wealth, and with respect to what they know and how they act. It has taken some of the tragedy, some of the magic and much of religion out of life. The constraints of everyday existence have increased as a consequence of this collectivizing process and many of these are 'social constraints toward self-constraint'. In the process people have learned to be more careful with time, money, goods and their own bodies; to take into consideration more desires of more people more often; to plan further into the future; in brief, they have become more civilized in the sense Norbert Elias attaches to the term. On the other hand, the collectivizing process still operates very much through external compulsion and does not rely on the self-steering capacities which human beings may possess: education continues to be imposed on children and social-security taxes on workers – the juxtaposition is not fortuitous.

New mediating elites have emerged in and around the extending state apparatus. The teaching body has never been able to gain the prestige or autonomy of a professional elite, but with state support it has succeeded in imposing a pedagogic regime upon the population for an ever-extending part of juvenile existence. Medical men have been successful in combining state protection and professional status in a medical regime which subjects almost everyone to continual screening and selection procedures and absorbs growing numbers of chronically sick and aging people into 'total' institutions. The medical example has been emulated, but never equalled, by other professionalizing groups, such as social workers: a welfare regime extends over the mass of claimants and potential beneficiaries of social security. Legal counsellors and fiscal consultants establish their regime over widening circles of laymen.

The medical profession achieved its present position through a 'reluctant imperialism.' Individual, enterprising doctors found new opportunities in socially controversial fields, where their intervention could reduce social conflicts to 'medical problems' – with the tacit complicity of the parties involved. The medical establishment, fearing internal dividedness, followed its vanguard hesitantly. In this manner, the medical profession was drawn into these new fields as much as it pushed its way in. (This is the subject of ch. 7.)

The contemporary state is very much the product of the collectivization of health care, education and income maintenance. And modern life, in its most intimate and pervasive aspects, is shaped by this collectivizing process. The recent welfare backlash and budget cuts affect the welfare society only superficially, even if they cause much individual distress and institutional upheaval. Cut-backs, also, are central interventions and in the end they may even contribute to centralization.

At present, the most pressing political problem is not the financing of collective institutions, but the ever-increasing control of the central state and its conglomerate of bureaucracies over more and more intimate aspects of life. With hindsight, it is clear that the nineteenth-century movement of small cooperative funds under self-management was doomed to failure: autonomous and voluntary associations exclude the neediest as 'bad risks' and when the state supports them, its aid tends to profit the more alert who need it least. (This is the subject of ch. 5.) Yet it may well be that the collection and distribution of money transfers is handled best by the central state – for reasons of distributive justice – but that the adjudication of cases and the administration of human services is better left to small, self-managing cooperative bodies of citizens.

11

The collectivizing process has not run its course; there has never been a single, necessary path for it to take, no hidden hand or divine plan to guide it. If it has developed along similar lines in different countries, this is due to the similar operation of capitalist competition and rivalry between states. The dilemmas of collective action are still with us, as pressing as ever, and operating on an even higher plane: with national states as the relatively autonomous, but interdependent, agents, aware of their interdependence, but as yet without a supranational collectivity to coordinate their actions effectively. The problems of poor relief, education and the sanitation of a polluted environment continue on a world scale.

Plan of the book

The subject matter of this book is structured along three dimensions: chronological, comparative and institutional. So as to organize it into a linear – and finite – narrative, each chapter is devoted to a critical episode in the development of an institutional field: poor relief, education or health care. These episodes are treated in roughly chronological order. Throughout the book, developments in various countries are discussed together; only in chapter 3, on Education, and 6, on Social Security, have separate sections been devoted to a discussion of events in each country, so as to show the dynamics of political conflict in the separate national systems.

Chapter 2 deals with the emergence of a charitable equilibrium at the parish level in the late Middle Ages and the establishment of poorhouses in early modernity. The subject of chapter 3 is the emergence of national communication networks and the spread of compulsory elementary education at a national level from the eighteenth century through the nineteenth. Chapter 4 addresses the problems of urban health and the establishment of citywide sewerage and water-supply systems from the mid-nineteenth century on. The rise and demise of workers' mutual funds in the late nineteenth century is the theme of chapter 5. Chapter 6 is devoted to the enactment of nationwide, compulsory social-security schemes from the end of the nineteenth century until the 1930s. The concluding chapter, 7, combines these themes in a summary and a discussion of developments in welfare states from 1945 to the present. Next comes a discussion of the transformation of the middle classes and the effects of bureaucratization and professionalization upon the means of cognitive orientation in everyday life (protoprofessionalization), on affect management (the civilizing process) and on moral stances (the emergence of social consciousness).

2

Local Charity, Regional Vagrancy and National Assistance

No matter how the poor have been defined throughout the ages, they were the ones who had less of whatever it takes to survive. Some of them worked to earn a living and needed more, many among them were without means of subsistence and lacked most. But always and everywhere the condition of the poor depended on that of their counterpart, the rich; or rather, the poorer depended on the richer for survival, the richer on the poorer to maintain their advantage.

1 Poverty, surplus and property

Where no surplus existed and everybody lived under conditions of subsistence, whether harsh or abundant, there was no poverty, just the precarious satisfaction of limited needs: 'Poverty is not a certain small amount of goods, nor is it just a relation between means and ends; above all it is a relation between people. Poverty is a social status. As such it is the invention of civilization.'[1] Resources are divided up as they are acquired, fairly or unfairly. Nothing is accumulated and nothing left to be divided among outsiders or in times of hardship.

Only when stocks and savings are kept, the danger of envy, beggary and robbery arises. Then the institution of property emerges as an amalgam of rights and defensive measures to ward off the claims and threats of others. The concept of poverty is thus doubly tied to the notion of property, implying at once the existence of a surplus and exclusion from it. What constitutes a surplus is a matter of sentiment and judgment for those concerned, and these depend again on the relations prevailing between those who have and those who have not.

Property is a defense against the poor and it perpetuates their poverty; but as soon as property is legitimated in terms that are also meaningful to those who possess less or nothing (and the legitimation is intended for them in the first place – the owners do not need it as much), their exclusion must be justified. No meaningful justification can avoid defining some form of entitlement for the poor also. A moral order that encompasses the poor, whom it must persuade of the rightness of property, in justifying their exclusion also establishes their claim to part of the surplus. The same god that forbids stealing also demands charity. A society that pretends to reward achievement must also compensate for lack of opportunity. Thus the existence of property and poverty imposes upon the possessors an obligation to give to the poor or to help them improve their condition.

The idea of poverty is thus doubly paradoxical: it refers to want in the presence of surplus and it refers to entitlement under conditions of exclusion. A discourse on poverty must explain at once this exclusion: the existence of property rights; and its limits: the entitlement of those who are in need.

The problem of the poor is to stay alive; the problem of poverty is a problem for the rich – the problem of distributing part of the surplus without altering the rules of its accumulation and conservation. In this perspective the solution is to distribute enough of the surplus to guarantee the long-term working capacity and reproduction of the working force, to pacify and terrify those who might attempt to change the rules of accumulation, and to prevent the ills from poverty – whether through crowding, contagion or discontent – from affecting the ranks of the well-to-do.

The dialectics of poverty and property already imply a measure of structured interdependence between those who have much and those who have little. Without such mutual ties they might have ignored one another or clashed in incidental raids in the way of primitive tribes living in a state of 'fragmented anarchy'.[2] But once people begin to settle in a common territory, to develop resources and build up stocks, they develop mutual dependencies which are rendered asymmetric, but in no way diminished, by the fact of unequal access to such opportunities.

The institution of property also constitutes a continuous defense against claims and raids that may be carried out by other rich; the concept of poverty adds complimentary notions of obligation and deference to this system of exclusion. Given a figuration of material surplus, of political authority and compliance, of military and economic domination and subordination, the problem of poverty exists as the problem of distributing a minimal amount of the social surplus without altering the patterns of dependency and exclusion which define the rich on the one hand, the poor on the other and all others in between.

What complicates matters is that the rich, wishing to protect their position with respect to the poor and to their peers, do not usually act in concert. All of them would much rather have their fellows take care of the poor: to the propertied classes the problem of poverty is in the last analysis a problem of collective action.

Although the well-off have often publicly decried the poor as profiteers, in private they may have accused their own kind of an equally bad sort of profiteering: allowing others to spend a good part of their resources on the poor while holding on to their own wealth and enjoying the benefits of social harmony for free.

To coordinate their efforts and exert convincing mutual pressure on their own kind, the rich needed rules for the partial redistribution of surplus wealth. Some sort of consensus was indispensable, since any system of voluntary distribution requires all benefactors to trust that their peers will act likewise. One charitable benefactor alone would soon find himself or herself overwhelmed by hordes of supplicants and doomed to bankruptcy if he or she were not soon to limit his or her generosity. Even holy men such as the wandering bishops of the early Middle Ages would surround themselves with dogs to ward off the obtrusive poor, a custom prohibited by the Council of Mâcon in 585.[3]

The fact that the rich needed some confidence in their peers, and some rules to abide by, does not imply that they usually did trust one another or that they always found such rules, or that, having found them, they kept them. But in general, when confronted with a sufficient number of visibly suffering poor or with threatening bands of the indigent, the established classes did realize that a coordinated effort was required – they found it much harder to persuade everyone in their ranks to participate in it and to agree upon a distribution of burdens.

2 Disability, proximity and docility

In order to maintain the exclusion implicit in the institution of property and at the same time to mitigate its consequences, rules for the redistribution of the surplus had to be designed and categories of poor people entitled to some form of assistance had to be defined. Such classifications were implicitly applied all along and had become a widespread subject of debate by the sixteenth and seventeenth centuries.[4] Of themselves they do not say much about the actual living conditions of the poor in all their variegation, but they do reveal much of what the rich thought about them.

The three criteria implicit in almost all classifications of poverty from very early on are *disability*, *proximity* and *docility*.

Disability refers to the incapacity to make a living through one's own efforts. This dimension constitutes 'need', the other two 'entitlement'. It is therefore the necessary condition, albeit rarely sufficient by itself.

Strictly speaking, no one can take care of himself or herself once a division of labor has developed; the best one can do is to make others take care in exchange for efforts of one's own.[5] The criterion can therefore only be interpreted within the context of the modes of production and exchange within a given society, and against the background of changing labor conditions. At this general level, disability refers to the perceived incapacity to perform any kind of activity that would create a socially valid claim to someone else's resources and stocks, or to his efforts. There is an implicit notion of reciprocity in all these exchanges, be they monetary or in kind. Disability, then, refers to the incapacity to deliver an equivalent as part of a reciprocal exchange. Deference and gratitude, prayers and blessings may be the rewards that the poor can bestow, or, negatively, abstinence from violence, offense, curses or spells.[6] Thus, there may exist a moral or a metaphysical economy which restores the reciprocity lacking at the material level. This goes to show both the socially constructed nature of seemingly factual categories such as disability, and the human tendency to construct interpretations that compensate for relational asymmetry.

Where agriculture predominated, an able-bodied person was one who could cultivate the land or assist the peasants in their work and earn a share of the produce in money or in kind. Even this criterion allows for a wide variety of skills, from herding – which may sometimes require little force or agility – to plowing or harvesting, which is often strenuous work, requiring a fully functioning adult body.

The second criterion refers to *proximity*. It defines a social area of accountability. The poor within it are charges of the rich, those outside of it are someone else's burden or no one's. Proximity may refer to both *kinship* and *residence*. Kinship is a major criterion of obligation up to this day – for example, in the mutual duty of assistance between parents and children, sometimes extending to grandchildren and first cousins. In small nomadic and early agrarian communities, it may have been the only criterion, but as sedentary agriculture developed and members of the same family no longer always lived closely together, it was supplemented and partly replaced by residence. Even the elementary criterion of proximity precludes one solution to poverty: simply chasing the poor away. Residence as a criterion permits the assigning of every poor person to a community of assistance so that responsibilities will be completely demarcated. This, of course, was the idea behind the famous Elizabethan Poor Laws and the edicts that preceded them on the continent, such as that of Charles V for the Low Countries (1531), or Ferdinand I for the Austrian Empire (1552), John George for Brandenburg (Prussia), or the Parliament of Paris (1535).[7] In essence, the criterion of residence had already been established by the Second Council of Tours (576): '*Ut unaquaeque civitas pauperes et egenos incolas alimentis congruentibus pascat secundum vires*' – that every community feed the indigenous poor and needy appropriately, according to its resources.[8] And even then, the bishops – gathered as a continental council – added a motivation which transcended the scope of the single isolated village economies of those times, but would become predominant at the dawn of European Modernity: '*quo fiet ut ipsi pauperes per civitates alias non vagentur*' – so that the poor will not roam from one community to another.[9]

Early absolute princes attempted to enforce local care for needy residents by combining it with the prohibition of vagrancy, of beggary and of almsgiving, and with a sharp demarcation between deserving and undeserving poor. This curious mixture of repression and relief characterizes social policy at the beginning of modern times.[10] Its failure would haunt Europe and America for many centuries.

There is a third criterion, disguised often as a moral or criminal judgment: *docility*. It refers to the degree of passivity or activity with which the poor attempt the redistribution of the surplus once they are excluded from it. At one extreme, there were the *pauvres honteux*, the decent and embarrassed needy who hid their misery and asked for nothing, accepting charity without begging for it.[11] In actual fact, this may often have been a quite active, but subtle, strategy of making covert claims for care and alms. A shade more active were those poor who did go out to beg, drawing attention to their miserable state and often exaggerating it ostentatiously.[12] Through subtle shades of comportment and expression a plea for alms might change into a demand, into a curse upon the miser, or a covert threat of attack, robbery and arson. There were also those who not only threatened, but actually did steal and destroy. At the extreme, there were the poor who united in bands to terrorize the peasants of the region. These shades of passivity and activity, of docility and rebelliousness, are rendered in sixteenth- and seventeenth-century language in moral terms, increasingly pejorative, from the *pauvres impotens et honteux* to the *coquins vagabonds*.

The 'weakly' poor tried to evoke pity, but often also fear. The hideous leper made as if about to touch – and contaminate – the passers-by. The

17

wretched old woman might whisper blessings, but if rebuked, hiss curses, or cast spells. The mutilated beggar would stumble close, smelling foul and soiling those he touched. Even children could threaten to reveal still more hideous sores than they were already exposing, and they might scoff and scold the bystanders, follow and embarrass them, or steal what had been refused. A wretch could put to shame the avarice and the callousness of those who would not give by exposing them to everyone's attention. The weak preferred to beg in public and with grand display, in squares or near churches. What was a matter of moral sentiment to the public was a question of technique for those who made their living by begging: attract attention, evoke pity, threaten exposure and, covertly, damage. The art of begging has a long tradition and its teachings are being recovered by social historians such as Aydelotte, Cobb, Geremek, Küther, Salgado and others. For those of the poor who would not wait shamefacedly at home for the dole and who considered their indigence as a kind of professional qualification, exposing and exaggerating their misery was the only way to earn their daily bread.[13]

The weak might also be dangerous; it does not take much stamina to steal from unattended fields or to pick from the orchards, milk a stray goat or worse – eternal fear – take revenge by setting fire to the barns or poisoning the wells.[14] But the least docile, the most active, were the able-bodied vagrants who united in bands, terrorizing an entire region. These bandits met some secret sympathy among the rural poor, as rebels; but it was the threat they posed, lasting deep into the nineteenth century in Europe and the United States, and here and there even into this century, that provoked many of the measures that contributed to the gradual transformation of local poor relief into a national system of correction and assistance.

The three dimensions of disability, proximity and docility interacted. But disability remained the major criterion, as it determined the options of the poor on the other two continua.

An able-bodied adult could work for a living, and whoever could work could also walk and fight. This was the fundamental equation of employment, vagrancy and rebellion. The fact that a person could walk made him into a potential vagabond, one who might leave the community, be ousted from it or intrude upon it as a wandering stranger. But such a 'sturdy' person was also capable of working and might therefore be put to good use, or refused relief as someone who needed no help. And whoever could work or walk, could fight and steal, rob, rape, burn and plunder. Such people had to be either appeased or confined, chased away or killed. Conversely, people who roamed the highways were suspected of being beggars or thieves; also if they professed a trade, as knife-grinders, jugglers, soothsayers, they could rarely make their living in that manner.[15] Even a plea for alms was often more a demand, exacted as a tribute, which few dared to refuse.[16]

It follows that those having no residence for any length of time had to be able to wander, had to be sturdy.[17] And it also follows that the more active – that is, the more reprehensible – demeanor was available only to these able-bodied poor. Until three or four generations ago, bands of vagrants were a common and frightening presence in the countryside, threatening travellers and terrorizing isolated peasants, continually harassed, but rarely eradicated, by the state's police forces. They formed a culture of their own with its intricate hierarchies and distinctions, its loyalties and codes. This underclass has often been quite numerous, although its numbers may have been exaggerated by contemporaries. The weak poor could only maintain themselves in their wanderings if they were believed to be potent in magic, frightful sorcerers and accursers: the spiritual gift – by attribution – might compensate for physical weakness.[18] Belief in witchcraft thus may have saved many more lives than it took, since it prompted people to give alms to elderly, wandering women.[19] But on the whole the strongest and the most desperate went to join the gangs of bandits hiding in the woods.[20] Küther considers these vagabonds in seventeenth- and eighteenth-century Germany a distinct social stratum, at times counting up to 20 per cent of the population, and sufficiently organized to confront state power time and again.[21]

At the dawn of modern times there were in Europe at one extreme the invalid, resident, passive poor, entitled to assistance on all three counts and, at the other end, the wandering, active and valid poor, to be combated three times over. Between the decent poor, on the one hand, and the sturdy vagrants on the other, there were a number of intermediate categories, as figure 2.1 illustrates.

Most tragic perhaps were the invalid poor without any residence. If they were few and docile, leading and begging their way, they might encounter some kind soul to help them on. But when they were many as a result of famine or plague, these silent, miserable throngs of sickly, starving peasants, driven off their land by catastrophe, became the object of stunned pity at first, and then of hatred and fear as their ranks swelled beyond help and they themselves became desperate and numerous enough to invade the towns and plunder the harvests. 'The permanent confrontation with the migrating possessionless became an obsession for the "right-minded" Europeans . . . One looks in vain for some trace of understanding, some vague feeling of sympathy.'[22] Often, the walls

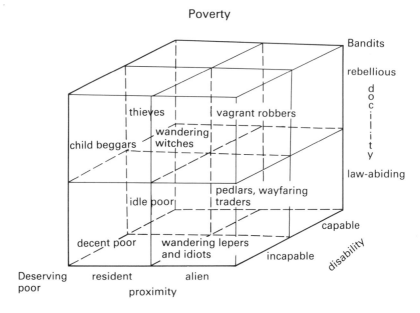

Figure 2.1 The three dimensions of poverty in early modern Europe

served as much to defend the towns against them as against enemy armies. Their ghost has now receded to the margin of European consciousness, only to be revived in images from faraway lands where famine and disease still haunt the populace: pictures on the screens of the settled population of the world's core, evoking humanitarian and gratuitous commiseration, solicitude hardly, fear not at all.

The invalid poor who had settled in the villages or found their way to the towns depended on local charity. As long as they were docile they were the first to receive alms. If they became unruly, they were easily controlled in small communities, but not so in the cities, where they constituted a reservoir of beggars overflowing into a pool of petty crime, theft and prostitution.[23]

There were of course also the able-bodied poor, living off the common lands in the countryside, or living in the towns, the *oisifs*, the idle, bearers of all the vices associated with city life. As resident poor, they were visible and exploitable. If they were also able-bodied, they were considered dangerous and reprehensible for whatever they undertook to improve their lot, unless it was not work for a wage: they were also the perennial object of concern and reform. Since they could walk, they might become vagabonds at any time, and many vagabonds who found the opportunity to settle joined their ranks.

The dimensions of disability, residence and docility allow a first and general characterization of the various forms of poverty, but they are not sufficient for a complete classification of its variegated manifestations from the early Middle Ages to the present times; they do, however, correspond to fundamental distinctions made by the authorities between the deserving and the dangerous poor.

3 Local charitable systems and the problem of collective action

Wherever sedentary agriculture developed, relatively durable relations of ownership emerged. The agrarian form of life almost always led to exclusive use of part of the land, exclusive claims to livestock, the use of one's own durable tools, and the availability of a food surplus, if only as sowing-seed for the next season. This rather exclusive disposition over livestock, land, tools and stocks had to be defended against the greed of others.[24] The Tenth Commandment contains a precise inventory of early agricultural property, not to be coveted: 'thy neighbour's house . . . thy neighbour's wife, or his manservant, or his maidservant, or his ox, or his ass, or anything that is thy neighbour's'.[25]

Among the possessors agreements emerged to respect each other's property – mutual obligations, or rather, a non-aggression pact. But property was also to be defended against the dispossessed in the community. This was done with preaching and admonition, if possible through enclosure and exclusion, if necessary with manslaughter and murder.

Such may not have been the exception, but it was not the rule either: the care of the poor was a Christian duty. It is customary to describe this care in terms of individual, altruistic motivations, as an affair between two parties, the charitable and the beneficiary, the giver and the receiver of alms. In fact, from early on care of the poor was the object of collective action and served a collective good.

In sedentary agricultural society, with its relatively enduring relations of property and exclusion, the owners and the disowned are tied together in a complementary relationship. The maintenance of these relations of entitlement and exclusion serve the common interest of the propertied within a given domain: the poor who could walk might go from one farm to another. They were potentially useful as workers, possibly dangerous as robbers or incendiaries, and both their usefulness and their dangerousness did not concern an individual peasant, but all those farms within walking distance.[26] In the confrontation between settled peasants and paupers, the latter would attempt to invoke at once commiseration and, covertly, fear. The peasants might follow their sense of obligation and charity and also try to ward off these vague threats. Christian doctrine contained a script for the management of such encounters which was known to both parties and to which both referred. These were the bilateral aspects of almsgiving.

But charity had other functions which concerned the peasant community as a whole. Charitable giving might keep the poor from rebellion and crime. It could prevent them from starving and falling prey to diseases that were contagious to the rest of the community. That may not always have been understood, but it was sensed in magical representations of uncleanliness and contamination. Even the invalid poor were to be feared, because of their maledictions and sorcery which had to be warded off by the practice of Christian virtue. The first collective function of charity was therefore the abatement of the threat represented by the poor.

The able-bodied poor also formed a reserve labor force, to be employed according to the season or the size of the harvest. A peasant community that allowed its sturdy poor to die off in the winter months would be short of hands in spring. Maintenance of this reserve army was therefore also a common interest with collective aspects.[27]

Moreover, poor relief might function as a form of insurance against future adversity for the settled peasants themselves. Most of the invalid poor were orphans and widows, elderly or handicapped. The fate that befell them might also be in store for the well-to-do peasant and his kin: '*hodie mihi, cras tibi*'. Finally, alms had the magical function of placating fate.

Peasants who would not contribute to charity might still enjoy the relative peace and order bought by the gifts of others. They too might hire in spring some of the poor who had survived the winter months on the handouts from other peasants. In this sense, collective action by the rich created a collective good from which all peasants profited, whether they had contributed to it or not. The security brought about by charity was very much an 'indivisible good' from which no one in the village could be easily excluded. To some degree this also applied to the maintenance of a labor reserve: even peasants who had not paid to maintain the poor could hire them when the season came. It applies much less to charity as a mutual insurance arrangement, since the survivors of a miserly peasant could be excluded from the dole in retribution.

Charity thus brought about a good, indivisible in important aspects, which no peasant could create on his own, while it could still be realized if some refused to collaborate. These were the conditions that made for the dilemmas of collective action as they applied to community charity.

Charity was a form of altruistic behavior *par excellence*: the sacrificing of money or goods for the sake of others; moreover it was a form of action that profited not only the receivers, but also the collectivity of possessors as a whole. While this beneficence may therefore be conceived of as a bilateral relation between the giver and the receiver, it must also be understood in the context of collective action on the part of the providers for the sake of collective interests, such as defense against threats and the maintenance of a labor reserve.

As sedentary agriculture and village communities became the predominant form of life throughout Western Europe from the ninth century on, mutual arrangements for the maintenance of the poor gradually emerged among the settled peasants in every intermediate form from individual almsgiving to compulsory levies for communal assistance. Whenever peasant communities could exist in relative peace and security, that is after the period of the great migrations, systems of caring for the poor developed with a more or less proportional distribution of burdens and a level of maintenance more or less sufficient to keep the poor alive.[28] That the poor remained poor nevertheless meant that the possessors succeeded in protecting their land, tools and stocks and in establishing more or less stable relations of ownership. This stability was, of course, also the outcome of military protection and pacification by feudal rulers, who usually left the peasants free to manage their own affairs, such as the care of the poor among themselves, as long as rents were duly paid.[29]

In the circumstances that prevailed in large parts of Europe between the ninth and fourteenth centuries, collective charitable systems might develop in peasant communities. The established members of the community contributed to a number of collective provisions for their 'own poor', without compulsion or taxation from a third party. The historical reconstruction of these arrangements is hampered, because what little has been documented about them was written down by clerics who had their own role and vision within these charitable arrangements.

The poor, like the settled peasants, had rights to the communal grounds. They could build a cabin, graze their animals, collect food and fuel on the lands that belonged to the undivided estate of the community. For the rest, care of the poor was allotted proportionally to the farmers of the village. From early on it was the local cleric's task to see to the proper exercise of the Christian duties of feeding and sheltering the poor by the established peasants.[30]

The simplest form of caring for the poor consisted in every farm allowing a proportionate number of needy to eat at the table or to sleep in the barn. But even this presupposed some consensus about the proper

23

share for each farm. As the church became established in the peasant communities, clerics would make collections and distribute alms to the poor, usually in kind – wheat or bread or beer, for example. Here and there, mostly in or near towns, hospitals were founded, where vagrants and orphans, the aged and the starving, the sick or the mad, were admitted. Such foundations were maintained with gifts and legacies, operated by lay brothers and, especially, sisters of mercy.[31] By then, the care of the poor had been institutionalized to some degree, books were being kept and the first complaints about ill-management and selfish expenditures by the regents and caretakers appeared in the records.[32] In the process, clerical charity became increasingly ritualized. Alms and donations were earmarked for special occasions, specific dishes were to be doled out at particular celebrations, and alms were more and more reserved for a ceremonial list of persons, quite irrespective of their condition, often by right of birth: the 'immatriculated' or *marguillers*.[33]

The care of the poor in medieval peasant communities remained rudimentary and, at least in part, voluntary. The church tithe did increasingly become a compulsory levy and was, in theory and in part, intended for alms.[34] But additional gifts and donations for distributions and hospitals remained voluntary. The theological meaning of this voluntariness was that only a gift from the fullness of one's heart counted as truly charitable and could contribute to the salvation of one's soul.[35] Its economic function may have been to spare farmers and craftsmen a fixed payment and to allow them to adapt their contributions to the changing proceeds of enterprise. The church and the feudal lords, on their part, found it difficult enough to collect their rents and tithes and hesitated to use their means of coercion for the sake of the poor also.

In the course of the thirteenth century, lay charities of a collective character sprang up at the parish level from Spain and Italy to the Low Countries, collecting the 'common alm' in the *table des pauvres*, managed by the local notables and supervised by the parish clergy and the communal authorities. Voluntary charitable systems also emerged in medieval towns, again with roughly the same threefold function of security, maintenance of a labor reserve and mutual assistance.[36] Guilds, fraternities (*confréries*) and sodalities instituted funds in aid of their 'own' poor.[37] Often, clerics and ecclesiastical foundations were charged with collections and distributions. The dole of alms attracted professional beggars from far and near, who made a living for themselves at the expense of the local 'decent' poor. In late-medieval towns begging and, equally, almsgiving were prohibited time and again, while the valid poor were ordered to work and assistance was promised to the invalid needy.

Fischer concludes: 'From early on, it was not only justice for the necessitous beggars that was at stake, but also the protection of the citizenry from those beggars, especially from those who had been classified as capable of work and excluded from the dole.'[38] None of these precepts carried much effect for lack of administrative capability, which would allow the maintenance of the decent poor, while excluding the able, but workshy, poor, and also because there was usually no employment to be found for the valid poor.

In late-medieval towns, too, collective charitable systems developed, based on voluntary contributions: 'there was no general poor tax.'[39] Even if royal edicts prohibited begging, forbade the poor to leave their place of settlement and ordered the townships to maintain them, they did not impose compulsory levies.[40]

Clearly, even if the poor were usually left to their fate, if they were not actually chased away, a panoply of voluntary and collective charitable arrangements did emerge throughout Western Europe in the late Middle Ages. This will hardly surprise those historians who explain human institutions by referring to the religious doctrine of the times. They are left to account for all those cases – the vast majority – in which Christian teaching did not persuade the believers to provide for the poor. But voluntary collective action does, in its turn, confront social scientists with a problem. How were the dilemmas of collective action overcome?

Welfare economists, and more recently neo-Darwinian ethologists, have tried to solve the paradoxes of 'altruism'. They have achieved a satisfactory explanation of 'kinship altruism' and of 'reciprocal altruism', in which the recipient of the sacrifice is clearly identifiable.[41]

None of these approaches, however, has produced an adequate explanation of altruistic behavior in groups, i.e. of the surrender of individual chances of survival or economic gain, for the sake of an advantage that accrues to all within a given collectivity, regardless of their own contribution.[42]

But these theories of group altruism and of collective action begin by postulating as the unit of analysis, i.e. as the actor, the smallest constituting element: the individual economic agent, or even the single 'selfish gene' as Dawkins has called it.[43] They then confront a paradox when the concept of collectivity or group is introduced into the argument.

So as to avoid these paradoxes, the analysis of collective action, for human society at least, must proceed in terms of a 'figuration' of people, bound together in a structured process of competition and interdependence. The information, resources, preferences and strategies of the human beings that make up this figuration are transformed as the figuration itself changes, mostly as an unintended result of their interactions. If grasped in these terms, the dilemmas of collective action may be understood as a transitional phenomenon, as a phenomenon which occurs in the process of transition from a collection of interdependent, but uncoordinated, human beings to a coordinated association which may effectively impose its policies upon the constituent members. A similar process may occur at higher levels of integration, where the constituent elements are, for example, villages or towns, capable of acting in a coherent and goal-directed manner, involved in the process of coordinating their actions at a regional, or even a national, level. And such a process may again be observed among nations in a world context.

It is in this transition from uncoordinated interdependence to enforceable coordination that the dilemmas of collective action occur. This enforcement may proceed through any kind of sanction – physical, monetary, religious, magical and so forth – and may be imposed by some central agency or by the collectivity in its entirety. But once the transitional nature of the problem is recognized, it ceases to be a paradox and turns into a sociological, rather than a logical, question.

The problems of charitable collective action on the part of the well-to-do in a community toward the poor cannot be understood on the basis of individual, goal-directed actions alone or from collective functions only; let alone by postulating a blind mechanism of selection favoring those entities that have achieved effective adaptations, as biologists usually do and historians or sociologists are wont to assume implicitly, when ascribing the emergence and survival of institutions to their successful adaptation, without explaining how such institutional adaptation was achieved by the human beings involved in it.

The problems of collective action, for instance in charity, emerge and disappear again because the *expectations* that people entertain about each other change with the relations in which they stand to one another. At this point *false* expectations may play a catalytic role: if they spread widely enough, they may well fulfill themselves, as Robert K. Merton has argued, elaborating an idea of W. I. Thomas.[44] Thus, if mutual distrust is general, it will lead to a refusal to participate in a collective endeavor: it turns out to be self-confirming. But if for some reason the expectation takes hold among some people that most will be ready for mutual collaboration, then this may inspire others with the confidence that collective action has a chance of success.[45] And even then, participants may decide again to desert the collective effort whenever this suits them better.

In the case of medieval poor relief the solution came from the Christian faith, but in a different manner than the believers believed.

The church preached brotherly love and taught that the wages of charity were the salvation of the soul in the hereafter: 'To him that giveth shall be given.' It was not even necessary that this message was believed by all, it was necessary that most people believed that others believed it.

At this point, the local clerics functioned as entrepreneurs in charitable affairs: they initiated, admonished and, above all, provided the occasions for visible and mutually inspectable acts of charity. They succeeded in making virtue public, even ostentatious. One person could know if the one next door was giving, and how much; those who shirked their charitable duties were confronted by their neighbors, despised, hated and damaged in every which way.[46] This public quality of charity and the corresponding social control set in motion a process of collective sanctions, the rewarding of duty and the punishment of negligence.

Public charity also became a matter of honor. The countless legacies doling out alms to the poor served also to honor the deceased and to increase the standing of their descendants in the community. Thus, a competition in liberality might ensue, in which benefactors made an economic sacrifice, but in doing so won honor for themselves above others, whereas the profiteer (no expression for this role exists that does not denote dishonor) lost esteem. Apparently, several forms of competition may proceed in human society, sometimes even at the same time: for money or wealth, but also for honor or prestige, or glory in battle.

Here another phenomenon appears, largely ignored in the theory of collective action, in which the collectivity is accepted as a given fact: the collectivity is itself, in part, the result of collective action. Thus, in their defense against foreign invaders, peasants united into a defensive community and developed methods of warfare that required collective action. Once having formed such firm associations, they took an assault on one of their number as an attack on everyone, and the enemy, learning to count upon a collective response, would not attack before amassing the numbers to match this defense, thereby necessitating, in turn, that the defense community maintain unity in its ranks.

In the case of poor relief, collective charitable effort also led to further community formation and impelled new forms of collective action: the relative security that came from pacifying the poor facilitated free movement and a more intensive community life. This in turn might prompt additional collective initiatives. At some point, one person's refusal to give was no longer considered as just individual callousness toward a particular poor person, but came to be experienced as an affront to the sense of community upon which the collective charitable system was built.

In conclusion: the collectivity was not a given fact, but grew out of collective action, which in turn became more feasible as mutual confidence in an increasingly effective collectivity grew.

Through the interaction of the expectations that people entertain about one another a slow spiral of charity is set in motion, always threatened by unilateral defection, sometimes in equilibrium as to the mutual distribution of burdens among the rich and as to the proceeds of charity and the needs of the indigent, always unstable because local adversity or external disturbance may provoke a stampede of desertion. False expectations of the rewards of cooperation, interacting with one another, may break the deadlock of mutual distrust and become self-fulfilling. In the last analysis, virtue rests upon expectations about the virtuousness of others.

4 The breakdown of local charitable systems

At the dawn of modernity rights of property and use had been established over the inhabited lands of Europe.[47] In times of peace and good harvests, in the absence of epidemics, some kind of equilibrium emerged in most areas: no plundering soldiers or discarded veterans, refugees from the plague or starving peasants roamed the countryside. Those who were denied access to the land had to seek employment on someone else's property or in the towns. Those who could not find work, or who would not, and those who were unfit for work were more or less known in their community. As long as their numbers did not suddenly increase, some kind of arrangement could be worked out. The church maintained homes for the orphans and widows, for the diseased, especially the lepers, and for the deranged. Poor families received alms from the parish or from concerned neighbors, and those who would not wait for charity went out to seek it by begging. It rarely was an idyllic state of affairs. But as long as no major disaster – plague, war or failure of crops – intervened, it was at least relatively stable.

This stability in itself allowed for a system of distribution to develop. In the course of time, precedents of support were created; long-standing clientele-relations, lasting obligations and enduring mutual social control could be established, allowing the well-to-do to compare the generosity of others with their own and compelling all to fulfill their part in giving aid. Such conditions of enduring stability were essential for a charitable structure to develop: it makes sense for contributors to continue giving as long as they may be assured that others will do likewise and that the collective effort will indeed maintain a measure of social harmony without undue sacrifice on the part of anyone in particular and without untoward profiteering by avaricious owners, who would share in the rewards of social order without contributing to the burden.

Even then, some may desert the common strategy of charity and so weaken the resolve of the others to keep it up. A feud may arise and destroy the precarious solidarity of the rich. The charitable system may break down and its demise will make it hard to build it up again as long as the memories of defection hamper mutual trust among the wealthy part of the population. Of course, the church played an important role in preventing such desertion and in recreating an equilibrium of mutual trust and common charity. But the charitable equilibrium was essentially unstable, since in the short run it rewarded the defector who was able to enjoy the social order at no expense.

At this point the question arises why the fortunate ever bothered to maintain the poor. Why not let them starve, kill them, nay, eat them? In fact, countless numbers of poor people, orphans, lepers, idiots, invalids were left to perish. And those among the needy who found the force and courage to resist, to demand, to steal and rob were often ousted, punished or killed off without mercy. But the poor did have numerous allies who could exert pressure on their behalf: those who, without being paupers, lived at a subsistence level and realized that they might be next. After all, those of the poor who clearly could not help their lot – children and their widowed mothers, the sick and the old, the mutilated – all suffered a fate that might befall everyone in a world where disease, accident and death might strike blindly anyone. As the money economy expanded and wage work became more frequent, laborers also learn that they might suddenly be without work or without an adequate wage through no fault of their own and they, too, might commiserate with their fellows who lacked employment.[48]

Thus, as long as the cause of their poverty was believed to be an adversity that they themselves could not help and that might befall everyone without riches, the poor could count on the lower ranks of society to identify with them. Small peasants, journeymen or laborers would demand hospitable and humane treatment for their less fortunate fellow men. Such demands could always be phrased in the common and commanding vocabulary of Christian charity from which the rich could not easily excuse themselves. Moreover, by clamoring and rebelling, the lower ranks of society drove the wealthy together in a united defense against them. This common counter-effort on the part of the rich may well have increased their solidarity, which next facilitated charitable collective action on their part. Such efforts would also be inspired by the fears that the rebellion had evoked.

*

So, partly as a thought experiment and in part also because it did in fact occur, the analysis may begin with assuming an equilibrium state, balanced on three counts.

First, there might be a relatively closed community, say a rural village or a small town living off trade in local craft products in exchange for the produce of the surrounding countryside. No major outside upheavals disturbed the patterns of dependency and exchange.

Second, within this community those who could not earn their own livelihood had entered into complex arrangements with those who could and received part of the surplus in food or money. The arrangements varied from incidental almsgiving to long-standing clientele-relations, sometimes direct, sometimes mediated by religious or secular authorities. The poor may have rendered some kind of service in return or they may have paid in deference and allegiance to their betters. What mattered was that each of the wealthy trusted that his peers had shouldered a more or less proportionate share of the burden and that anyone's failure to do so could be corrected by gossip, shaming rituals, discreet reminders, priestly exhortations and all the other devices of social control in a tightly knit community.

Third, the poor were being maintained at a level sufficient to prevent starvation, rebellion or the departure of able-bodied and capable workers who might be needed at some other time. Of course, such standards of maintenance in a community developed gradually in proportion to the available surplus, the living standards of the employed workers and land-holding peasants and in accordance with the prevailing ideas of neighborly duty and human dignity. On the other hand, the level of maintenance should not be so high as to tempt poor people to abandon their own quest for subsistence – for example, by hunting in the waste lands, gathering food and fuel, performing odd jobs and seeking more durable employment. Charity should certainly not increase to levels at which it might attract outsiders to the fleshpots of the community.

Thus, there was a triple balance: a relatively undisturbed balance of trade between the community and its surrounding area; an equilibrium in the distribution of charitable duties; and a balanced level of maintenance which did not decimate the poor through starvation or increase their number by attracting outsiders or by discouraging willing or capable residents from work. The first equilibrium was beyond the control of the local community. The third, the level of maintenance, could be manipulated to a degree. Whether it endured depended on the persistence of the second equilibrium state: the mutual confidence among the wealthy that all of them would contribute their share. This was not a stable configuration. The defection of any party might have brought the charitable consensus down. Yet, in the course of time, the bonds of tradition, mutual trust and social control might secure the equilibrium.

The most likely cause of a breakdown of the charitable equilibrium would have been some outside disturbance that suddenly increased the claims on charity: the disturbance might work anonymously, through price fluctuations of wheat or salt; it might come in the form of an epidemic which sent people fleeing in panic ahead of the plague (and spreading it), or through the failure of crops or the havoc of war, manifested by peasants from the nearby lands deserting their fields and seeking refuge in the villages and towns.

If the wealthy could not agree on how to divide the burdens, so suddenly increased, they might unite in defense against the claims being made upon them. The first measure would be to send away strangers who came into the community to beg for food and shelter. The next might be to reduce assistance to the increasing ranks of the local poor, to quell any attempt at disturbance, and to chase the new or the unruly poor away. In such a situation a voluntary charitable system betrayed its essential weaknesses: individual desertion by contributors paid, or rather saved, in the short run. Mutual loyalties might prevent defection, but by the same token these inveterate bonds were not easily adapted to the requirements of crisis control.

When the system broke down in one community on account of an external disturbance, a collapse was likely elsewhere also for the same reason, and accelerated by the failure of neighboring villages. At this point it suddenly became obvious that the local communities had never been independent of one another; rather, the local equilibria had prevented the poor from one locality spilling over into adjacent communities. Catastrophes such as war, famine, plague would remind the towns and villages of their common fate and the subsequent movements of the victims from one place to another would in turn involve those communities that might have been spared disaster at first.[49]

Thus, the supralocal or regional equilibrium that endured because of the charitable autarchy in all communities might be undermined by any local or regional breakdown. A village could reap short-term advantages from the expulsion of its resident poor, and from the exclusion of vagrants expelled by neighboring villages. The regional equilibrium, therefore, was also unstable. As it started to disintegrate, a general *sauve qui peut* might ensue at all levels. The rich withdrew their aid in the face of actual or alleged desertion by their peers, once the specter of larger burdens was raised. The poor who could still walk were chased out of town or left of their own accord in search of a better fate. The prophecies of doom were self-fulfilling: as bands of starving and diseased people began to roam, they would descend on any township that had a reputation for hospitality, and as they arrived, they crushed the very charitable system that had attracted them. In anticipation, the towns and villages closed their gates on them before the poor could even come near. The very fact that the poor began to wander and seek a better place sufficed to abolish these better places.

Events have taken this course time and again. They still do, unless a compulsory system of assistance which encompasses the full area of interdependence has come into being. But in the absence of such an effective central authority, the breakdown of the initial unstable regional equilibrium leads to the emergence of another stable equilibrium of neglect and misery.

At the local level a charitable balance may have been restored after some of the poor had gone or been ousted; the communal authorities might try to maintain the local balance literally by closing the gates on the vagrant poor in the area, and in so doing helped to maintain the regional state of distress.[50] No community was tempted to defect from this equilibrium by opening its doors to the roaming poor for fear of being overwhelmed by hordes of miserable beings who had nowhere else to go. No unilateral defection from the collective strategy of exclusion would have occurred, and if it had, it would have been quickly corrected, by the villagers if they still could do so, or otherwise by the demise of their community. At local level such a proposal was not very likely to be adopted as a course of collective action.

Why did medieval and early modern society not disintegrate into an archipelago of small fortresses with vast stretches in between, where the poor were left to roam and perish? In fact, it did more than once, for considerable periods and in large parts of Europe, particularly in the aftermath of the Black Death in the fourteenth century. But sometimes such impoverished and partly devastated areas were conquered or resettled and a new ruler would impose taxes in return for a measure of protection against roving bands, thus permitting the revival of agriculture and traffic with the towns and establishing for himself a source of revenue in the process. After a period of relative regional stability a new charitable equilibrium might form in the area, more or less along the same lines as before, each village taking care of its own poor and accommodating the few vagrants still at large.

5 The emergence of a regional relief equilibrium

During the Middle Ages institutions emerged, e.g. courts and and abbeys, that were not immediately tied to interests at the local level and that accumulated a surplus of their own. Monasteries might admit the needy when disaster struck the area, thus relieving the burden of nearby villages and towns and allowing them some time to maneuver back to a charitable equilibrium. Feudal courts might do likewise, and for the same reason: to prevent the complete breakdown of the system of production and commerce which yielded the taxes they depended on. They would use part of their accumulated surplus to safeguard their tax-base in times of hardship. Religious admonition and appeals to feudal loyalties beyond the local sphere might slow down the rate of desertion from the charitable equilibrium at the communal level and persuade some townships to accept a share of the vagrant poor. By transcending the strictly local perspective and by applying their economic, political and moral resources they might prevent the fatal stampede to local isolationism. If they succeeded in weathering the storm, and if they were widely believed to be able to, their integrating presence might itself help to transform the figuration of local autonomy further in the direction of institutional coordination at the regional level.

By the sixteenth century large cities such as Amsterdam, London, Paris, Lyons, Berlin, Rome and Vienna had begun to play a similar role in maintaining a charitable equilibrium in the region surrounding them: the municipal poorhouses would accept many thousands of vagrants, sufferers and beggars, acting as a clearing station and a buffer zone for the autonomous local communities in the area. Accepting a disproportionately large share of the burden, they tried to preserve their central and dominant position in the regional network of trade and traffic. Each city found itself compelled to protect the equilibrium of poor relief in the region that produced its food so as to prevent a resurgence of banditry endangering its supply-lines. Being open cities moreover, they did not find it easy to check the flow of people or to refuse at the gates those who would not be able to support themselves or to oust those who had become a burden to the urban charities. As a consequence, the cities were flooded with relief-seekers.[51]

In the sixteenth century, the impetus of legislation was toward the confirmation and reinforcement of an encompassing charitable equilibrium among autonomous local authorities. The movement known as *le grand renfermement* in sixteenth-century France was, first of all, an attempt to put an end to vagrancy by confining the poor to local institutions, often former *léproseries*, fallen into disuse, as Foucault has argued.[52] Such poorhouses, hospices and asylums housed orphans and widows, the aged and the infirm, the invalid and the destitute, lunatics and idiots, prostitutes, rogues and petty thieves, as well as the able-bodied poor who were without means of subsistence. These institutions emerged in the large cities, wealthy enough to attract the poor and to support them. But even there, in times of scarcity the authorities would try to rid themselves of poor strangers, dumping them whenever they could.

The sequence of Elizabethan Poor Laws which resulted in the Act of 1601, although very different in their provisions, aimed at a similar reinforcement of the equilibrium of relief, both within each community and among the communities within each region.[53] The law of 1601 imposed standards of care for the needy and of relief for the able-bodied poor, requiring each parish to levy an adequate poor-rate from its property-owners. It thus replaced the unstable local equilibrium of voluntary collective charity by a system of compulsory taxation and shifted the tasks of collection, coordination and disbursement from church agencies to local elected overseers of the poor. Most importantly, it assigned the care of persons without means of subsistence to their community of residence or birth: the parish could refuse settlement to anyone who might become 'chargeable', or remove him before he could become so, back to the parish he came from. The preamble of the law was clear on the prevailing predicament:[54]

> . . . by reason of some defects in the law, poor people are not restrained from going from one parish to another, and therefore do endeavour to settle themselves in those parishes where there is the best stock, the largest common or wastes to build cottages, and the most woods for them to burn and destroy; and when they have consumed it, then to another parish, and at last become rogues and vagabonds. . . .

This refers to the 'open-field' villages with common lands, many of which would not be enclosed until well into the eighteenth century. Until that time, poor people could find many resources outside the market system and without individual property title – a degree of independence often begrudged them by established citizens. Enclosure made matters worse: 'For whereas have been a great many householders and inhabitants, there is now but a shepherd and his dog . . .'[55] And the process was self-accelerating, for those who had been ousted by enclosure now beleaguered the commons of the remaining 'open' villages.

Compulsory, rate-financed poor relief was the essence of the Poor Law[56] and it was meant to solve the dilemmas of voluntary charitable collective action within each parish. Geremek aptly characterizes the general policy. Urban reforms, whether they proved lasting and efficient or not, always employed the same means – compose lists of the needy, expel most of them as vagabonds, select and mark beggars to be assured of relief, centralize asylums and charities under supervision of municipal authorities, secure the funding of assistance, most often through a special tax.[57] And, it may be added, at about the same time citizens were being prohibited from doling out alms to the poor or offering shelter to the homeless on their own account.[58]

In colonial New England, a similar arrangement was worked out after the Elizabethan example at the level of the town-meeting.[59] The responsibility for taxation and relief remained with local authorities. The colonial government issued general instructions for care, standards of taxation, guidelines for collection and administration, and – most importantly – laid down a rule for the division of the burden of relief by assigning all indigents to their locality of birth or residence. But the temptation to oust the needy and unburden them onto adjacent communities remained as strong as ever, especially since the new standards of relief made it harder to abandon the poor once they had been formally accepted as charges of the local community.

The *archers* and the *chasse-gueux* in seventeenth-century Lyons would chase away wandering beggars. The town 'constables' in colonial New England would 'warn off' or 'pass on' vagrants.[60] 'A shortsightedness, however, marred this decision. The town was rid of the disease, but without concerning itself about the spread of the contagion to others.'[61] In Prussia, under the articles of the *ältere Heimatrecht*, the ancient Home Law, German and Austrian troops escorted throngs of vagrants out of the principalities, back to their alleged place of birth where they were often refused access and sent on again: farcical disputes ending all too often in tragedy for the deported poor.[62] As such banishment only shifted the vagrants off to the next community, the Dutch Estates General ordered the Generalities to send those poor who had been banned elsewhere away from their province, thereby only increasing the scale of the problem.[63] Trattner concludes: 'It was the problem of the "unsettled poor" in times of trouble that led to the first important change in the practice of local responsibility.'[64]

The Elizabethan Poor Law and its offshoots in colonial America and the urban asylums in France did much to abolish the charitable dilemma within each community. They also entailed a secularization, a *laïcisation*, of poor relief, as Foucault has argued, and a systematic repression of the poor. Foucault continues: 'Poverty slides from a religious experience, sanctifying it, into a moral conception, condemning it.'[65] These changing conceptions may have been closely connected with the transition from a charitable equilibrium out of voluntary donations under mutual social control to a relief equilibrium out of legally enforceable taxes. The new compulsory arrangement tended to weaken the spirit of religious charity and to replace it by a sense of civic duty.

The new approach to poverty within each community did not guarantee a stable equilibrium at the regional level: it still paid to exclude, and even to exile, the indigent. Throughout the seventeenth century and after, 'complete parochialism'[66] prevailed in England as elsewhere. But the new legislation did reinforce the local relief system and thus diminished the odds of regional breakdown by making local failure less likely. It also stabilized the regional equilibrium by promulgating a general rule of assignment, the settlement requirement. That every parish maintain its own poor – no matter how ambiguous a rule – did become a 'focal solution'[67] in the sense that, barring disturbances, parties tacitly gravitated toward adherence. Yet the rule did not preclude movement of persons who might still become burdensome to their new community of residence. As manufacture and mining began to develop and enclosures spread, the traffic of persons increased. It was impossible to distinguish an able-bodied worker seeking employment from a sturdy beggar posing as a laborer. And working men, too, might become indigent with time.[68]

Gradually, the working of the Poor Law in England, the asylum system in France and the poor relief of town-meetings in colonial America provoked increasing intervention from higher authorities. Since they had promulgated the Poor Laws, these authorities were confronted time and again with requests to amend or adapt them and magistrates were besieged with suits concerning the assignment of chargeable poor to this or that locality. Also, since an obligation was imposed by central authorities upon local communities, the latter could always protest to the authorities responsible for these regulations that they were incapable of implementing them for lack of funds or because of an avalanche of relief-seekers. This prompted incidental amendments and occasional grants-in-aid from higher authorities or attempts to distribute the burden of relief over several parishes at once or to form unions of parishes to carry a common load.[69]

Thus, by pronouncing upon the subject and by laying down standards, the central authorities had made themselves accountable for the implementation of their precepts, and found themselves drawn more and more into the direct administration of poor relief.[70] But until the nineteenth century, none of these efforts amounted to anything like a coherent or effective national policy.

The problem of vagrancy acquired ever larger proportions in the eighteenth century. In France:

In the 1780's their numbers, already large as a result of the rigid social and economic structure of the *Ancien Régime*, were swollen by population increase and economic crisis. In the country round Paris in 1788–1789 the armed forces were hard put to hold them down and keep the roads open. It was the same in Languedoc where brigands and bandits multiplied.[71]

Not only was vagrancy on the increase, it was feared even more than before: as cities grew in population, local epidemics broke out and vagrant 'distracted persons' were believed to spread contagion, which, most likely, they did. This too increased awareness of regional interdependence among localities.[72] The colonial governments in North America, where the Indian wars caused upheaval, or the absolute monarchies of Western Europe, plagued by economic and demographic crisis,[73] were incapable of dealing with problems of such scope directly. They had no police force to seek out and destroy criminal bands, let alone to arrest vagabonds at large in the realm.[74] Most of the time they could only issue harsh penalties for vagrancy, and sternly admonish the towns to lock up wandering beggars and keep them confined, an option the municipalities resented because of the effort and expenditure of constant patrolling and supervision.[75] The towns preferred banishment and corporal punishment. In Lyons, the penalty for first-time vagrancy was a public whipping, for second-time the stocks or the irons,[76] and third-time offenders might be sent to the galleys or hanged. In England, wayfarers were forcibly recruited into the navy.[77] It was to no avail; vagrants could always pose as wandering sheep-shearers and flayers, knife-grinders, peddlers and quacks. The authorities might always suspect that no decent living could be made on the road and that the itinerants supplemented their income by begging and stealing. But often local peasants came to the defense of an arrested vagabond, out of pity or hatred for the authorities, but often also out of fear of revenge from his mates.

6 Regional vagrancy and local authority: an *n*-person game-model

Once local communities had solved their internal dilemmas of collective action and worked out a consensual or compulsory scheme of distribution of burdens, they could be considered as coherent actors, capable of pursuing a consistent policy within a regional figuration. In a regional context of this kind all local authorities were confronted with the threat of vagrancy and banditry, while each one was concerned to keep its relief expenses down. A figuration of this sort may be analyzed as an *n*-person game with all the characteristics familiar from the so-called Prisoners' Dilemma game: cooperative strategies will result in a situation beneficial to each and every one of the actors involved, but such a state of affairs is not 'self-policing' in the sense that a single defector may go unpunished and profit from his solitary noncooperative course at the expense of the loyal parties. When others follow the defector, a situation may ensue which is much worse than the one that resulted from general cooperation. It is, however, stable in a formal sense: since no actor can improve his situation on his own initiative, there is no temptation to defect.

These game-theoretical notions may serve to analyze the dilemmas of poor relief for relatively autonomous local authorities in a context of regional vagrancy. To begin with, it is assumed that within a region of many small communities no single community could through its actions affect the overall situation perceptibly, on analogy with the assumption of perfect competition in free markets. Thus, if one community were to decide to cooperate, this would not change the total situation of banditry and vagrancy in the region, although it would expose that community to an invasion of relief-seekers. By the same token, if one community were to withdraw from a policy of regional cooperation, the effects on the regional situation would be negligible, although its own gains might be considerable.

For reasons of simplicity, the game-model is collapsed into a two-person game which takes place in the imagination of a community, called 'We'. This community tries to visualize the consequences of the different courses of action open to it – that is, of either excluding indigent outsiders or adopting them. The local authority attributes the same options to all other communities in the region, which are introduced as one aggregate actor, 'They'. The community reasons: when 'They' *adopt* the vagrant poor, the regional problem of vagrancy and banditry will disappear. Since the actions of 'We' do not make much difference on a regional level, 'We' might as well profit from the general generosity and *exclude* the needy that might come for relief. Or on the contrary, 'We' might admit the vagrants, thus helping to preserve regional stability for Kantian or Christian reasons.[78] If 'They', on the other hand, decide to *close* their gates, widespread banditry and vagrancy will result. If 'We' open the town to these hordes, it will have hardly any effect on the regional situation, but it is very likely to cause a breakdown of our own relief facilities. This fate may be avoided by sticking to a policy of exclusion while the regional problem of vagrancy and banditry continues unabated. These options are rendered in a 2 × 2 matrix (fig. 2.2).

Charity, vagrancy and assistance

If they:

	(1) admit	(2) exclude
If we: admit (1)	−5 −5	−11 −15
exclude (2)	−5 −1	−11 −11

Figure 2.2 Local authority and the problem of the vagrant poor

Note: It is assumed that 'We' make calculations, also about the preferences 'They' might hold: these are rendered in the matrix. 'We' cannot change the overall situation in the region through 'our' options; only 'They' can if they all act in the same way, which 'We' assume them to do.

The lower left-hand entry in each cell stands for 'Our' evaluation of the outcome in that cell, the upper right-hand entry for the evaluation 'We' attribute to 'Them'. Figures have ordinal meaning only (implying only 'less' or 'greater than' comparisons).

The costs of admitting the poor by a single locality are set at '5', the costs of vagrancy and banditry are set at '10', the costs of exclusion are set at '1'. Cells are identified in the text by the pair of numbers of, respectively, the horizontal and vertical strategies whose combined outcome they represent.

At first sight, the matrix seems to reproduce a 'game against nature' (viz. human nature). What 'They' do completely determines the regional situation and is in no way affected by what 'We' decide; it is a given fact in any situation. But the council that decides on the strategy for 'Us' is aware that 'They' are made up of very similar communities with corresponding interests and comparable councils. Therefore 'They' are likely to reach the same conclusions as 'We' will: the very suspicion of any one council's defection will precipitate everyone else's.

If, in the course of time a distribution of burdens has been achieved throughout the region, for example through the adoption of the distribution rule that each community cares for its resident poor, a cooperative equilibrium prevails: cell (1,1) in figure 2.2. Defection – cell (2,1) – is tempting: it saves the community the costs of relief, '5'; it appears not to affect general security within the region in the short run, and all it requires is vigilance at the gates, at a cost of '1': paying the *chasse-coquins* or the constables. But at this point 'They' are assumed to make the same calculations and reach identical conclusions as 'We' did. If, however, 'They' decide to abandon collaboration *en masse*, the situation portrayed in the second column results: havoc in the countryside, plunder of the harvests and supplies, '10', plus the costs of local vigilance, '1', adding up to '11'. Because any defection may provoke this chain of events, 'We' will think twice before shifting from (1,1) to (2,1), since it might instigate the stampede to (2,2): general exclusion of the vagrant poor with all the attendant destruction. What is worse, situation (2,2) is stable: no community can revert to an open-door policy, without being flooded by desperate alms-seekers, since vagrancy in the region continues unabated – the result would be (1,2), at the cost of '15'.

In other words, when an unstable collaborative equilibrium has been achieved (1,1), the temptation of defection remains. Since all the actors are aware that the same temptation exists for others too, they know that another dismal, but stable, equilibrium may be the final result. Their suspicion of others may prompt them to be the first to desert, their fear that others will follow suit may dissuade them from a profiteering policy.

Clearly, there is a dilemma. Some kind of focal solution, recognized as 'obvious' or 'fair' by all, may be adhered to by all as long as it is expected to be adhered to by everyone. And this is not a tautology, but a vicious circle, halted only by mutual trust. Neighboring towns may pressure a community into doing its part, central authorities may try to persuade the would-be defector, judges may order him to do his share. As soon as a system of compulsion becomes effective, the dilemma is solved and the figuration changes into one of subordinate, rather than autonomous, actors. But even among autonomous communities the unstable equilibrium need not break down, as long as no major upheavals interfere with the pattern of traditional distribution of burdens, with mutual persuasion and trust. On the other hand, once a general pattern of exclusion takes shape for whatever reason, it is stable and very difficult to change back to mutual collaboration, since one-sided open-door policies are self-destructive.

The policy of *grand renfermement* in France and the Elizabethan Poor Law in England may be understood as focal solutions, providing a fair distribution of burdens among the local actors, without imposing it coercively, for lack of central authority, police and funds. In times of catastrophe or in especially heavily burdened areas, central authorities might intervene with grants-in-aid, such as *le don royal*, or establish their own institutions, as they did in Paris and Lyons. This might always provoke other communities to demand additional aid and to relinquish their own support to the poor. Thus, while the fragility of any equilibrium prompted state intervention, experience would teach time and again that such intervention would quickly have to be expanded in order to quell the defections it provoked elsewhere. An unstable cooperative equilibrium provokes central intervention, but as it risks being burdened with an increasing part of the costs, central authority will be wary of intervention: a dilemma very similar to the one confronting the separate communities.

On the basis of these options and the calculations about the options of other parties, a system of equations might be constructed, indicating some optimal or equilibrium solution. But the parameters for such a system of equations are unknown. The costs of relief per capita may be reconstructed, but the numbers of the needy, the resources of the various communities and the propensity to migrate to more generous localities are unknown, even to the authorities of that time. The exercise would therefore be strictly formal and add no insight into the calculations of historical actors, nor would it allow any postdictions that might then be tested against known data.

7 Regional vagrancy, workhouses and central authority

Up to this point it has been assumed that all communities within a figuration were equally small and that none could affect the regional situation on its own. In fact, in the course of the seventeenth and eighteenth centuries some cities grew to such a size that an entire region and all communities within it were oriented toward this center, supplying it with local produce, buying its manufactured and luxury goods and following its political lead. A metropolis of this kind could affect the overall conditions of vagrancy in the surrounding lands and would in fact be ready to act if its supply-lines were threatened. Mancur Olson has shown that if there is a 'large actor' who will profit sufficiently from a collective good to make it worth his while to establish it on his own, he will do so even if he cannot force others to contribute to it or prevent them from enjoying it.[79] This was more or less the situation of the capital cities of Europe in the absolutist era. They might resent having to carry the burden on their own, but it still paid them to do so. Thus, from the middle of the sixteenth century on, a number of cities with very extensive and sensitive trade networks admitted itinerant paupers, attracting them as workers, accepting them halfheartedly as relief-seekers.

The existence of such centers acts on the surrounding communities as an incitement to cut their own relief outlay and oust their needy, saving costs without endangering the overall peace of the region, which was safeguarded by the admission policy of the central city in the first place. This reliance of the surrounding communities on poor relief from the big city provides an instance of what Olson has called 'the exploitation of the great by the small'.[80] As a consequence, urbanization became self-accelerating; and the availability of urban poor relief explains part of the demise of rural relief and the attendant desertion from the countryside.

When these large cities were also the residence of the national court which had a similar interest in the pacification of the realm, metropolitan relief was hardly distinguishable from early relief from the central state.

When disaster struck, however, large cities, too, would send away the alien poor and even their own, so as to ward off famine and contagion. Those who had been expelled would swell the ranks of beggars and bandits at large, aggravating the disorder in the countryside. Tilly quotes instances from sixteenth-century Venice, Marseilles, Naples, mentioned by Braudel, and adds:[81]

In Rome, about the same time, the Pope's men threw out the beggars . . . a classic case of fighting an evil by expanding it, since the control of important parts of Rome's supply area by bandits had helped to create the shortage and the exiled beggars often joined the bandits. As was so often the case in early modern urban administration, the interests of the long run and the exigencies of the moment collided head on.

Nevertheless, by the seventeenth century, European states were deeply involved in the finance and administration of poor relief and asylums. This swift transition was facilitated by the introduction of a quite novel kind of institution, a scheme which suggested to each individual community a strategy that might liberate it from the dilemma of exclusion or admission of the poor, because the new course of action promised results preferable to either. Since it was a dominant strategy, i.e. better, no matter what others might do, any community might safely expect its neighbors to adopt it also and thus a new equilibrium was expected to emerge.

The new strategy turned out to rest upon an illusion. But by the time this became apparent, a new equilibrium had been established because of these false expectations. Once the illusions had been dispelled, individual defection might again seem rewarding, but it could be bought off by small, judiciously distributed grants-in-aid from the central authorities.

The new invention was the workhouse. All able-bodied vagrants were to be confined there. Those who accepted placement thereby proved themselves to be decent poor and were rewarded with employment, food and shelter; those who resisted induction thus betrayed their laziness and were deservedly punished by forced labor or excluded from any support at all.[82] Since idleness was thought to be the cause of vice and vice was believed to be the root of poverty, diligence would comfort the decent and educate the indecent poor. 'Work could and should replace assistance as much as possible.'[83]

What counted most, the workhouse would pay for itself through the yield of the inmates' labor. Thus, moral arguments, considerations of economy and of public order all pointed to the establishment of workhouses.[84] Arrangements could be made at the level of the parish or the small town; no broader coordination was required. The initiative rested with the political institutions most capable of acting and most ready to act in their own interest. Moreover, it was expected that admission to the workhouse could be tightly controlled. By manipulation of the conditions of work and accommodation, the workhouse could be made more attractive or more of a deterrent, as the control of regional vagrancy and local poverty might require.[85] At first, it was thought that the local government only needed to give out a license and that private entrepreneurs would establish and manage the workhouses. But risks proved too great, problems of discipline too demanding and profitability too uncertain to leave the matter to private initiative. Local authorities took over for what they thought would be a preparatory and transitional stage, until the poor became law-abiding and willing to work, ready to enter the labor market on their own account.

The conditions in the workhouses varied very much from one place to another. The depiction of their horrors became a fashionable literary genre in nineteenth-century England.[86] In seventeenth-century France they were *lieux redoutables*, lugubrious prisons – the poor risked their lives staying out rather than accepting work there.[87] In Prussia they were known during the same period as *Hochschulen des Verbrechertums*,[88] or 'colleges of crime' as English contemporaries called them. Yet life in these institutions may not always have been so dismal: elsewhere wardens were reported to be kind, discipline lax and work light or not required at all.[89] This gave rise to citizens' complaints of idleness, laxity and of the taxpayers' money being squandered.[90]

The workhouses never did become a financially sound proposition: 'Authorities founded them with high hopes of a reduction in rates but discovered after a few years that the overhead costs outweighed any savings gained from the workhouse test', Oxley writes.[91] Expenses sometimes amounted to four times the cost of outdoor relief.[92] Complaints about the venality of wardens and the corruption of suppliers were familiar.[93] 'And yet, notwithstanding these shortcomings, the charity workhouses did constitute an effective means of fighting beggary.

What is more, they put in practice one of the novel ideas of the eighteenth century – assistance through work.'[94] In this respect they represented a break with the seventeenth-century asylums and work-houses which merely kept the poor for the purpose of sustenance or punishment without any other attempt at betterment than through religious instruction. The eighteenth-century workhouses were aimed at converting the poor into citizens through the discipline of work, and, this at least presupposed their essential humanity, their potential to become human beings like all others. In this sense, these new schemes issued from greater sense of identification with the poor on the part of the initiators, a notion that they were not just barbarians, but victims of circumstance who could become honest and industrious people if properly reformed. The workhouse may in turn have helped to spread this sense of identification with the poor among citizens in general.

The workhouse has often been interpreted as an institution for regulating the labor market under early capitalism. The notion is ambiguous; it may entail that workhouses served to recruit workers from the pre-proletarian vagrant masses in times of high demand for labor, 'transforming non-wage-workers into wage-workers'[95] by cutting off alternative means of survival outside the market and forcing work upon the idle until they were ready to offer their labor force for a wage.[96] But the same notion may also imply that workhouses served to sustain wage-workers, laid off by capitalists in times of slack, thus maintaining a labor reserve until demand for labor picked up again.

The first idea, that workhouses recruited hands among the idle in times of high demand for labor, is on the whole not borne out by the facts.[97] Almost throughout the epoch of early capitalism unskilled labor such as the workhouses could supply was plentiful. The second idea, that workhouses served to maintain a reserve labor force, seems more plausible in the light of historical evidence. Piven and Cloward have suggested a more complex connection:[98]

> Relief arrangements are ancillary to economic arrangements. Their first function is to regulate labor, and they do that in two general ways. First, when mass unemployment leads to outbreaks of turmoil, relief programs are ordinarily initiated to absorb and control enough of the unemployed to restore order; then, as turbulence subsides, the relief system contracts, expelling those who are needed to populate the labor market. Relief also performs a labor-regulating function in this shrunken state, however. Some of the aged, the disabled, the insane, and others who are of no use as workers are left on the relief rolls, and their treatment is so degrading and punitive as to instill in the laboring masses a fear of the fate that awaits them should they relax into beggary and pauperism.

This Marxist-functionalist account correctly identifies the functions of poor relief in the regulation of the labor market, although workers tempted by laxity might have been as much intimidated by the conditions outside the poorhouse as within. But the 'police' functions of relief are wholly subsumed under its economic functions. Moreover, the identification of the economic functions does not explain the emergence of the arrangement among mutually distrustful local authorities confronted with regional vagrancy – a political problem first of all.

Indeed, when the Lyonese silk business was slack, the *charité* opened its doors to the workers to maintain them until business should pick up, preventing them from deserting to other countries and divulging the secrets of the silk trade.[99] Conditions in the asylum had to be kept favorable enough for the workers not to emigrate elsewhere and harsh enough to prod them back to work when need for them arose. The *recteurs* (regents) were quite explicit about these considerations. However, these regents served more than one master: apart from the silk-manufacturers, they had to heed the king's instructions which corresponded with an interest of the burghers of Lyons also, even if this was sometimes at odds with that of maintaining laid-off silk-workers: to absorb vagrancy in the surrounding area. The hospitals of Lyons had to accept a share of the vagrant poor in the *généralité* as a whole. They did what they could to keep this share at a minimum; however, by chasing too many beggars away they risked overburdening the asylums in the smaller towns of the area, while a breakdown of the regional relief network might result in mutiny, plunder and havoc, as it had so many times before. On the other hand, too generous a policy on the part of the Lyons regents would attract vagabonds from the entire region and beyond, overtaxing the city's facilities and the generosity of its citizens. But too low a level of assistance would drive the unemployed silk-workers out of town.

A modern government would make sure of distinguishing between different categories, such as unemployed silk-workers on the one hand and foreign poor on the other hand. But at the time, this was quite beyond the capacities of government.[100] Even today, with a corps of trained and loyal civil servants, advanced techniques of administration and inspection and with a reliable civil registry, the segregation of foreign newcomers from unemployed residents remains a problem. Recently, South Africa has made a consistent effort at maintaining the distinction and the Soviet Union has probably been effective in this too. In eighteenth-century France it was almost impossible, nor was it always felt to be justified. Thus, Lyonese assistance, like poverty policy in eighteenth-century Europe in general, did 'regulate the poor': its regents were well aware of the alternative policies and of their consequences.

However, they had to regulate several systems at once – both regional vagrancy and the local labor reserve – and they were incapable of keeping one from flowing into another.

Workhouses were founded to counter the threat to public security posed by both the unemployed and the unemployable. '*L'internement . . . est chose de "police"*', says Foucault[101] – 'police' should be understood in the broad sense of those days. These workhouses had to be run in such a manner that life inside was 'less eligible', as the English phrase goes, than outside for anybody who had the choice. This simple principle goes far toward explaining the conditions in camps, prisons and other closed institutions for the able-bodied and potentially dangerous up to the present. Conditions may often have been intolerable, but most often only slightly worse than outside.

8 The workhouse as a dominant solution

The model presented in this section illustrates the implicit dynamics of the figuration, rather than the actual development in historical societies. In the first place, almost 250 years elapsed between the establishment of the first workhouse in 1596, the 'Rasphuis' in Amsterdam and the heyday of the institution in England and America. Second, the term 'workhouse' was used indiscriminately for a variety of institutions, ranging from the tiny asylums of the English countryside in the eighteenth century to the huge *Hôpital Général* of the 1650s in Paris. The term applies more to the expectations of the founders than to the activities of the inmates: most workhouses were populated by a miscellany of people who, for whatever reason, were thought to be in need of shelter or confinement: lunatics, petty criminals, the idle sons of the rich in need of correction, orphans, widows and the aged, the infirm and the invalid and so forth. The able-bodied poor were usually in the minority.[102] Although work was widely believed to be the avenue to moral betterment, prayer, religious instruction and discipline usually took first place. The valid poor did what they could to stay out of the workhouse, which therefore tended to end up with those least fit for work.

Able-bodied beggars and vagrants, for whom these institutions were set up in the first place, tried hard to stay out and were often avoided by the regents since they required close supervision and strict security to prevent escape. Workhouses in the narrow sense of boarding houses for those without employment, yet fit to work, with adequate facilities for productive labor and a full schedule of work, were the exception rather than the rule. With hindsight, it comes as no surprise that the institutions so often failed to realize the hopes of their founders. Everyday pressures tended to bring in those most in need and least able to resist induction, and to exclude those who would have been best capable of working and continued to be most of a threat outside.

Even workhouses that were run like factories-cum-boarding houses were ill suited to finance themselves: if business was slack, so it would be for the products of the workhouse; if demand was brisk, free enterprise might as well respond to it. If the house was run rightly it would compete with private business on unequal terms, and if it was not it would operate at a loss. The same dilemmas tend to frustrate work projects for unemployment even in this age.

In the seventeenth century, workhouses were adopted with high expectations by one town after another. The workhouse provides a good example of 'conscious cultural diffusion',[103] of the purposive adoption of a scheme from one community by others: the Amsterdam scheme by towns in the Dutch Republic,[104] by the Hansa cities and on to Vienna[105] and by the city government of Paris,[106] from where it spread throughout France, and influenced in turn German, Dutch and Spanish projects.[107] The purpose in adopting the scheme was to solve the pressing problem of public peace, threatened by hordes of beggars and vagabonds, and to lessen the burden of relief which until then had to keep the poor from starvation or evil. Time and again minor corrections in the scheme seemed to hold a promise of efficacy. But each new arrangement turned out to present new shortcomings.

Esentially, the workhouses served as intramural centers for the detention and treatment of the invalid and not so able-bodied needy who contributed what little they could to their own upkeep, if hard pressed to do so. City authorities simply lacked the will, the technique and the resources to enforce the regime on those who could work there, but refused to. For most of its history the workhouse was less a panopticon than a pandemonium.

Only by the time that the Industrial Revolution was well under way and national government had become capable of the effective policing of the highways and of keeping reliable registers on criminals, beggars and vagabonds, could the able-bodied poor be locked up and made to work. By that time, the institution had turned into a punitive instrument, a house of correction to teach the discipline of steady work to first-time offenders and recidivist idlers.[108] The workhouse tradition had run its course and was succeeded by a process of differentiation into many specialized institutions such as orphanages, old-age asylums, hospitals, insanity wards, maternity houses and prisons.[109]

The attempt to enforce labor discipline upon unwilling inmates became outdated by the effects of the factory system and the operation of the labor market; under the impact of literary indictment it began to seem incompatible with the humanitarian ideas with which it had always been coupled. It took much more effective techniques of administration and policing, and the ideological notion of the 'enemy of the state', to enable the central authorities of Nazi Germany and the Soviet Union in the twentieth century to lock up millions of people for enforced labor. And, yet

> the industrial, almost military *regulo* that still exists now not only in prisons, but in hospitals, schools and welfare institutions bears painful testimony to this adherence to a tradition in constant need of reappraisal. This kind of perpetuation is physical, in that the original institutions are still utilized or used as models for replacement, but it is also psychological, in so far as one's familiarity with the institutions makes it difficult to reconceive an alternative.[110]

Nevertheless, the expectation of employment for the idle poor and of a self-financing system of relief turned out to be of great consequence. It seemed to offer a way out of the dilemma of exclusion or assistance which plagued the relatively autonomous communities in modern Europe. The towns were more ready to admit considerable numbers of beggars and vagabonds, since they could always lock them up in the workhouse, where they would cause no trouble and no expense – or so they thought.

The process may again be illustrated by a game model. Of course, no

If we:	If they: (1) admit		(2) exclude		(3) put to work	
admit (1)	−5		−11		0	
		−5		−15		−5
exlude (2)	−5		−11		0	
		−1		−11		−1
put to work (3)	−5		−11		0	
		0		−10		0

Figure 2.3 Local authority and the solution of the workhouse.

Note Workhouses are assumed to operate at no cost: '0'. For further explanations, see fig 2.2.

town could put an end to banditry and vagrancy in the entire region by acting on its own. But it could make a beginning, and in doing so it would improve its situation no matter what 'They' did. Thus 'We' might opt to establish a workhouse – strategy (3) – whatever condition prevailed in the region: if a general equilibrium of local assistance prevailed, the scheme would still cut a community's cost of assistance, from '5' to '0', while regional order continued: cell (3,1). If the figuration had deteriorated to a state of general exclusion, with disorder rampant in the region, the town could not end overall chaos by establishing a workhouse, but it could at least cut the costs of exclusion and vigilance, '1', while still suffering the costs of unavoidable regional disturbance, '10': cell (3,2). Other communities would come to the same conclusion and establish workhouses in turn, in the process restoring peace to the region and saving themselves and others the costs of relief, ending up with '0' in cell (3,3). Clearly, the workhouse equilibrium (3,3) is an optimum – yielding for every actor a better outcome than any other strategy – and it is stable in the sense that no defection on its own is rewarding. It is hardly surprising that the illusion found such willing diffusion.

It is interesting to infer from the matrix what might have happened when the workhouse began to disappoint, when its returns remained below its costs and the sturdy poor continued to stay outside. As peace in the region continued to be disturbed and the burden of assistance decreased less than expected, some cities might begin to consider closing their institution, opting for defection from (3,3) to (2,3), exclusion or (1,3), outdoor relief. Again a dilemma emerged. Defection was tempting, also because it might occur to others and should therefore be anticipated. On the other hand, because it might precipitate desertion on the part of others, such defection could result in a general exclusion of the poor (2,2), with all its dire consequences.

It was at this point that central authorities were able to achieve great results with small means. A grant in the operating costs of the workhouse might make the move to (2,3) less tempting and the subsidy only needed to cover the difference between the – increased – costs of maintaining the workhouse and the costs of excluding the poor. The central government or the capital cities might step in to establish an institution to deal with the sturdy, but unwilling, elements in the region, something the regents of local institutions were loath to do once they learned that it involved the costs of tracking down vagrants, rounding them up, incarcerating them and enforcing a permanent regime of compulsory labor. Yet a central government with some means at its disposal could persuade the local authorities with grants-in-aid to do so in order to maintain or restore order in the region.

The analysis does demonstrate the dynamics of admission and exclusion within a figuration of autonomous communities confronted by a regional problem of vagrancy and banditry. Such figurations have gradually given way to those with a central state regulating the communities within its territory through legislation, taxation and policing. Usually, this state intervention is explained by developments external to the process within the regional figurations. Quite often, increasing intervention by a central authority is accounted for by the impact of humanitarian ideas and reformist campaigns, or the increase in fiscal, regulatory and police capacity of the state serves to explain why central authority began to intervene in the regional figuration.

But the figuration of regional vagrancy and relatively autonomous local relief displayed a dynamics of its own which prompted increasing state intervention and in this way contributed to the process of state formation.

From the sixteenth century onward central authorities had reacted to the growing problem of regional vagrancy by issuing 'focal' legislation which left the actual persecution and detention of vagrants and the financing and management of workhouses to the local authorities. Nevertheless, these central agencies were goaded into more direct intervention, imperceptibly and incrementally, through incidental, but all the more pressing, appeals from imperilled local communities. The very fact of a grant-in-aid provided by the state would tempt the recipient local authorities to relinquish their own efforts and others to clamor for an equal share. This mechanism gradually increased the involvement of the central state in combating vagrancy and relieving the poor.

Thus, at some point a central agency emerged with sufficient internal cohesion and external connections to develop a policy and promulgate it throughout the realm. It was capable of recognizing the regional, or even national, character of a problem such as vagrancy and to issue a rule that was at once intended to guarantee public security, its mission, and to spare it the costs and efforts of implementation, its weakness. The burden remained with the local communities, but the supralocal-distribution rule had to be adjudicated by the state or in its courts of law. Next, the central agency found itself drawn into attempts to enforce its verdicts upon local communities. And in a further stage it was seduced into facilitating adherence to its policies by immediate, albeit incidental, intervention. Under conditions of competition among local authorities, these isolated interventions tended to multiply and to replace local efforts, often against the overall intention of the central authorities that were drawn into it, and against the broad intentions of the local authorities, jealous of their autonomy.[111]

This figuration of relatively autonomous local agencies pressed by need and mutual competition to submit to a central authority which expanded accordingly, is reminiscent of Elias's 'unfree competition regulated by the monopoly apparatus', a model which refers primarily to the relations of interdependence between the landed nobility and the royal court in the latter stage of transition from feudalism to absolutism.[112] Increasingly, the dilemma of collaboration or defection in the uncoordinated figuration of local relief was replaced by competition for support from the central state at the price of local independence. The state, while gaining in influence as a consequence, had to underwrite the costs of relief, and all the time it was caught in the dilemma of either accepting the burdens passed on to it or letting the encompassing relief equilibrium deteriorate through local negligence.

In this instance, state formation was furthered by the internal dynamics of political competition itself, a complement to the external competition among states which contributed to the same process. This extension of state intervention must be understood against the background of the relatively autonomous processes of capital accumulation and urbanization, to which it contributes in turn. These long-term processes are mostly left implicit in the present account, discussed only when they touch directly upon the main theme of the sociogenesis of state care. Here, the internal dynamics of state formation in the field of poor relief are at issue.

What the workhouse brought about was, in the last analysis, a cooperative equilibrium based on illusions. But once it was achieved, disillusionment did not necessarily undo the unstable balance, since state and metropolitan agencies by then were capable of preventing defection by judiciously acting as stabilizers. In doing so, they unwittingly helped to transform the figuration of autonomous local authorities into one of centralized policing and relief.

The game was never played exactly like this from beginning to end. But many times, in fact almost everywhere, parts of it were enacted and historical episodes may be better understood with these dynamics in mind.

3

The Elementary Curriculum as a National Communication Code

At the present time all over the globe about one billion children go to school for the better part of every working day – the numbers and the percentages of children in school have been on the increase now for two centuries, and so has the time that each child spends in school.[1] What all these students learn in the first six years is surprisingly similar over the entire globe, and so is the classroom setting where this effort occurs.

In elementary schools everywhere, children learn to read and write, very often in a language which differs greatly from their local speech: a standard version, current over an entire region, a nation or even a continent.

The students also learn another kind of language, one more restricted in its use, but shared by almost all of mankind: arithmetic – a code for buying and selling, for measuring property and assessing taxes, for calculating distances and measuring time.

All children are also taught their place in the world – the location of their habitat in relation to adjacent settlements, within the region, the country, the continent, the globe and even in space: geography. And they are taught to view their own lives as the latest in a long chain of generations which have all contributed to some coherent development of which they now are also part: history.

Finally, educators all over the world attempt to inculcate in their pupils' minds ideas of good and evil, of rights and duties, implicitly through a 'hidden pedagogy'[2] and explicitly through religious and ideological instruction. This *formation* or *Bildung* has become a dominant issue wherever an elementary-school system has been established, so much so that the considerable consensus over 'education' proper has often been overlooked.

All told, reading, writing, arithmetic, some geography and history, and a great deal of ideological or religious formation, make up the bulk of the elementary curriculum all over the world. Other subjects are offered on the side: physical education may have become almost universal; in most places poor children receive some vocational or domestic instruction and rich children are educated in the arts, languages and sciences, but these are mere embellishments of one basic program of instruction which has occupied and transformed mankind for the past two centuries.

Yet at the dawn of the elementary-school movement, around the end of the eighteenth century, a preliminary issue divided minds in Europe and America: the proponents of popular education confronted many opponents who thought it unnecessary, if not downright pernicious, to teach children, especially girls and the offspring of the poor and lowly, anything at all beyond an outline of the Holy Bible and, if need be, some practical virtues and skills.

It testifies to the momentum and pervasiveness of the educational transformation that barely a century later the matter was settled once and for all and that today boys and girls of every rank everywhere receive elementary education.[3]

It is not easy for the contemporary reader to imagine what objections could be raised to teaching children the 'three Rs' of reading, writing and arithmetic. This opposition must be understood in the context of traditional European society, where the great majority lived in rural villages. In these small communities most people worked the land, as peasants on a small plot of their own or as tenants, farmhands or journeymen on someone else's property; most people were landless and many were unemployed for much of the time. Most countryfolk could not even write their own name, some could read, others had learned by heart a few verses from the Bible or lines from the catechism. Many did not understand the language of the realm, but spoke a regional dialect which was unintelligible to the inhabitants of the neighboring region. They could not add or multiply, but they could count on their fingers, measure a surface or a distance by the traditional standards of a morning's labor or a day's march, mark the passage of time by the sun's position, the coming and going of the seasons, or the year's holidays.[4]

1   The uses of literacy

The difference between the illiterate, uncouth peasants and the gentry appeared enormous and unbridgeable, almost as if they belonged to different species.[5] It simply did not occur to the cultured and enlightened minds of those times that their notions of liberty and human rights might also refer to these 'proletarii' or 'rascals'. The English moral philosophers excluded the poor and the peasants by omission.[6] There was no need to mention them, since to the eighteenth-century audience it went without saying that these inalienable rights did not apply to the poor[7] – they were excluded as thoughtlessly as children are omitted from such a discussion in this century.

Throughout the eighteenth century a lively interest in educational matters prevailed in Europe, but the issue of educating peasants and paupers was hardly raised: 'Members of the enlightened community could hardly conceive of a radical improvement in the lot of the people', writes Chisick on France, and he adds: they 'were remarkably consistent in describing the effects that such an education would have on the laboring poor: they regarded it as "dangerous".'[8]

The peasants' lot was unrelenting toil and unending poverty; 'the members of the enlightened community' were convinced that it must continue so: 'This was the great *non-dit*, the generally unspoken but universally understood presupposition on which the entire debate on popular education rested.'[9]

Politics was the world of the printed word and there was no other way of keeping abreast of the news than through print: an added reason not to teach the common people to read. Literacy would give them access to newspapers and Bible-tracts, and draw them into controversies which could only confuse and excite their immature minds. To the practical demands of daily peasant life literacy appeared wholly irrelevant. Nor would the workers in the new factories have any use for it: they needed fewer skills than the traditional crafts had required, as Adam Smith had already signalled.[10] Educating the lower ranks of society would not profit them or benefit society; rather the opposite: it might turn workers and peasants away from their appointed course in life, inspire discontent and awaken higher aspirations. This was a fear that continued to plague the upper classes: 'the spectacle of an incalculable and vaguely threatening multitude which so greatly alarmed the employing and governing classes'.[11] And Schama notes of the Dutch by the end of the seventeenth century: 'Perhaps surprisingly, the urban patriciate which gave so generously to keep the poor out of sight were less disposed to provide for their education. There seemed no point in training them for stations in life which their incorrigible immorality disqualified them from occupying.'[12]

Since the days of the Reformation and Counter-Reformation the churches had been almost exclusively in charge of formal education. The wealthy, the landed gentry and the merchant bourgeoisie did appoint private tutors and governesses for their children until they were ready to go to a Latin school or *collège*, run most often by the clergy. For the remaining vast majority of the population there were parish schools which demanded a small tuition and offered a – very limited – education for a few hours a day, a few winter months every year and in a child's life a few years only. Even such schools were too expensive, too remote and too demanding for many peasant and pauper families. The vast majority of the population received hardly any instruction at all. If the local population could spare the tuition, or if there was an endowment, the money was used to pay for a classroom and a schoolmaster. The children were taught to recite Bible texts from memory, to memorize the alphabet and to read Biblical and spiritual fare aloud and in unison. Schools were custodial, rather than educational, institutions and what little education was provided aimed at religious indoctrination by rote learning and chanting *en masse*.[13] It was brutally repetitive. In Prussia the catechism had to be repeated from beginning to end every six weeks, and this on the orders of Frederick the Great's progressive minister of education.[14] Even as late as 1836, Anglican schools required the children to make a genuflection each time they read 'Christ': every ten or twenty syllables.[15]

The problem of discipline was always paramount in the single classroom, overcrowded as it was with unruly children, of widely different age and accustomed to the space and the movements of country life. Classrooms were often dark, damp and filthy; on many occasions they served a variety of other purposes, as gathering rooms, living quarters for the teacher's family or even as barns or stables.[16] But for most children conditions at home were hardly likely to be much better; for some they could be much worse.

The village priest had the final say in everything that concerned the school and the teacher was expected to assist him with chores such as grave-digging or bell-ringing. Often the teacher also ran the local sick fund, or doubled as a land-surveyor, bookkeeper, innkeeper, or constable.[17] Schoolmastering was not considered a vocation, not even an occupation, it was mostly residual employment for men who were considered unfit for anything else. After all, for men without property or skills there were very few jobs that did not require heavy physical effort; discarded veterans or disabled working men could not be employed at much else than guarding the young. 'Most teachers and "social welfare workers" at that time, it is well to remember *were* paupers, employed by the parish.'[18]

Nor were peasants, servants and paupers particularly anxious to have their children educated. From a very early age children were needed to help at work or earn some money.[19] And then parents did not think literacy would have much practical purpose in their existence, and, in fact, it hardly did. Peasants acquired the skills they needed through practice and most merchants and craftsmen learned their trade in apprenticeship. The notion that education might be a means to individual improvement in life hardly occurred until well into the nineteenth century. Even a lengthy formal education would not open social avenues which at the time still required wealth, rank and connections.[20] In Drucker's words: 'Throughout the ages to be educated meant to be unproductive.'[21]

Even so, peasants and craftsmen sometimes did make the effort to have their children educated. The classrooms served a custodial purpose by providing a place where children were kept out of trouble and where they were sometimes more comfortable than in their parents' shacks or out in the cold. The teacher, even though lacking most other qualifications, could be expected to teach the children some discipline and regularity of habit which parents found difficult to impose. The children, on their part, may have cherished the opportunity to be with their age-group in a situation that left many opportunities for escaping the teacher's vigilance.[22]

To pious parents it was, of course, very important that their children should be taught religion. The students were made familiar with religious texts by recitation and rote learning. But reading and writing – even if restricted to excerpts from the Bible and the catechism – were a different matter, one which inspired great ambivalence among clergy and laity alike. On the one hand, literate believers could read the Scriptures among themselves. This allowed much more frequent and dispersed gatherings than any one clergyman could hold. On the other hand, left to their own wits with the Scriptures, the faithful might develop their own readings of the text and they might come across tracts and pamphlets of different inspiration.[23]

Bible-reading had been a major proselytizing strategy of the Reformation, allowing scattered congregations to celebrate and keep alive the new faith. The great educational effort made by the Catholic teaching orders was prompted strongly by the specter of Protestantism,[24] but it never went so far as to allow independent reading of the Scriptures in the vernacular.

Religious competition, rather than religion as such, has been a driving force in the spread of education. Wherever an established church, comfortably connected with the landed aristocracy and securely supported by the central state reigned supreme in education, schooling of the working people and the poor stagnated, as it did from the end of the seventeenth century in England, France, Italy and Spain. But wherever denominations forced one another to compete for adherents and for support from the civil authorities, schools improved[25] – most strikingly so in New England and the Low Countries, and to some degree in Prussia where Frederick II could never be certain that 'sie doch nicht katholisch werden' – that they would not turn Catholic if he did not insist on Lutheran catechization.

On the whole, elementary education of the lower estates was superior in Protestant lands, because there the faithful were encouraged to study the Bible in the vernacular translation. Moreover, wherever Protestantism spread, it encountered religious competition, spurring its efforts to improve education.[26]

Change in literacy rates among the rural population was slow and uneven throughout Europe and North America and formal education of the poor remained scanty and scattered.[27] Although the eighteenth century was an era of great innovators in pedagogy – Locke, Basedow, Pestalozzi, Rousseau and Helvétius – the new insights hardly affected the practice of the village schools. The reformers never addressed the preliminary, practical problems of managing and financing elementary education on a large scale. The incorrigibility of the situation is perhaps best illustrated by the sorry fate of all grandiose schemes to improve the schools. Among the French *philosophes* and their public, the discussion of educational reform was a perennial topic, but it did not produce actual reforms.[28] Frederick II of Prussia prepared a long sequence of reform bills and even convened a Wednesday Society of enlightened intellectuals to discuss the prospect of mass education for the peasants and serfs.[29] These discussions had little practical result and even if a law did reach the books, it failed to score much actual effect. Yet these debates did serve to prepare the ideological ground for the profound changes to come in the wake of the French Revolution.

What French enlightened discussion and Prussian legislative proposals did reveal was a profound ambivalence toward the education of the lower ranks of society.[30] The issue was not yet perceived in terms of a curriculum of skills which would prove of practical value in adult life, as such skills were normally passed on by parents to children and by master craftsmen to apprentices. If the idea of teaching domestic or artisan crafts came up, its purpose was not so much to prepare children for the labor market, but to render them virtuous, patient and industrious through the practice of traditional arts.[31] This lofty disregard of the actual demand for skilled labor was one cause of failure for the *Industrieschulen*.[32]

The seventeenth-century reformers could not easily conceive of a world where educated workers would be required in vast numbers: labor was manual; literate people did not work with their hands, artists and printers excepted; even doctors avoided touching their patients, leaving such physical treatment to the lesser surgeons. The bureaucracy was still miniscule and absorbed only a small number of merchants' and farmers' sons in the lower and middle positions. The officer corps was almost entirely made up of noblemen and tended to resist administrative and technical innovations, nor would it normally accept cadets for their skills alone, irrespective of birth. There was as yet no industrial production, requiring engineers to control the machines, or clerks and supervisors to help in managing the enterprise. Thus, if the subject of mass education came up, it was predominantly in the context of moral, religious and political enlightenment on the one hand, and of the control of unruly peasants and paupers on the other. Those of a conservative bent warned against the dissatisfaction and the rebelliousness that might come from the acquisition of literacy. Others, leaning toward a more rationalist view of mankind, trusted that education would dispel prejudice, obstinacy and sedition among the peasants, abolish idleness and vice among the young and prevent mob action by promoting a better understanding of the sound foundations of society. This profound and enduring ambiguity among the established ranks of society with regard to the issue of educating the lower classes had expressed itself earlier in the doubts about teaching them to read the Scriptures on their own and in their own language: at once a means of propagating the beliefs of the dominating groups in society, and a medium through which dissident and radical ideas might enter and take hold. The same ambivalence reappeared when education was discussed in more secular terms, as an avenue to moral improvement and political participation, as it was in the eighteenth century when practical considerations of labor qualification did not yet count for much: the school would teach the lower orders the conceptual foundations for much of civic virtue, and authority, but it might also make them accessible to revolutionary ideas of equality, liberty and fraternity.

Between 1750 and 1850 these doubts gradually dissolved and were replaced more and more by a split between various groups holding either the one or the other view of education. Individual ambivalence was resolved in social conflict between two groupings which did not wholly correspond to social classes or to a single opposition of interests, but which were very much defined by their position in the figuration of communications relations which connected and isolated people within an emerging nation. An increasing number of citizens came to depend for their livelihood either on the state bureaucracy or on trade in national and international markets. These people, officials and entrepreneurs, did not live off their landed property and were therefore much less connected with a particular local or regional community. On the contrary, they stood to gain from the greatest freedom of movement and the most unencumbered exchange of messages between regions.

Most of these officials and entrepreneurs lived in the metropolis and sought access to the surrounding population, whether for purposes of taxation and recruitment or in order to buy and sell goods and recruit labor. They stood to profit from the emergence of a national network of communication and therefore supported the teaching of the standard language throughout the land. They themselves spoke this lingua franca when at work, and often also at home. Their business, keeping books and files, drafting contracts and statutes, was transacted in writing, and they wrote in the standard version of the language. They also constituted the natural audience for an expanding group of intellectuals who developed and elaborated a literary version of the lingua franca – a *Kunstsprache* – for this public.

These officials and entrepreneurs moved in circles where everyone was literate and fluent in the standard language. The situation was very different in the countryside. The village community, and frequently even the larger community of a provincial town with its surroundings, represented a relatively closed network of communication and exchange. Its population did not participate in national politics directly, but through the mediation of its traditional representatives – local aristocrats mostly. Its peasants and craftsmen did not themselves buy and sell on the national market, but were connected to this exchange through local middlemen, the landed nobility among them. And finally, very little information from beyond the region reached these people directly. Being ignorant of the lingua franca, most of them depended entirely on messages in the regional dialect, and being illiterate they had to rely on word of mouth from travellers or local literates. In a figuration where the lingua franca was unintelligible to the great majority of people on the periphery, as it was in the south of France, the east of Prussia or the north and west of Britain, or where the rural majority was illiterate, as it was all over Europe, local elites had a quasi-monopolistic function of mediation in communication between their clientele and the metropolitan network. This mediation corresponded in part with monopolistic middlemen functions in trade and politics.[33]

Of course, the situation varied over time and between such extremes as the East Prussian estate with its illiterate Polish-speaking serfs tied to the land, on the one hand, and on the other, the provincial towns of eighteenth-century England, where 'the King's speech' was understood by all and communication relatively free and easy: but even there illiteracy isolated many from the wider traffic of facts and ideas and kept them dependent on mediation by the literate elite.

It is in this context of local networks of communication, connected directly or indirectly to a metropolitan network and more or less accessible to it, through a lingua franca and through literacy, that the emergence of elementary mass education will be discussed in the following paragraphs, first in a theoretical and formal fashion, and next, in a brief presentation of the historical development in separate countries.

2 The floral figuration of communication networks

The history of education has been studied first as a history of pedagogic ideas; second, as a history of parliamentary legislation; and thirdly as a history of educational reform movements. Most of all, educational historiography has been concerned with ideas: pedagogic, political and religious. Usually, it has presented the slow, but irresistible, victory of the ideals of enlightenment, civilization and egalitarianism against reactionary obscurantism and authoritarian oppression of the lower classes.

But this is not the whole story.[34] Without doubt, the movement for the establishment of an elementary-school system proceeded mainly through public debate and propaganda; almost nowhere did it result in armed struggle, violence was the rare exception and even lockouts and boycotts occurred only seldom. It was in fact a process of ideas, carried on with words. Such ideas were cherished even more tenaciously as they corresponded with the efforts of social groups to maintain or improve their position in society against the similar efforts of other groups. The rise of literacy and the emergence of a school system were the outcome of societal conflict and in turn affected the relative positions of the social groups involved in the contest.

The rise of elementary education appears to be so universal a phenomenon and so similar in different countries, that it can only be related to profound social transformations which in fact occurred everywhere, notwithstanding the national variation in ideas, issues and forms or organization. One elaboration of this view is to be found in the structuralist-functionalist approach, which explains educational institutions among others in terms of the persistent functional needs of the social system in which they occur, or, as Talcott Parsons[35] defined the task: 'an analysis of the elementary . . . school class as a social system, and the relation of its structure to its primary functions in the society as an agency of socialization and allocation'. Where the encompassing developments in various societies are similar, corresponding systemic needs will give rise to similar institutions, educational institutions among them.

Vaughan and Archer have criticized this approach[36]:

> Thus the selective mechanism determining educational change is located in the broad and undefined area of social needs . . . However, since the whole concept of 'need' is undefined, their deterministic influence on educational development can only be detected *ex post*. Consequently, the role of individual reformers or activist groups is ignored, unless their purposes happen to correspond to social needs. Conflict is regarded as a symptomatic, rather than as a formative process in its own right.

A surprisingly similar approach in terms of systemic requirements has been adopted by Marxists who define these needs as the necessary conditions for the rise of the capitalist mode of production. Although historical-materialist in inspiration, this approach is often functionalist in method.[37] It involves an attempt to explain the rise of the elementary-school system from the functional requirements of shaping and reproducing an adequately qualified proletariat and avoiding the emergence of an articulate and knowledgeable working class. Factory owners, the argument goes, needed a disciplined and governable, more or less skilled workforce, and the schools would produce just such cohorts of literate, docile and punctual workers.[38]

The nineteenth-century school regime does reveal some unmistakable similarities with the factory regime of that time: standardization, formalization and the imposition of punctuality and discipline were paramount in both. But this analogy nevertheless fails to provide an explanation, for two reasons mainly. First, even though employers may have profited from the presence of elementary schools, they often did not do much to help in their foundation, sometimes even actively opposing it, if only because they wanted the children to be available for factory work. Many other groups in society campaigned with more zeal for the establishment of a school system: educators, civil servants and working-class organizations among them. In other words, it remains unclear how the functional requirements of capitalism were fulfilled, if it was not through the efforts of those most closely associated with them. And second, the functionalist account cannot deal with the problem of timing: in most countries, such as France and the Netherlands for example, the growth of literacy and the establishment of elementary public-school systems preceded industrialization by many decades.[39] Apparently, the functional requirements of industrial capitalism were effected without any special effort from the party most concerned, the industrialists, and long before the system whose needs were thus to be served had itself emerged.

The historical-materialist-cum-functionalist account suffers from the same shortcomings as more traditional structural-functionalism and, moreover, tends to reduce the emergence of an elementary-school system to the requirements of the capitalist economy, ignoring its cultural and political implications, its functions for the figuration of communication networks and the process of state formation.[40]

A more adequate explanation of the rise of the elementary-school system should proceed in terms of the conflicts between social groups attempting to maintain and improve their position against one another. One aspect of these contests was the issue of control over the educational institutions. Such an explanation 'should take account of profound educational conflict without either assimilating the parties involved to conflicting social classes or attributing to the ideas involved some order of ascendancy or subordination according to social needs.'[41]

Vaughan and Archer proceed to elaborate this perspective in terms of a conflict over educational control between 'dominating' and 'ascending' groups in society. In the cases studied by the authors – those of France and England in the nineteenth century – the initially dominant groups were the established churches, Catholic and Anglican respectively. The assertive groups came from the ranks of the middle classes: 'the assertive policies of the French bourgeoisie depended on their political and that of the English middle class upon its economic role and interests.'[42]

This approach has the merit of taking seriously the conflicting ideas, interests and strategies of the parties involved, without reducing them prematurely to the metaphysical workings of system requirements or the equally opaque impact of class interests only. It is, therefore, essentially a sociological approach, which places the ideological conflicts in the context of a power struggle for control over the most important institution for the transmission of culture: the school.

The approach of this study equally focuses on group conflict, but from the general theoretical perspective upon the sociogenesis of the welfare state. The emergence of a nationwide public elementary-school system is treated as one aspect of that larger transformation. In dealing with education also, the focus will be on the emergence of collective arrangements which remedy deficiencies and adversities. The deficiency that matters at this point is ignorance, or, more specifically, incompetence in the standard language and illiteracy. The external effects of spreading literacy gradually turned illiteracy into a deficiency: as reading and writing became more common, those who lacked these skills found themselves increasingly incompetent in everyday interactions. Conversely, illiteracy formed an impediment to the projects of officials and entrepreneurs who began to seek collective remedies for a deficiency that also hampered them.

Ignorance or illiteracy cannot be considered an adversity, as they do not strike suddenly or randomly; but in an increasingly literate society they tend to become conditions of deficiency. The notion of 'external effects' is clearly relevant in this case. And although the 'uncertainty of moment and magnitude' plays little role in the analysis, the 'uncertainty of effect' does: a child's education is a relatively costly and protracted enterprise of uncertain outcome and in more than one sense a risky, long-term investment.

Elementary education was first of all a means to convey fluency in the standard language and literacy in its written version, thus providing access to a corresponding communications network.[43] Literacy in the standard language provided unmediated access to a national network of written communication. But in many countries, albeit in widely varying degrees, there was a prior necessity to teach some fluency in the standard language to children who spoke a dialect or a different language. Only by learning to speak and understand the standard language could they acquire unmediated access to the national network of oral communication – a very loosely connected network of conversations and speeches which became truly significant and united only with the advent of the electronic media in this century. And all along, of course, understanding the standard language was a necessary condition for learning to read and write it.

The point of departure of the argument is a figuration of local or regional speech communities, hardly intersecting with one another, but all of them linked to one central or national language community through the mediation of bilingual and literate local elites.

Throughout the Middle Ages the lingua franca that connected all of the Christian Europe was of course Latin, the means of communication among the clergy of every regional speech community. As central states emerged in early modern Europe, in every country a regional vernacular emerged as the language of the court, of administration and law, science and literature; it became the standard language, serving the function of communication among the elites of the various regional speech networks within the realm. Between these regional communication networks there was little or no exchange except in this lingua franca.

In other, more formal terms, there existed a set of sets of regional speakers with little or no intersection between them. All these sets did intersect with one other set – that of lingua-franca speakers. This may be called a 'floral figuration of languages', for no other reason than that the most convenient graphic representation of such a figuration is a flower, with the regional speech communities as the – barely overlapping – petals, and the category of lingua-franca speakers as the heart, which does overlap with every petal. Part of this central set may not overlap with any other, or to put it plainly: some lingua-franca speakers might not speak any regional language and thus perform no mediating services for a regional clientage, although they depended on regional mediating elites for access to the regional dialect speakers.

This 'floral' model of communication may also be applied to a figuration in which it was not language diversity that formed the barrier to mutual exchange, but illiteracy. Oral communication between various regional networks was possible, as regional parlances were mutually intelligible ('intercomprehensible'),[44] but it was restricted to the immediate environment. The written word travels light and far, but oral communication requires face-to-face contact and was in the past hampered even more by physical distance and the difficulties of travel. In this version of the floral diagram, the petals overlap more than they do in the model of language diversity, since oral communication between regions could occur over short distances. But although the large majority of the population understood the standard language, only a minority in every region was capable of reading and writing it. This literate elite in every regional network of oral communication could communicate in writing with its peers. The literate minorities were therefore also part of the central set of readers and writers of the standard language. Illiterates were dependent on these educated mediators to communicate in writing, e.g. for official purposes or in order to bridge long distances. In this case, too, there were members of the central set who did not belong to any regional network of oral communication, not because they never spoke to anyone, but because everyone in their network was literate and they had no clientage depending on their mediation services. In other words, in contrast to the bilingual or literate elites belonging to regional networks of oral communication, these 'metropolitans' had no dependent clientele of their own, while they did need the services of regional mediators to reach a mostly illiterate population in the country at large.

The figuration of language diversity and that of illiteracy are similar in many respects; both a lingua franca and written communication serve to link various regional networks through mediation by bilingual or literate elites. The population of a region needs elite mediation to communicate in the national network, whether it speaks a regional dialect or the standard language, but is still illiterate. And in either case, the metropolitans depend on the regional elites for access to populations in the periphery. But there is one major difference between the two figurations: linguistic diversity may be overcome by speakers of one language learning the other and vice versa; illiteracy is overcome in a one-way process: illiterates learn to read and write.

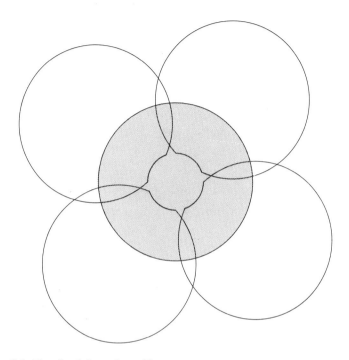

Figure 3.1 The floral figuration of languages

Note: The outer circles represent the users of the regional languages; the shaded area represents users of the standard language. Those in the unshaded part of the outer circle speak only the regional language. Those in the core star (the metropolitans) speak only the standard language. The bilingual mediation elites are to be found in the overlapping areas of the shaded central circle with the outer circles.

The shaded area may also be interpreted as representing all literates, the outer circles as regional communities of oral communication.

To sum up, there existed a floral figuration of barely, or loosely, connected regional networks of oral communication; the 'petals', together making up the 'periphery', separated by mutual unintelligibility of dialect, *or* by the impediments of distance in the case of a shared spoken standard language and continuing illiteracy. All these regional networks were united by a central set, the 'heart' of the floral diagram, which contained bilinguals or literates belonging at once to a regional network and to this central set. Finally, a third category, 'the metropolitans', also in the 'heart' of the figuration, belonged to the central set, but to no other.

What are the communicative interdependencies between the categories of language speakers in this floral language figuration? A simple formal model may serve to analyze their strategic positions. In this analysis of multilanguage figurations, the floral figuration forms a special case.

Three kinds of opportunity appear especially germane to determining the interests and interdependencies of communication in multilanguage figurations: (1) the chances for a given speaker of communicating with another in a shared language, i.e. the opportunities of 'direct communication'; (2) the odds for a given speaker of encountering a second speaker with whom there is no common language *and* of finding a third speaker, a translator, who has a language in common both with the first and the second speaker and may thus mediate between them, i.e. the opportunities of 'passive translation'; and (3) the probability for a given speaker of finding a second speaker with whom there is a common language *and* a third who shares no language with the second, but shares another language with the first, i.e. the opportunities of 'active translation'.

Next, the floral figuration of languages will be discussed as a special case of this multilanguage figuration. The focus will be on the consequences of the second-language learning for the strategic positions of the various groups. The analysis produces a number of factual generalizations which are especially relevant for the present subject: the spread of codes for national communication.

2.1 A probabilistic model of communication opportunities

Imagine a system S of different languages and of the persons speaking them. All languages are mutually unintelligible.[45] Two persons having no language in common may nevertheless communicate through an interpreter who speaks the languages of both. Persons may speak any combination of languages in S. Speakers who are all competent in the same combination[46] of languages form a uniquely defined subset of speakers.

For example, in a four-language system $S = \{E, F, G, H\}$ there exists one and only one subset of speakers $a_h = \{x_1, x_2, x_3, \ldots\}$ who are competent in the two-language combination $c_h = \{F, G\}$. The number $n(a_h)$, of speakers in a_h as a proportion of the number of all speakers, N, in the system may be written as f_h:

$$f_h = n(a_h)/\Sigma_i n(a_i); \quad 0 \leq f_h \leq 1.$$

Every speaker in S belongs to some set a_i and no speaker to more than one: the partition of groups of speakers in S according to the combination of languages they speak is disjoint ($a_i \cap a_j = \emptyset$ (for $i \neq j$) and exhaustive ($\Sigma_i f_i = 1$).

When the focus of interest is not only on the combination of languages in which speakers are competent, but also on the order in which they acquired them, i.e. one as a first language, the other(s) as second or maybe even third and fourth languages, sets of speakers may be defined according to the specific variations, or ordered combinations, of languages, o_i, that characterize them.[47] When the analysis centers on language acquisition, o_i may be a more appropriate characteristic than c_i, but the formal properties of the model remain the same and the version for variations will not be presented separately.

Although every combination of languages c_i (or variations o_i) corresponds to a set of speakers, some sets may well be empty, $a_i = \emptyset$ and $f_i = 0$: no speakers in the system have been found to be competent in that particular subset of languages. As a rule, the sets of speakers of a single language will not be empty, and most sets that correspond with two-language combinations will also not be empty (otherwise sufficient translation would not be available and the system would fall apart in disjoint subsystems). But three- and four-language combinations usually correspond with only a few speakers, or sometimes none at all.

At this point, the focus of analysis is the strategic position of speakers of some combination of languages within the system S. Following Greenberg, it is assumed that pairs of speakers are formed randomly.[48]

2.1.1 Opportunities of direct communication

The present focus is on the strategic position of *speakers* within changing systems. Here the question is, what is the probability that some speaker x_h who belongs to some set a_h with frequency f_h and language combination c_h is a member of a random pair which shares a common language and thus may communicate directly? The pair x_h and x_i will share at least one common language on condition that the language combinations c_h and c_i, spoken respectively by the speakers in the sets a_h and a_i, will have some element(s) in common. Thus the opportunities for direct communication u_h of some speaker belonging to a set of speakers a_h may be written as:

(1) $u_h = \Sigma_i f_i$ for those c_i such that $c_h \cap c_i \neq \emptyset$;

Note that i may or may not be equal to j.

Up to this point, the argument has been analogous to Greenberg's, it will now be carried further.

2.1.2 Opportunities of passive translation Apart from direct communication, a person in the system S has other opportunities. In encounters with other persons with whom there is no common language, a third person may be found who can translate for them. This requires the formation of a *triad* instead of a pair. Again, in order to assess the odds of this mediated form of communication the probability may be assessed of randomly forming a triad in which the first and second members have no language in common, while the third member shares one language with the first person and another with the second. The opportunities for passive translation v_h of a member of the set a_h may now be written as:

(2) $v_h = \Sigma_i \Sigma_j (f_i . f_j)$ for $c_h \cap c_i = 0$ *and* $c_h \cap c_j \neq 0$ *and* $c_i \cap c_j \neq 0$

Note that, by definition, $h \neq i$, $h \neq j$, $i \neq j$. The translators are members of a_j.

2.1.3 Opportunities for active translation Finally, multilingual speakers in a system S may be in a position to translate for others and this opportunity is again a component of their overall strategic position within the system. This situation occurs when a triad is formed with two other speakers who have no language in common, given that the first speaker shares a language with each of the former. The opportunity for active translation w_h for some speaker in a_h, is:

(3) $w_h = \Sigma_i \Sigma_j (f_i . f_j)$ for $c_h \cap c_i \neq 0$ *and* $c_h \cap c_j \neq 0$ *and* $c_i \cap c_j = 0$

Note that, by definition, again $h \neq i$, $h \neq j$, $i \neq j$ and that the translators are members of a_h.

2.1.4 Overall strategic opportunities Depending on the purposes of the analysis, the probabilities (1), (2) or (3) may be taken to characterize the strategic position of some speaker in the system S. The sum of these measures provides a significant indicator of overall opportunities for a speaker in a_h:

(4) $y_h = u_h + v_h + w_h$

Note that $0 \leq y_h$, but under some circumstances $y_h > 1$ (in fact, max $(y_h) = 2$).

2.2 The formal characterization of a floral figuration

Some systems may display characteristic patterns of connections between the constituent languages. These connections are formed by the sets of multilingual speakers 'linking' two or more languages.

In a 'random' system, these connections appear purely coincidental. In a 'proportional' system they are a function of the frequencies of the sets of single-language speakers ($n(c_i) = 1$) that they connect.

A pattern that is more likely to prevail is one of 'contiguity' in which languages spoken in contiguous areas are more strongly connected by bilingual speakers than those whose areas do not share a border.

A 'floral figuration of languages' is characterized on the one hand by a number of 'peripheral languages', which are not only mutually unintelligible, but which each have only a small number of translators between them, and on the other hand, by one central or metropolitan language which has a considerable number of translators in common with each of the peripheral languages. This central language is called 'L', for 'lingua franca'. In general, the sets of multilingual speakers tend to be small, say $f_i \leq m$, *unless* L is an element of the corresponding bilingual combination, and $f_i > m$. The number of elements in a set may be written as $n(c_i)$. Accordingly, a floral figuration is defined by:

(5) $f_i \leq m$ for $L \not\subseteq c_i$ and $n(c_i) \geq 2$; $f_i > m$ for $L \in c_i$ and $n(c_i) = 2$

2.3 Analysis of transformations in multilanguage figurations

We now have a very powerful, simple and general model of language figurations and of speakers' communicative opportunities within them. The next challenge is to study the transformations in these figurations, or as it is sometimes called, 'the dynamics of the system'.

For the present purposes, the key process is language learning by persons within the figuration. At this stage of the analysis, it is easier to study a subsystem with only two languages, say F and G, and accordingly only three sets c_i: $\{F\}$, $\{G\}$, and the bilingual set $\{F, G\}$, to be called c_1, c_2 and c_3 respectively.

What happens when a_3, corresponding to $c_3 = \{F, G\}$ begins to grow, because people are learning a second language? That depends on who does the learning. For the remaining monolinguals, say those in a_1, speaking only F, opportunities for *direct communication* do not increase if some speakers of their language acquire competence in the other and join a_3: they could communicate directly with them all along. But for the members of a_2, the speakers of the other language, G, opportunities for direct communication do increase as they may now communicate directly with the new bilinguals who came from a_1 to a_3 by learning G. Clearly, it is a very comfortable situation, in which speakers of other languages learn one's own language. In a floral-language figuration in which second-language learners from all peripheral language groups adopt the central language L as their second language, monolingual speakers of L (the metropolitans) are therefore in an especially favorable position: their opportunities for direct communication increase without any effort at language learning on their part.

But for the bilingual speakers already in a_3, opportunities for direct communication do not increase as their ranks grow, since they could already communicate with everyone in the two-language system.

In formal terms: since a_3 grows at the expense of a_1, $f_1 + f_3 = c$; and as $f_1 + f_2 + f_3 = 1$, $f_2 = 1 - c$. By substitution in expression (1) for u_h:

$u_1 = f_1 + f_3 = c$ (F in common); u_1 remains constant;
$u_2 = f_2 + f_3 = 1 - c + f_3$ (G in common); u_2 increases with f_3;
$u_3 = f_1 + f_2 + f_3 = 1$ (F and G in common); u_3 remains constant.

What is the impact of an increase of bilinguals in a_3 at the expense of F-speakers in a_1, on the opportunities for *passive translation*, v_h, as defined in expression (2)? For those monolinguals remaining in a_1, an increasing number of translators become available to mediate with the constant number of speakers of G only in a_2. For the monolinguals in a_2 a growing number of translators is available to mediate with a dwindling number of F-only speakers in a_1. For the bilinguals, in a_3, passive translation is irrelevant.

By substitution in expression (2):

$v_1 = f_2.f_3 = (1 - c).f_3$; v_1 increases with f_3;
$v_2 = f_1.f_3 = (c - f_3).f_3$; v_2 increases as a parabole up to $f_3 = c/2$, then decreases until $f_1 = 0$, $f_3 = c$, and $v_2 = 0$: everyone speaks G ($u_2 = 1$);
$v_3 = 0$. Passive translation opportunities are irrelevant to bilinguals. But *active translation* oportunities are all the more salient for this group (and irrelevant to a_1 or a_2).

Again, by substitution, this time in expression (3) for w_h, the opportunities of active translation become:

$w_3 = f_1.f_2 = (c - f_3).(1 - c) = -(1 - c)f_3 + c(1 - c)$

The active translation opportunities w_3, for the bilinguals in a_3, show a linear decrease: the very first tranalator ($\lim f_3 = 0$) obtains $w_3 = c - c^2$. But as the proportion f_3 grows toward its upper limit c, w_3

decreases from $c - c^2$ to 0. This is because there are fewer and fewer monolinguals in a_1 left to translate for in encounters with members of the – constant – set a_2. But this implies that speakers who are already bilingual *lose* by an increase in their numbers, even as every individual speaker may stand much to gain by joining their ranks. This loss for the original bilinguals is not made up by an increase in their direct communication opportunities u_3 which throughout have equalled 1, nor by a gain in opportunities for passive translation v_3 which do not apply to them.

Finally, as a_3 grows at the expense of a_1, while a_2 remains constant, the overall communication opportunities, $y_h = u_h + v_h + w_h$, show the following pattern:

$y_1 = u_1 + v_1 = c + (1 - c).f_3$; linear increase with f_3;

$y_2 = u_2 + v_2 = 1 - c + f_3 + (c - f_3).f_3$; parabolic increase from y_2
$= 1 - c$ for $f_3 = 0$ to $y_2 = 1$ for $f_3 = 1$.

$y_3 = u_3 + w_3 = 1 - (1 - c).f_3 + c(1 - c)$; linear decrease with f_3.

It follows that those monolinguals in a_1 who do not learn a second language nevertheless gain in overall opportunities as others from their ranks do learn another language. As overall opportunities are concerned, the monolinguals in a_2, none of whom learns a second language, also gain when members of a_1 learn their language. Thirdly, those who are bilingual at any moment, the members of a_3, only lose in overall opportunities by an addition to their ranks.

Finally, any individual moving from a_1 to a_3 by learning a second language, gains in overall opportunities:

$y_3 - y_1 = 1 - (1 - c).f_3 + c(1 - c) - \{c + (1 - c).f_3\} =$
$(1 - c).(1 + c - 2f_3)$.
The gain is positive since $(1 - c) \geq 0$ and $(1 - f_3) \geq 0$ and $(c - f_3) \geq 0$; the profit decreases as f_3 grows: late learners win least.

2.4 *Factual generalizations on the basis of the model*

On the basis of this analysis some general statements can be made about multilanguage figurations.

(1) A population of monolingual speakers stands to gain if people speaking their language learn other languages, not because of increasing opportunities for direct communication but because of growing opportunities for passive translation.

(2) A population of monolingual speakers stands to gain if people speaking other languages learn theirs, because of increasing opportunities

for direct communication and up to a point by growing opportunities for passive translation, beyond that point overall gains continue at a slower rate.

(3) People learning an added language will increase their opportunities for direct communication by gaining access to the speakers of this additional language (these gains always outweigh the loss of opportunities for passive translation which have become irrelevant); they will also increase their opportunities for active translation, the more so, the fewer other translators are yet available.

(4) Multilingual speakers have more opportunities for direct communication than the monolinguals in any of the languages which these multilinguals speak, but these opportunities are not increased if the number of speakers of their particular combination of languages increases, and by this addition they actually lose opportunities for active translation.

Of floral language figurations it can be said in general that competence in the central language provides special advantages of direct communication, since this is the language adopted by most or all second language learners; it also provides special opportunities for passive translation, since translators to every peripheral language are available and becoming more numerous as second-language learning proceeds. For these reasons acquisition of the central language may become a self-accelerating process.

If it is assumed that individuals and language groups act so as to maintain or increase their communication opportunities, these five general statements produce a process of group conflict in multilanguage, and especially in floral-language, figurations. Monolinguals will favor language learning, especially of their own language by others. Individuals may greatly increase their opportunities by learning an additional language (but the cost may often be prohibitive). Third, multilingual speakers will oppose others learning the languages between which they translate (but they may welcome others learning one of those and another language). Finally, among populations in which much second-language learning goes on, a pocket of monolingual speakers may remain, when actual opportunities for passive translation have increased and the prospective gains of active translation have decreased to a point where second-language learning appears no longer worth the effort (even though in the circumstances the costs of second-language learning may have gone down considerably).

The acquisition of literacy may be studied in terms of the model as a special case of language learning. Of course, learning goes in one direction only, toward literacy, all literates being already competent in the spoken version of the language. The illiterate population is divided into relatively disjoint groups, each with its own network of oral communication, but mutually separated, not so much by unintelligibility of languages (although that may well be the case, also), but by distance and the costs of transport. Written communications move throughout the system, but only among literates. The literates may 'translate' for illiterates by reading or writing for them. They will resist others becoming literate, as that might dilute their mediation gains. In terms of the model, written communication functions very much as a lingua franca. And similar predictions hold: illiterates gain by learning to read and write, and if they themselves do not do so they still gain from others learning; literate local elites lose opportunities for active 'translation' if illiterates among their clientele learn to read and write; literate metropolitan elites, for whom such active mediation is less important for lack of an illiterate clientele of their own, only gain from people learning to read and write as this increases their opportunities for direct communication, in writing.

Thus, in a floral figuration the speakers of the central language and the literates occupy a pivotal position. Others will strive to learn this central communication code. If the users of the central code are competent and active in that code only, like the metropolitans, they will support the spread of it for the sake of direct communication. If they are competent in both the central code and another code, as the regional elites are, they will oppose the spread of either code for the sake of maintaining their gains of active mediation. But they, too, profit when the speakers of a third code – outside their sphere of mediation – learn the central code. Although mediating groups have similar interests, they have no common interest – a fatal source of weakness.

It is manifest from the analysis that a state apparatus would tend to promote knowledge of a central code L for the entire territory, since this would enable its officials to approach the citizens directly – that is, without local mediation.[49] Equally, it was inherent in the position of those involved in supraregional commerce to support the promulgation of national codes of communication, of the standard language, of standard measures and currencies, of elementary arithmetic and geography, so as to facilitate exchange.[50] The same did not necessarily apply to industrialists who, especially in the early phases of industrialization, often operated on local markets for labor, raw materials and finished products.

For similar, but opposite, reasons it was inherent in the position of local and regional elites to oppose the spread of the standard code in their sphere of influence,[51] so as to safeguard the allegiance of their clientele and maintain their advantages of monopolistic mediation.[52] But they might well be favorable or indifferent toward the promulgation of that code in other territories than their own. This impeded collective action on the part of regional elites.

The communication interests between regional dialect speakers or illiterates and bilingual speakers or literates in that region are also divergent: in actual history they probably closely paralleled other patterns of cultural, economic and political cleavage. It is not far-fetched to imagine the bilinguals or literates as coming from the local gentry, the clergy and the *notables*;[53] while the monolinguals or illiterates may be identified as peasants, journeymen and workers. The patterns of communication of course may well have corresponded to patterns of commercial, political and cultural interaction (people, after all, tend to communicate about something). Although the lines of communicative intersection and exclusion did not always completely coincide with those other patterns of exchange, they were of importance to these other interests, too, and so, no doubt, people at the time conceived of them.

The floral-figuration approach allows a redefinition of the role of the 'forever rising' bourgeoisie as the bearer of educational reform. The bourgeoisie as a whole did not necessarily support nationwide elementary education: *notables*, such as small-town lawyers or notaries public might vehemently oppose it. Industrialists who were predominantly oriented toward regional markets sometimes preferred an alliance with members of the local establishment. On the other hand, aristocrats in national commerce and – more importantly – in the bureaucracy of the central state were prone to join those supporting elementary education for literacy or fluency in the standard language.

The different groups in the floral figuration are defined according to their position in the communication process. But a common position is not sufficient to transform the members of such a group into a coherent actor, capable of collective action. Local elites were often linked together by intermarriage, commercial interests, common sociability and the church. Most important, however, their power base usually coincided with an institutional, political entity: an incorporated town, a county and so on. This allowed the leadership to enforce common policies and it enabled local elites to operate as cohesive political actors. At times, coalitions of regional elites even gained control of the national government. There they found themselves in an ambivalent position in matters of education: the state apparatus they now controlled would increase in effectiveness by expanding national elementary education, but its gain would be at the expense of the original power bases of the local elites. As they neither could nor would undo the national system, they tried to imbue its curriculum with traditional values and allowed local authority and clergy to supervise instruction.

For peasants and the rural working class, it was much more difficult, if not impossible, to manifest themselves as a political entity in their own right. Insofar as they were organized at all, it was precisely in those institutions that the local elite controlled. This fact alone goes far to explain the weakness, or sometimes even the absence, of peasant initiative in seeking direct access to national communication networks and demanding elementary education for their children.

The metropolitan elites were in a better position to operate as coherent actors, especially when they could gain control of the government, or at least of the ministry of education and the inspectorate. But when they could not, members of the metropolitan elite had to rely on voluntary collective action to found and support schools for their own children and those of others. At this point the ambiguous character of education becomes salient: on the one hand, a child's education is an individual good, a long-term investment by parents in their offspring. On the other hand, not only do joint educational facilities reduce costs enormously, schools being much cheaper than tutors, but all parents within a given social category have a collective interest in the transmission to the next generation of uniform and shared codes for communication, a coherent body of knowledge which each one may assume the others to be familiar with.

With their voluntary tuition fees, parents bought an education for their own children, and on top of that, they contributed to the costs of their collective school system as a whole in order to increase the currency of the curriculum their children were to be educated in. Again, religious and poitical zeal, mutual social control and increasing institutionalization had to overcome the dilemmas of collective action, and, once more, clergymen acted as entrepreneurs in collective education. Here too, the collective campaigns to establish congenial schools helped to constitute the collectivities which the schools were to serve and reproduce.

The floral model provides a rough and simple scheme in which people are affected, favorably or adversely, by other people's acquisition of a second language or of literacy. These externalities represent a linguistic interdependence, which may imply concert as well as conflict. As such, it provides a first approximation of the various interests involved in language-learning and alphabetization. The parties are identified by their communicative positions within the floral figuration. These positions may often have corresponded closely to class positions, they almost always corresponded to geographic location, and they may well turn out to have correlated with religious affiliation. In other words the dynamics of a figuration of communication networks closely corresponds to the dynamics of class, religious and regional conflict.

3 Language unification in Europe and America

The French historian Marc Bloch has characterized medieval society with one grand linguistic contrast:[54]

> On the one hand, the vast majority of the illiterate, each immured in his regional dialect, restricted in his literary baggage to a few profane poems transmitted through oral recitation and to those pious chants that well-intentioned clergy composed in the vernacular for the sake of simple folk and which they sometimes wrote down from memory. On the other, the small handful of cultured people who, oscillating ceaselessly between everyday speech and the learned universal language, were truly bilingual. For them, the great works of theology and history, uniformly written in Latin; the understanding of the liturgy and of business documents. Latin was not only the language of instruction, it was the only language taught. The ability to read was the ability to read Latin.

The functions of Latin were gradually replaced by the languages of the central courts; Latin maintained itself for some centuries as the language of scholarship and in the end only as the language of the Catholic liturgy. The advent of the printing press accelerated this process: 'Printing preserved, codified, even created certain vernaculars . . . Having fortified language walls between one group and another, printers homogenized what was within them, . . . assigning a new peripheral role to provincial dialects.' And Elisabeth Eisenstein concludes:[55] 'Typography arrested linguistic drift', as would classroom instruction by centrally trained teachers, and radio and television in this century.

But the court languages, which were to expand into national languages as nation states evolved, succeeded only slowly, and never completely, in driving out the regional dialects. The royal court imposed the use of the court language upon the landed aristocracy and as a result the local elites usually became bilingual, using both the regional dialect and the court language, which thus began to function as the modern lingua franca. Those who could not read or speak this language remained confined to the local, oral community and cut off from the cultural and political life beyond it: 'the village community . . . was politically isolated, save for those at the head of the community; the squire and sometimes the parson were the links between the village and the nation.'[56]

Historical maps of linguistic diversity in early modern France[57] and

Britain (or Russia and Spain for that matter) display a floral pattern: a large, central patch indicates the area where the standard language was current and includes a very large metropolitan area around the capital city, London or Paris. At the periphery, these maps show regions where dialects, and even distinctly different languages, were in use. Such outlying zones had often been conquered or acquired more recently, having long remained independent, like Scotland and Wales, or been part of another realm, like Catalonia[58] for example, while others continued to be contested, even into this century, as Alsace was between France and Germany.[59]

The pattern of language diversity in what is now the United Kingdom is well characterized by the expression 'the Celtic fringe':[60] the great arc of Scotland, Ireland, Wales and the Isle of Man, all with a different Celtic language, surrounding the English-speaking heartland. The anglicization of the elites in Scotland began as early as the thirteenth century; in Wales it had its origins in the Union of 1536. Especially in Wales, the gentry 'went at great length to dissociate themselves from their rude and barbaric countrymen' by adopting English speech and manners.[61] The anglicization of the common people of Scotland began with the proselytizing efforts of the established church[62] and was taken up in Wales with renewed energy in the nineteenth century, when the Anglican Church at first, the central government later, founded elementary schools. The Dissenting School Society, competing with the Anglicans, tended to favor local speech and was accepted more readily for it among common Welshmen.[63] Official educational policy and the advent of industrialization, which stamped English as the language of progress and opportunity, led to the gradual decline of the Celtic languages in public life first and, with the introduction of mass media, almost completely in private situations also.[64]

The linguistic geography of France under the *ancien régime* represents the paramount example of a floral model of languages. The pattern has survived well into the nineteenth century, as Eugen Weber has documented: 'a wealth of tongues' prevailed.[65] The French kings insisted on the use of French in the transaction of official business, but were not much concerned with the speech of the common people. 'Burghers of the bigger towns, men of law of course, nobles, and clerics became bilingual or multilingual.'[66] At the time of the French Revolution, Grégoire's investigations showed that out of some 25 million people only 3 million were fluent in French and 6 million did not know it at all.[67]

With the Revolution began the campaign for language unification, carried out through the establishment of state elementary schools. The Catholic Church and local priests resisted, motivated more by a concern to maintain their local control and to safeguard the religious curriculum than by a commitment to local speech. In this respect they reflected, rather than led, local resistance. But, as Eugen Weber remarks,[68] 'One of the greatest enemies of patois was simply its own parochialism.' Elementary schooling and military conscription finally overcame regional language diversity and by 1900 peasant children had come to despise their local dialect and preferred to learn the language of mobility and opportunity.

In the German lands, where political fragmentation persisted much longer, the linguistic pattern was surprisingly homogeneous. Local dialects differed considerably, but as early as 1500 German was the vernacular from the Ostsee to the Danube and from the Oder to the Maas, with only one enclave of Sorbic, a Slavonic language, around Lützen, south of Berlin.[69] A written version of the language was widely used for official purposes. Only on the fringe of the area that was to become the German Reich, different languages and clearly distinct dialects persisted, related to Czech, Polish or Danish, and in the extreme north to Frisian, which was also spoken in the north in the Low Countries.[70]

With the Prussian annexations of Polish territory in 1772, a large heteroglottic population came under German control. For the next century official language policy was 'pragmatic', 'liberal' and 'cautious'. Polish remained the vernacular of the large majority in a mostly rural society. The nobility was the first to become bilingual, German being the language used by the Prussian officials and the courts and in interregional trade.[71] Germanization, always an implicit and remote objective, became the manifest and energetic policy of the Reich after 1871. Language unification then proceeded, as in other places where regional languages had survived, as part of the campaign for compulsory elementary education: 'alphabetization as an instrument of language policy'.[72] The Catholic clergy opposed this German influence: initially siding with the local squires in rejecting any Prussian initiatives in education, later in the century it began to support elementary schools with a Catholic curriculum and Polish as the language of instruction. In this case linguistic and educational conflict became part of a national struggle which in this century formed an issue in two succeeding world wars.

The Netherlands, too, were relatively homogeneous with respect to language. In the Republic, contact between the various regions was mediated mainly through the urban elites; the peasantry and the common people had little or no part in it. The speech of the Amsterdam patriciate served as a standard.[73] As national integration proceeded in the Netherlands, the speech of its vanguard, the bourgeoisie, came to be accepted as 'general civilized Dutch'. This standard language served the function of communication in an integrating society, especially in secondary relations – among strangers and within formal institutions. But, as Goudsblom has pointed out, it also provides a standard of civilized behavior by its strict regulation of speech forms, thus linking people together while at the same time increasing the distance between people with 'refined' and 'rough' manners of speech.

In the southern and northern fringes of the Netherlands distinct dialects are still in use. In Limburg, in the south, a dialect persists which was once felt to be a variation of 'high' German and is at present perceived to be a dialect of its close relative, Dutch, or low German;[74] Frisian survives in the north of the Netherlands; recently revived as a language of instruction, law and politics. But on the whole, regional variation in speech has gradually disappeared without much conflict in the Netherlands and contemporary mass media now impose a country-wide standard of spoken Dutch.

At the beginning of the twentieth century, national language unification had almost been completed in Western Europe, at least when it came to written communication. Clearly distinct language communities existing next to one another within one national territory now persist only in Belgium and Switzerland: all petal and no heart. But, except for Swiss Rhaeto-Romanic, the languages spoken in these countries are regional versions of the national languages in adjoining realms; both countries have survived as independent political units at the intersection of much larger political entities.

The United States has also developed into a unitary linguistic community. Native American languages almost disappeared with the conquest of the continent by European settlers and the Indian wars. The languages once current in the more recent acquisitions, Louisiana, New Mexico, California, belonged to different linguistic empires, France and Spain respectively. But not much of this language diversity survived into the nineteenth century.

In America, immigration was another important source of linguistic variation, but this did not last long either. Linguistic assimilation proceeds very differently and at a much faster rate among migrants than it does among sedentary populations such as constitute an established language community. Immigrants, after all, have made the decision to move to another place and are usually ready to adopt the culture of their new environment. Moreover, they confront the new culture separately or in small groups of settlers, uprooted and cut off from their communities of origin. Given the overwhelming advantages of linguistic assimilation to the new environment and their orientation toward upward mobility, immigrants tend to abandon their original language within two or three generations at the most. As a result, the 'United States, ethnically the most heterogeneous nation, is one of the most linguistically homogeneous.'[75]

Migration played a major, but mostly forgotten and unrecoverable, role in European language unification also. As in the United States, rural folk who came to town gave up their local speech, and townspeople who gravitated to the metropolitan area equally adopted the standard language. But in England and France, reverse migration also played an important role. Officials and entrepreneurs who came to the peripheral regions acted as unintentional missionaries for the standard language and contributed to its ascendancy by their prestigious presence. Soldiers quartered in garrison cities and skilled workers coming to the new industrial zones – for example the mining areas of Wales – also spread the word, conveying an aura of innovation and modernity to the metropolitan language (which, therefore, was often as despised as they were). Here, as in Ireland, or in the French countryside, the local population in great numbers abandoned its speech for the standard language, just as American immigrants did, since it was the prerequisite for social mobility. '*Who* speaks the language is ultimately far more important than *how many*', writes Dorian, and she adds elsewhere: 'the adoption of a dominant-culture language (even at the exclusion of their own) by the members of a subordinate or peripheral culture is an adaptive, or coping strategy.'[76] One may add that the *strategic* position of a language community as the one that links together all other linguistic groups in society may be most important in the end.

By 1800 all these nations had seen the establishment throughout the land of a system of government agencies and law courts, where the standard language was required for transacting official business and drafting legal documents. Postal-relay systems carried instructions, letters, books, tracts and newspapers to every outpost of the realm, almost all of them written in the standard language. Cultured, learned, legal and official discourse all required knowledge of this central code, in both its written and its spoken versions.

Local elites and *notables* were fluent in the standard language, having learned it at school, if it had not been their first language right from the nursery. Some of them had even forgotten, or affected not to know, the local speech. Latin still survived as a lingua franca, but only among clergymen and scholars. Throughout the eighteenth century, French functioned abroad as the international language of diplomacy and high culture, and also as the first or second language of the court, the aristocracy and part of the *haute bourgeoisie* in the Netherlands, Germany and Russia (where German also fulfilled similar functions).

The use of French by these elites extended their communication network to include the elites in other nations, but it mainly served the purpose of social distinction from the lower bourgeoisie and the working classes. In the same vein, the members of the higher bourgeoisie in the early nineteenth century supported the revival of Latin as the language of higher education and the professions in order to distinguish themselves from the lower strata, once the latter also began to attend secondary schools. Clearly, the value of such codes did not only reside in the number of their users and in the availability of translation to other languages: they also provided direct access to a transnational network linking together national elites – their strategic function. And, these exclusive languages allowed preferential access within the corresponding elite networks, since users of the exclusive code were given priority over others who might also communicate directly, but in a vernacular which was accorded lower status. In the same manner, the professional vocabularies which have superseded Latin in the twentieth century now function as exclusive codes. To account for the phenomenon of these 'contained languages' the floral model should be modified by the incorporation of the aspect of 'competition for access' into direct communication.[77]

By the end of the eighteenth century the metropolitan population as a whole and the gentry and *notables* of the peripheral regions were fluent in the standard language. This speech remained unknown to the poor, the working people and the peasants in large parts of the outlying regions, in France and Britain especially, and to immigrants from abroad. From the French Revolution on, central governments were to make a persistent attempt to introduce the standard language as the vernacular for all classes in all parts of the land. Local elementary schools were to be the instruments of this campaign, which involved in one grand effort instruction in reading, writing and arithmetic, national history and geography.

The history of linguistic assimilation and unification remains to be written. First of all, it is very difficult to reconstruct the degree of mutual intelligibility between various dialects and the 'holosystem'[78] of which they were part. Second, such statistics on self-reported linguistic competence as are available at all are scanty and unreliable, if only because people considered it socially undesirable or, on the contrary, politically opportune, to profess ignorance or, as the case might be, knowledge of the regional or the standard language.[79] Third, it is almost impossible to trace back the actual patterns of usage or of 'language shift' that prevailed among different sections of the population and at different occasions for a given area and a given historical period.[80] Fourth, actual resistance against the imposition of the standard language was mostly passive, tacit and covert. People affected not to understand whenever it suited them best. The Dutch colonial expression 'East Indian deaf' nicely conveys this suspected simulated incomprehension of the imperial language. A more eloquent protest against the neglect and wilful abolition of regional speech was not to emerge until regional languages appeared to be in danger of extinction. It came first from emigrants who had left for the city and, having made good, now turned back to look at what they had left behind. These regional-cultural revival movements strongly romanticized the threatened heritage and tended to exaggerate the tenacity with which the local population clung to it.[81] Such regionalism became a political force only in combination with resistance to the economic domination of the regions by metropolitan entrepreneurs and politicians. Most contemporary literature on problems of regional languages breathes an indignant romanticism, as if regional language were *per se* superior to standard speech and had disappeared without any complicity on the part of regional speakers.

In the nineteenth century, the conflict between linguistic diversity and unification was almost entirely subsumed under the conflict over elementary education as the vehicle of language assimilation. The advantages of fluency in the standard language completely coincided with those of literacy, which by then had come to mean literacy in the national language.

On the whole, local elites opposed the extension of elementary education to the lower classes, thus resisting implicitly the propagation of literacy and of competence in the national language among their heteroglottic clientele, as the floral model would lead one to expect. But contrary to the model's predictions, the local peasants and working people were often not overly eager to have their children learn to speak, read and write the standard language. This was partly because those who were oriented toward the new opportunities of the market and the civil service voted with their feet and left for the cities. It was partly, also, out of the sheer necessity and traditionalism: they could not afford to do without their children's work. Parents often did not see what advantages learning would yield, and in fact, in stagnant communities it did not do much to increase opportunities. Finally, many parents feared the rebellion of children who had become wiser than their elders; they identified with the ancient order of things, with authority and with traditional local manners and speech.

The impetus for the unification of the language, for alphabetization, and thus for the spread of elementary education, came from the metropolitan circles around the growing state apparatus and the expanding national market, from the speakers of the central language only, who, in terms of the model, stood much to gain from others learning the lingua franca. And once the metropolitan campaign was under way, the momentum was kept up by its vanguard: the schoolteachers recruited to carry out the actual task.

4 The churches: local monopoly and state support

The school was the most important, but not the sole, institution for the acquisition of fluency and literacy in the standard language. And other subjects in the elementary curriculum – arithmetic, history, geography and even religion – may also be interpreted as codes facilitating communication in a wider context.

The issue whether the children of the lower classes should learn to speak, read and write the standard language, may be interpreted in terms of exclusion from, or access to, the central communications network. This matter had, of course, immediate consequences for the monopolistic position of the mediating elites in regional networks, elites which usually were in a position to control local education.

In multilingual figurations almost everywhere, the clergy, generally literate and very often fluent in the standard language (in Catholic countries also in Latin), formed an important part of the mediating elites. From early times, churches had taken a special interest in education: in Europe and the United States the clergy came close to monopolizing control over the schools until the end of the eighteenth century, usually in concert with, or in the service of, the rural elites.

Although in a figuration of linguistic diversity or widespread illiteracy the local clergy performed monopolistic mediating functions, this does not imply that the church organization in its entirety identified with the position of local mediators. As an organization, it had as its first interest in education the maintenance or the increase of control over the schools, to ensure that its teachings were being spread there. If the church leadership believed its position to be strong enough to maintain its educational monopoly even in a unified national network of communication, where a single standard language and general literacy would prevail, this would be its option of first preference. In actual history such a position of monopoly in national education always required strong state support and, if they thought such support likely, established majority churches would opt for a 'maximalist' strategy: a state-supported monopoly for church-controlled elementary education of all children in the reading and writing of the standard language.

But if the state could not be counted upon to support a monopoly, elementary education in the standard language and in reading and writing might break open hitherto secure local networks of oral communication, undoing the monopolistic mediating position of the local clergy in alliance with the gentry, and allowing other denominations or lay educators to proselytize in the provinces of the established church. For these reasons – denominational competition and regionalist interests – a church that saw no chance of securing a state-supported monopoly in education would opt for its second preference: complete state abstinence from education and full reliance on regional elites to maintain local monopolies: a 'minimalist' stance.

The two, apparently wholly contradictory, stances were in fact quite close to one another, a matter of different estimates of the policies that might be adopted by the regime in power. But either position, maximalist or minimalist, presupposed a strong base in many regional networks. This dilemma presented itself to dominant denominations and established churches, such as the Catholic Church in France, the Lutheran Church in Prussia or the Anglican Church in England. For minority denominations the situation looked rather different. Since they did not stand a chance of obtaining an educational monopoly with state support, they would vehemently oppose the maximalist stance of the dominant church. Their first inclination was to side with the minimalist position of no state interference whatsoever and to rely on their own local networks. But some of these denominations were more ambitious in their proselytizing educational efforts: they began to claim some support from the state. One type of denomination was particularly likely to obtain such aid: a creed with many adherents among the 'metropolitans' who had no clientele of their own in a local communication network. Once any minority denomination succeeded in obtaining privileges from the state, all other churches might claim the same: a 'most-favored denomination' status. This, then, was the third stance, the 'pluralist' strategy: state support for church-controlled education by a multiplicity of denominations, according to some rule for the distribution of subsidies, which then became the subject of contention.

In this argument the position of the churches with regard to mass elementary education is defined quite independently of their respective substantive teachings. Almost every mature denomination possesses a body of doctrine sufficiently complex to justify either state support or state abstinence: religious monopoly in education or religious variety or denominationally neutral education with additional voluntary catechization.[82]

In other words, the role of the Catholic Church cannot be inferred from the Catholic faith – its policy was vastly different depending on its position in the figuration of communication networks in France, England or the United States, and it changed with changes in the figuration. Thus the policy of the Catholic Church in France was much more reminiscent of the Anglican Church in England or of the Lutheran in Prussia than of its policy in the Netherlands or in the United States – its course depended mostly on its estimates of the chances of monopolizing control with support from the state, or having to accept other denominations and lay schools as equally favored competitors.

The position of the churches in the struggle over elementary education was dictated by considerations of strategy in the competition for control over schools, supported either by the state or by regional power bases.

In countries with a variety of denominations, or with a large nondenominational minority, a curriculum emerged, containing only those religious, moral and 'civic' elements that would be acceptable to parents of every persuasion: a general Christian *paideia*.[83] Such a 'highest common denomination' was at first vehemently opposed by almost every church out of fear that it would come to replace religious instruction completely. This fear proved to be well founded. The universal code for the avoidance of religious offense in the end helped to produce an etiquette for confrontations between strangers which showed the irrelevance of religion to most modern social pursuits.

5 Lower and middle classes, primary and secondary schools

Three major movements mark the development of mass elementary education: the spread of a standard language for oral and written communication; the encapsulation of religious conflict, either by the establishment of separate schools for different denominations or by the separation of religious teaching from the standard curriculum; and, thirdly, the differentiation of the educational system into primary and secondary streams, and more recently into a tertiary stream at university level.

Before elementary education became accessible to the great majority of workers' and peasants' children, the sons of the regional and metropolitan elites were already being educated, at home, and more and more in *Gymnasiums*, *Realschulen*, *lycées* and *collèges*, *académies*, Latin and public schools, etc. In the course of the nineteenth century, elementary classes were often set up as preparatory extensions to these elite schools. Children from the upper classes did not attend the popular schools, and workers' or peasants' children who had completed their elementary education were rarely admitted to these secondary schools. Instead, a few years of extended primary education, mostly technical and vocational, were added to the career in the popular school. Thus, the popular 'primary' stream was never made to connect with the elite 'secondary' flow.[84] On the contrary, as popular education took off, the elite curriculum was differentiated even further from the mass program. Latin enjoyed a revival as the language of secondary instruction,[85] and by the time this classic lingua franca was abandoned again, other 'codes' served to maintain social distance between 'lower-class' and 'middle-class' children, as they were known by then. The metropolitans had indeed succeeded in establishing a national communication network which allowed direct access to all citizens in the written standard language as it was by then being taught to practically every child. But as this was being accomplished, and regional elites were losing their mediation advantages, they and the metropolitan bourgeoisie sought to secure their social privileges by restricting access to new positions of income and status, especially in the professions and the civil service. Since these modern careers had come legally within reach of every person duly qualified, irrespective of rank or birth, the qualifications had to be monopolized; this was the new function of the secondary-school system. The renaissance of Latin has been explained by the concern to protect access to these expanding career opportunities, e.g. in law, medicine and the civil service.[86] The reborn elite language did not connect people who would be unable to communicate without it, as it had in the Middle Ages; now everyone could speak, read and write the standard language, and Latin provided no advantages of mediation to its users. But as a 'contained' language, it served very effectively to impede access for the great majority. Although everything that had to be communicated among the literati could be said in the standard language, and many new concepts were very difficult to articulate in Latin, it served the purpose of distinction and exclusion.

In the end, Latin did not keep its key position as the exclusive language of the professional and bureaucratic elites, even though it was used until well into the twentieth century. Technological and economic expertise also opened up elite career avenues (their jargon being as impenetrable and exclusive), while the humanistic schools gradually abandoned Latin as the language of instruction, continuing to teach it as a foreign language.

A different code, less conspicuous and circumscribed, emerged instead and served as effectively to exclude the uninitiated. In a society of universal suffrage, class differences became more subtle, more pervasive, without ever losing their bite as marks of distinction. Basil Bernstein has demonstrated how a 'hidden curriculum' may implicitly convey communication skills especially suited for communication between diverse elites in society: this 'elaborated code' serves as a means of communication in a wide gamut of social relations and over a broad range of topics: 'An elaborated code is universalistic with references to its meaning in as much as it summarizes *general* social means and ends. A restricted code is particularistic with reference to its meanings in as much as it summarizes *local* means and ends.'[87]

The concept of a lingua franca, allowing exclusive communication among elites in different, disjoint networks, has gone through a number of phases by now. The idea was applied quite literally to the floral figuration of mutually unintelligible regional languages intersected by a lingua franca spoken among the bilingual elites in each region. The position of the lingua franca was then taken up by literacy, uniting the literate in each regional network of oral communication, relatively isolated by the paucity of transport. 'Lingua franca' was used as a metaphor when it was applied to the general Christian *paideia* which allowed members of all denominations to communicate while avoiding religious offense. The same concept of a central communication code may finally be applied to the 'elaborated code' which Bernstein ascribes to the middle-class curriculum. No doubt, this 'elaborated' code again excludes those who use the 'restricted codes' and who are therefore much less capable of managing encounters with strangers or dealing with matters at an abstract and universal level, for which the 'elaborated code' is especially suited. One function of the 'elaborated code' is the management of people within an organizational context. Other than Latin, the 'elaborated code' does indeed permit communication in ways and with people that are inaccessible in a single restricted code, and these restricted codes are mutually isolated to a great degree. In this sense, diffuse as it may be, the elaborated code does function as a communication code for the central set, providing mutually connected elites with the advantages of mediation among their respective clienteles.

6 The beginnings of elementary mass education in Western Europe and the United States

In the process of European state formation, the elementary education of peasants and workers in national codes of communication represented the most significant inroad on the mediation monopolies of local elites – the first breakthrough to a national network of mass communication. The landed nobility and local clergy confronted the metropolitan elites of officials oriented toward the central state, and of entrepreneurs geared toward a national market: their conflict may be analyzed in terms of the floral figuration of communication.

All the time, however, other conflicts also played a part in the struggle about elementary education. In the United States, as in Europe, immigrants were felt to threaten the established urban order; industrial workers demanded opportunities which middle-class parents tried to monopolize for their children; and as new religious and political organizations emerged, they soon acquired vested interests of their own. The school struggles contributed, in turn, to a revival of religious loyalties and a strengthening of denominational ties, sometimes regional in character, often also at a national level.

The following sections briefly describe the development of national systems of elementary education – an exploration of the relevance and validity of the perspective developed in the preceding sections.

6.1 Prussia

In Prussia more than anywhere else school reform was an object of government policy. In order to finance his military exploits, Frederick the Great (ruled 1740–95) required an ever increasing tax-flow and intended to raise it by promoting trade and industry. This, in turn, demanded improved education: 'It should seek to awaken a certain commercial genius or drive and delight', wrote Bergius, the administrative scholar or 'cameralist' in 1768.[88]

The development of a German standard language was another objective: 'without such a national language, no art or culture,' Frederick II wrote (in French).[89] 'Now there is only a half-barbarian tongue, with as many ways of speech as there are provinces in Germany.' In the parish schools the stress should no longer be solely on catechization for the raising of good Christians, but there would also have to be a 'civil catechism' to educate good citizens.[90] But even zealous reformists, who expected education to raise loyal and productive citizens, at the same time feared for its potential to awaken ambitions that would be wholly incompatible with the order of a predominantly feudal, rural society: 'for the countryside it will do when they learn to write and read a little. But when they know too much they will only run away to the cities and want to become clerks or something like that.' Thus Frederick II wrote to his minister of education, Von Zedlitz, and he warned him that 'the peasants should not run away from the villages, but stay nicely put.'[91]

These concerns neatly define the limits of eighteenth-century reform schemes in Europe. Nothing came of Frederick's plans, for lack of funds in the first place, and because even cautious improvement of peasant schools proved unacceptable to the estate-owners.[92] This preoccupation with the emancipatory potential of mass education was echoed all over Europe: 'it must not elevate the common man above his estate,' the Dutch reformers warn;[93] nor should it breed dissatisfaction with the peasant way of life. In 1770 the Anglican Bishop Goldsmith rhymed: 'If to the city sped, what waits him there? / To see profusion that he must not share.'[94]

The reform proposals that appeared functional at one level, that of the Prussian state, were considered most dysfunctional at the other level, that of the Prussian estate. Frederick's reforms were paralyzed from the outset by the threat of a confrontation between the feudal aristocracy of the estates and the bureaucracy of the emerging national state. As yet, there was no commercial middle class of sufficient number and wealth to tip the balance in favor of the metropolitan bureaucrats and their proposals for educational renewal.

The reform proposals envisaged an educational system which was tiered according to the class divisions of Prussian society. The lowest schools, the *Volksschulen*, were intended for peasants or all those others who were considered fit for manual labor only and 'whose condition in life education should not render insupportable', as Von Zedlitz expressed it. Another kind of school, the *Realschule*, was to be established for the *Bürger*, and the nobility would attend the *Ritterschulen*.[95]

In terms of the floral model of communication, the peasants would stand to gain by unmediated access to the national network, and education would provide them with it. But they stood entirely outside the political process, controlled as it was by the rural lords. However, the few times that they did make themselves heard, they demanded the preservation of traditional religion and the inherited ways. In Nassau it even came to a rebellion, the so-called 'ABC war' against the introduction of new, more 'enlightened' textbooks.[96]

With hindsight and from a rational viewpoint, elementary schooling promised to increase the communicative opportunities of the peasantry.

But the realities of traditional rural life, and certainly of Prussian serfdom, precluded such ambitions: 'apathy toward schooling was a rational stance for most early modern families,' writes Mary Jo Maynes:

> Agricultural families everywhere relied heavily upon seasonal child labor. There was little free schooling available, so sending a child to school meant a strain upon often marginal family budgets. Economic payoff from schooling was minimal for most peasant families, although elementary education was undoubtedly becoming more relevant with growing commercialization of the rural economy.[97]

Moreover, in traditional communities, peasants, serfs included, strongly identified with established authority and may well have feared that their children educated without God or law, would turn against them. Their lords were even more conservative: when Von Zedlitz proposed 'to put some geography in the peasants' heads', he was accused of inciting the peasants to desertion by teaching them the map of the area.[98]

Eighteenth-century attempts at school reform remained almost entirely without practical effect, but they did lay some of the theoretical and administrative foundations for the establishment of an elementary-school system in the following century.

First of all, the principle of universal and compulsory education, which had been promulgated many times since it was first written into the ordinances of Magdeburg in 1658 and which each time had remained a dead letter,[99] had gained wide acceptance by the end of the eighteenth century.[100] It was also accepted that basic education would have to proceed in the standard language of the realm, German, rather than in Latin, the lingua franca of pre-modern times, which long remained the language of instruction in the higher *Bürger-* and *Realschulen*.[101]

The elementary curriculum in eighteenth-century Prussia had concentrated on catechization of the most automatic kind. But it also conveyed a degree of literacy in the standard language. And a sustained effort was made to educate the children of the poor and of the soldiery in reading, writing and also in practical domestic skills and crafts so as to instill a sense of industry and obedience.[102]

Yet, as long as serfdom continued, any direct access to national culture, trade and politics was out of the question for the rural masses. And when, after 1791, it was formally abolished as a consequence of the *Allgemeines Landrecht* and subsequent legislation,[103] the local lords remained in secure control of the local schools, supported at the national level by the conservative parties, and at the village level by the *Deputation* that controlled the local school,[104] hand-picked by the village squire.

Throughout the nineteenth century the central state and the local landed elites agreed that rural elementary education should serve to inculcate loyalty both to the nation and to the local lords and they went to great lengths to ensure that nothing untoward was being taught.[105] This concern apparently overrode religious differences, as Catholic schools rarely protested against this close supervision by the Lutheran state, its inspectors or the local deputies.[106] By mid-century, opposition came more often from Lutheran teachers who resented the constant meddling of the authorities: 'Protestant teachers as early as 1848 overwhelmingly demanded that schools be autonomous' and advocated schools that would be nonconfessional.[107] Educated and upwardly mobile as they were, the teachers, who were often stationed in the villages against their will, sought access to the metropolitan network.

Through literacy, elementary knowledge of arithmetic, history and geography and by a thorough immersion in Christian morality, the rural masses of Prussia became minimally competent in communication with the central state, and increasingly also with the merchants and entrepreneurs who operated on the national market. But at the same time their actual opportunities for social mobility remained greatly restricted, largely because of the almost caste-like, three-tiered school system.

In this manner, the lower ranks of the population had become directly accessible to the state as taxpayers, recruits and, later on, as voters (in a public ballot). Yet they found little opportunity to use this national network for their own purposes. On the contrary, the lords and the Prussian state used the schools as a vehicle for incessant indoctrination in civic loyalty. In doing so, however, they could not avoid creating a potentially rebellious teaching body[108] and supplying the urban poor and the rural peasants with communicative skills which would one day help them to organize for political emancipation.

Throughout the eighteenth century the attempts at educational reform by the Hohenzollern court were aimed at establishing immediate access to the peasant population and breaking the hold of the rural lords over their clientele. In large measure, this was a struggle for military control: soldiers for the King's army were supplied by the *Junker* from among their serfs and tenants, and these local lords might not always be forthcoming.[109] The French Revolution spurred on the attempt to bring the rural population under the direct control of the central state. The Prussian court saw itself compelled to mobilize a national army and a national productive effort against the French menace. Part of the effort to free the country's human and economic resources from feudal bounds was the drive for mass education which would instill loyalty toward the Prussian state.[110]

With the French revolutionary armies defeated, and a conservative alliance in power in almost all of Europe, the Prussian estate-owners succeeded in taking over control of the state apparatus. From this vantage-point they tolerated the expansion of mass education, while restricting the curriculum to the requirements of raising loyal subjects. Thus, although education was the subject of central legislation, control over finance, the curriculum and the disciplining of the teaching body remained with the local authorities, while the popular and the higher school systems continued to be carefully segregated.[111]

The conservative coalition was strong enough to tide over the March revolts of 1848 and survive the foundation of the Reich in 1871, until it broke down with the defeat of 1918.

In the case of Prussia, the persistence of local power was assured because local elites had coalesced to capture state power. But as they exerted this central control, they could not avoid developing precisely those centralized bureaucracies, such as the army, the civil service, and the school system, that would gradually undermine the traditional autonomy of the local institutions which formed the original power base of the *Junker*. Elementary education consisted in large part of indoctrination in the traditional values of loyalty to the Lutheran Church, the feudal estate and the Prussian – later the German – state, but it also produced citizens fluent and literate in German and quite capable of participating in the national communication process. In the end they put this competence to new uses, in the trade unions and the liberal or radical political parties.

6.2 France

What was unique to the beginnings of elementary education in Prussia was not so much the content of the reform proposals, but their origin in the crown itself. The next time educational reform was to be debated in the very center of state power, it was in France, not by the king, but among the regicides of the constitutional assembly.

Before the Revolution, writes Gontard,[112] the school used to be no more than an annex to the church, the teacher first of all a man of God, an assistant to the priest. From 1724, state inspectors had gradually gained in significance:[113] the actions of the *intendant* still remained limited in scope and discreet in manner, to avoid a clash with the church, but they were effective.[114] With its inspectors, the state had acquired a power of veto in the establishment of schools, which remained the prerogative of the Catholic Church.

This almost complete control of education by the established church the French revolutionaries set out to abolish at one stroke and to replace with an entirely new system of universal, secular, free and compulsory elementary education. Even today this episode remains contested among French historians and educationalists. Both parties agree that the revolutionary proposals were entirely impractical and that all schools deteriorated under the Republic. Allain, who published his *L'Œuvre scolaire de la Révolution* in 1901, squarely blames the revolutionaries for the destruction of the schools: 'Destruction was inevitable; the confession must be remembered and these three words reveal the entire genius of the revolution.'[115] But Gontard, writing from a secular point of view more than half a century later, considers the demise of the schools an inevitable consequence of the Revolution, since their existence was inextricably tied to the *ancien régime* of church, aristocracy and the monarchy.[116]

The initial proposals envisaged a state-financed school system without tuition, where all children would be nourished and instructed, with the parents as the enforcers of attendance (this was apparently where the authority of the state ended), and with French as the language of instruction,[117] 'so as to strengthen the unity of the Nation through unification of the language.'[118] Eugen Weber remarks:[119] 'All this was easier said than done,' and 'what survived from the shipwreck was the principle.' As Weber has documented, patois was still widespread throughout France as late as the 1870s and beyond, and even at that time many French peasants spoke no French at all. Yet in 1794 the Convention decided that *instituteurs* were to be expedited immediately to every community in the regions where other languages than French were current: 'Let the language be like the Republic; from the north to the Midi, all over French territory, tongues and hearts should be in unison.'[120] In other words, dialects and foreign languages were to be abolished and French imposed by revolutionary decree. As Eugen Weber remarks, it was the principle that mattered. Thus successive conventions proposed a series of aggressive reforms for breaking down local mediation monopolies by abolishing regional speech in favor of standard French and by making instruction in reading and writing compulsory.

The Revolution engaged in a battle which it abandoned halfway, whereas Frederick II had not even started it: the dismantling of the local schools under the control of the clergy and village nobility and their replacement by a unitary system of free, public, compulsory, secular, elementary education. The French Revolution invented the administrative techniques of the *levée en masse* and the supply of mass armies, as Frederick II had developed the techniques of managing standing armies over a long period of time. The organizational capacities for a nationwide overturning of the school system may well have existed among the French revolutionary ranks, but foreign wars required all available resources, effort and enthusiasm.

The reform attempts by the Prussian royal court were blocked by the *Junker*, and the revolutionary French parliaments had failed for lack of funds and administrative resources. Yet these failures pointed to a deeper shortcoming. The apparatus and the techniques of central government required to carry out such a massive operation had not yet been developed. What Frederick II and the French revolutionaries were capable of, each in their own way, was an unparalleled military effort. Both regimes had grappled with the budgetary, logistic and administrative problems of maintaining a formidable fighting force. Prussian policy had been aimed at promoting industry and commerce so as to raise taxes to pay for a standing army. Educational reform was initiated as part of this overall project. The French had succeeded in drafting a mass army, supplying it and transporting it over long distances – once on its way it supported itself in the traditional manner of plunder and requisition. This was the state of the art of central military administration by 1800. But universal elementary education would have posed new problems of governance: it required the development of techniques for raising and allotting funds, building schools throughout the realm according to population densities, developing and imposing a standard curriculum, overruling entrenched local and religious opposition, training and examining teachers for certification, inspecting the condition and performance of each school, disciplining the new and expansive teaching body (which might pose for a government many of the problems that armies are prone to create, including intellectual armies), prodding the local school authorities and getting the children to attend the school, not just on paper, but in person. As a matter of fact, military mobilization might have been a good training ground for an educational *levée en masse*, which was more or less how the Convention went about it, sending its *instituteurs* into the villages in the same way as its recruiters and quartermasters. But it was only a half-hearted attempt: the Convention had other, more pressing business to attend to, and although it passed a series of decrees, they were drafted carelessly and debated only perfunctorily. And the *instituteurs* met staunch opposition in the villages where they had to face the priest on his own ground.

Nothing much came of educational reform in the following years either.[121] And yet the Revolution had laid down the guidelines for educational reform for the century to come: secularization, civic indoctrination, and national unity. In the early nineteenth century centralization was partly a response to the strength of the centrifugal forces of regionalist particularism. And in the meantime, the Catholic Church patiently attempted to regain its hold over the elementary schools.[122]

Under Napoleon, neglect of elementary education became intentional policy: 'Keeping the masses systematically ignorant, so as to subject them better to his tyranny, such were his principles,' writes Godechot.[123] The emperor left the entire enterprise of elementary education in abeyance: 'the schools, like the teachers, are in a state of misery', Gontard comments.[124] The emperor was indifferent to the issue, except when it came to the training of an administrative and military elite: for this purpose he established an Imperial University (1808) which would control the entire system of universities and secondary *lycées* and *collèges* through a rigid mechanism of teacher certifications and central examinations. With the Restoration control of the university was turned over to the church, only to be contested time and again in the years to come.

In the new Bourbon kingdom (1815–30), the initiative in elementary education was with a group of educationalists, united in the very influential *Société pour l'instruction élémentaire*, who propagated the *école mutuelle*, explicitly modelled upon the English Lancasterian or 'monitorial' system which provided for advanced pupils to teach the younger ones under the master's supervision.[125] The Catholic teaching congregations protested that the *Société* wanted to do away with religious instruction, and replace it by a vague moral education, leaving it to the priest to teach the catechism after school hours. Louis XVIII, who supported the Lancasterian proposals, guaranteed that the Catholic religion and no other would be taught in the new schools. With the English influence on pedagogical method came the adoption of the Dutch model of school organization in the Law of 1816.

A long-drawn-out struggle between the *Société* and the church ensued, blocking further legislation, but mobilizing public opinion on a grand scale throughout the land. The church was forced into popular education, even though 'to the half-educated brought up without God it preferred the completely ignorant, who were at least resigned and compliant.'[126] But challenged, the church could not back out without loosening its grip on education, a hold it had regained from the revolutionary epoch with so much effort. Everywhere the Catholics were pitched against the lay population: 'in many communes where before no one would have bothered to establish a school, now they wanted one just because one lot of villagers wanted to have one of the other kind.'[127] But the teachers' pay remained as miserable as it always had been.

As both sides in the struggle were more or less evenly balanced, the vicissitudes of educational policy depended on the politics of the cabinets that succeeded one another. By 1830 the number of schools, the number of school-going children and the state grants for the establishment of schools had greatly increased[128] and a far-reaching regulation of elementary education had been passed with the Act of 1830, without much practical effect, however.

During these years the church gradually abandoned its maximalist stance of claiming a teaching monopoly and full state support, in favor of a policy of 'freedom of education', the second-best, minimalist option, 'even though it deplores the abuse others would be wont to make of it.'[129] The change of position came with the realization that either the monopoly could be maintained only at the price of painful concessions to the state, or a state-controlled system of church schools might one day pass into hostile hands.

It took a *coup d'état* to break through the political stalemate. The July monarchy was openly anti-Bourbon and anticlerical and counted on elementary education to raise a generation of citizens that would support liberal bourgeois democracy, since 'in numerous rural regions the authority of nobleman and priest, acquired from the discarded sovereign, still reigned in favor of ignorance and superstition.'[130] Louis Philippe, the 'citizen-king' not only feared the reaction, just like the English middle classes of that period, he was also anxious to appease the emerging urban proletariat.[131] Another tug-of-war ensued over educational legislation, but this time the liberal bourgeois circles and their vanguard, the *Société pour l'instruction élémentaire*, got the upper hand and with the *Loi Guizot* of 1833, a system of universal, elementary education was established[132] with compulsory attendance (under parental consent), free parental choice between public or private (mostly Catholic) schools, free tuition for the poor, teachers' certification by the state and financing through a system of school committees in each *département*, *arrondissement* and commune.[133] The law proved effective and was further strengthened by its success.

The *Loi Guizot* was only the beginning of very many new conflicts, this time at the village level. The local *notables* feared that the literate peasants would not need their services anymore and that the educated youngsters would prefer the city to the village.[134] The nobility and the clergy did what they could through endowments, intrigue and slander to frustrate the efforts of the public schoolteacher. And the antagonism was mutual, the mayor siding with the public schoolteacher who often doubled as his secretary. Both sides tried to pack the school board and the communal council.

The Revolution of 1848 produced an abortive attempt at radical educational reform, but once Louis Napoleon came to power the tables were turned again in favor of the church with the *Loi Falloux* (1850), a law adopted 'to moralise education too cut off from religion'.[135] The difficult life of the school teacher became miserable. 'Isolated in his village, subject to the pressure of local notables, cut off by salary from the middle class and by education from the peasantry, the *instituteur* was a prey to retaliatory persecution, encouraged by successive government measures.'[136] Yet, as an occupational group, the teachers had long since become a force to be reckoned with. Liberal governments supported them against parents and the church, conservative governments could not do without them to teach the children of the poor obedience and orthodoxy.[137]

The teaching orders and the nuns moved back into the villages. 'The factor determining the failure or success of the clerical campaign in such a dispute was whether or not it could attract the support of influential local notables who could not merely supply funds but continue to pressure their dependents – tenants, customers and so forth – into supporting the Catholic school.'[138]

However, in the long run, the religious inroads on rural public education inspired such anticlericalism among the peasants (who also feared and resented the new tithe levied for the Catholic school), that their progress was stopped. Moreover, Napoleon III, for political reasons of his own (the Ultramontane question) began to loosen his ties with the church.

In the meantime, in the cities the bourgeoisie played its part in undermining the egalitarian and universal impetus of the *Loi Falloux*. Since the law provided free instruction to the poor, but left financing to the local authorities, the quality gap between poor and working-class schools on the one hand and bourgeois schools on the other widened, and the middle class now concentrated its efforts even more on secondary education. The *lycée* would perpetuate the class differences by providing opportunities for careers in government and business, thus enabling the bourgeoisie to transmit its class-advantages to the next generation.[139]

In the end the village nobility and the clergy were bound to lose their grip on rural education: as state finance became increasingly important, and as the peasants departed in ever greater numbers to the cities, literacy and modernity increasingly undermined traditional authority. Yet the emerging system of universal and compulsory elementary education tended to reproduce in its different tiers the corresponding class divisions, thus effectively perpetuating class differences in subsequent generations.[140] In secondary education internal upper-class divisions were also reproduced to some extent, because the *lycées* catered for the bourgeoisie and the – mostly Catholic – *collèges* attracted the children of the *grande bourgeoisie* and the rural nobility. Apart from class divisions, there also remained the old distinction between metropolitan and regional elites. Very broadly speaking: 'Catholic schools, with a clientele drawn from the landed nobility and the peasantry, stood for the values of the rural world, while the state schools were urban.'[141] While older and more recently established groups in society thus made sure that the higher reaches of the educational system would serve to provide selective advantages to their children, the mass base of the system was extended steadily to encompass all French children in one communication network: free, compulsory, and secular public education finally came with Ferry's laws of 1881–2 and 1886.[142]

In France, as elsewhere, the conflict over education was fought on the grounds of religion. From early times the Catholic Church, had been in control of rural education and it stuck to its maximalist stance throughout the Revolution and its aftermath. It became the ideological vanguard of the local elites who wished to restore and maintain their authority. As the church had been organized on a nationwide scale all along, it was able to function as a political institution at the national level.

The metropolitans campaigned for free, compulsory, universal secular education. Although the program was tainted by its origins in the Revolution, it received cautious support even from Louis XVIII, who was sympathetic to the *Société pour l'instruction élémentaire*, which became the bearer of educational reform after 1814. The Catholic Church, however, took an uncompromising position and maintained its full maximalist stance, until the Revolution of 1830 turned the tables. But even with a bourgeois government in power and a progressive law – Guizot's – on the books, the struggle continued at the local level. Napoleon III's legislation – the *Loi Falloux* – was again more favorable to the church while at the same time facilitating elementary education for the poor.

In this religious conflict, the language issue was almost completely lost. But the unmistakable message of regional control which the church conveyed implied that local speech would be tolerated, and even encouraged, under its aegis. Linguistic conflict seems to have taken place in the form of stubborn, mute resistance on the part of rural students, parents, and often also teachers: the refusal to speak French outside the classroom, the rejection of the standard language whenever it was not directly imposed by the authorities, as it was in courts of law and for official business. But from the available evidence, it appears that the French school struggle was in large part a conflict about local versus national control of the elementary schools, a conflict of interest within a floral figuration of communication networks. The local elites in their traditional monopolistic mediating position resisted a national network of communications which would allow their clientages immediate connections with the expanding state apparatus and the growing national market. The metropolitan elites, on the other hand, with a power base in the state apparatus, sought to expand direct access to the population at large by expanding elementary education whenever the regime in power would allow it.

6.3   The Netherlands

Surprisingly, the administrative innovations that for the first time produced a national system of elementary education were introduced by a divided and defeated nation under French imperial rule: the Dutch.[143]

The enterprise was carried out by the pro-French 'Patriotic' Movement with an evangelical enthusiasm for the moral regeneration of Dutch society from the stagnation and corruption of the periwig regents.

In December 1794 French armies had invaded the Dutch Republic and brought to power a regime manned by radical Patriots, in tune with the ideals of the French Revolution: they proclaimed the Batavian Republic and ran the first governments of a centralized state which marked a sharp break with the federalist traditions of the Dutch Republic.

For some ten years the *Maatschappij tot Nut van het Algemeen* – the Society for the General Good – had been propagating schemes for educational reform, inspired by the ideas of Basedow and Pestalozzi, and by a strongly moralistic brand of enlightened Christian pietism. Once the Patriots were brought to power on the bayonets of the French in 1795, the *Nut* began to solicit the Assembly to establish universal public education. Only a few years later, from 1801 on, most of these proposals were embodied in the orders issued by the *Agent* of national education, Van der Palm. What was new was that these instructions were in fact carried out. The Batavian Republic, after all, was set up as a unitary state, and the Patriots intended to exploit the possibilities with which the new centralism presented them. The 'regents' of the towns and the gentry of the countryside could still muster a formidable opposition, all the more when the church joined them in protesting against the intrusion of a secular, revolutionary government into the province of religion. Educational reform had provided for the examination of all schoolmasters and for the dismissal of those found incompetent. This measure provoked clashes with the local squire, deacon or regent who considered a particular teacher his appointee and protégé. The Dutch Reformed

Church, on its part, was wary of any deviation from its orthodox teachings and loath to accept young teachers just because they had passed their certification exam. And thus, local authorities delayed what they could.

But the opposition from the local elites and clergy was in great part overcome, mainly through the astute exploitation of local conflicts by the volunteers of the *Nut* and the energetic intervention of the *Agent*'s inspectors in the deliberations of the local school committees.[144]

Seigniorial and church prerogatives were abolished one after the other, albeit not without opposition.[145] The success of the movement rested on a singular combination of a strongly centralized government bureaucracy, capable of enforcing its decisions, and a mass movement providing a program, an evangelical inspiration and a corps of dedicated inspectors, teachers and voluntary board members. In the process, the reform developed its own *paideia* – Christian without being sectarian, nationalist while posing as nonpartisan, aiming at the highest common denominator of a highly fragmented culture, striving to accommodate everyone without alienating anyone. But 'to the regents who fought a rearguard action against its acceptance, it amounted to the substitution of the familiar community by the monistic authority of the state.'[146]

Thus school reform, animated by a zeal for moral regeneration,[147] was carried out in a struggle between Unitarists in government and Federalists in the country, pitching the *Agent* and the inspectorate against the traditional local authority of the *heren* (squires) in the villages and the regents in the merchant towns.

In the Netherlands, the urban regents had been established as a ruling patriciate since the seventeenth century. They had long since joined their fate with the Calvinist Dutch Reformed Church, supporting a somewhat more liberal wing. The regents had made their fortune not in agriculture, but in international trade, and they represented the very example of a ruling bourgeoisie – a hereditary oligarchy – rather than a nobility. They operated on the international market from a very restricted urban base and contented themselves with keeping their hinterland quiet by means of the federal government, the *Staten-Generaal*, which they dominated. National integration, mobilization of the rural peasantry or urban paupers would only threaten their hold over this fragmented system.

The Dutch case displays many of the features of the model: the vested elites with their local power bases are represented by the town regents and village squires, closely connected to the Dutch Reformed clergy, and tightly controlling their pauper and peasant clientele with charity handouts and tenancy bonds respectively. The assault on this figuration of limited-access networks was carried out by a nonsectarian, evangelical, nationalist movement which gained access to a new, centralist state apparatus in need of direct connections at the level of the local communities. Language was not a major issue in the Netherlands,[148] but direct access to a national network of communication was. Literacy was already at an exceptionally high level.[149] The new, central government was eager to activate the skills that would allow it to recruit the masses of the Dutch population as citizens ready 'for participation in the new national commonwealth'.[150]

Yet the final result of the reforms was by no means a 'state monopoly'.[151] It left the churches (and the *Nut*) free to establish their own schools, albeit at their own expense. The public schools were intended mainly for the poor.[152] Even these public schools, although subsidized by the central government, were not completely controlled by it. Teachers might still be appointed by the *départements*, even though nominally on condition of certification by the central inspectorate, which did not always have its way.

In all public schools teaching was permeated by 'general Christian principle', but sectarian instruction was ruled out – doctrine could only be taught in special classes 'after school hours'.

Once the Dutch Reformed Church was forced to abandon its maximalist stance, all churches could agree upon the minimalist position of support to none. The Catholics, after centuries of discrimination in the northern Netherlands, readily accepted these terms, since they, too, were allowed to establish schools if they paid the costs.

The schemes of 1801, 1803 and 1806 were a compromise on the issue of religious education and also on the matter of regional autonomy, leaving much to be settled by the authorities of the *départements* (later the provinces) and by local agencies. For all intents and purposes the formula worked quite well;[153] it became a model for educationalists abroad and survived more or less intact until the 1870s.

From the 1840s on, however, Calvinists and Catholics became increasingly dissatisfied with the 'general Christian' content of the state-school curriculum.[154] This created a dilemma for the more liberal Protestants: should they opt for a maximalist strategy, and insist upon strengthening the Christian content of the public curriculum, or should they take a pluralist stance of demanding state support for church schools, even if this meant that other denominations might also profit? Because of their ambiguity and because of the sympathies among political liberals, the public school continued to be the only one enjoying state support: and, significantly, court circles opted for the 'general Christian public school' as a place where all denominations could meet freely. But when growing religious zeal spawned the Protestant *Reveil* movement and churches began to mobilize their adherents, pressure mounted. The Catholics grew further apart from the Liberals who had helped grant them equal rights under the Constitution of 1848 and began to agitate against the Protestant character of the general Christian curriculum in the public schools. The Protestant fundamentalists and the Catholics finally overcame their traditional hostility and after the extension of the suffrage succeeded in forming a series of coalition governments from 1888 on.

Yet denominational schools remained without subsidies; the faithful had to establish their own schools at their expense. This prompted them to resist any improvement in the public-school system which might help to draw children away from the private schools. They resented paying taxes that went to finance the public schools and contributing at the same time to denominational schools for their own children. Nevertheless, attendance at denominational schools increased steadily, from 20 per cent in 1860 to more than 40 per cent in 1917, just before financial equality was granted, and from then on to 75 per cent in 1970.[155]

After more than half a century of school struggle, a 'pacification' was brought about with the Education Act of 1920, committing the state to maintain at an equal level both public schools and all denominational schools: a model of pluralism which has survived more or less intact until the present day.

One aspect of the school struggle had been the resistance of local, rural fundamentalism against the metropolitan, 'general Christian', national school system. But this was not simply a movement of rural elites against the central network. It was also a movement of the petty bourgeoisie and the peasantry in favor of sound religious instruction against the evils of modernism and the threats of a secularized, urban working class. Public schools had in practice often strayed from general Christian principles, and in later years the poorly paid teachers were increasingly prone to radicalization. These 'proletarians among the intellectuals' came from the popular ranks of society, as a teacher's career was one of the few avenues to upward mobility. Nor did they always hide their radical convictions in the classroom, thereby antagonizing religious parents.[156]

By the end of the nineteenth century, the faithful had been mobilized *en masse* on the school issue. Religious and political leaders succeeded in reorganizing these movements into denominational political parties and social organizations which became the vehicle of mass politics in the new democratic state. As in France, through the school issue the church modernized itself and succeeded in setting up the agencies that democratic politics required. In the Netherlands, the various denominations gradually formed tightly controlled networks of separate associations in almost every field of social life, and so did the 'non-denominations', Socialist and 'General', the latter to a lesser degree. Trade unions, employers' unions, peasant organizations, newspapers, broadcasting associations were set up separately for every (non-) denomination and affiliated with the corresponding political party.

The result of this 'pillarization' was a transition from networks of local control to a series of national networks, once for each 'pillar', connected at the top through bargaining among the various elites.[157] However, notwithstanding political and religious differences, in public and private schools the elementary curriculum promulgated a single, national communication code which allowed direct mutual access among all Dutch citizens. In the end, this contributed to the gradual dissolution of pillarization in the second half of the twentieth century.

6.4   Britain

In Prussia, France and the Netherlands, metropolitan elites around a centralizing state promoted educational reform. Initially, the attempt succeeded only in the Low Countries, with the aid of a mass movement which encouraged and supported the administration. But early in the nineteenth century in all three countries the state had become deeply involved in elementary education, no matter how contested its role may have been. In England, on the contrary, the central government stayed out of the field and what little renewal was achieved came from voluntary societies established for the purpose. As in the Netherlands, the French Revolution made a great impact on English public opinion, also on the issue of public education. Those who opposed the Revolution also rejected its educational ideas, but among the supporters and waverers the Convention's proposals for elementary education made a great impression.[158] In England also, a movement for school reform got under way, inspired by evangelical and philanthropic ideas, drawing from the ranks of the Dissenters, especially from the Methodist Church which had proselytized among the urban workers and of late also among the bourgeoisie in the cities. The movement stressed personal spiritual growth and the humanitarian improvement of institutions, advocating education as a means for both.

Early industrialization had produced a large urban working class and a wealthy and self-confident entrepreneurial bourgeoisie, even while control of local and central government long remained in the hands of the aristocracy. The urban bourgeoisie and the 'workers' aristocracy' – the best educated and best paid among the industrial workers – often belonged to dissenting denominations and they sought a more adequate education for their children outside the pale of the Anglican Church. Until late in the nineteenth century even workers often preferred private schools – less disciplinarian and more congenial – to public or church schools.[159] The upheavals of the Industrial Revolution and the impact of the French Revolution caused intense concern with the social problems of the day; this combined with nonconformist zeal to create a passionate interest in educational innovation which found its institutional embodiment in the British and Foreign School Society of 1814 (formerly the Lancasterian Society). It was founded initially to propagate the monitorial scheme of elementary education which employed advanced pupils to teach their younger peers so that the teacher could manage the instruction of many hundreds of pupils at once. The emphasis was squarely on the three 'Rs', of reading, writing and arithmetic. Religion was played down; instead the general formation of Christian character was stressed, much to the dismay of the established church, which disparaged these teachings as 'Sunday-school religion'. Even before the Lancasterian movement had transformed itself into the British Society, the Anglicans had set up their own version of the monitorial system (inspired by Bell) and established the National Society for the Establishment of Schools According to the Teachings of the Established Church. Henceforward the Anglican Church was 'the rightful schoolmaster of the nation'. The established church insisted upon its monopoly in education, adhering to a rigidly maximalist stance and rejecting the claims of other denominations to teach with the support, or even the consent, of the state, as this would result in 'placing the blasphemous Jew, the idolatrous Romanist, the Unitarian denying this Christ, or the sensual Turk on the same level as the humble and adoring believer of the Son of God.'[160]

Initially the British Society had widely found favor also with the king who considered granting it mailing privileges, essential in those days to carry on nationwide communications at a bearable rate,[161] but the National Society, the vehicle of the established church, protested against these privileges.[162] The competition for state support had begun in earnest and it would last until 1870 before making way for a system of public education.

As elsewhere, the initiative for educational reform came from the metropolitan elites, oriented toward the national market and dissenting from the hegemonic creed. And in England also, it provoked a revival of religious fervor and educational zeal among the ranks of the established church, which then sought to mobilize its resources by activating its ties with local authorities sensitive to the value of religion, tradition, deference and whatever else would perpetuate their control over the clientele.

> [In England] the rise of popular elementary education was very largely an incidental by-product of the struggle between Anglicans and Dissenters for the allegiance of the lower classes. For a long time the Anglican establishment had been indifferent or even hostile to the education of the poor . . . By 1800 this was no longer true, if only for reasons of enlightened self-interest.[163]

The development of elementary education in the first half of the nineteenth century was determined by the competition between the two school societies, pressuring one another at the slow pace which their private means allowed[164] to establish schools and maintain teachers throughout the kingdom: 'While the political elite positively dissociated itself from educational extension, the church was forced to engage in greater educational activity by the increasing pressures of dissent.'[165]

Gradually, and often reluctantly, the state was drawn into this process. It first awarded small grants for the establishment of schools to both societies and gave into the dissidents by creating an inspectorate of the schools.[166] This agency turned out to be manned by activists under the leadership of the indomitable Kay-Shuttleworth,[167] who by their bureaucratic bent and reformist zeal would pressure especially the established-church[168] schools to improve the quality of teaching and who, with their yearly reports, drew the public's attention to the derelict state of popular education.

Around 1830 matters came to a head. The middle classes, with massive support from the working classes, agitated for electoral reform and attacked the representation of 'rotten boroughs'. At the same time the British Society, recruited from similar circles among the bourgeoisie, the Dissenters and the most skilled workers, attempted to break the local education monopolies held by the Anglican Church. The political-reform movement prevailed with the Reform Bill of 1832. But Roebuck's Education Bill of 1833 failed, as did succeeding attempts. In part, this was the result of a split in the reformist ranks: the alliance between the bourgeoisie and the working class disintegrated in much the same way as the collaboration between the bourgeoisie and the popular masses in France, once the July Revolution had brought the middle classes to power.[169]

The workers' movement continued to agitate on its own against child labor and for shorter working hours. This alienated an important sector of the middle class, which feared that compulsory schooling would prevent children from working in factories or as domestics. The Factory Act of 1833 represented a compromise: 'two hours of schooling became compulsory for child labour.'[170] But as long as the question of working hours and child labor had not been legally settled, every scheme for elementary education was doomed to failure.[171] The Chartist workers' movement thus concentrated on political and industrial reform in the first place.[172]

The attempt at educational reform had also failed since both the National Society and the British and Foreign Society turned against the Education Bill of 1833. The Anglicans demanded that any school operating with public funds teach the Anglican catechism. The Dissenters rejected this condition: 'Thus dissent acted as the strongest break on the formation of a state educational system, and instead accelerated the formation of a great denominational system, relatively independent of Parliament.'[173]

The competing school societies went on to found schools and appoint teachers, each side trying to remain ahead of the other. In the meantime, the government enacted laws on the working conditions and education of factory children, without, however, providing funds or appointing inspectors. It also slowly increased its grants to the societies. But nothing more happened. 'For much of the century each side was to demonstrate that it had the power to block any educational scheme which appeared to give advantages to the other.'[174]

Education remained with the societies and voluntarism meant in practice that the required tuition fees excluded the children of the poor from all but the most basic instruction, condemned the children of the working class to inferior schools and provided with adequate education only those who could afford to pay the going rate.[175] Yet the dialectics of the situation provided the established church with an advantage from backwardness: inherited endowments, a tradition of charitable donations and of free instruction by clergymen enabled it to hold Sunday schools where millions of English working-class children had their brief encounter with literacy – learning to read the Bible – but nothing more, not even writing. Even this rudimentary instruction was no part of the Tory program, but rather the mostly unintended byproduct of catechization among a proletariat thirsting for worldly knowledge. Conservatives feared working men's education as a source of sedition. And not entirely without reason: many Chartist leaders had learned to read at Sunday school, where they got their first taste for Biblical rhetoric.[176]

Yet among the more progressive members of the middle classes the events of the 1830s in England, as in France, had somewhat abated the old fears of popular education as a source of unrest and inspired a new confidence in elementary schooling as a means of solving urban problems and training qualified workers.[177]

Even the 'deeply felt dread of rebellion and disintegration'[178] increasingly prompted others to support universal elementary schooling as a means for inculcating discipline and subservience – the Tory point of view – or as a way of persuading the working classes of the merits of capitalism and of the virtues of the middle class, so that they would support its supremacy.[179]

In the meantime the state slowly became more involved in elementary education. The British and Foreign Society had sought privileges of the kind that the established church had received long before, while the Anglican establishment had furiously protested against granting them to its rivals. Yet this created a dilemma for the Church of England. If education was to expand at all, it would cost more. State support might help the church in defraying the costs, but the state was likely to impose conditions in return, and it might grant the same support to other interested parties also. Once it became clear that a maximalist position – unconditional state support to the Anglican Church only – stood no chance of acceptance, some Anglicans veered to the second, 'minimalist', position, a wholesale rejection of state support (and of the conditions that might go with it) for any and all denominations.[180] The church could count on its endowments and donations and on its connections with local or central authorities to tide it over the upsurge of reformist zeal.

The minority churches, more or less united in their support for the British and Foreign Society, took a third, 'pluralist', position, on the whole favoring state support for all denominations, as long as they would not be forced to teach anything contrary to their doctrines (such as the Anglican catechism). Gradually, the conviction took hold in these circles that instruction in a particular creed was best left to special hours and classes, to be taught by a clergyman, while the remaining curriculum, free from sectarian teachings, should be pervaded by a general Christian spirit, promote Christian morality, and avoid offense to anyone in particular. It took deist and rational theology to produce this sort of highest Christian common denominator. And its acceptance implied that each church would have to take a step back from daily life, from its special province, the education of the young. Religion would have to be set aside as a special topic for a special class, rather than reign supreme as the ultimate purpose of all education.[181]

This development of a nondenominational Christian curriculum was immensely practical and effective: it allowed the preservation of the Christian heritage for general education and yet avoided sectarian strife. The general Christian teachings became a lingua franca of religious interaction, providing a minimal etiquette for encounters between strangers and allowing the establishment of shared Christianity while avoiding sectarian friction. Briefly, it was to the various denominations what a standard language was to the regional dialects.

The great compromise came about with the Elementary Education Act of 1870, providing for the establishment of school boards which could found schools wherever existing forms of elementary education did not meet the needs. The Act 'did not introduce free or compulsory education, but it made both possible.' The costs were to be borne in equal parts by tuition fees, local rates and state grants. When local schools were unable to collect the 'school pence' from the poorest children, the state saw itself compelled to pay for them, especially as in the course of the 1880s it made attendance compulsory throughout the country and poor children had to be admitted by law.[182]

As elsewhere, the elementary system barely connected with the system of secondary and higher education, the 'educational ladder' was narrow and steep and, moreover, short for the working classes. The term 'elementary' had a strong lower-class connotation, and the middle classes objected to extending the education of the poor, which they had paid for, to the secondary level where their own ranks were being recruited.[183] Although the boards were democratically elected, working-class people rarely participated in them, as the task was demanding and meetings were often held during school hours, when they were at work.[184]

Board schools were mostly nonsectarian in composition, but tended to opt for compromise, usually the general Christian curriculum, derisively called 'School Board religion'.[185] And thus almost a century of competitive strife came to an end:

> Paradoxically, the near *absolute* failure of the nonconformists to establish an adequate spread of schools gained them their objective of a rate-supported system. The *relative* failure of the Anglicans, which had embodied an enormous effort, was not sufficient to prevent, from their point of view, this feared outcome.[186]

In England, as in France, the struggle was against the stronghold of the established church; in both countries an urban bourgeoisie formed the vanguard of educational reform, but the English middle class had acquired wealth in commerce and industry, while the French had found a power base in the state bureaucracy and the professions. On the issue of religion, the Dissenters confronted the Anglicans in England, while in France the *laïques* opposed the Catholics. In the one country industrialization had occurred early and with vehemence, in the other a new state apparatus had emerged with even greater upheaval.

Vaughan and Archer have argued convincingly that the differences in educational development between these two countries cannot be explained by reference to industrialization only. The functionalist argument based upon the needs of industrial development and the Marxist version postulating the capitalist need for a qualified workforce are not persuasive, since they would have required England, the first to industrialize, to be the more advanced in educational achievement. The opposite is true for the nineteenth century.[187] The case of the Netherlands provides even stronger evidence in support of the criticism made by Vaughan and Archer.

The authors explain the educational history of the two countries in terms of the 'assertion' and 'domination' of competing social groups, which do not neatly coincide with social classes. Since the state was the power base of the French educational reformers, each change in government should have affected the course of reform there much more than in England, a supposition which seems warranted by the events.

But in France also, for a long time after the Revolution, the state's role was limited to encouragement and supervision, leaving the communes to their own resources and relying on voluntary societies, the Catholic Church paramount among them. Only gradually did the central government become directly involved in primary education, albeit earlier and more intensely than in England.[188]

The underlying attitudes toward the education of the poor and the working classes were 'strikingly similar' in both countries. The French bourgeoisie tended to favor it all along, until the laboring classes turned against the state in 1848. British middle-class opinion tended to be more cautious, but gradually came to accept the schooling of the poor on condition that it be a proper moral training.[189]

In both England and France, as elsewhere, the gentry and the established church with their local power bases opposed a national elementary educational system which might undo their traditional mediation advantages. Those parts of the middle class that were oriented toward the national market and the national state tended to favor a nationwide system of elementary education, although industrialists were often ambivalent about it as it might limit the supply of cheap, unskilled labor, especially child labor. Since entrepreneurs dominated the English middle class, their hesitation tended to weaken the educational zeal of the bourgeoisie. Middle-class officials strongly favored educational expansion and this vanguard of the metropolitans had gained a foothold in the state apparatus in France after the Revolution of 1789, whereas in England it found itself forced to organize on a voluntary basis and to engage in exhausting competition with the Anglican Church, penetrating the state apparatus only slowly through the newly created branches of the civil service, especially the ministry of education. But once they occupied positions of power, their policies were very similar to those of their French counterparts, and even the timing was not so very different: the forsaken promises of 1830 and the final establishment of a compulsory, free and national system around 1870.

6.5 The United States of America

Until deep into the nineteenth century the 'little red school house' remained the model of elementary education in America. The village school originated in New England, and remained closely connected to the churches, supervised by a board of parents and financed through tuition fees and endowments, often in land. Lawrence Cremin nicely captures the essential functions of elementary education in providing direct access to the encompassing communication network:[190]

> The school performed many functions: it provided youngsters with an opportunity to become literate in a standard American English via the Webster speller and the McGuffy readers; it offered youngsters a common belief system combining undenominational Protestantism and nonpartisan patriotism; it afforded youngsters an elementary familiarity with simple arithmetic . . . It eased their way into productive work outside the Household, where literacy and punctuality, adherence to rules and procedures, and the ability to cooperate with people of varying ages who were not kin would be expected. It made possible various uses, and misuses, of printed material . . .

The colonial government and the provincial authorities rarely intervened in education, nor did the states or the federal government in the early phase of the Republic. Government limited itself to ordering local authorities to establish a school, leaving its management, financing and curriculum to them.

The impetus for educational expansion came from the heirs of the colonial clerical elite, who sought to defend their position against the 'barbarians' in the frontier states and the 'aliens' immigrating to the eastern ports. They found an ally in the emerging commercial middle classes.[191]

Around 1800 however, the various denominations began to force one another into a minimalist stance of rejecting even such state intervention in education as had seemed acceptable at an earlier time, out of fear that competing sects might profit from it too.[192] The result was a stalemate on educational politics.

As small towns grew into cities, the village schools survived more or less intact, run along the same principles of parental control and religious affiliation. In the frontier territories the redbrick schoolhouse appeared as soon as settlers had gathered in sufficient numbers. However, when populations in the West and in the expanding cities became more heterogeneous in religious conviction, strict sectarianism as an organizing principle began to be abandoned for 'interdenominationalism', the highest common denominator of various traditional Protestant persuasions.

The school boards tended to be quite conservative in educational matters and reluctant in financing expansion. As a result, immigrants in the growing cities found themselves excluded from these restricted educational facilities. The new brand of 'schoolmen' increasingly came to oppose community control of schools as an obstacle to pedagogic reform and expansion. They began to organize and to campaign for educational improvement with state support. In New York, for example, the Quakers founded and dominated the Free School Society, which promoted nondenominational schools with government subsidy and under professional control.[193] By mid-century, 'Friends of education' appeared in every state, forming a network of 'schoolmen' throughout the United States and campaigning for the establishment of elementary-school systems by the states. On this issue they confronted local elites: 'neither the ideology nor the technology of political control at the state level had been developed to the point where it was seen as a replacement for political control at the district, town, or county level.'[194] In Virginia they confronted 'the relentless opposition of eastern landowners' and populists.[195]

In many respects the Friends may be regarded as 'metropolitans' promoting a nonsectarian, universal and compulsory system of elementary education which would break through the barriers of denomination and transcend differences of ethnic origin, so as to establish 'the one best system'[196] which would socialize all into one grand national culture. 'The goal of all these systems was the creation of a literate American public.'[197] Kaestle writes:[198]

> The systematization of the schools would also solve the problem of scale. Once the system was established, it was recursive. No matter how many new children appeared, poor or rich, immigrant or native, the system would simply provide more identical schools and train more identical teachers.

The attack on the traditional schools also came from a different quarter: the Catholic Church. In New York City, at least, this opposition was exacerbated by the victory of the enemy of its enemies: the Free Society, or after 1826, the Public School Society. By 1818 the Society had succeeded in convincing the State of New York that subsidies for elementary schools were a dire necessity and that they should not be granted to church schools, but to Society schools only. As a result, the Catholic Church lost whatever chance it had of establishing schools of its own with government support. In a predominantly Protestant country any maximalist ambitions were out of the question. Since the Catholic hierarchy had as yet almost no schools under its own control, the minimalist stance of rejecting government support for all churches would not do either: the Protestant church schools had enjoyed such subsidies and the 'nondenominational' (but also in fact generally Protestant) schools still received them. The Church of Rome was forced to opt for seeking a most-favored-denomination status – to demand equal treatment – and it stubbornly insisted on government support. It thus took a pluralist position at a time when most Protestant sects had come to accept nonsectarian education and nominally secular public schools.[199] For the time being, the Catholics decided to found their own elementary schools at their own expense. In fact, their movement turned out so successful that separate Catholic school systems have survived until this day in many American cities, next to a public-school system largely financed by the government. Ater the formal disestablishment of churches in 1833, schools and churches became increasingly separate, and the schools thus became 'the public's agencies for creating and re-creating publics'.[200]

As in other countries, in the United States an encompassing elementary-school system began to emerge in the course of the nineteenth century, and here too it imposed a standard version of the written language upon practically every child of school age.[201] In colonial times linguistic diversity was a minor problem, as only some German and French and a few Dutch communities insisted upon teaching in their own language.[202] But in contrast to other countries, the language issue became more acute with time, as new cohorts of immigrants began to demand instruction in the speech of parental origin. As elsewhere, the language question was closely intertwined with religion and the maintenance of traditional life-styles, but in the United States the proponents of linguistic and cultural diversity were not the established rural elites, white Anglo-Saxon Protestants, but on the contrary, recent immigrants in the large cities, most of them working class and of peasant stock. The informal leaders of these immigrant communities, often Catholic clergy, as in the case of the Irish, the Polish and the Italians, championed the cause of separate religious education, and as the case might be, of teaching in the language of origin; the German immigrant communities succeeded best in maintaining their language at school.[203] Such nonconformism provoked a 'nativist' campaign against ethnicity, immigrant subculture, immigrant 'machine politics' and minority languages. It was carried on with the same zeal and the same ideals as the campaigns against regional traditionalism and urban pauperism waged by metropolitan reformers in Europe. But in America the metropolitans were the established group and their efforts were mainly preventive: to avoid the development of minority institutions in the field of politics, economics and culture.

Internal immigration within Europe from the countryside to the city was not so very different from transatlantic migration from the European countryside to American cities, although it was much more dramatic for the immigrants concerned and more dramatized in the popular imagination of those days and the present. The task of assimilating succeeding waves of immigrants into American society was in many respects equivalent to the work of acculturating the peasants to the exigencies of urban industrial society in Europe. And on both continents the schools were expected to achieve this feat of acculturation. In retrospect, the educational system was quite effective in assimilating paupers and newcomers to metropolitan culture. It was much less successful in bringing about greater equality:

> Nineteenth century cities can perhaps best be thought of as railroad stations with waiting rooms for different classes. Although the population of the station constantly changes, those departed were replaced by people with remarkably similar characteristics. And, though their populations constantly increased, the proportions in the various waiting rooms remained about the same.[204]

The massive influx of newcomers, new to the streets and to the ways of the city, caused great anxiety among the established city-dwellers. The threatening presence of swelling hordes of landfolk caused concern for the safety and the respectability of the settled townspeople and inspired much of the nineteenth-century zeal for reform which led to the establishment of such collective arrangements as elementary schools, hospitals, penitentiaries, medical and police services and so forth. In this perspective the establishment of an elementary-school system represents the response of expanding open cities to the problem of poverty, once the charities and church schools of the old, relatively closed towns could no longer deal with accelerating migration.[205]

The appearance of young vagrants in particular caused great dismay; this was a relatively new phenomenon in the cities – on the farms there was always something for the young to do and, if not, they were quickly out of sight. In the old towns, poor children became servants or apprentices. But as the crafts declined, so did apprenticeship, being only partly replaced by factory labor. The new overcrowded apartment houses provided no room for children and so they spilled out into the streets where their play might quickly pass into mischief and then into petty crime. Juvenile criminality inspired intense concern: child offenders would surely grow up to be robbers and murderers. If immigrant parents were despised for their rough and peasant ways, their children were feared as hooligans and future bandits. At this point the school was to become a sort of policing. Long before attendance was made compulsory, truancy officers patrolled the streets on the lookout for young absentees. The schools functioned as centers of preventive detention for these children: their sheer presence in the streets during school hours was sufficient reason to round them up and deliver them to the neighborhood school, 'for their own sake'.[206] Teachers, however, were not at all eager to have these troublemakers in their classroom: separate classes were established for the refractory cases, and later special reform schools, a hybrid offshoot from the educational and the workhouse systems, specialized in disciplining the young.

The concern caused by the street children was transformed into a loud clamor for more and better schools for the children of the poor, especially of the immigrant poor. Professional educators saw an opportunity to realize their schemes by playing upon these fears and demands. As the school system expanded, so did the ranks of the teaching body, which, well organized and articulate as it was, became a strong, relatively autonomous force for the further expansion and bureaucratization of the school system.[207]

Elementary education came to the frontier states in the wake of the ordinance of 1784, providing 'that one lot in each town be reserved for the maintenance of public schools.' Initially, land was plentiful and did not bring much revenue, but as settlements became more densely populated, rents from the endowed land should have increased more or less at a par with the increasing costs of education, had the proceeds not been dissipated through corruption.[208]

As rural communities were established one after the other, commercial farming led to the formation of a peasant middle class. Itinerant Methodist and Baptist preachers came to the villages to spread the faith. 'Along with religion, and frequently in the persons of the same entrepreneurs and congregations, came education.'[209] In this manner, the model of the village school could be adopted all over the rural regions of the continent. Education prepared for the general skills of national citizenship and in the absence of a landed aristocracy no mediation monopolies stood in the way.

Public education reached the southern states as part of military and political occupation in the aftermath of the Civil War.[210] Again, 'metropolitans' from the North seemed eager to circumvent monopolistic local mediation by establishing a school system in the southern states. They were confronted by local elites whose mediation monopolies, already sorely damaged, were further threatened by educational reform. The regional elites generally prevailed against the 'northernness' of public education. It was not until the end of the nineteenth century that an autochthonous movement of 'Friends of education' began to campaign for reform in the South also, supported by a 'flood of capitalist philanthropy' from the North.[211]

In one respect, the American system of elementary education differed profoundly from its European counterpart: in the persistent segregation of blacks, which lasted into the third quarter of this century.[212] In terms of the floral model, metropolitan entrepreneurs and officials would be expected to try to establish direct access to these local, rural clientages, as they did in the period of the Civil War and its aftermath.

Around 1890, in many southern states black enrollment almost equalled that of whites. But this educational achievement was effectively rolled back, once black political power began to decline in the South. Education for southern blacks did not improve until the early 1950s.[213]

Those blacks who went north initially also did quite well in the schools, their median level of educational attainment coming close to that of native whites.[214] This development was sharply reversed in the 1930s, when the educational gap began to widen.[215] Southern blacks who migrated north during the Depression years found employment only at the very lowest levels, or none at all. Immigration from abroad was severely limited during those years, and workers of European stock further protected their position by closed-shop union policies. As a result, for blacks educational achievement hardly seemed to matter in selection for jobs and this in turn discouraged black parents from sending their children to school, while poverty further impeded the attendance and the achievement of young blacks.

The civil-rights movement, in an uneasy alliance with the federal government, finally succeeded in abolishing legal and institutional barriers to the education of black children and in ensuring their enrollment at least at the elementary level of the educational system. In some respects – their national orientation, their metropolitan origins, their dissident creed – the civil-rights activists were reminiscent of their nineteenth-century predecessors. And after all, they were carrying out a nineteenth-century program, though somewhat delayed.

The history of American education is also more variegated than that of

European nations because the federal government remained aloof for so long.[216] Rural schools stayed under local control, and only in the large cities did an elementary school system begin to develop, differing from state to state, from one municipality to another and for a long time even between wards. The predominance of English-speaking Protestants mitigated the school struggle; sectarian conflicts occurred on the small scale of the village and the ward. With the exception of the southern states, there existed no landholding aristocracy, and the corresponding clientele relations and mediation monopolies were equally rare.[217]

Conflict over education occurred in the big cities, where a modern school system emerged in the context of urban immigration. None of these immigrant groups ever formed a serious challenge to the hegemony of English, with the possible exception of organized Catholic ethnic groups. But even these were in no position to maintain a separate linguistic identity, if only for the simple and classic reason that their very separatism precluded solidarity with other minority groups who set themselves similar goals.[218] Thus the Poles abandoned their claim for Polish as the language of instruction once they realized that the Italians would then insist upon the same privileges, just as the Dutch and the Germans had abandoned it before. Moreover, city life effectively prevented any attempt to shield the youngsters against 'foreign' influence, since their parents themselves had already 'to the city sped.'[219] Finally, the advantages on the labor market of fluency and literacy in English were all too blatant to be ignored for long.

7 Conclusion

What seems to have propelled the spread of elementary education more than anything else was the presence of metropolitan elites who could capture control of the relevant parts of the state apparatus. Middle-class entrepreneurs supported educational reform as a means to gain access to rural populations. But industrialists could not always be counted upon in the short run, if they feared a shortage of child labor. Government officials, however, promoted elementary education as a means to extend the reach of the state apparatus directly into the population at large. In this effort the metropolitan elites confronted the opposition from the land-based gentry and the established clergy: local coalitions which in the course of the conflict were forced to organize on a national basis and finally to establish alternative, but equally nationwide, systems of elementary education, no longer distinct in the substance of their curriculum, but only by their religious orientation.

Competition between metropolitan entrepreneurs and officials on the one hand and local gentry and clergy on the other over control of access to local populations could produce an early victory for the metropolitan elites, unless the regional elites banded together and in so doing brought about what they initially wished to avoid: an educational system that transcended local and regional loyalties. The established churches, which were thus mobilized into an educational counter-campaign, in turn provoked competitive efforts from other denominations. In none of the countries studied did the dominating church succeed in obtaining a state-supported educational monopoly for any length of time. Protection and subsidies from the state were provided at the cost of the church's autonomy and were challenged by other religious groups which demanded equal favors from the government. In reaction, the majority churches withdrew from their original maximalist stance to a minimalist position of rejecting state support for all denominations. This attitude had to be abandoned again whenever another sect appeared to be successful in obtaining government aid. As a result, a system of equal treatment of various denominational and public schools had developed in most countries by the first half of the twentieth century, with the exception of the United States, where a separate and private Catholic elementary-school system survived in the cities without government aid, side by side with a public-school system permeated by a nonsectarian 'general Christian' ethos.

In the course of a long century of competition, local autonomy and idiosyncrasy disappeared and a single national standard curriculum prevailed, with variations in religious coloring. The struggle between traditional-local and metropolitan elites around a centralizing state was fought out in terms of denominational versus secular control – that is, as a conflict about religion – the only denominator that could bring regional elites together in a national coalition.

The outcome was a compulsory national elementary-school system where all children are trained in the basic skills of communication in a standard code valid throughout the nation: speaking, reading and writing the national language, manipulating the basic operators of arithmetic, understanding space and time in terms of a national geography and history. Within this unified communication network and with these uniform codes appeared the mass audiences for twentieth-century politics and modern electronic media. Control over communication networks has passed long since to national centers of political and economic power.

4

Medical Police, Public Works and Urban Health

In the course of the nineteenth-century, a number of cities in Western Europe and North America began to grow at an unprecedented rate.[1] Around 1800 urban mortality still exceeded birthrates, but this trend was reversed by the second half of the century.[2] Moreover, increasing numbers of country-dwellers and people from small towns migrated to the capital cities. The commercialization of farming had rendered many hands superfluous and had made it harder for the landless to survive in the country. Traditional factories, powered by wind or water, had usurped some of the surplus labor in their area. With the advent of steam engines, industrial activity began to concentrate upon harbors and coal- or steel-mines. In the capital cities, major centers of finance, commerce and management developed and new industries sprang up in their vicinity. All this activity attracted migrants from the small towns and villages. And, in turn, the availability of cheap labor in the growing cities drew new enterprises.[3]

But for young and enterprising people the city held other attractions: for youngsters who would not inherit their parents' farm or who had learned more than they could find a use for in small-town careers, for unemployed farmhands and rural paupers who could afford the trip, for the relatives of people who had left for the city and made good or sent word that they had. For all of them the big cities held a spell of riches, advancement, opportunity and excitement, liberation from the shackles of small-minded village life and from the omnipresent supervision of elders and masters. The metropolis promised adventure, chance encounters, erotic fulfillment, cultural stimulation. Lack of economic opportunity may have propelled the migrants to the cities, but an appetite for cultural and emotional experience drew them.[4] Up to this day, the metropolis attracts young people, it is the place for adolescents, and adolescence as a stage of life is a modern and an urban phenomenon.

The nineteenth-century cities of Europe were the internal frontier, the zone of expansion and opportunity for the uprooted rural populations, as they still are today in Asia, Latin America and parts of Africa. In America, the cities on the eastern seaboard, New York most of all, functioned as a transcontinental frontier for immigrants from Europe. About these nineteenth-century cities Dyos wrote:[5]

> Here, new opportunities for communication intersected, new patterns of human relationships began to form, new institutions sprang up, new values, sensations, conventions, and problems were expressed; while older perceptions, behaviour and limitations changed their pitch or disappeared altogether: everywhere a flickering failure of absolutes in ideas and attitudes, a stumbling advance towards free association between people, a more democratised urbanity.

Millions flocked to the cities and whenever the labor market could not absorb the influx, a mass of penniless, and often homeless, paupers would form, cramming the back alleys, the courts, attics and basements of the old centers, or simply squatting in makeshift huts on abandoned lots, depending on charity handouts for survival and threatening the security of the established city-dwellers.[6]

In the course of this urbanization process, people come to live together in a different state of aggregation, more dense, more structured and differentiated than earlier forms of society. Proximity and a high functional interdependence characterize the urban form of social life. Autarchy was, and is, out of the question for the city as an economic entity, and so is self-subsistence for its individual dwellers. In this tightly packed environment no open space was left where one might eke out a living in relative independence, beyond the reach of the money economy. No niches remained where one could hide from the twin controls of employment and charity, except in the urban underworld.[7] No one in the city could avoid daily involvement in his neighbor's business; each person's activities increasingly became a necessity and also a nuisance to others.

1 Migration and the struggle for urban space

Urbanization is a continuous process of absorption of immigrants, an ongoing struggle between the 'established' urban population and the newly arrived urban 'outsiders'.[8] To the settled citizens these newcomers represent both opportunity and danger: they were useful as workers, profitable as customers, recruitable as political supporters, and themselves often ingenious entrepreneurs – an often forgotten aspect of urban migration.[9] But at the time these immigrants were also felt to be a threat, they were looked upon as 'barbarians, savages, nomads' who deserved no place in the city.[10] Their country manners – considered rude and uncouth – clashed with the more urbane ways of the city. As newcomers were the first to be suspected of theft and robbery, they were held to be a threat to urban security. The old urban proletariat feared competition from their cheap labor.[11] The most widespread and fundamental attitude of the established city-dwellers toward these newcomers was that they ought to disappear as quickly as possible, either through physical removal,[12] or through a social transformation into city folk like everyone else. But since the city could neither exclude nor oust the new immigrants,[13] they had to be accommodated somehow in the expectation that sooner or later they would assimilate to city life. This increasingly came to mean that the poor and the immigrants were segregated in distinct urban areas. Even when the ostensible goal of urban-reform policies was the social improvement of paupers and newcomers, the net result was usually to further this social and spatial segregation.

Individual citizens could not force their new neighbours to leave, nor could they do much to transform them. Yet the close proximity of these uninvited and unfamiliar inhabitants caused a continual vexation, a permanent fear of social offense and physical assault.[14] It was this constant friction between the established and the outsiders in the expanding city that prompted people to make individual moves and join the collective movements that have so much shaped contemporary urban life and contributed to the emergence of the medical and social services that preceded the present welfare state.

Modern city life consists of very many encounters which have to be coped with in such a way as to minimize conflict and vexation. In part, this has been achieved by bringing about new separations and establishing clearer boundaries between the people packed so closely together. In early industrial towns, the rich and the poor often lived in the same places. Work and family life also took place in the same or adjacent premises. Streets were a natural extensions of homes, and the dwellings of the poor were barely separated from the common courtyards, privies, stairwells and corridors. This may have functioned more or less, as long as people knew what to expect of one another, could recognize the status and occupation of their fellow citizens by their dress and appearance, respected their betters, accepted their own station in life and abided by the rules for the use of common spaces and the avoidance of nuisance.[15] And even then, it may not have worked very well.

City life has always meant constant mutual aggravation. The quite sudden influx of newcomers made matters much worse, not only because more people now had to share the same space, but also because the immigrants gave offense, ignoring as they did the fine urban art of avoiding nuisance (or getting away with it). And finally, although city people had grown accustomed to all sorts of vexations, the very speed and scale of urban immigration caught them unprepared and disturbed them precisely because it caused new and unaccustomed nuisances.

Increasing numbers of people were packed together in the large mansions and hotels in the city's center, occupying every nook and cranny.[16] The ground floor usually housed a bourgeois family, on the higher floors a petty-bourgeois family might live, a teacher, a clerk or a shopkeeper and his kin. On the top floors, small dwellings were boarded off for a salesman, a governess or a tailor. The attic was divided up into tiny cubicles where an apprentice, a maid, a seamstress, a student could put a bed and a chair. The basements also began to be tenanted, and pauper families often lived in moist cellars eight or ten to a room, without light or fresh air.[17] They all had to use the same facilities, if there were any. Families cooked on coal fires and somehow had to get rid of the smoke, the ash, the dust and the waste, they had to find a place to wash themselves and discard the water, they had to dispose of their excrement. Conditions might be worse, with people using a room alternately, one shift at night, the other during the day. There might be no water supply at all, no place to defecate but the dung heap, the gutter or some hidden backyard corner.

Among the poor, most of family life took place within sight and hearing of others. People did their laundry in the courtyards, met their friends in the street, made their deals and had their fights or their pleasure in the common corridors and staircases. They were not accustomed to keeping their affairs to themselves, indoors, and they hardly had the room to do so even if it had made any difference, since almost everything was overheard next door anyway. People, especially poor people and immigrants, tended to be loud, quarrelsome and boisterous and often to drink a lot. None of this could be hidden, nor was it considered particularly intimate or secret. Domestic life was carried on quite openly, thus scandalizing others who felt that such behavior was shameful and, if engaged in at all, should at least be hidden from the neighbors. Those who took offense felt the proximity of their social inferiors to be somehow abasing to themselves: a 'fear of social contamination'[18] which may well have been a more powerful motive than vexation at the actual nuisance. What was and is socially humiliating in such situations is the manifest powerlessness of established citizens to control the surroundings within which they perform their social role and to protect this performance from intrusion by disparate elements. The 'decent' families felt that they were tarred with the same brush as their 'improper' neighbors. And it may safely be supposed that most rural immigrants and urban paupers, in turn, felt patronized and hemmed in by condescending and meddlesome busybodies who thought themselves superior to them.

Not only at home, but also in the streets, social distance had to be maintained or recovered under conditions of physical proximity. Only the very rich could afford to encapsulate themselves in their mansions and to move through the streets of the city sheltered in their carriages or shielded by their servants. And even they sometimes had to suffer ignominy, snide remarks and offenses from passers by. The lesser urban dwellers could not avoid the rough and tumble of the city streets and had to face the daily risk of unpleasant encounters and constant interference from peddlers and beggars. They had to protect their person from assault, their property from theft and their dignity from ridicule and offense.[19] For still others, often the same persons on different occasions, public spaces provided opportunity for rough entertainment, exciting encounters and sometimes quick profit, booty or romance.

Nineteenth-century city streets, most of them unpaved and with open gutters, were filthy, strewn with garbage, narrow and overcrowded, noisy and permeated with all sorts of smells from refuse, kitchens, sidewalk workshops and open sewers. Animals, dogs, but also chickens, goats and pigs, ran around unattended: at least they ate up more waste than they produced. Most streets remained unswept, and if there were any sewers at all, they were usually open gutters which ran down the middle of the street, filled with animal and human excrements.

City life was made worse by the abundance of small workshops among and within the tenement buildings. A butcher might slaughter his animals or a tanner treat his skins in the courtyard, a tinker or a smith might ply his noisy trade on the front steps, a carpenter or a cobbler set up shop on the pavement blocking the entrance. There were noises, smells and fumes everywhere and there was offal and garbage wherever one went. The factories, often in the very center of town, made their deafening noise and spewed forth their black fumes, dumping their foul waste in the city's rivers and canals. Traffic was even more hectic and noisy than today, as carriages rattled over the cobblestone streets, bumped into stray stones or gutters and got stuck in the mud.

Human misery was visibly, often ostentatiously, present in the streets of the city.[20] Large numbers of people were totally indigent, without any hope of improvement, many of them ill, deformed or disabled: they sat on the pavement, slept in doorways or under bridges and often died there. Young people, illiterate and unskilled, loitered in the streets in the hope of finding something to eat for the day. Children, neglected and undernourished, roamed the streets, with nowhere to go. Infant mortality remained appallingly high until late in the century. Elderly people were often left to their own devices, with no pension or medical care and no one to look after them. In fact, the misery of the Victorian cities became a nightmare to the nineteenth-century mind, the subject of a literary genre of indictment and reform.[21]

It was really hard to maintain one's poise in such surroundings. Women especially risked unwanted confrontations and this was often sufficient reason for them to avoid visiting public places unaccompanied altogether. Where restrictions prevailed on the appearance of women alone in public, those women who did move about the streets could only be less than decent and this assumption provided men with an excuse for accosting them.[22] Such license in turn prompted the women who could avoid it to shun public places without a chaperon.[23]

Public transport, boats and horse-drawn omnibuses brought together people from very different backgrounds in cramped quarters and this again was often perceived as an infringement upon their personal dignity by those who considered themselves above their fellow passengers, yet could not afford to avoid travelling by these common means of transport and could not prevent strangers from coming too close. In these streetcars clerks, shopkeepers, craftsmen and their wives, often for the first time in their lives, found themselves packed together with people of lower station, such as street vendors, factory hands, fishwives or longshoremen and this alone was cause for great vexation and status anxiety.[24]

To sum up: immigration into urban areas created unaccustomed adversities and deficiencies in the lives of both newcomers and established citizens in addition to more familiar ones. The very facts of spatial density and economic connection intensified and magnified the external effects of individual adversity and deficiency, making it almost impossible, except for the very rich, to isolate themselves from the consequences of the actions and vicissitudes of others. By the same token, it was often quite difficult to exclude others from the benefits one had secured and paid for oneself.

City life thus generated uncertainties of its own: crime, mob violence, rebellion, the unpredictable cycles of the urban-industrial labor market, and mass epidemics. None of these adversities could be remedied in any sort of reliable manner.

Lengthening and tightening chains of interdependence bound together the urban population, increasing the externalities among them. And although the awareness of these externalities was often only patchy at best, the fact that mutual dependency tied together the rich and the poor, the established and the outsiders, in one figuration, escaped no one. In nineteenth-century urban consciousness, this state of affairs acquired a new and haunting expression in the specter of mass epidemics, most of all cholera.

2 Cholera as the paradigm of urban interdependence

In his already classic study of the impact of epidemic disease on human history, William McNeill writes:[25] 'The first and in many ways most significant manifestation of the altered disease relationships created by industrialization was the global peregrination of cholera.' Although yellow fever had struck Barcelona in 1819, there had been no major epidemics in Western Europe since the last outbreak of the plague in 1720 in Marseilles.[26] The first outbreak of cholera thus surprised and terrified the nations of Europe. The wave in 1832 created 18,000 victims in England and an equal number in Paris alone.[27]

'Cholera – the very name spread panic!'[28] In their helplessness the authorities could only appeal to higher agency: 'Whereas it has pleased the almighty God to visit the United Kingdom with the disease called the Cholera . . .'[29]

In the public imagination of those days the specter of cholera brought together in one grand obsession the preoccupations with the predicament and comportment of the poor, with the sanitary dangers these implied for the established citizens and with the need for urban sanitary and administrative reform. Nearly all urban concern for order, decency and cleanliness could be collapsed in the paradigm of infectious disease and at the same time this notion hinted at a program of prevention. Moreover, mass epidemics provided a striking image of interdependency between fellow city-dwellers, poor and rich, established and newcomers, ignorant and cultivated alike. Thus, to put it in the terms of the Introduction, the cholera outbreaks served as an object lesson in the external effects of individual deficiencies, in the uncertainty of moment, the magnitude of adversities and the uncertainty of effect of individual remedies. It all seemed to point to the necessity of citywide, collective and compulsory arrangements to combat the risks of mass contagion.[30]

At first, the threat of infectious disease inspired only mutual loathing between the poor and the rich – some slum-dwellers even suspected that cholera was the result of a plot on the part of the governing elite to poison and exterminate them.[31] The rich, on their part, blamed the victims:[32] they were convinced that infection was a consequence of vice and dirty habits among the poor; that it was the immorality of the poor that brought the plague upon their houses, even endangering the health of the rich themselves. Thus increasingly, one person's way of life, nutrition, hygiene, housing, sexual and drinking habits might no longer be just pitiful or offensive to others, but might actually constitute a source of danger to them. The external effects of the private lives of the poor were felt to extend far and wide into the lives of the rest of the citizenry: as far as miasmic substances might go, or germs might travel.[33] The more practically minded among the city officials and medical doctors realized that these epidemics somehow had to be a result of urban squalor and that any attempt at containing them would require cleaning up the slum areas.

But mass epidemics were not the only threat that haunted nineteenth-century city-dwellers; there were also the ubiquitous fears of rebellion, mob violence and crime. These anxieties also set the established against the dispossessed, causing suspicion and hatred, and at the same time they too provided an idiom in which to articulate vague intuitions of mutual dependency. The poor suffered a sorry fate, maybe through their own fault, but these sufferings might one day be revenged upon the rich: through collective action by violent uprisings against the urban order, in rebellions or through equally concerted action against specific targets, in mob violence against hated magistrates or profiteering shopkeepers.[34] Such outbursts might occur only once or twice in a lifetime, but they were acutely and continuously remembered, always present at the edge of urban consciousness.

By the end of the century, once the proletariat had become better organized, these violent upheavals were succeeded by a more controlled form of collective action – strikes – not always peaceful in nature, but less disruptive of the urban order.

Petty crime was another omnipresent plague of city life: it too was understood as a concomitant of poverty; necessity might drive the poor to theft, or their immorality was believed to be at the root of both their indigence and their criminality. Most crimes were committed as individual actions or by very small groups: the collective enterprise of robber bands was mostly a rural pursuit and the heyday of organized urban crime came only later, near the close of the century. Crimes hit people one at a time, striking single passers-by and separate family

125

homes. But the typical nineteenth-century response to urban criminality was pre-eminently collective: increased vigilance by the newly established standing police forces.

Epidemics, too, were believed to be a consequence of individual actions, albeit sins of omission rather than deliberate misdeeds. There was no clear understanding of the mechanisms by which diseases spread. Yet, in nineteenth-century notions 'gross negligence' certainly was considered to be a cause of disease: people who spread filth, caused stench, created rubbish piles, or defecated in the streets were believed to increase the risk of epidemics in the entire area. And the aggregate, but unintended, effect of such individual action, or individual lack of foresight, did create a danger to the collectivity.

Rebellion, mob violence, crime and epidemics were the four horsemen of the urban apocalypse. And against all these evils the urban community responded with a clamor for police. At the time the term did not denote only vigilance and repression, but also broad and incisive measures of prevention. Nor were its connotations restricted to security in the modern sense of protection against theft and violence, they encompassed the full range of public safety, including tasks which later were separated off, such as sanitation and hygiene or even information. The eighteenth-century German term *Polizey* is best translated as 'administration' and the meaning of the word 'police' in the early nineteenth century approximates to that of the contemporary terms 'inspection and enforcement'.[35] Except for France, a standing police apparatus for the protection of public order was a novelty early in the century.[36] Around that time, permanent bodies of 'medical police' were established in various countries to inspect sanitary conditions and enforce measures of public hygiene.[37] Both kinds of police constituted a collective response to the threats of urban living: a citywide, public arrangement entrusted with coercive powers and financed from compulsory rates. The medical police force in the large cities of Europe and the United States had as great an impact as the urban police force. Not only did it impose sanitary discipline on the poor, it also dared to pressure the rich, especially the real-estate owners, to accept its directions.[38]

Both medical and urban police increasingly enabled the urban authorities to control those aspects, and many they were, of the citizens' behavior that caused untoward external effects. But the city also began to provide services which helped to change the conditions of urban life: illumination of the streets, construction of hard pavements (against mud and pools), supply of fresh drinking water, removal of human waste, collection of garbage and refuse from homes and streets, public-transport systems, public schools for the poor and the not so poor, and later gas, electricity and telephone systems, and, most recently cable TV. Most of these urban provisions were set up as networks, connecting every user to some major supply installation through a system of pipes, cables, wires, roads and tracks.

There are thus two key concepts in nineteenth-century urban collective arrangements: the idea of police and the idea of a network. As collective goods, they each have their distinctive arithmetic for the allocation of costs and benefits. A police force is, in theory, the more purely collective good: its vigilance benefits all citizens in a given area without exception, no one can exclude himself or herself from its attention, nor can anyone be excluded from the security it is supposed to convey. A police force is universal in its benefits, specific only in its punishments, or so it ought to be. A network, on the other hand, consists of quite specific connections which may provide individual subscribers with certain advantages, excluding all others who have not paid the price. Yet, as we shall see, these network connections did create external effects for those who had not subscribed, while those who remained un-connected might cause external effects for the subscribers. Moreover, the necessary capital outlay for the infrastructure of the network – the central installations and the main connections – required large-scale financing which also created specific problems of collective action.

The specific nature of the service to be provided and the particular features of the urban environment determined the problems which the city government faced in establishing urban networks. Much depended also upon historical circumstances, upon the balance of power between the various urban classes, upon the strength of the urban administration, the readiness of the central state to support local administration and subsidize its schemes and upon the wealth or poverty of the urban community in its entirety. And, no doubt, the hydrological and demographic layout of the city played an important role in the shaping and timing of urban provisions.[39] But everywhere the conditions of urban life itself exerted constraints of their own and provided new opportunities for the collectivization of protection against the threats of urban existence.

The overriding fact of urban life was that people of different classes could not avoid confrontations with one another or extricate themselves from mutual dependencies. In the economic relations between capitalist entrepreneurs and workers, the latter depended on the former to earn a wage in exchange for their labor, just as the former, the entrepreneurs, were dependent upon those classes to find the hands that would work the machines. Similarly, the large real-estate owners needed the immigrants to rent their dwellings and these newcomers would find no roof without them. But, of course, these dependencies, though reciprocal, were not at all symmetric: for a worker the difference between finding a job or not finding it was one between subsistence and starvation; whether an employer could or could not find a suitable man only made the marginal difference of keeping a machine in operation or not. The same applied to a family seeking a roof and someone trying to turn a mansard to an added profit. Yet, in their totality, employers as such are as dependent on workers as vice versa and this also goes for the interdependence between all landlords and all renters. Even then, the dependence of employers and house owners is less acute and immediate than that of their opposite numbers, workers and renters, since the former have more resources to fall back on in times of adversity and tend to be better organized, more capable of coordination, and to have greater access to the political arena.

But apart from these rather general interdependencies, there existed others, specific to the conditions of urban life, connected with public order and the use of urban space.

3 Individual coping strategies, networks and collective goods

It was the very vastness, the deadly heaviness of urban poverty that made it seem unavoidable and insoluble: 'those vast, miserable, unmanageable masses of sunken people'.[40] The enormity of the problem prompted those who were better off to look the other way, to forget about it or to find some argument that would shift the blame from their conscience to the poor themselves or to some cabal of manipulators and monopolists.

Whoever could afford it would move out of the areas where the poor lived. The dominant strategy of nineteenth-century city-dwellers was to move to wealthier, cleaner, roomier and safer districts – it was a strategy of individual isolationism. Any family who could rent or buy a home in a better area would opt for this solution. And by doing so, these individual isolationists unwittingly helped to reproduce the problem of urban poverty in different forms, with new and further-reaching external effects. The aggregate result of individual isolationism was collective spatial segregation: the separation of different social classes in distinct residential areas. In the course of this process the unit of analysis shifted from individuals with varying social positions to urban areas of different social composition. The struggle over urban space was no longer fought between individuals on the square meter, but among the inhabitants of different areas of the city, each trying to keep out cumbersome newcomers and ward off vexing activities, each trying to defend and improve the status of the neighborhood community as a collectivity. In this struggle some areas could scarcely defend themselves for lack of social cohesion, economic resources and political impact. And thus, the rest of the city would deal with these areas according to its interest, allowing them to deteriorate, unloading its least desirable elements and most troublesome business there, thus contributing to the emergence of the urban-blight zones which have become so familiar a feature of modern large cities. As an alternative, the slums were simply cleared up to construct thoroughfares and luxury housing as in the 'Haussmanization' of Paris, or tracks, docks and warehouses as in the London West End.[41]

The great social-geographic trend of urban development was from spatial homogeneity and social heterogeneity toward spatial differentiation into socially more homogeneous areas, 'neighborhood communities' as they have since come to be called. This transformation occurred through individual decisions to move elsewhere within the city – choices prompted by the results of preceding decisions by some to come to the city and settle wherever cheap dwellings were available and of others to abandon the deteriorating areas for newer, better neighborhoods.

With this global transformation of the city went a change in the demarcation and uses of public and private space of streets and dwellings. Daunton has described the development for early nineteenth-century England:

First, the private domain of the house moved from a *promiscuous* sharing of facilities to an *encapsulated* or self-contained residential style. Secondly, the public domain of the city lost a *cellular* quality which had entailed an ambiguous semi-public and semi-private use of space, and took on a much more *open* texture. The dwellings became more enclosed and private, whilst the external space became 'waste' space or connective tissue which was to be traversed rather than used . . . The boundary or threshold between the two became less ambiguous and more definite, less penetrable and more impermeable.[42]

Conscious city planning was rare, the great demolitions and re-constructions in central Paris, London and Vienna were grandiose exceptions.[43] Official policy was usually restricted to the designation of areas in the outskirts of the city for new housing and for slum clearance in the city core. Project developers and construction firms mainly reacted to the manifest need for dwellings among those who wanted to move out of the overcrowded downtown areas. And this manifest desire was inspired by the vexations of city life, noise, filth, stench, overcrowding, crime, but underneath it all, by a fear of social contamination, a desire to be further away from, and thus further above, the city's poor.[44]

The resulting spatial segregation into homogeneous subpopulations made a great difference in the provision of collective goods. At every turn one must ask of a collective good which collectivity it refers to. The residents of the new areas constituted the potential agents of collective action and the potential consumers of collective goods; as collectivities they became increasingly homogeneous in their interests and resources. Moreover, spatial segregation allowed the exclusion of potential free riders among other layers of the population through sheer physical distance. Thus, the inhabitants of a reasonably wealthy neighborhood might be willing to accept an increase in the rates to pay for improved police vigilance in their area or for the creation of parks in the vicinity. The poor, being exempted from the taxes, were also excluded from these benefits, as they lived too far away. It remained for the municipality to make sure that the actual advantages of its services would go to the rate-paying public; this became all the more feasible now that the taxable citizens lived in well-demarcated areas.[45] The policy could hardly be avoided, since the well-to-do not only paid the taxes, their representatives also manned the city government.

City politics were initially dominatd by aristocrats and *grand bourgeois* who also often owned the better part of the land and the mansions in the central area of town. Professional men, minor officials, shopkeepers, merchants and craftsmen either owned a house of their own or rented space in the large buildings that belonged to the great real-estate owners and where people of smaller means occupied the less comfortable dwellings. This close and intimate proximity between people of divergent class and style was often praised as a means of civilizing the newcomers and watching over the poor, to discipline and protect the workers through close supervision from their bourgeois neighbors and to ensure mutual aid and support in times of need. But it also helped to distribute the burden of the poor rates among a greater number of taxpayers in the core areas.[46]

The density of habitation increased, and so did rents. Landlords profited from this development, and this was another reason why conservative opinion in the city stressed the civilizing effect of the proximity between petty-bourgeois and working-class families on the one hand and newcomers and paupers on the other. But those families who found themselves forced to live near the poor suffered from the rent increases and also from the vexations and indignities of having to live with the uncouth – they preferred to move whenever they could.

The creation of collective service networks was very much determined by this segregation. In a formal sense, such service networks are hierarchical or tree-like in structure. A number of endpoints are all connected to a node, without being directly connected to one another. The nodes, again unconnected to one another, are all connected to higher-order nodes, and so on, until the heart of the system has been reached. This is usually a large installation such as a water basin, a sewage mill, a gas factory, a power station or a telephone exchange. Only public-transport network lines have interconnections and are not supplied by a single central installation, except for electrical power.

Individual consumers could be excluded from these networks, or admitted against payment for services used: in this respect, the urban service networks did not constitute a collective good. A private entrepreneur or an enterprising city government could build a transport system, or a water-supply network, organize garbage removal or construct a sewerage system, and charge its users at the going rate. Major capital outlays were required to build the system of pipes, cables or tracks and the central installations. At the time, the new railroad companies were providing a – controversial – lesson in raising the necessary funds on the developing capital market. Nevertheless, the interdependencies of urban life eluded the price mechanism: urban-transport systems created intractable external effects, and so did sanitary conditions. Subscribers could ensure their own domestic hygiene, but they were still exposed to the risks generated by others who would not, or could not, pay the price of subscription. The dilemmas of collectivization continued.

4 The creation of the 'venous-arterial system'

During the second half of the nineteenth century medical and custodial institutions multiplied, the elementary-school system was greatly extended and a series of service networks were established: for public transport, for gas supply and somewhat later for electricity and telephone communication. For the present purposes the most important network provisions of the time were water supply and sewerage. Urban sanitation represents a special chapter in the sociogenesis of the welfare state: within fifty years or so a very costly and highly effective system developed in all large cities, initially on a private and voluntary basis, but in its final stage as a compulsory arrangement under public control.

Urban sanitary conditions had been deteriorating during the first half of the nineteenth century as a result of increasing population:

> the primitive sewage systems which served ineffectively in previous centuries, deteriorated under the pressures created by the greatly enlarged populations of the industrial towns . . . but what was even more serious in

relation to exposure to infectious disease, it led to further pollution of the sources on which the towns depended for their water.[47]

The groping attempts to remedy these evils finally resulted in citywide public systems of fresh-water supply and sewerage. Along with the improvement in the quantity and quality of food supply, sanitary innovation was the main factor in the large reduction of mortality at the time, according to McKeown.[48]

Mass epidemics epitomized the facts of urban interdependency to the contemporary mind and urban sanitation represented the most massive and consistent effort to control the external effects of infection through common and collective measures. As noted in the preceding paragraphs, epidemic diseases were believed to strike the poor and those of immoral behavior much more severely than 'fit and proper persons'. Nevertheless, not even the most respectable and well heeled of town-dwellers felt safe. Moreover, epidemics caused great upheaval: there were mass panics and people fled from the city in great numbers, travellers and commerce from affected areas were held in quarantine, while business and industry threatened to come to a halt. The most squalid slums and boarding houses were cleaned up, or even evacuated, the streets were swept and rinsed in grandiose, emergency campaigns which were abandoned with equal suddenness when the danger seemed to have passed. But, even if the established classes did not fear for their lives, which most of them did anyway, they had every humane and material reason to fear the apparition of contagious disease.

A number of conflicting ideas circulated about the spread of disease, and of cholera especially. Overriding in the early-nineteenth-century mind, was the general idea of filth and dirty living which was not yet neatly separated in microbiological, as distinct from moral, categories. Most people sensed that poverty and squalor were somehow associated with ill health and epidemics. Mainly because of these suspected effects upon urban health, the living conditions and habits of the poor became the subject of moral discourse, political debate and scientific enquiry. And in the prevailing popular conception of disease, the danger was not so much an individual carrier of germs who might be identified and isolated or treated, but rather a diffuse, general uncleanliness and immorality among the poor and among immigrants or aliens. Thus, initially, the problem of urban health was inextricably associated with the specter of urban poverty and both issues were seen as essentially moral matters.

This view had two opposing implications: on the one hand the problem seemed enormous and unmanageable, its solution appearing to require no less than a sweeping reform of the way of life and the living conditions among the vast masses of the urban poor. As this seemed entirely beyond reach, this conception inspired a certain resignation and passivity. On the other hand, if measures were to be taken at all, they clearly had to be collective in scope, and this insight directed the search for remedies by reformist urban administrators and urban hygienists. But before they could put any of their ideas into practice, the reformists had to come up with much more specific and practical measures.

The medical experts of the time were sharply divided on the causes of epidemic disease and the ways to prevent them. A great debate raged between the 'contagionists' and the adherents of the 'miasma' theory. Although positions in the discussion were not nearly as neat as the terms suggest and although the concepts themselves were not at all mutually exclusive, the thrust of the contagionists' approach was to locate the disease-carrying agent in living organisms which were passed between persons. The 'miasma' approach located the cause of disease in places where filth exuded noxious vapors.[49] The two therefore inspired quite different policies. On the whole, the contagionist view prompted people to increase their own immunity through healthy living habits and the avoidance of possibly contaminated persons. In advocating quarantine, the contagionists continued the ancient medical tradition of the Mediterranean harbor towns. Accordingly, they were resented by businessmen for restricting trade. Their fellow experts often considered them outdated or even reactionary.[50] The contagionist approach, moreover, pointed to individual remedies and thus tended to further the private practice of medicine.

By the beginning of the century, some researchers had suggested a correspondence between epidemic disease and the squalor of urban poverty.[51] Polluting substances were believed to emanate from foul air, decomposing waste and stagnant water. This 'miasma' might itself go undetected by the senses, although stench was a certain sign of its presence. Thus, vapors had to be driven out and fresh air circulated, stagnant pools were to be eliminated, fecal matter, garbage, dirt and dust cleared away. All this seemed to point first of all to a massive cleaning operation of homes and streets. The next phase would require the demolition of unhealthy dwellings, the construction of adequate housing, the continuous removal of garbage from the streets and the installation of a network of pipelines to supply clean water and remove human waste: in short, a complete program of enlightened urban management, advocated in medical and technical terms by doctors, engineers and civil servants as the means of preventing disease.

What was new about these sanitary reform proposals was how they redefined the problem of pollution: initially it was a matter of individual misbehavior to be corrected by official admonishment or city ordinances, but by mid-century the question had changed into a collective problem of urban waste from domestic life and industry which could be remedied only by a combination of official inspection, legal compulsion and above all, public-work projects.

By thus specifying a practial program, the sanitary reformers reduced the issue to manageable, albeit still enormous, proportions: what used to be seen as the tragedy of urban existence, as a political and moral issue in the first place, was redefined as an administrative and engineering problem which the urban hygienists would duly solve. As they considered it their mission to bring health to a diseased community, and as they evoked science and reason as their only guidelines, they felt justified in laying down the law in the most intimate and exacting detail for each and every citizen: 'Hygiene turned itself from an instrument into a legislator.'[52]

The cholera epidemics of 1832 and 1849 alerted the general public to the urgent necessity of urban-health measures. But even the panic of these years was insufficient to bring about the required reforms. Once the mass outburst of cholera abated, sanitary emergency measures were quietly abandoned again and health boards were disbanded or robbed of their discretionary powers. This happened after the great epidemic of 1832 and again after that of 1849. But by that time administrative and medical opinion in Western Europe and the United States was leaning toward 'miasma' theory: cholera and other infective diseases were believed to be caused by emanations exuding from filth, stagnant water and foul air – the inseparable concomitants of urban poverty. And if poverty could not be abolished in the short run, then its side effects might at least be limited. This was to be done through the introduction of the new techniques of urban water supply and sewerage construction. From mid-century on, the 'miasma' theory began to lose ground and was gradually replaced by an improved and empirically grounded version of the contagionist view, which until then had widely been considered as outdated. Yet, in the meantime, the 'miasma' approach had dictated a much more radical and effective program of reform than the essentially individualist approach of the contagionists ever could have.[53] A number of enterprising engineers, medical men and urban administrators had worked out sweeping schemes of urban hygiene: Virchow in Berlin, Von Pettenkofer in Munich, Villermé and Parent-Duchâtelet in Paris, Liernur in Amsterdam, Shattuck in Boston and, most important, Chadwick in London.

They all agreed that filth and human waste had to be removed from the city instantly and constantly. Gradually they realized that this required a constant and adequate supply of fresh water to rinse the streets and carry filth, waste and excrement away.[54] That clean drinking water, too, was an absolute necessity for public health dawned more slowly upon the authorities. Only by the 1860s did this become a matter of incontrovertibly established scientific fact.[55] And it added one more decisive argument in favor of a finely branched, running supply of fresh water which henceforward had to be of higher quality than required for rinsing and carrying purposes only. The authorities now also began to realize that the enormous increase of waste water used to carry away urban refuse added to the pollution of the sources for the city's water supply. As a consequence more care was taken in dumping waste water, which was to be piped further downstream or further away from the city, while fresh water was carried in from more remote and purer sources.

It testifies to the complete success of the urban-hygienist movement that no one now would dream of allowing drinking water to be polluted with sewerage water. But a century ago such contamination appeared much less of a threat than the danger of miasma, the emanations from dungheaps and stagnant pools. Even the newly constructed sewerage installations often discharged their contents only a small distance upstream from the inlets for drinking water. Chemists charged with testing the water found no harmful substances – their instruments did not yet register them.[56]

In France, the hygienists had adopted the battle cry of 'tout à l'égout', to promote the removal of all waste, including human excrement, through street gutters and the underground sewerage system, to be carried off by a generous supply of water.[57] In Paris, as elsewhere, there was much vehement debate whether waste water, street dirt, domestic waste and human excrement ought to be carried separately or in one grand sewerage system. If there was any provision for human waste at all, it usually consisted of cesspools which leaked their contents in the surrounding soil, or of containers ('privy-pans') which might be removed periodically. Farmers from the vicinity would come every once in a while and clean the cesspools or empty the tanks and take away the contents for use as manure. From early times, human excrement had been considered valuable substance, to be saved and used as fertilizer. Today's city people want their faeces to disappear as quickly, completely and unobtrusively as possible and a certain attachment to one's excrement is thought to betray a fixation upon infantile anal tendencies. But in the not so remote past it was common practice to hoard faeces for use as manure or sell it to farmers who came around to collect it. Excrement was indeed money and this explains, with the costs of sanitary improvement, the opposition to sewerage connections which would rob people of their own production and make them pay on top of that. Only by the time that this interest in one's anal excrement had lost its evident social functions, Freud came to identify the enduring concern with faeces as an individual psychological 'fixation'. Gleichmann points out that urban sanitation went with a 'sanitation of speech':[58]

> As the distance to dirt and to human excrements increases, as people create lengthening chains of interaction between themselves and their waste, as more and more sanitary specialists come between them and their excretions, people have less and less occasion to speak about these matters.

But in the meantime, accumulating filth increasingly became a problem to the urban public:[59] 'Excretion obsesses the urban imagination', writes Corbin,[60] noting 'a lowering of the threshold of olfactory tolerance' in terms reminiscent of Elias's description of the general, long-term decrease of the 'threshold of embarrassment', which he considers one aspect of the civilizing process.[61] No doubt, at the beginning of the nineteenth century, living conditions in the teeming cities were quickly changing for the worse for many people, but this fact is of itself insufficient to explain why people began to take offense at smells and sights that had long been the omnipresent concomitant of city life. Filth began to be associated closely with pauperism and strangers, with everything that was 'foreign' and 'low'. Doctors were instrumental in connecting urban low life with vice and filth, and with disease. Once clean water became available to the rich in sufficient quantity to wash, rinse and flush, they could afford to distinguish themselves from their social inferiors by bodily and domestic cleanliness and the absence of odors. Social distinction could now proceed in terms of cleanliness, and the 'other half' began to be thought of as 'the great unwashed'.[62]

The proposal to have human faeces removed swiftly and without trace encountered unexpected vehement and indignant opposition which can only be understood from these archaic attitudes towards bodily waste.[63] And, surprisingly, the most innovative and radical reform scheme transposed these same notions from the individual human metabolism to the metropolis as one huge circulatory organism.

The findings of the German chemist Liebig had added solid scientific evidence to the old ideas of the utility of human excrement and other organic waste as fertilizers. It was the English reformer, Chadwick, who included these findings in a complete scheme of urban recycling: 'the venous-arterial system'. A constant supply of fresh, clean water should be pumped into the city and distributed through a system of ever finer mesh to each individual household, where it would be used for cooking, drinking and washing, next to be carried off through a matching, but strictly separate, sewerage network in which human excrement might also be flushed with running water; industrial waste and street dirt, rinsed away with freshly supplied water, would also flow into these sewers. The waste waters would then be carried out of the city and processed, and the organic contents would be spread over the surrounding fields as fertilizer in liquid form or as solid pellets. The lands fertilized in this manner would yield an improved harvest with which to feed the expanding city: a perfect cycle of urban metabolism.

5 How collective arrangements became citywide

At this point a generalization may be proposed. Urban provisions such as police surveillance or water and sewer networks served the wealthier citizens in the first place. Spatial segregation allowed the construction of service networks for quite homogeneous areas of private subscribers. The poorer areas mostly remained unconnected, until the urban area had become almost 'saturated' with network installations. In the meantime, negative external effects from these poorer, unconnected areas continued to affect the wealthier parts of town. At this final stage, with the central installations and mains in place, urban service networks could be extended to the poor areas at marginal cost only: it was a matter of weighing these added expenses against the continuing externalities. At some point in time, the municipal authorities made connection compulsory throughout the city and began to provide the service as a semi-public good. User rates were imposed as a kind of tax, largely independent of the actual costs of individual connection and often even independent of the volume of individual use.

Individual isolationism and the resultant social segregation served to transform the interdependence that urbanization had brought about between rich and poor individuals. They mitigated the immediate external effects of poverty and squalor upon the wealthier ranks of the citizenry. In the process of segregation poor and rich neighbors no longer affected one another so immediately, but poor and rich neighborhoods did so increasingly – first of all, because through segregation some areas improved very much, while others deteriorated since they now also had to accommodate the poor who were being driven out of the renovated zones;[64] second, because the same segregation necessitated increased traffic between areas, some of which had become specialized industrial zones, while others functioned mainly as central shopping districts or exclusive residential neighborhoods. This compelled people to commute from one part of the city to another, as their daily business required. Urban-development projects and transport schemes quickened the pace of demolition of older working-class and slum areas, thus splitting the population into those who could afford public workers' housing and those who had to huddle ever more closely together in the remaining slums. The more marginal commercial activities were also increasingly cut off, street vendors or peddlers no longer found customers in their own areas and were excluded from the commercial and residential areas. Boarding houses were closed one after another for reasons of sanitation and public security. This again added to the number of roofless, seeking refuge in the streets or the casual wards. Thus the specter of petty crime, epidemics and rebellion remained unabated, even if the typical external effects of the first phase, nuisance, had disappeared in large part.

Throughout the nineteenth century, urban reforms were the subject of vehement discussion and of a succession of innovative schemes. They did take a long time to materialize, but in the end all major cities established a series of urban provisions, more or less at the same time and very much in the same manner.

The various innovatory schemes proposed in early-nineteenth-century cities all served to combat ills that were conceived of as collective threats, and they all involved the establishment of collective goods through collective actions, but each of them in a quite different way.

In general, the schemes may be compared in three respects. The first consideration was whether or not they required sizable initial capital outlays. If they did, considerable long-term loans had to be raised, either by private capital or by the city government: an example of collective action in the face of uncertainty of remedy. The second question was whether such arrangements required most citizens in a given area to cooperate in one way or another. Such relative 'jointness of production' of the collective good would necessitate some form of compulsory regulation on the part of the city government. Any proposal imposing novel compulsions was certain to be controversial.

And finally, there was the matter of the exclusion of those who declined to pay for the proposed services. If such exclusion was not feasible for economic or technical reasons, then the opportunity to take a free ride at the expense of those who provided the service might tempt a sufficient number of citizens to undermine the financial base of the scheme: in such a case the scheme had to be financed by the imposition of a fee on everyone, regardless of actual use, either by special rates or from the general tax fund. In the course of the century, the process of spatial segregation unintentionally provided the solution to this free-rider problem, by separating willing subscribers from those people who would be most tempted to eschew the costs of connection.

Since urban areas were becoming more homogeneous, their in-habitants tended to share the same views on the problems of urban life and to agree upon the remedies. In many respects, the 'neighborhood community' became the agent of city politics. This certainly applied to matters of policing, the most collective of urban provisions: although, in theory, no one could exclude himself or herself from police vigilance, nor could anyone be excluded from its protection, in practice policemen guarded property most assiduously where there was most of it and watched people most intensely where there were most of them.[65] It also applied to urban-service networks, even though these were less collective in character, since exclusion and self-exclusion were indeed feasible. But here, too, external effects operated. If one household remained unconnected to the sewerage system, its waste might cause a nuisance for the neighboring dwellings.[66] If one owner refused to subscribe to a garbage-removal service, his rubbish would clutter up the pavement for his neighbors also. And finally, if some inhabitants remained unconnected to the supply system for fresh water, it might still taste as sweet to the people next door, but they might worry about their neighbor's health and their own risks of contagion: epidemic disease was the great externalizer of the effects of private life.

In this respect, gas and electrical networks are the least collective in nature, since it matters much less for one household whether others are connected or not.[67] The same applies to the more recent telephone and cable-antenna networks. Accordingly, policing, water supply, sewerage and garbage removal have become public services almost everywhere, whereas gas, electricity, telephone and antenna networks remain privately owned in some countries and subscription often remains voluntary.

Poverty, squalor and disease convinced the urban population of the general necessity of sanitary reform; the recurrent cholera epidemics testified to its compelling urgency. There could be no doubt that the living conditions of the poor did affect those of the well-to-do even after they had moved to segregated neighborhoods. 'Unsanitary' areas could still affect other districts through their 'miasma'. The main task was therefore the removal of human, animal and industrial waste from dwellings and pavements throughout the city. By mid-century it had become clear that this was to be implemented by a constant and abundant supply of fresh water to rinse the streets, flush domestic waste and carry all of it away. As the water was also going to be used for drinking and cooking purposes, it should be of high quality. New engineering techniques, scientific ideas and administrative schemes all pointed towards a grand solution, the venous-arterial system of water supply and waste disposal.

But all these necessary conditions together were not sufficient to bring about the reforms. It took the determined commitment of a small vanguard of dedicated and enlightened civil servants and professional men with the support of the progressive middle-class vote. And even then the new system could only be completed in a rather roundabout and unforeseen manner.

First of all, water supply and sewerage installations were costly, even if money might be lent against the rates to be paid by subscribers. Second, the administrative map of the urban area nowhere corresponded with the hydrogeology of the region, that is with the flow of potable water and the drainage basins. Conflicts of competence paralyzed the reform at every point. And finally, the well-to-do who had moved to better quarters could also manage their water and waste household privately, buying fresh water by the bottle or having it piped in by private companies, and disposing of their garbage and waste through the services of independent collectors. This accorded quite well with a general opposition against government interference, a permanent fear of rate increases and a profound suspicion of innovations which would introduce alien pipelines into the citizen's most private corners and connect his household so intimately to the body public. It may well have been the invention of the water closet that finally persuaded the well-to-do citizens to accept the system. After a period of trial and error this contraption turned out to be completely effective in preventing odors or sights associated with defecation.[68] And as these smells and scenes had become so closely associated with poverty and disease, the elegant management of defecation became a sign of wealth, health and cleanliness. But the relatively simple system of the water closet did require a constant supply of flushing water under some pressure and a permanent outlet connected to a larger waste disposal system. The water closet became the immediate connection between the private citizen and the collectivity.

As installation was easiest in open lots, newly built houses were usually the first to be connected to the piped-in water supplies and the underground sewerage system. Water closets became a major sales point for the new real-estate projects. The relatively well-to-do inhabitants of these new areas were ready to pay the rates for water supply and sewerage.

Although this was a matter of much debate at the time, with hindsight it did not matter very much if the services were run by private enterprises with a license from the city government or by city-owned agencies which had to be financed with bonds. And in most cities publicly licensed, but privately operated, water and sanitation companies were taken over in due time by the city government. Designing and financing the operation required all the available expertise of the time.[69] Railroad construction served as a precedent, as both a warning and an encouragement. It had taught how to build an extensive network without sharp bends or slopes (water and sewerage networks must of course constantly slope slightly downward, avoiding sharp corners, so as to keep the water running: a major engineering challenge which was at first not always foreseen). Railroads also provided an example in raising the vast sums of money required for a long-term investment to be paid back from users' rates.

Things were much more difficult in the older parts of town where installation was more costly and the population more heterogeneous: most schemes required the landlord to pay the subscriptions and this made for strong opposition from an influential stratum which – in England – organized as the 'dirty party'. Nor did matters improve very much when in the older mansions up to a score of people had to use the same facilities (the more private these became, the harder it was to scrutinize their users).

The water and sewerage companies had to build central purification and pumping installations, mains and side-channels for the neighborhoods they served. Gradually a large part of the city was connected to the system and mains installed underneath the greater part of its surface; the specific outlay of the city, the location of the water sources, the discharge areas, the water levels of the various neighborhoods, the situation of the richer in relation to the poorer areas, all these considerations determined the growth and shape of the system and therefore which areas would remain unconnected or what the added cost of connecting them would be.

In this manner a water supply and a sewerage system were initially constructed in most nineteenth-century cities as a common, i.e. a divisible, good: the central installations were paid for by loans against the revenues from subscriptions, while those who would not pay the rates might be excluded from the network. This approach became feasible in the new, socially homogeneous, residential areas where everyone could be expected to subscribe on moving there. The danger that some people might choose to remain unconnected to the sanitation system, to profit from the clean environment themselves and to spoil it for others with their unprocessed waste, was minimal in these relatively wealthy neighbourhoods; city ordinances requiring subscription either were superfluous or could be easily enforced as a condition of the lease or the sales contract. Thus, no matter how large and costly, the networks were initially paid for and provided as private, albeit common, goods. Their considerable external effects were more or less evenly distributed, given the social homogeneity of the user population in the new areas. Private home comfort was the main consideration in subscribing to them and was made possible, once the short-term and nearby external effects of the squalor of others had been warded off through social and spatial segregation.

The collective interest in public hygiene – the prevention of mass epidemics – set the ideological tone for much of these sanitary activities. But it did not determine the timing or the course of network building, which were shaped mostly by private demand. The economics of network construction were and are governed by marginal cost accounting. Gradually the city became saturated with pipes and channels until only a few areas, usually the older and poorer zones and those that were harder to reach, remained unconnected: 'Class divisions thus had hydrological dimensions', writes Berlanstein.[70] The centrally located, impoverished districts represented the most acute threat to urban hygiene and they were usually the cheapest to connect once a large network had been established. By that time, technical and administrative experience had eased the troubles of installation and management, the city government had gone through a learning process and statistics now demonstrated how fresh drinking water and efficient waste disposal improved public health beyond the highest expectations. At this point the coalition of engineers, health experts and administrators, supported by enlightened public opinion, were able to push through legislation to subsidize water supply and sewerage for these remaining pockets of ill health which endangered the health of the citizenry in its entirety. Thus, only in its last phase did the system become a true public good, extending to all citizens, from which no one could be excluded, or excluded themselves. It was financed from compulsory rates, calculated independently of installation costs, either as flat rates or connected to volume of use. Water and waste management had once and for all been transformed from a private concern to a public affair at the level of the city administration.[71] The new sanitary arrangement proved so successful and effective that it has become uncontroversial and slipped out of public consciousness and private awareness within a few generations. What has lingered on and become acute again are the problems of pollution and environmental protection, but this time at a higher level of integration, that of the national state and, even more pressing, at the supranational level.

5

Workers' Mutualism: an Interlude on Self-Management

At a time of deep poverty and wide uprootedness – during the period of early industrial capitalism and accelerating urbanization – a form of voluntary mutual aid emerged which lent new life to old traditions of reciprocal support.

Factory workers in the cities could no longer build upon time-honoured customs of kinship and neighborliness, on the traditions of guilds or sodalities. They had to find alternative arrangements, based on voluntary cooperation and adapted to the conditions of urban life. This proletarian experience of mutual aid and self-management stands out as a unique example of autonomous collective action in an industrial urban setting.

Workers who had drifted from the surrounding towns and villages to the new factory cities joined together in mutual-aid societies which in some respects continued the traditions of the apprentices' funds from the guild era, but industrial workers were neither compelled nor protected by the municipal guild ordinances of earlier times.[1] In the free-market economy of rising capitalism they stood empty-handed, with nothing to offer but their labor-power. In the sprawling factory towns they had no other resources to fall back on than the kindness of a relative or neighbor from their home village or the support of fellow craftsmen.[2] And yet, before long, working men began to form associations to provide in times of need and put aside a few pennies a week from their penury for the common fund to ensure a decent burial, often for children who had died at an early age.

Many Friendly Societies extended their provisions to unemployment dole, sick pay, medicine and medical treatment.[3] Sometimes they also succeeded in disbursing pensions for disablement and old age, and even for maintaining the surviving kin of deceased members with a widow's mite.

The individual Friendly Societies tended to be small in membership and capital, but taken together the workers' mutual funds comprised millions of subscribers: 'by mid-century it was estimated that almost half the adult male population of England and Wales belonged to a society.'[4] Anatole Weber presents figures for France that indicate a rapid growth of the *sociétés de secours mutuels*: an increase from a quarter of a million to 2 million members between 1852 and 1903.[5] Tennstedt reports 45 per cent of the population of Prussia as ensured for sick pay in *Krankenskassen*, each of minute size, 100 members on the average.[6] Starr mentions estimates of 25 to 30 per cent of American families belonging to 'fraternal orders and benefit societies'. many of which provided some form of insurance.[7] Mutual-insurance arrangements in Amsterdam covered 40 per cent of the population by the end of the nineteenth century.[8] The figures quoted cover more forms of insurance than just the workers' mutual societies, but taken together they do provide a rough indication of the size, growth and importance of the phenomenon. And yet, the impression prevails that workers' control was already on the decline by the turn of the century and that the bewildering multitude of funds protected the working classes only against a small fraction of the risks of death, disease, disability, old age and unemployment.[9]

Very few of these countless small, autonomous aid funds have survived till the present day.[10] How is the demise of this form of mutual aid under independent, joint management to be explained?

Little is known about the day-to-day management of these small funds. Few descriptions or minutes of their meetings have been left for posterity. The working people who made up the membership lacked not only the habits of formal meetings, but also the skills of methodical administration. Moreover, they usually resisted outside intervention or inspection of their books.

However, 'meticulous attention to procedure and institutional etiquette' prevailed, writes E. P. Thompson under the heading 'The rituals of mutuality', and he adds, 'the discipline essential for the safe-keeping of funds, the orderly conduct of meetings and the determination of disputed cases, involved an effort of self-rule as great as the new disciplines of work.'[11]

The collection of weekly dues represented another 'social constraint to self-constraint'.[12] In this respect, the workers' mutual society continued a tradition of the guild apprentices' funds which also stressed modest and respectable comportment to prevent pandemonium during meetings and to gain the confidence of patrons and city authorities.[13] In the Friendly

Societies, frequent plenary gatherings were indispensable. They served first of all to shame in front of everyone such members as had not yet paid their fees. Drinking, smoking and talking together also helped to instill a sense of togetherness which was not yet firmly established among the new proletarian city-dwellers.[14] Accordingly, the workers' mutual societies were also social clubs which continued the apprentices' tradition in this respect too. Members frequently supported one another during crises, in childbirth or illness, in times of need or in quarrels with bosses and landlords. The members of the Friendly Societies educated one another to share in an emerging workers' culture and a proletarian solidarity which found its ultimate expression in the union movement.

Yet, because of a number of essential shortcomings, these workers' mutual societies perished in a relatively short time and their providential functions were taken over by new, much larger arrangements: the nationwide, state-controlled, compulsory institutions of social security. Precisely the characteristics that held such appeal for nineteenth-century workers, and explain the enormous growth of the mutual funds, also made for their weakness and caused the demise of the friendly societies.

1 Informal togetherness – fraud, strife and mismanagement

The mutual-aid funds were small, but internally weak and vulnerable. Actuarial science – still in its infant stage – was unknown to them. They had no access to statistics and only the faintest notion of the distribution of risks to be insured. Adequate mortality or morbidity tables for their population were nonexistent.[15] As a result, the required fees could not be calculated, but were set according to vague rules of experience and the estimated paying capacity of the members. Since insight into the distribution of risks was lacking, the funds tended to exclude persons considered less decent, of an irregular walk of life or in hardship, since their punctual payment could not be counted upon. Moreover, hardly anyone among the members was accustomed to managing relatively large amounts of money for a long period of time. Those who might resist the temptation to take something for themselves, in a burst of generosity might regale others who were in a bad way.[16] Quite often the local clergyman or the inn-keeper acted as treasurer, since the former was generally trusted and the latter believed to be competent in financial matters.[17]

It was also new to the funds' members to decide who was entitled to an allowance and who was not. They found it hard to control for malingering or to treat like cases alike, irrespective of kinship or friendship ties. In a personal context, without guidance from formal regulations or the shelter of expert authority, it was difficult to disburse to one member and reject the claims of another without raising suspicion and envy.

Corruption, fraud and favoritism were no exception in the small mutual funds. And worse, they were often paralyzed by mutual suspicion and interminable conflicts. To overcome these ills would have required skilled administrators, trained and detached visitors of the sick and needy, external inspection of the books and formal rules to define entitlement to benefits. Small societies, however, lacked the money to hire professionals and the expert knowledge to draft regulations. But in the large societies which could afford such expert helpers and outside advice, self-management would quickly lose its meaning.

2 Homogeneity of membership – the accumulation of risks

The original burial societies and sick funds were formed by men who worked at the same trade, or who originated from the same region,[18] and had migrated to the city at about the same time and who therefore were often about the same age. Many lived in the same area or frequented the same pub.[19] This very similarity greatly strengthened the sense of mutual identification and of reciprocal solidarity. But the homogeneity of membership also carried with it similar risks: workers in the same trade ran the same danger of occupational disease and often lost their job at the same time. The inhabitants of one neighborhood were exposed to the same contagions. People living in one street, having settled at the same time and belonging to one generation, grew old together. Those in charge of the funds, however, were reluctant to demand higher fees from elderly members, or to attract younger members with lower fees, as it appeared inequitable to them. As a result, many young workers would not join and this increased the average age of the membership as years went by. The social homogeneity which made for mutual solidarity among members also caused a concentration of risks and sooner or later an accumulation of claims which might doom the fund to bankruptcy. Only the dispersion of risks could prevent such a failure, but this required a heterogeneous membership. Diversity, however, tended to weaken mutual identification and solidarity.

3 Cooperation among equals – the exclusion of inferiors

The Friendly Societies, *Krankenkassen* and *sociétés de secours mutuels* proved to be inadequate for still another reason, one that concerned not only their own members, but also a larger social context. Once a number of working men had combined to found a mutual-aid society, they were strongly tempted to exclude henceforth what they considered 'bad risks'. For lack of medical or actuarial knowledge, people of lower station, looser habits or lesser means were believed to run greater odds: status determination took the place of risk calculation.

It was from these 'lowly' and 'mean' persons that the 'decent working men' wanted to differentiate themselves in their effort to emancipate their own stratum of regularly employed and settled workers.[20] They did not identify at all with casual or itinerant workers or with all those others whom they too saw as the 'dregs of society', who would only undermine common solidarity and increase the risks borne collectively.[21]

In other words, small, voluntary, collective care arrangements such as the workers' mutual funds tended to be closed in a downward direction – they would refuse people of lower status and lesser means. And, in fact, to these paupers, wretches, *lumpen*, the pressures of daily survival were often too great for them to afford a penny a week for the burial society, let alone for the sick fund. Excluded as they were from the mutual funds of the better-off workers, they could only have combined with their companions in misfortune who could spare as little and would need as much.

A system of small, autonomous, collective provisions always excludes a substratum – this is a sociological regularity of much wider validity than for this subject alone.

But at the upper end, the opposite occurred, this time as an unintended function of government intervention. Local authorities might often be wary of any coalition of working men, but they usually welcomed the mutual funds, expecting them to alleviate the burden of municipal relief. The established bourgeoisie hoped to save on the poor-rates and believed that the funds might uplift the morality of the lower classes. For these reasons, the mutual societies were allowed certain privileges and exemptions, on condition that they opened their books to inspection and facilitated adequate supervision.[22] The societies were loath to allow such interference with their autonomous management.

The advantages of registration and recognition were often considerable: exemption from stamp duties, for example, or the opportunity to invest on favorable terms in municipal or government bonds.[23] But these

147

opportunities prompted an entirely different brand of people to combine under the cover of mutualism in order to secure for themselves the privileges granted to the working men's societies. In this manner for example, the English clergy succeeded in financing their life insurance.[24] The same occurred with savings banks[25] and housing societies.[26] The advantages the government offered to associations of working men were adroitly exploited by middle-class citizens who combined for this purpose, while the poorest ranks were excluded from these arrangements all along.[27] Government measures intended to mitigate the downward exclusion by small, autonomous, collective entities thus tend to profit the social stratum just above them.

To sum up: the mutual-aid societies represented a form of authentic solidarity and collective care, widely and densely spread, and managed on a small scale by the autonomous members. Yet these very characteristics also accounted for their shortcomings. Personal involvement went with a lack of financial expertise or professional detachment. Homogeneity of membership made for mutual solidarity, but also caused an accumulation of risks instead of a complementariness of claims and resources. And autonomous collective arrangements resulted in the exclusion of the less privileged, while government support tended to favor the somewhat better off.

4 The demise of the mutual funds – the rise of state insurance

Today, only a century later, not much more remains of this vast archipelago of working men's associations than some faded banners, yellowed papers and here and there a union or an insurance company that can trace back its pedigree to some friendly society long since defunct.[28] What made these workers' funds, once so numerous and lively, perish so quickly and completely?

A nationwide, collective and compulsory arrangement emerged which provided people with greater security for the same fee and liberated them from the dilemmas of voluntary collective action by compelling all workers to contribute to a single scheme, largely irrespective of each one's personal odds. But the rise of state care also meant professionalization, bureaucratization, extension of scale and legal compulsion.

Professional expertise and bureaucratic techniques allowed the routinization of decisions according to fixed rules and impersonal procedures. Financial management and administration of personal records became tasks for skilled specialists. Actuarial knowledge and improved statistics allowed a precise calculation of risks and an adequate assessment of fees and benefits. Insurance physicians and specially trained visitors of the sick were able to gain information about each and everyone's physical or living conditions and to make due recommendations irrespective of personal ties, unhampered by the bonds of friendship which had held together the funds' companions in earlier days. Social workers would fill out identical forms for every case, making each comparable to all others, and make recommendations according to the standards of their profession. The regulations, written by lawyers, were tried and refined in the jurisprudence of appeal courts. The financial resources were aggregated and brought under the management of experts who operated not as treasurers of 'the box', but as managers of an abstract capital which left much less opportunity for self-enrichment and almost none for spontaneous largess.

Even today, insurances are not managed without effort and strife. On the contrary, almost every aspect is controversial, notwithstanding all regulations and expertise. But anyone who envisages the rapid development and the enormous size of these insurance and allowance systems, the hundreds of thousands of officials, the millions, tens of millions of claimants, and the capital of hundreds of billions, even trillions, must also realize the relative insignificance of corruption and disputes within these gigantic organizations, even in times of economic slump and retrenchment.

The development of a public system of social insurance has been an administrative and political innovation of the first order, comparable in significance to the introduction of representative democracy and greatly underestimated as an achievement of administrative technique.

State intervention in insurance introduced three unique and novel elements: permanence, national scope and legal compulsion. The state was the oldest and most creditworthy risk-bearer, one function that by the end of the century the churches could no longer fulfill to the same extent. The state also was the largest and most encompassing organizational structure that functioned effectively at the time. Joint-stock corporations coming anywhere near it in size developed only later. And, most important of all, the state could exert effective and legitimate compulsion and thus impose obligatory insurance upon the vast majority of wage-earners.

This compulsion, even if it was at times experienced as oppressive, also implied liberation from another pressure: the temptation to exclude bad risks and thus maintain and secure one's own membership against competing funds through fees kept low by exclusion.

The latter feature appealed especially to organized workers, as they were increasingly confronted with yet another form of insurance against adversity and loss of income: commercial companies. The commercial insurances showed themselves well capable of organizing their affairs on a grand scale, to calculate their fees sharply, manage their capital expertly, take on clients after physical examination only and adjudicate payment decisions in a consistent manner. After an initial period of swindlers and bankrupts spoiling the market for commercial insurers, a number of companies succeeded in building up expertise and gaining the public's confidence, to win clients among the small bourgeoisie and eventually among working men too.[29] The exclusion of 'bad risks', a temptation for the workers' mutual societies, was to the entrepreneurs a matter of business acumen only. As a result, their insurance conditions and premiums attracted precisely the younger, healthier and more 'decent' workers who were so indispensable to the adequate functioning of the workers' funds. Only the – actuarially – least attractive members would remain in the societies that were thus doomed to eventual bankruptcy.

As modern means of communication and publicity created a nationwide market, commercial insurers began to reach out to a public which had traditionally supplied the members of the workers' funds. The mutual societies found themselves outpriced, their potential clients usurped by the commercial societies and their actual members increasingly isolated on relatively unfavorable terms. The commercial-insurance market threatened to do to them what the autonomous mutual-aid funds had done before to a lower social stratum: exclude them and join on better terms with more attractive company. This perspective forced the workers to abandon mutualism and opt against commercialism in favor of the one most encompassing and least voluntary solution: compulsory national insurance under state control.

Apart from its own material stakes, the principles of solidarity, voluntariness and self-management made the choice especially difficult for the mutualist movement.[30] But the worker amateurs realized that they could not match the advantages of professionalism and the increase in scale. In the face of commercial competition, they were forced to amalgamate their funds and to abandon small-scale autonomous management. But what they feared most was the inexorable process of risk selection and differentiation of clientele which would tear apart the infant workers' movement. Confronted with these perspectives, many organized workers opted for a state insurance system. For those trade unions that also offered insurance to their members the choice was even harder, since these 'side benefits' helped to strengthen the loyalty of individual members and provided the leadership with an employment opportunity and a power base in their own workers' insititutions.

By the turn of the century, the dynamics of a nationwide economy and a national state was increasingly interfering with the workings of the small-scale, voluntary and autonomous funds. What had once been viable principles of cooperation now generated more and more perverse effects. The main weakness of the mutual societies was their overall redistributive effect. Their strength was, and may still be, in the supply of personal services adapted to the differentiated needs and preference of small and varying clienteles. Central regulation is required to ensure redistributive justice. Professional standards may be necessary to guarantee adequate quality. But under those conditions, small-scale collective management of service provision by the clients themselves may yet help to adapt the supply to a greater variety of needs and preferences.[31]

6

Social Security as the
Accumulation of Transfer Capital

In the course of the past century a nationwide, compulsory and collective system of protection against the economic hazards of urban-industrial life has developed in the democratic capitalist nations: 'while the rate of total government spending in industrialized nations has grown perhaps 80 to 90 times in real terms during this period, the rate of spending on social policy has probably mushroomed by 5,000 to 6,000 times.'[1] And although this expansion has levelled off during the past ten or fifteen years, and in some countries even been reversed, most workers in Western Europe and North America today live in the awareness that they and their families are covered in one way or another against the risks of income loss from disease, disability, unemployment, old age or death.[2] They have come to share 'the equanimity of the welfare state'.[3] To them the state of providence is first of all a state of mind: they have grown accustomed to sizable taxes levied on their payroll in exchange for a guaranteed income in times of hardship. In this respect, wage-workers – who now form the vast majority of the labor force – have grown more similar to the propertied classes: today's sacrifice brings security for tomorrow. But there are differences: saving in the bourgeoisie is self imposed, it is state-enforced among wage-earners; and: privately accumulated savings may be freely disposed of by the beholder, but the payroll taxes levied by the state yield only specific entitlements which cannot be transferred to anyone else. Whatever is accumulated by wage-earners through their contributions, it is not theirs to dispose of. It is tutelary property, kept for them until 'really' needed. If the contributors 'own' anything, it is a claim to future transfers upon specified conditions of adversity or deficiency.[4]

Such claims have no market value,[5] they are not transferable, yet their value may be estimated by calculating the odds and capitalizing the expected transfers: the resulting sum represents the 'net worth' of a contributor's claims, his or her 'transfer property'.[6] The total of all these claims upon public agencies might be called the 'transfer capital' of the population. To the agencies committed to pay these transfers in the future the transfer capital represents a liability very similar to the national debt and covered in much the same way.[7] For the holders of these claims their transfer property is the functional equivalent of private property in one major respects – as a protection against future adversity and deficiency: transfer property shares with private property its providential function.

Wage-earners are well aware of this. They may often be able to reproduce no more than a few acronyms denoting laws and agencies, but they know very well that they and their family are covered against the major financial risks of working life; they may have a fair idea of the level of provisions, a slight notion of the premiums deducted from their wages, and some hunch of the conditions imposed for disbursement. And, in a significant way, this subjective knowledge may correspond more closely to the structural realities prevailing in these countries than the insistence of specialists on national differences between systems.[8]

In a long-term developmental perspective, the synchronicity and parallelism are the most striking facts about the accumulation of transfer capital. Henri Hatzfeld concludes: 'In the end the central powers intervened . . . the differences could not mask the deep similarities.'[9]

What must be understood and explained first of all is the emergence of compulsory and national collective insurance systems against the major adversities confronting wage-earners.[10] Such arrangements were established in all countries under discussion somewhere between 1883 and 1932 – a time-span of barely fifty years. But the similarity does not mean that like effects were begotten by like causes, or that differences are unimportant.

Social-security arrangements are collective remedies against adversity and deficiency. They provide for reimbursements in specified cases of income loss. What distinguishes these modern institutions from prior arrangements is their nationwide, collective and compulsory character. They have developed only in societies with a highly effective central state and in connection with a growing sense of national identity. Moreover, as arrangements for the compensation of income loss, they were to remedy the adversities that befell wage-earners who had no property of their own to fall back on in times of hardship. These arrangements could only emerge in societies where regular employment for a money wage had become the normal condition of working life.

1 Private saving and collective accumulation

Social security presupposes a highly developed monetary economy in which wages and benefits are paid in money. It also presupposes that a sizable portion of the working population is employed under similar conditions which allow uniform administrative handling. And it requires an awareness that workers may lose their income through no fault of their own and cannot anticipate such adversity by individual providence alone.

The adversities of working life first had to be understood as recurrent and inseparable aspects of the industrial mode of production, affecting the majority of workers in modern society, and not just as a transitional phenomenon concerning only an ill-adapted minority. Workers, on their part, had to realize that what happened to others today might well happen to them tomorrow. They had to develop a sense of collective fate. But others also were to understand that massive poverty among industrial workers would threaten their existence. Strikes would damage the interests of entrepreneurs, riots those of politicians and both would disturb the general public. What was required was an awareness of the generalization of interdependencies among people in industrial society, a 'social consciousness'. This interdependence may well have been experienced most of the time as anxiety or anger, where once only indifference and contempt prevailed.

The sensitization to problems in terms of social issues did not bring about new institutions of its own. But the spreading social consciousness did prompt the search for institutional solutions and inspire articulate programs for political reform.

By the end of the nineteenth century and the beginning of the twentieth the debate centred upon the notions of property and providence. Private accumulation of wealth had become the means to provide against future adversity and deficiency. This reliance on property, and more and more on money, to secure an uncertain future was itself a result of the security from violent attack which had been the major hazard of an earlier epoch. As societies had become increasingly pacified in the process of state formation and the monopolization of violence and taxation within extending territories, people could engage in exchange and accumulation more safely that before. Attack and defense alliances for mutual protection and joint conquest declined in importance. Under the generalized protection of the state these specific protective relations gave way to specific relations of property. The research for security through reliable alliances with others by bonds of marriage and clientage continued in changing forms. And property, also, may be conceived of as a claim to the future services of others, more abstract and more generalized as relations were monetarized.

In this process, the nature of property changed. Land and buildings had once appeared to be the most secure holdings, but in the course of the nineteenth century financial markets developed and more people than before began to invest in riskier enterprises, such as railroads, mines, factories, without, however, directly involving themselves in their management. Those who sought more secure investment found an alternative in government loans. The expanding state guaranteed the security of its bonds with all the authority and mystique it could muster.

In other words, security now appeared to be a matter of private property. The prior necessary condition of pacification and security from violent attacks was taken for granted – it is even ignored by most scholars. The prefix 'private' became almost inseparable from property and suggested that wealth made its owner independent of others, whereas in fact the dependence upon the efforts of others continued unabated, but in a more abstract and generalized form. In a sociological perspective, no one is 'of independent means', no one can provide for himself. Wealth only helps – very much – to make others provide for one's needs, now and in the future. Nevertheless, the notion of autonomy, of being in control of one's own life, is essential for an understanding of why people have so tenaciously insisted on individual property when confronted with the option to collectivize it. And state collectivization is precisely what social security is about. It is what constitutes its relative novelty.

The struggle over social security was one for and against this enforced collectivization of property as a protection against future adversity. The extension in scale to entire nations and its compulsory imposition by the state are necessary corollaries of the collectivization of providence.

This collectivizing campaign was opposed by those people who could expect to provide against adversity through private accumulation in a monetary economy under the generalized pacification by the state: small entrepreneurs, shopkeepers, craftsmen, traders, farmers and professional men. It was supported by those who could not hope to do so and who increasingly realized that this was not their individual peculiarity, but part of the common conditions of their working life: the industrial workers. More and more, large-scale industrialists, politicians and administrators came to share this view and accepted the collectivization of provision not for themselves, but for the workers.

By the end of the nineteenth century the state apparatus had grown much larger than ever before. State bureaucracies ran standing armies, supervised poor relief on a national scale, provided mass education throughout the land and supported urban sanitation, police and transport networks. The state now seemed capable of accomplishing administrative tasks on the scale the new insurance schemes would require.

2 The accumulation of transfer capital in a four-sided figuration

Social-security institutions were established by an activist regime for electoral purposes in the short run, and so as to expand the hold of the state apparatus in the long run, but never in a void: the politicians and administrators in power who made up the regime had to seek support both to secure acceptance of their legislation and to ensure its implementation among workers and employers. They did so by forming coalitions, sometimes with the moderate wing of the organized working class, sometimes with reformist circles among the entrepreneurs, sometimes with both.

The strength of the opposition from the property-owning petty bourgeoisie very much determined the moment and the momentum of social-security legislation. Its resistance was hardly strategic, it did not organize for the purpose, nor did it formulate alternative proposals: it was opposed. But the independently employed declined in numbers throughout the period. Even in their own lifetime, many of them entered employment in large firms or government departments or saw their children become workers or functionaries. Among the ranks of the new, employed, middle class there was scarcely any opposition to collective, or even compulsory, protections against income loss. They only insisted that it be visibly distinct from, and superior to, the arrangements for the working class: more generous, and if need be, more expensive. Time worked for social security: as the independently employed or their children became dependent wage-earners, their attitudes towards private provision changed accordingly.

Every step and every choice in the process was laborious and contested. Intricate administrative machinery had to be designed and tried before it could cover millions of people and process huge sums of money. Creating social security was hard political work. It demanded strategic coalition-building and tactical parliamentary and bureaucratic maneuvering. The coalitions that carried social security through parliament, and made it acceptable to the workers and employers concerned very much determined the nature of the arrangements: the division of control and the distribution of costs.

But even the most innovative schemes had to be realized within a matrix of ongoing practices, existing institutions and prior legislation. This did not always imply continuity: sometimes earlier experience prompted the rejection of anything resembling it, for example the workmen's *carnets* in the French pension legislation of 1911, or the hatred against the Poor Law dole that led to the rejection of noncontributory unemployment insurance in England. Moreover, sometimes a 'law of arresting advance', as the Dutch historian Jan Romein has called it, operated: where the voluntary collectivization of provision had preceded very far and mutual societies or unions had built up extensive institutional networks of their own, they tended to resist any takeover by the state and to oppose compulsory arrangements.

Finally, social security required legislation and subsequent implementation, and it was very much molded by the dynamics of the political process and the structuration of the bureaucratic apparatus. Where the working class became enfranchised, its preferences became immediately relevant for the electoral chances of politicians, whereas without the vote these preferences were only dimly anticipated. It also mattered very much whether social cleavages, and accordingly electoral calculations, prompted politicians to discuss the matter of social security in terms of strongly opposed interests and ideals, or whether they could trade with one another, and with the interest groups concerned, in an incremental manner. Equally, it is very plausible that strongly centralizing policies were better adapted at bringing about uniform, nationwide social-security arrangements than those of a more centrifugal nature, and that states with strong and extended bureaucratic agencies could more easily implement an effective social-security system than those that had to set up such networks for the first time.

The emphasis in this chapter is on those critical episodes in which nationwide, compulsory and collective arrangements to provide for income loss were established in a country for the first time. The *moment and momentum* of these episodes is explained by identifying both the coalition that carried the scheme and the opposition against it by the property-owning groups. The small owners together formed the 'brake' upon this development, the coalition of an activist regime with moderate union leaders or progressive industrialists represented the 'motor' driving it.[11] The shifting balance of power between the stalling, but dwindling, petty bourgeoisie and the gradually extending reformist coalition determined both the moment and the momentum of legislation by an activist regime; the *division of control and cost* of the scheme depended mostly on the composition of the support coalition.

The regime was the one necessary actor. Without its active efforts, no legislation. But the regime needed support both in parliament and in the country. It could not pass or implement a scheme against the overt opposition of the majority of organized workers, because it needed both their votes (or their political pressure) in parliament and their compliance in realizing the scheme. Working-class acceptance very much depended on the financial terms of the scheme, but, more importantly, working-class-leadership support depended on the degree of institutional control the scheme would allow it. The regime could hardly go against the unions, but it could accomplish much without them if the employers were willing to pay a sizable part of the costs and cooperate in the administration of the scheme. The regime could, however, override very strong employers' opposition if it could count on massive working-class support. A regime might do without employers' contributions and rely on its own administrative apparatus or on workers' institutions, financing the scheme from general tax funds (collecting workers' contributions was and is an almost impossible task without the collaboration of the employers). Thus, an activist regime was indispensable; employers could be missed if workers' support was strong; if employers' support was strong, the tacit and passive consent of the workers' movement was sufficient. How strong the reformist alliance had to be in order to get legislation adopted was determined by the strength of the parliamentary opposition from parties of the petty bourgeoisie. Once a law had been enacted and the stage of implementation had come, this opposition no longer mattered very much. Small employers could escape inspection and many schemes therefore simply exempted domestic employers and farmers, at least initially.

In the main, four parties made up the figuration in which transfer capital was institutionalized, and they themselves were transformed in the process. The independently employed property-owners opposed any attempt at the compulsory collectivization of providence. They resisted most other extensions of government activity and at the same time fought the growing competition from large-scale industry. But they suffered desertion from their ranks to these large enterprises and to government bureaucracies.

Large-scale entrepreneurs identified with their smaller brethren and rivals, but had much to lose from labor conflicts. They were accordingly divided on the issue of social-security legislation. Workers stood most to gain by the introduction of social-security schemes, but their leadership was much more ambivalent. And finally, the government was the indispensable fourth party.

In the course of industrialization, unions, employers and government bureaucrats found themselves compelled to deal with one another more and more on a regular basis, and in the process they developed similar conceptions of personnel administration, factory regulation and the interdependencies of a national economy in international competition. In this evolving balance of dependencies, an activist regime, bent on extending the sway of the state apparatus and securing the political loyalties of the growing working class, might succeed in organizing sufficient support to overcome the political opposition of small property owners and employers. If and when a regime decided to contest the issue, it might seek support from employers and at least anticipate workers' influence (the German case), it might seek support among workers and only anticipate employers' demands (as in England and America), or it might form a tripartite coalition (as in France and the Netherlands). With the composition of the coalition went the terms of the agreement. All parties concerned tried to maximize their control *and* to minimize their costs: they demanded to be represented in the management of the social-security system and they insisted on the other parties bearing the expenses of the scheme. Whenever they came to an agreement, paying the costs turned out to be the price of control.

The history of social policy is a history of great issues, great needs and great men and women against a backdrop of great transformations in society. In this vast conglomerate of causes and actions which brought about such complicated and encompassing structures as modern social-study institutions are, one limited, but still vast, question may be singled out for clarification: why were collective and compulsory arrangements of nationwide scope adopted as a remedy for the financial adversities of wage-earners and what accounts for the timing and growth, the modes of finance and control, the scope and level of coverage, of these insurance systems?

'Collective', 'compulsory' and 'national' are the keywords here, as they have been throughout this study, and the critical episodes are those in which a government decides to adopt an income-insurance scheme for the industrial workers in the nation. Such schemes were collective, insofar as resources were pooled and benefits paid out of the common fund, independently of individual contributions;[12] national, because the schemes transcended the boundaries of specific occupations and industries, overrode local and regional governments and covered wage-earners throughout the land; compulsory, because taxes were levied and benefits defined, not by mutual consent among the parties involved, but by authority of the state, imposed upon all those concerned, whether they wished to join and contribute or not.

These new arrangements instituted a novel relation between citizens and the state: a *transfer bond* which tied individuals as contributors and as potential or actual claimants to public agencies committed to honor their claims under specified conditions. They constituted a functional alternative to the security private property could provide, a 'social security'. They were also a functional alternative to the coverage that commercial and mutual insurance had to offer, a 'national insurance'. All prior arrangements relied on a propensity to save, the new schemes did not. If contributions were levied, as usually they were, they were deducted from the payroll even before it was handed to the worker. Equally, benefits were not paid in a lump sum, but parcelled out by the week or by the month.

It was assumed from the outset, and it has been accepted ever since, that a sizable part of the working class was incapable of saving to provide against adversities to come. An earlier illusion had to be dispelled: that the proletariat might disappear of itself, once wage-earners had put aside enough to establish themselves as independent craftsmen or shopkeepers, leaving only a residue of improvident workers whose enduring indigence reflected their defective character. Until the end of the nineteenth century many people believed that an industrial proletariat was a transient phenomenon, bound to disappear in a generation or so, either because general wealth would grow swiftly enough for wages to increase to a level that might guarantee a 'decent', that is a petty-bourgeois, way of life, or because in the course of their lives individual workers would buy their freedom with their savings and begin for themselves. Many skilled workers and employed craftsmen entertained similar hopes and joined forces in voluntary, collective savings and insurance funds to obtain through their joint efforts the protection the propertied classes sought in private savings. But as the century progressed, it became increasingly apparent to informed public opinion and to the workers themselves that most of them were in no position to provide by their own means for protracted periods of disability, for old age or for their surviving kin. On the contrary, industrial workers showed every sign of having abandoned that hope: instead, they began to organize into unions, to support working-class parties and to agitate for reform and even for revolution. Clearly, the proletariat was not going to dissolve, industrial workers were not going to pass *en masse* into the petty bourgeoisie or to adopt its forms of providence. On the contrary, a workers' movement emerged, ready to fight collectively for institutional changes that might serve the needs of the wage-earning classes.

3 The compulsion to save

For the bourgeoisie, the 'social question' was initially: why didn't the workers save to protect themselves against life's vicissitudes? Was it from improvidence or for lack of means?

This question already implied a profound change in attitude towards the poor, at least to the new poor in an urban-industrial setting. Poverty in industrial society increasingly came to be regarded as an amoral category, one inflicted by blind fate and devoid of any transcendent meaning that might anoint it with spiritual redemption for the victim and his benefactor. It also began to be considered as essentially a remediable condition, rather than the outcome of inscrutable divine design. This new kind of poverty was gradually reduced to a single, bare fact: lack of money.

As long as the weekly wage was duly earned, most working-class families could manage a regular existence, but one that was bound to collapse within a few weeks if for whatever reason no pay was forthcoming. Thus, poverty could strike in the midst of an industrious life or after a lifelong working career; and in many cases it appeared to be caused clearly and solely by a loss of earning capacities or opportunities, devoid of any connection with the victim's character or walk of life. Urban-industrial poverty, moreover, was more visible, less easily camouflaged than the traditional rural misery. Paradoxically, as Harris points out, this new realism and the increased visibility often also tended to harden attitudes towards the poor as poverty now seemed so massive and unalterable.[13]

The age-old distinction between the honest and the dishonest poor was transformed into one between working men, impoverished through no fault of their own, and the others, who would not work for some reason which had to be bound up with their moral person and social milieu. Such persons – new terms were coined for them throughout the nineteenth and twentieth centuries and continue to be invented – had to be punished, or, later, reformed or re-educated, and, finally, treated and cured. Thus, this residual category of the poor remained the object of interpretational effort and remedial practice: of penitentiary theoretization and correction first, pedagogic constructions and re-education next and finally of medical and psychotherapeutic treatment: victims they still were, if no longer of fate, then of their own misguided volition.

This gradual reworking of the conceptions of poverty was connected to the emergence of a working class, of a category of people who did not possess land, stocks or machines, but who were nevertheless regularly employed and lived a steady life: people who, unlike the peasants and laborers of old, spoke the vernacular, could often read and write, who were in almost every respect undeniably human, might even become entrepreneurs, home-owners and voters themselves, if they would only put away some savings and buy themselves a business or some property.[14] The one thing that was hard to understand about them was why they did not save and invest like any decent citizen; such lack of foresight did, after all, reflect badly on their character. If only working men could be persuaded to lay away some savings, they would surely be able to weather the vicissitudes of life in modern society: 'The Republic . . .should follow the worker in every phase of his existence and, almost taking him by the hand, conduct him step by step to the possession of capital, of property, the real wage of liberty, the material sign of his emancipation.'[15]

Contemporary students of the industrial working class agree with the radical labor leaders and expert investigators of those days that workers simply did not earn enough to build up a nest egg for bad times ahead.[16] Saving among the lowest income groups, especially in tightly knit communities is also difficult, because relatives and friends will demand support from someone they know to have something on the side. Such claims can hardly be refused. This alone is sufficient reason for not even trying to save. But the bourgeois of the time and many workers with them believed that in order to save workers needed not just higher wages, but more discipline. Didn't the poor squander a good part of their money on liquor or tobacco?[17] The question was where and how the workers were to learn the required self-restraint. Religion, with its incessant insistence upon abstinence, although not necessarily on material frugality, may have helped to instill a more parsimonious life-style. But apart from admonition and exhortation by priests and lay moralists, there were the attempts by workers themselves to strengthen their resolve by seeking the company of well-intentioned peers: they hoped to help one another to save by coming together for the purpose – the mutual-savings and insurance funds served to increase their members' propensity to save. Pooling these savings also increased their efficiency as an insurance against adversity. The voluntary workers' mutual-insurance funds constituted a mechanism of mutual social control expressly set up for the purpose, and members joined of their own free will in order to reinforce mutually their intentions to save. Such joint and purposeful establishment of an agency of mutual compulsion and the voluntary submission to its dictates represents in itself a stark contrast to the traditional institutions of social control of village life in which a person found himself absorbed by birth and from which he could hardly divest himself if he could bring himself to reflect upon them at all. It is a clear example of the Parsonsian transition from status to contract. The mutual funds represented a transitional stage from individual accumulation to the accumulation of transfer capital under state compulsion, and as such they displayed all the paradoxical features that go with such transitory collective action, as has been demonstrated in chapter 5.

The mutual associations meshed very nicely with liberal-capitalist concepts of self-help and the collective nature of the effort fitted well both with patriarchal-religious notions of community and with more radical ideas of working-class solidarity. They seemed a veritable panacea.

Yet, for reasons already discussed, in the larger social context, even when widely and densely spread, the workers' mutual associations proved to be inadequate to protect the industrial working class against the vicissitudes of working life under capitalism in an urban-industrial context: the specter of poverty remained in individual workers' lives, most of all for the lower strata that could not even afford the dues of mutuality.

Contemporary bourgeois opinion nevertheless continued to articulate the problem in terms of spending discipline rather than in terms of wage increases. Increased earnings would only be dissipated by undisciplined spenders. More importantly, wages were considered to be the outcome of free competition on the labor market. They could not be increased by anyone's dictate and if they could, this would only interfere with the competitive advantages of the industry. It would delay the accumulation of capital from which alone could come a true increase in national wealth and a lasting improvement in the conditions of the working classes themselves.

Since the problem was defined by bourgeois opinion in terms of individual resolve and discipline and could hardly be discussed in other terms, new ways had to be found to increase the saving propensity of the working classes for their own good. If exhortation did not work and mutual encouragement was not enough, then – and only then as a means of last resort – there had to be a law. The state ought to intervene and compel the workers to spend their money in the way they really wanted, but could not bring themselves to abide by. 'Does a man have the right to be improvident', the French Minister of Labor, Viviani, exclaimed in 1901, 'when at the very moment that he abandons the ties of solidarity, he profits from them?'[18]

What economists call the propensity to save is a clear example of the control of affective impulses, of the pleasurable impulse to spend according to one's whims as they come. Management of household income is also a management of affect; financial restraint is a form of emotional restraint. The classical sociological characterization of middle-class mentality as one of deferred gratification implies this arduous abstinence from immediate pleasures.

In his analysis of the civilizing process Norbert Elias has stressed the correspondence between stage formation and domestic pacification on the one hand and on the other the increasing affective restraints that people imposed upon others and themselves: the social constraint toward self-constraint.[19] As Elias has pointed out, the very 'pressures from below' exerted by the lower classes forced the middle strata to increase their own self-restraint and thus maintain social distance. Similar efforts to increase social distance against pressures from below prompted the upper layers of the working class, the 'fit and proper' working men, to adopt in turn many canons of bourgeois behaviour to distinguish themselves from the rough and uncouth immigrants, casual workers and paupers.[20] The Friendly Societies, which so stressed decorous conduct at their meetings, contributed to this distinction within the working class, which was greatly reinforced by the effort of the providential associations to increase their members' orientation towards the future by their insistence on collective saving.

In the course of middle-class socialization, the external constraints towards self-constraint in spending and saving seem to have been inculcated so effectively that adults appeared to need no more prompting from others, and to save on their own account as a matter of character. In this perspective, the mutual societies represented the perfect example of such external constraints toward constraining oneself: voluntary, yet collective; based on individual consent under pervasive peer pressure.

With the transition to compulsory insurance, this balance shifted quite decisively from self-constraint to external constraint, that is to compulsion by the state. Subsequently, the imposition of external limitations on spending was no longer restricted to a dwindling proletarian rearguard, but, on the contrary, it was extended to all wage-earners, functionaries and personnel included, and finally even to the self-employed. The overall effect of this almost universally imposed foresight has been a diminishing of contrasts, a levelling off between life phases of relative wealth and indigence. High payroll taxes and relatively generous benefits have dampened the financial effects of life's vicissitudes for the vast majority of modern citizens. In this respect, the compulsion to participate in the accumulation of transfer capital has laid the economic base for a superstructure of diminishing contrasts in social life, and has helped to increase foresight by facilitating long-term career, family and financial projects on the secure foundation of transfer property. Again, there is an analogy with Elias's analysis of domestic pacification, imposed forcefully through the monopolization of violence by the state and thus facilitating more self-restrained forms of behavior among people who no longer have to be constantly prepared for violent attacks. And just as the monopolization of violence and its corollary, the emergence of the monopoly of taxation, are major aspects of the process of state formation, so the accumulation of transfer capital by means of taxation is a major aspect of a later stage of state formation: the sociogenesis of welfare states. This theme is taken up again in chapter 7.

Even today, the reliance on collective and compulsory arrangements rather than on private accumulation may well be the most important difference between bourgeois and proletarian mentality, one that opposes the working class *and* middle-class employees to what is left of the old middle class of independent entrepreneurs. In this respect what has occurred is not at all an *embourgeoisement* of the proletariat, but rather a proletarization of all wage-earners, the new middle class included, opposing both to the remnants of the old middle class.

None of this came about by design. What motivated people at the time was mass discontent among increasingly organized workers who apparently were in no position to provide for almost unavoidable periods of income loss. Neither individual nor collective saving seemed to promise adequate remedy. Therefore, some proposed that the state should intervene, as it had done before in poor relief, education and sanitation: it should institute compulsory insurance.

This was a crass interference with personal liberty indeed, and so it was perceived by many citizens, bourgeois and working-class alike. It would moreover involve at the very least a vast administrative effort of collecting weekly dues and paying out benefits, an enormous legislative and regulatory task in setting contributions and, even worse, determining entitlements, but, most of all, it threatened to saddle the state with the responsibility for a financial venture of unprecedented and, most likely unmanageable, magnitude. This prospect appeared all the more forbidding when it was suggested that the state should bear part of the costs, or even that the entire scheme should be financed from general taxes, without any specific contribution from the workers at all, as the radical wing of the labor movement insisted.[21]

The transition from individual providence by private saving via voluntary collective forms of insurance against income loss to nationwide compulsory social-security arrangements involves a transition in the forms of property. Next to private property, transfer capital emerged as the functional equivalent of private property in its providential aspects. It is in this perspective that the emergence of social security is to be approached in this chapter.

There is an analogy between the entitlement of citizens in modern capitalist democracies to an income from the state under certain conditions and the rights of property owners to the returns on their capital. But the participants in social security cannot dispose of their share in the transfer capital: transfer property is not transferable. They can exert a measure of control only in their capacity of citizens or union members, voters who – in theory – can influence decision-making on social-security taxes, benefits and conditions of payment. In this respect their position is somewhat similar to that of shareholders, who can only indirectly influence the ways their investment is used, and not much more effectively so than voters in a democratic polity. The emergence of joint-stock companies with the attendant separation of rights to share in profits and rights of control may well have influenced thinking about national-insurance systems, which would give workers 'a stake in the country', to quote Churchill's 'Bismarckian utterance.'[22]

There is, however, one great difference: shares can be freely bought or sold, savings placed or withdrawn, but the entitlement to social-security payments is not for sale:[23] it constitutes an inalienable right – and an inescapable duty. In fully fledged systems workers' contributions are compulsory and levied as payroll taxes: enforced savings earmarked to ensure income maintenance in case of need. And in this latter respect only are they a functional equivalent of private property.

As a functional equivalent of private property, social security tends to grow at the expense of private saving because payroll taxes diminish available household income:[24] and this was once a favorite argument against national-insurance schemes. But, indeed, social security as it expands becomes more necessary, not only because people – having less to spend anyway – will leave it to 'the state' to help their needy neighbors, but also because the income it absorbs might otherwise have been saved by each in his own way as a hedge against hard times ahead. This argument unmasks yet another uneasy truth about social-security arrangements: the worker's best judgment is not thought good enough for his own good. Apparently, wage-earners are not to be trusted with their own wage, but must be compelled instead to protect themselves and their kin. Social security is tutelary property.

State compulsion was to make up for the discipline which workers were believed to lack. Even the workers' champions, who argued that wages were simply insufficient to make provision against future adversity and that funds had to come from elsewhere, from the employers or the state, agreed that the money should not be left to individual workers to dispose of freely.

This issue did not oppose employers workers, or conservatives and radicals. Anarcho-syndicalists sided with small property owners, mutualist workers and many trade unionists in resisting compulsory contributions, while conservatives of a patriarchal hue, large-scale industrialists, moderate union leaders and social democrats tended to favor legal coercion.

But while the discussion proceeded almost compulsively in terms of 'discipline' versus 'improvidence', or 'liberty' versus 'compulsion', immediately below the surface it was involved with the anxieties aroused by the specter of the dispossessed masses of industrial society, or in more analytical terms, with the external effects of mass poverty and with the dilemmas of collective action any attempt at solution would create.

In these terms the problem was that inactivity might lead to deterioration, and finally to chaos and rebellion, to the detriment of all who identified themselves with the existing order of society. Activity on a voluntary basis, however, would either exclude the neediest (and at higher levels of integration, the poorest industries, union branches or regions), or require third parties to shoulder the burden of others of their own free will. Compulsion, finally, would force a majority to pay for an indigent or improvident minority unless even the pennyless were somehow forced to pay their share. This would involve a kind of policing and repression which no one thought palatable or feasible: plucking feathers from a frog. But allowing some to enjoy benefit without paying dues might tempt many to try a free ride, and thus undermine the system yet.

These dilemmas weighed very differently upon the various classes of society and upon different groups and individuals, according to their position.

4 Changing relations in the four-sided figuration

In each country, the small property owners, the industrial entrepreneurs, the industrial workers, and the regime in power together formed a figuration of changing balances of power and interdependence. These figurations had emerged in an even broader context in international competition. States formed in mutual rivalry and national economies developed in the competition for foreign markets. This, in turn, transformed the relations between the petty bourgeoisie, the industrial classes of employers and workers and the regime in power. In such constellations of shifting oppositions and coalitions, the institution of transfer capital emerged as an alternative to the providential functions of private property.

4.1 The petty bourgeoisie

The petty bourgeoisie, for whom private accumulation was the pivot of economic life, resisted the imposition of collective insurance schemes most bitterly and tenaciously. And this for much more than economic reasons alone – an entire life-style was at stake. The small entrepreneurs, feeling threatened by the rise of large corporations and mass commerce, suspicious of all state interference, clung to their autonomy, to being boss in their own shop, to hire and fire as they saw fit, and accordingly, they opposed all legislation that would curtail their sovereignty.[25] Even as industrial workers and industrialists were being converted to the merits of social-security schemes, independent entrepreneurs, farmers and professional men resisted them throughout; they formed the 'brake' on social reform: it was against their opposition that social security had to be established.[26]

But there was more to this resistance to all interference, no matter how benignly it presented itself. It was a rejection of egalitarianism, but not so much on the part of the aristocrats or the *grande bourgeoisie*, the big owners and entrepreneurs. They did not fear the working class at all as potential equals and rivals. The differences that government intervention might equalize were much smaller and the distinctions based on them accordingly much more tenuous: what was at stake was the small distance that kept independent artisans, tradesmen and entrepreneurs, France's almost proverbial *petits et moyens commerçants*, just above skilled and employed workers.

Property meant security and this security was what distinguished the bourgeois from the proletarian, it was what he could promise his bride and what he did his best to bestow on his children, what made him and the likes of him better than 'them'.

In order to understand why the lower middle classes so strongly opposed state intervention for protection against income loss, one must not ask what they stood to lose, but what the social group that threatened them most, the one just below them, might stand to gain: a small advantage which might yet obliterate the distance that made for their superiority. The petty bourgeoisie redefined what looked to others like a variable-sum game from which all might profit, into a zero-sum game in which the workers' gain was their loss, because they reckoned in terms of social prestige. It was a politics of jealousy, or in more sociological terms, but with the same meaning, a politics of denying to others what they already possessed for the sake of maintaining social distinction.[27]

Social historians have been so busy studying the mentality of the victimized, but victorious, industrial working classes that they have neglected research on the losers in the drama, the independent middle classes, the petty bourgeoisie. Most of their shops, stores and offices have disappeared, and with them the memory of the pride and courage that went into running them, the anger and the anxiety evoked by anything that might threaten them: it was not a noble and not a revolutionary cause, just a bourgeois, even reactionary, concern.

The small property owners lost the battle, but they put up an obstinate fight. They opposed social insurance because they saw it as the gradual erosion of prudence and responsibility by a massive system of coercion for one's own good, regardless of cause or intent, indifferent to achievement or merit, imposing blindly on all the equality of potential victims.

The small entrepreneurs did not so much change their opinions on social policy, they changed class first: as they or their children became employees in large corporations or government bureaucracies, their attitudes tended to change accordingly. They came to prefer company and government schemes to private provision, especially when the level of white-collar schemes was markedly superior to workers' insurance, as it usually was.

Much more than a history of 'working-class strength', the emergence of social security is the story of the waning power of the small, independent bourgeoisie and the decline of private-property accumulation. And much more than a history of class struggle between proletariat and bourgeoisie, the development of social security is the result of a conflict between the petty bourgeoisie on the one hand, and varying coalitions of organized workers, large-scale employers and an activist, reformist regime of politicians and administrators in power. In this sense, social security is the result of a 'class struggle', but one with reversed alliances.

4.2 Employers

Attitudes changed especially among large-scale employers and among workers in the advanced industries. They, of course, were most familiar with the conditions of industrial life and they were the first to experience, each side in a very different way, the immediate consequences of economic coordination on a much larger scale than before.

Initially, large-scale employers, like small entrepreneurs, argued that the poverty problem would resolve itself once industry had brought prosperity to the nation, the workers included. For industry to expand and to weather competition with other nations, wages should not increase above their present level. Employers tended to look at the issue mostly as a problem of charity and humanitarianism, or as one of enlightened personnel management. It was, first of all, a matter between them as patrons, sovereign in their own shop, and individual workers. When scarce, specially qualified or reliable workers were concerned, they would be much more inclined to bridge over periods of sickness or incapacity and to keep them on the payroll even in times of slackness.

In the meantime, the workers should be taught to save and provide for their own future. The employers agreed that voluntary mutual funds might stimulate workers to seek coverage for sickness, disability and old age, but they tended to be suspicious of any form of workmen's organization, as it might always be a cover for union activity or worse – political conspiracy. They were especially wary of unemployment insurance, which, they feared, might easily turn into a strike fund.[28] Company funds, financed by workers' contributions, controlled by the company management, and sometimes subsidized by it, appeared the more reliable alternative.

The first to establish collective insurance schemes for their employees were the largest enterprises of the time: mines[29] and railroads, the former hazardous, the latter requiring special punctuality, both more closely connected to the state than other industries. Because of their central position in the economy, these were also the first industries in which government intervened to set standards of contributions and benefits. Growth industries, such as the textile producers in Northern France, also set up insurance schemes of their own which served as a model for other enterprises.

But entrepreneurs had to acknowledge that their company schemes would leave out workers in less prosperous industries or in smaller shops and that workers' savings ran the risk of being lost in the event of company bankruptcy.[30] The latter danger prompted them to join in amalgamated funds, at the price of having to accept common standards of provision – even these combined insurances turned out to be vulnerable in times of crisis.[31]

To those companies that could afford it, the advantages of a corporate scheme were considerable: it constituted a bonus in recruiting workers, it did not have to be financed directly and reserves could be invested in company ventures; it allowed management to define the conditions of disbursement, and, *summa injuria* to the workers, tied them to their job, since upon dismissal or termination a worker's claims were annulled without his accumulated contributions being restored. For these same reasons company schemes were greatly resented by the workers unless they came under their control.

In the long run, however, even large and affluent corporations risked being burdened with more extensive disability and pension obligations than they had bargained for, burdens which threatened to weaken their competitive position in relation to companies that had established such schemes at a later date or not at all. By the end of the nineteenth century workers' average life expectations increased faster than anticipated when the original fees had been set, and thus, disabled or retired claimants remained longer on the company's rolls than expected. The same demographic development also brought many friendly societies into trouble, in Britain especially.[32]

Thus, modern entrepreneurs, familiar with the techniques of personnel administration and wage accountancy, accustomed to large-scale and long-term financing, and eager to maximize control over their workforce, quite easily accepted the idea of a collective and obligatory insurance plan for their workers, on condition that they would remain in control: the workers were to bear the costs and the government would remain aloof.[33] In an era of rapid concentration of capital, entrepreneurs also managed to find ways to amalgamate insurance funds and thus reinsure their risks. And if they had reason to believe that the workers were about to organize their own insurance fund, this worked as an added inducement to forestall them with a company plan.

The next step, from the collectivization of provision against income loss by companies to the compulsory imposition of such insurance on a nationwide scale by the state, was much harder to take: state regulation might wrest from management the control over its workforce on the everyday issues of factory discipline. Whenever organized employers were confronted with a national insurance bill, they sought to gain control over its implementation, if necessary at the cost of paying part of the dues. Only an awareness of wider externalities and long-run consequences could reconcile industrialists to national insurance.

4.3 Workers

By the middle of the nineteenth century, workmen who could afford it at all were quite willing to join collective insurance schemes, whether in the form of mutual societies, union funds, communal chests or company plans. But the working class by no means supported national insurance as one man. One radical tradition in the workers' movement resisted all social reform as mere tinkering at the margins of capitalist oppression, which would only delay the coming of the revolution. Close to this position were the maximalists in the workers' movement who wished the state to impose and pay for compulsory insurance against all risks of income loss and tax the rich for it, rejecting anything less. But other groups equally opposed state interference, albeit from a minimalist position. They insisted on the autonomous management of workers' institutions: the anarcho-syndicalists because they believed the independent working-class associations to be the seeds of proletarian self-government,[34] the more conservative adherents of the mutualist movement because they saw in these institutions the avenue to worker respectability and wished to retain control of what they had built with so much effort.[35] For trade unions there was an added reason to resist state intervention: they often offered insurance as an individual incentive to membership in an organization of which the main purpose was collective: improvement of wages and working conditions for all workers. For these unions insurance was a major way of solving the dilemmas of collective action, that non-members would receive the advantages union members had fought for, while avoiding all the costs and risks that militancy then entailed: union insurance provided members with an advantage from which non-contributors could be excluded. Such selective benefits accordingly played a major role in persuading members to join the union and remain in it.[36]

Employees individually may also have welcomed the advantages a company plan could provide: anything was better than no coverage at all; but workers' organizations quickly realized the opportunities for control it presented the management with and thus remained suspicious of corporate schemes unless they could secure a say in their management.

Control over insurance institutions had immediate and penetrating ramifications. First of all, entitlement decisions involved a redefinition of working relations: what constituted rightful absence of work, who was to be considered sick, when, for how long, and who had the final say in such matters? Which diseases should be considered a consequence of working conditions, which accidents were a 'professional risk', who was to be held responsible and who liable? What were acceptable grounds for dismissal, what kind of work should be considered adequate replacement, against which wage? Could jobless workers be required to break strikes or cross picket lines? Were common-law spouses or illegitimate offspring to be considered to be surviving kin? Should pregnant women and young mothers receive leave of absence or sick pay?

A third party, the insurance, threatened to intrude upon the permanent and pervasive struggle over work discipline on the factory floor. Since it was in a position to make up for wages lost or denied, it might end up transforming the balance of power between workers and management. As the scope of insurance arrangements extended, and especially when national schemes had been established, whoever was in charge of their administration was in a position to determine the day-to-day course of social policy and enforce it throughout the land in every insurance office and on every factory floor. The aggregate result of all these interventions was to impose greater conformity in factory practices, working habits and even in family affairs.

But there was more than this in insurance control. The institutions quickly grew into bureaucracies which offered jobs to men with some administrative skills, a talent for dealing with conflicts and experience in industrial working relations: shopfloor leaders. Appointment as an insurance official could mean promotion, prestige, increased earnings and security. Whoever could bestow these rewards had a strong hold on the workers' spokesmen, and the unions especially needed this opportunity since their activists put their jobs on the line and they had little else to fall back on.[37] The recruitment of workers' leaders into the social-insurance bureaucracy had major and unintended consequences for the domestication of the working-class movement, most notably among the social democrats in the Kaiser's Germany;[38] it also very much increased resistance to nationalization in those countries where local or sectoral schemes had already become established and employed large numbers of former union activists.

Thirdly, transfer capital accumulating in the insurance funds constituted an enormous resource of financial and economic power: it might be loaned to the companies concerned or invested in government bonds, used to build workers' housing, or even as a strike fund. As the capital market expanded, transfer capital grew at an even faster rate. Today, it may well constitute the largest source of investment funds in the economy.[39] These considerations were not lost on the union leadership, even when the rank-and-file membership was not always fully aware of the implications.

Finally, whoever controlled the insurance funds could also command the loyalty of the workers who had contributed to it throughout their working lives and drawn its benefits in times of disablement. Such attachments again constituted a mighty resource both in the power struggle within the company and in the political conflicts on the national level.

Thus, on the whole, the relatively privileged strata of the working class – skilled workers, regularly employed, in advanced industries – supported voluntary schemes and even company plans, but by the same

173

token they often tended to resist more encompassing, and especially compulsory, forms of insurance, which would abolish their relative advantage, burden them with the risks of the less advantaged workers and diminish their control over the arrangements that had covered them exclusively.

There was yet another reason why unions often neglected to press for social-security legislation: a generation gap. The workers' movement, and especially its militant wing, was future-directed: the young were in the vanguard and at the center of attention.[40] Insurance against disease, disability and old age or survivors' pensions were more of a concern to the elderly. They concerned a phase of life that many workers believed they might never reach. Higher wages, shorter working hours and better work conditions promised immediate relief. Thus, the issue of insurance required a degree of foresight which young workers were slow to develop.

For the workers' movement to proceed from promoting the collectivization of risk protection to advocating its nationalization required some confidence in the state and its administrative potential; but unions needed most of all to develop nationwide organizations and a national orientation. Trade unions, was well as employers' associations, had to develop an effective branch structure throughout the land with sufficient administrative unity and ideological consistency to make themselves heard in national politics. As long as they remained locally fragmented, they were in no position to grasp the ramifications of problems at the local level for the national economy and national politics. Much less could they be expected to develop nationwide institutional solutions, let alone support such proposals when they came from other parties. Organization thus preceded and determined programs.

Unions had to abandon the hopes either of self-help or of imminent revolution and to transcend the restricted identifications of locally and occupationally defined membership before they could be converted to national insurance. But this broader orientation could only come about in connection with a broadening of the organization. Different occupations had to join forces, sectarian divisions were to be bridged over, local branches were to federate at the provincial, regional and finally the national level. As so often in this process of integration, the driving force was conflict: a struggle with opponents who equally found themselves forced to form large entities in the process. Strikes and lockouts were of course a prime reason for both employers and workers to seek collaboration with their peers. If one company hired workers locked out by its competitor, the stratagem would be self-defeating. If some workers performed jobs refused by their colleagues on strike elsewhere, the struggle would be lost at the outset.[41] The process of amalgamation and federation of employers' and workers' organizations reveals many traits in the dynamics of state formation: it is an example of a figuration in which opponents compel one another to evolve to higher levels of integration.

The intervention of the state apparatus in industrial relations also contributed to the expansion of the organizational scope of workers' and employers' associations. Workers, employers and succeeding regimes were together involved in a continuing learning experience. Factory laws affecting working hours, woman and child labor, product quality, noise, pollution and so forth prompted countless intrusions by government inspectors and officials in the ongoing relations between workers and management. These state bureaucrats introduced national rules and considerations of nationwide relevance into their dealings with unions and companies and demonstrated the potential of compulsory regulation by the central state.

Employers and workers organized one another and were organized by the state as it in turn was drawn into industrial affairs. Employers, administrators and union leaders grew accustomed to dealing with one another, whether they liked it or not. Government intervention forced employers or workers to combine and articulate their interests at the central level. With big towns and big industry came big government, no matter what the strength of protest or denial at the time.

4.4   The regime

By the middle of the nineteenth century a novel breed of bureaucrats and academic experts were developing a practical science of public administration and many were eager to experiment with the exciting and powerful new machinery of government: inspectorates, nationwide agency networks, registries and so forth. This evolving state apparatus provided unprecedented career opportunities to young men who had no inherited means of pedigree. The heroes of nineteenth-century government expansion often came from lowly, bourgeois ranks and fought their way up on the strength of their expertise, tenacity and commitment, against aristocrats who still believed it was all a matter of honorary sinecure.

But politicians could hardly afford to be adventurous: they had to balance their budgets and win the next vote. Where suffrage was extended or where its extension was the scope of agitation, working-class opinion began to matter more and more in politics. Activist administrators and reformist politicians contemplating the political potential of workers' support envisaged a regime that might mobilize the coercive, administrative and financial resources of the state in a new venture: the establishment of compulsory national insurance.[42] Without such an activist regime no legislation could be proposed, let alone implemented; government was the necessary partner in any coalition that would establish national insurance. But an activist regime *per se* was not sufficient: it would still need support in the legislature, and thus in the country at large: either from industrial employers or from organized workers or among both.

No doubt, this renewed reformist activism among political elites was motivated not only by the enfranchisement of the working class, but also by the experiences and the anticipation of war: findings on the defective health of recruits prompted a well-orchestrated campaign for the improvement of the living conditions of the working class.[43] The loyalty of soldiers in the new popular armies had to be secured by promises of social reform. But, above all, mass mobilizations necessitated a regimen of total provision and taught governments the administrative techniques of large-scale health care or, in the aftermath of war, of extensive veterans' pension systems: by the end of the nineteenth century such pensions were the major instrument of welfare in the US;[44] by 1926 they made up 13 per cent of total government expenditure in France.[45] The total character of modern warfare also affected civilian populations and thus compelled governments to take encompassing measures of rationing and protection, which facilitated subsequent government intervention in peacetime.[46] In this manner, the rivalry between states and the internal oppositions between classes have both contributed to state formation, and especially to the development of welfare states.[47]

Summing up, farmers, small entrepreneurs and professionals, roughly the petty bourgeoisie, were opposed to the nationalization of insurance throughout the period. Their opposition had to be overcome by a coalition that would be effective both in the legislature and in the country. Without a sympathetic and committed regime no national insurance could be brought about. Such a regime had to wait until the working class had gained enough political weight, until resistance from large-scale employers had subsided sufficiently or even turned into active support, and until administrative capabilities appeared adequate to carry through the project against opposition from the small bourgeoisie. The regime thus occupied a pivotal position in a balance of power between the small property owners and the industrial classes which tended to shift towards the latter with the momentum of industrialization.

The institutional character of the insurance system depended on prior forms of institutionalization, but also very much on the nature of the coalition that brought about national insurance. The regime might join with large employers and create a system that would keep control away from workers as long as they were exempt from paying dues. It might also join a coalition with the unions, granting them a considerable amount of control and levying contributions either directly from the insured or from general tax funds so as to avoid having to rely on the employers' collaboration. Finally, the regime could build up a coalition with both employers and organized workers, resulting in a tripartite system of control and finance. The latter required all three parties to accept national insurance, whereas the other two strategies were feasible even if one of the industrial parties involved was not willing to support a compulsory nationwide scheme: opposition from employers might be overcome if they could be bypassed in the implementation and financing of the scheme through direct administration by state agencies and funding from general taxes or directly paid beneficiaries' contributions. The regime might also combine with employers, leaving the unions out: but for the scheme to be effective workers' preferences had to be anticipated.[48]

Out of this four-cornered struggle grew the state arrangements for the accumulation of transfer capital in the half-century between 1880 and 1930. The process was very much complicated by the presence of all sorts of insurance institutions at a lower level of aggregation; commercial, union, company or mutual societies who fought to maintain their acquired privileges and established positions and had to be bought off by the regime or incorporated into its national schemes. One occupational group, moreover, played a very special part in the development: the medical profession which was to provide treatment for the insured and non-partisan expertise in all cases of disability. But the basic dynamics in the establishment of social security resulted from the slowly shifting balance of power between the petty bourgeoisie and the industrial classes, with the regime in a pivotal position.

5 The adversities of working life

The risks that threatened to disrupt the wage-earner's life were fourfold: disability, old age, disease and unemployment. In many countries the financial burden of children was also considered to be a collective concern.

5.1 Disability insurance

The first adversity that was recognized to be unpredictable in each separate instance, yet predictable from the working conditions within an industry in its entirety, was disability as a result of accidents at work. Here the improvidence of the needy worker was not a matter of moral judgment, but the concern of formal legal investigation. Liability proceedings were to establish in each case whether the employer or the worker (or his colleagues) were at fault, and only if the first was shown to have been negligent was compensation awarded. Paradoxically, never was so much effort spent to demonstrate the claimant's irresponsible behavior and fraudulent simulation as in these lawsuits, which often dragged on and on until the victim's meager resources were exhausted in suing his employer. It was common practice for factory owners to discourage workers from claiming damages through intimidation, by making them waive the right when signing up for the company insurance plan, or by buying them off with a pittance (and suggesting that in accepting it they had forfeited their right to bring suit). By the last quarter of the nineteenth century these compensation procedures had fallen into disrepute everywhere.[49] Obviously, parties were too unequal for the legal machinery to function properly and the notion of individual liability began to appear increasingly irrelevant to the realities of the industrial division of labor where the chains of causality might involve so many people in any single accident. As a consequence, in many countries the doctrine of *risque professionel* was introduced, waiving proof of the employer's culpable negligence and replacing it with the legal pre-sumption of his liability unless there was clear proof of the worker's fault or no connection with work conditions could be proven at all. As a result, the industrialists were forced to insure themselves against workers' claims. This, in turn, strongly stimulated employer interest in industrial safety.

Legal reform very much improved the chances for a worker to win damages, even if they were often pitifully low. What remained a vexing problem was the assessment of the residual capacity for gainful and appropriate employment. This became the specialty of medical men, and thus one of the first fields where medical expertise served to isolate and neutralize, with the complicity of the parties involved, what was essentially a conflict of interests between them, by redefining it as a technical problem to be resolved by 'non-committed' experts (see also chapter 7).

Once instituted, disability insurance quickly expanded beyond sheer accident coverage. For lack of old-age provision, workers continued working as long as they could and when they could not go on any more were indeed permanently disabled. Chronic occupational disease and the wear and tear of working life also came to account as disability, covered by the employers' liability and accepted as grounds for disbursement.

Thus, the working men's disability schemes functioned vicariously as old-age pensions plans. Once the parties concerned and the wider public could be persuaded that most industrial accidents and occupational diseases hit workers through no fault of their own and that such risks were indeed structural features of the new industries, these incidents came to be exempt from the moral discourse of the times as adversities of a special kind for which special measures were appropriate. It might still be hard for a farmer or a blacksmith to imagine that an accident could occur through nobody's fault in particular, but as long as legislators left agriculture and small shops unregulated, opposition from this side was more moderate than on other insurance matters. As legal precedent changed in favor of employees, employers more and more sided with employees to seek legal reform.[50] To the degree that liability was imputed to employers, the risks were theirs and so would be the costs of a national insurance scheme. In return, employers insisted on maintaining control over the new administrative agencies. Compulsory employment insurance would help them solve the problem of companies shirking coverage and thus saving on labor costs, while discouraging their rivals from improving their schemes. It would also facilitate the adoption of a contributory system which might tax the unsafest companies most heavily.

Unions, on the other hand, while insisting that the liability, and thus the cost, be borne by the employers, were loath to leave the adjudication of disability cases to employers or their appointees. They realized that some say over the management of the agencies would afford them a chance to appoint union activists and to establish new links with a working-class clientele. However, the employers could arrange disability insurance very well without them, if they could solve their problems of competitive advantage and the repartition of burdens among themselves. Thus unions often supported national schemes as a means of gaining at least some say in the control over the arrangements.

5.2   Old-age insurance

Retirement in old age is a relatively recent phenomenon and it had no part in traditional working-class culture.[51] If factory work became too exacting, workers would seek quieter jobs, return to the village they came from to work on the family plot or move in with their children to help out with household chores. The traditional specters of old age were disease, poverty and loneliness: to be helpless without someone who cared.[52] In and of itself advanced age seemed no reason to withdraw from active life, nor a ground to claim benefits. It was physical deterioration, often setting in at a relatively early age, that made some people more dependent as they grew older.

Yet the reality of late-nineteenth-century poverty was such that the aged made up the bulk of the most indigent. Rural communities complained about the burdens the returning elderly workers imposed upon the village chest. Investigators of the poor showed time and again that many old people after a lifelong working career suffered abject misery. This may have been due to the faster pace of industrial work and urban life as compared to rural conditions, to the weakening of the ties of kin and neighborly traditions of care and also to the fact that by the turn of the century many more workers survived into old age, many of them weakened without, however, qualifying for disability benefits on account of injury or disease. This survival caught most workers unprepared. Old age now became a social problem in its own right.

One problem, moreover, that was particularly hard to deal with: actuarial statistics could only measure the average life-span at a given moment, not predict it ten, twenty, forty years ahead. And probably because of improved sanitation and nutrition, people survived longer than statisticians and insurers had expected them to. Disabled workers continued to live longer with their impairment than had been calculated and their benefits weighed heavily upon the funds. The elderly who had no specific disablement found themselves without any livelihood but charity and the dole. Any arrangement for old age would have to guarantee its benefits fifty years or more ahead, if young workers were to put their trust in it. This uncertainty of remedy required institutions of exceptional robustness over time. The alternative was, of course, to make people who were then working pay for the pensions of the aged at that time. But this required either uncommon altruism, or the same uncertainty of remedy had to be dealt with by guaranteeing that the contributors would benefit later from the contributions of subsequent generations. The notion that one and the same compulsory pension scheme could ensure the future pensions of those presently working and pay out of current contributions the pensions of the presently retired seemed a frivolous, if not fraudulent, sleight of hand to the solid, saving public. But obviously, both a fully capitalized scheme in which contributions are accumulated and reserved for the generations that paid them, and a revolving fund, in which current benefits are paid out of current contributions, involve a guarantee lasting a lifetime. Not only the experience of the mutual associations, but also the record of commercial insurers and company pension plans showed that this was a very long time-span to bridge without failure. Only the state, which had long been in the business of issuing bonds with the promise to pay them back in thirty or fifty years, seemed to be an institution with sufficient permanence to inspire such confidence.[53]

Employers had little reason to oppose pension schemes: such plans enabled them to ease out elderly workers and relieved the company of pressing obligations to its retired employees. It counted of course, that payroll contributions, levied one way or another, would add to wage costs, but this did not affect the terms of competition among equally labor-intensive companies within one industry and it even gave large companies with a lower labor-capital ratio an edge over small enterprises.[54] Their concern with the consequences of increasing labor costs for the international terms of trade at times united large employers against a pension bill, but it rarely seemed to outweigh the advantages of a secure and loyal workforce.

To large-scale employers and to ambitious, activist regimes the overriding attraction of a national pension scheme was the opportunity it offered to establish lifelong links with individual workers, tying them to the company and to the state by giving them a stake in the accumulating transfer capital. What stood in the way of the project was the sheer enormity of the numbers and sums involved, an unprecedented financial venture which began to inspire general confidence only when it was seen to work.

5.3   Health insurance

Disease, as an involuntary and transient state of incapacity to work, constituted a risk which was relatively easy to insure: it would be expected to strike at random, and thus quite evenly, among a population, its costs at the time were limited to some medicine, a little treatment if any, and – most important – cash benefits to replace earnings lost. Almost everyone had been sick at some time in his life and could expect to fall ill again, so that participants in a scheme could readily identify with the victims and claimants in their midst. Problems arose with contagious diseases which tended to afflict a sizable proportion of participants at the same time and thus exhaust the funds' resources in a single stroke. But in times of epidemic municipal and central governments might intervene with emergency relief. Greater difficulties were created by chronic conditions, such as the degenerative diseases of advancing age, especially since nineteenth-century factory workers were more prone to these afflictions than were the more comfortable strata. The main problem was that workers survived longer than expected when the rates had been calculated in mid-century, and that they often survived with a chronic affliction or a permanent disability which entitled them to benefits. Only where accident insurance was extended to cover permanent disability from any work-related cause could sick funds transfer these liabilities to other agencies, if and when the ills could indeed be shown to be connected to working conditions.

The insurance of chronic disease is thus very closely related to disability and old-age insurance: costs of treatment and income maintenance increased sharply with age and as people lived longer and more medical remedies became available, the increase became so much steeper.[55]

The poor, too, represented bad risks for health insurance. But once infectious epidemic diseases became prevalent, the correlation between poverty and ill health weakened, and inclusion of the lowest income groups became less of a threat to the funds' solvency, if means could be found to finance their dues, and the elderly, again, formed a growing part of the very poor.

The feasibility of health insurance on the one hand and its importance on the other very much depended on the risks covered; if chronic and degenerative diseases were insured under other schemes a relatively straightforward actuarial set up remained. Accordingly, most countries have insured the risks of lasting disability by other means, usually with considerable government participation.[56]

Free competition among relatively autonomous sick funds would still result in the exclusion of the most vulnerable, unless the state compelled the funds to admit them. But an obligation of this sort could only be made to work if the government compensated the additional costs of insuring the poor, which it usually did, sometimes through a national equalization fund.[57]

Health insurance has nevertheless remained controversial for two reasons mostly: participants may take a few days off with a minor complaint, which in the eyes of others may not warrant their absence from work. Countless measures have been devised against such unjustified absence: the custom of not paying for the first few days of illness, the *Carenzzeit*, for example. But this penalized genuine patients and was greatly resented. It was gradually abolished in most countries. What remained was the obligation to remain at home for a visit by a medical inspector.

This touches upon the second source of perennial conflict in health insurance: it depended from first to last on medical doctors and continues to do so to this day. Doctors had to decide whether illness did in fact justify absence from work, doctors had to prescribe the treatment and medicine the funds were to pay for and doctors and pharmacists supplied it.

Medical insurance transformed the latent need for care into an effective and informed demand for medical services, and doctors organized into a profession which obtained a state-protected monopoly for their supply. The health insurers, on their part, also formed an oligopoly or a monopoly with state protection, but instead of limiting demand, they increased it enormously. Accordingly, the medical profession and the health insurance needed each another and resented their mutual dependence. A tenacious power struggle ensued: in some countries, for example France, Germany and the Netherlands, the medical profession succeeded in gaining considerable say over health insurance and in controlling the demands, as well as the supply side, of a medical economy financed by continual rate increases; in other countries, such as Britain or Italy, doctors became the employees of a national health system, although there too, they maintained a degree of control over their terms of employment and practice. In many less advanced economies and in the United States the medical profession secured a state-protected monopoly, but continued to resist a state-controlled health system, even if it meant that demand among lower-income groups lagged for lack of finance.

Much depended on timing: initially many individual doctors of a progressive bent supported health insurance. But intervention by the government or the societies provoked countervailing organization among doctors. Professional leadership was usually recruited among the most prestigious practitioners, who identified strongly with private practice in a competitive market and accordingly opposed the collectivization of medical care. If a strong and unified system of health insurance had developed in the meantime, it could overcome the opposition it had itself engendered. If the system was more fragmented, the medical profession succeeded in setting the terms (see also chapter 7).

5.4   Unemployment

Of all the hazards of modern industrial society, unemployment is the most difficult to insure. First of all, it is not an event that strikes one person independently of another; rather, like contagious disease, one case increases the odds that others will follow. Unemployment, like epidemics, comes and goes in waves, which may be cyclical, but remain unpredictable. This makes for a very uneven accumulation of risks with all the actuarial problems that come with it. Commercial companies have therefore avoided unemployment insurance and left it to unions and mutual associations which were especially ill suited for the task, as their members usually shared the same occupation.

Secondly, it is difficult to decide whether someone is in fact involuntarily unemployed and whether he does not secretly work on the side. These problems of adjudication and investigation have become the province of specialists, but not of an academic profession which by its authority might have shielded administrators and applicants from one another, in the way doctors function as arbiters in sickness and disability insurance. Moreover, an unemployment fund may be used for resistance pay for dismissed activists and to support workers during a lockout or a strike. Employers and authorities were accordingly suspicious of such funds and often did what they could to disband them. Finally, unemployment benefits put a floor in the labor market below which wages can not sink. Opponents have objected that such benefits only serve to increase unemployment since wages are kept artificially above the level where demand for labor would increase again and of itself absorb the unemployed. Others have argued to the contrary, that these benefits have a 'multiplier effect' by increasing effective consumer demand and thus stimulating business.

The very term 'unemployment' suggests that continuous, regular employment is the normal state of affairs: anybody who is not sick, disabled, very young or very old, or busy taking care of a family, is expected to hold a steady job. The bourgeoisie of early industrial society could not bring itself to believe that people might be out of work through no fault of their own.[58] Nor did the canons of classical economics do much to relieve its suspicions: in a free market an oversupply of labor would be absorbed once wages began to fall and demand picked up. If, nevertheless, sizable numbers of people remained without work, they had to be unwilling to seek it. During the 1880s such simplistic ideas were refuted by a series of investigations among the poor. Moreover, economists were discovering the trade cycle and showed that unemployment was a characteristic of the economy in its depression phase, and thus the outcome of a societal process rather than the result of an individual disposition.

Nevertheless, the unemployed were treated as the other poor, but with a penalty for being sturdy and healthy: their condition had to remain worse ('less eligible') than that of employed workers, the incentive to work was to be instilled through stringent relief conditions and under the threat of the workhouse. Incessant admonition, education and inspection were to stamp out all remaining sloth and vice.

By the turn of the century philanthropic attempts to raise the morality of the poor and idle began to seem increasingly irrelevant as the economic causes of unemployment became more apparent. Reform of the labor market seemed to make more sense and labor exchanges were set up for the purpose. Some officials even played with the idea of public-work projects for the unemployed to keep them from the relief rolls and to prevent radicalization and disorder. At the beginning of the twentieth century municipalities on the continent began to subsidize trade-union unemployment insurances: the 'Ghent system'.[59] Such schemes were voluntary and covered only the better-off workers which made up most of the union membership. The unions, on their part, resisted extension of these plans as it might tempt the 'bad risks' to sign up, pay a few weeks' dues and next claim benefit. Disbursements tended to be very low, but even at those levels they quickly exceeded the unions', and even the municipal, means since unemployment tended to concentrate in specific occupations and localities.[60] For the great mass of the unemployed there was not even insurance, only charity and the dole.

Employers by inclination resisted arrangements that tended to keep wages above the market level. And in the single firm, of course, risks were accumulated, not spread. Independent company plans thus played scarcely any role in unemployment insurance: companies that were laying off workers could least afford to support them.

In the end, there remained no alternative to the state as the final carrier of unemployment insurance. But even ambitious administrators shrank away from the risks involved in a nationwide unemployment scheme. The early laws, in Germany and England, were passed in a mood of optimism during times of economic boom, and once the financial pressures of mass unemployment made themselves felt, they had to be supplemented with massive relief grants. Only in the United States was an unemployment insurance scheme enacted in the midst of the Depression; France and the Netherlands weathered the crisis of the 1930s with grants-in-aid to municipal and union schemes and with massive, but niggardly, poor relief: these countries adopted a national unemployment insurance only in the fifties, in a period of unprecedented economic growth and national consensus on social security. By then, Keynesian theory, the experiences of the Great Depression and the wartime economy had taught governments how to use public expenditure to maintain full employment. And here another fundamental difference from other forms of social insurance emerges: disease, disability and aging are quite independent of government policy, but unemployment can be manipulated by government intervention in the economy. Full-employment policies turned out to have their price: inflation. At present, the total volume of unemployment is no longer considered an external risk, but rather a dependent variable of total economic policy: the costs of unemployment benefits enter the calculations as one item among others in the determination of policy.

As a result, those who cannot find jobs increasingly consider themselves victims not of fate or of the market's hidden hand, but of government policy, especially since the government itself has become the largest employer by far, an insistent promoter of economic investments and a habitual subsidizer of companies in economic distress. Unemployment insurance, which never functioned very well when it was really needed, may now be better understood as a system of special taxes and refunds in and out of a general reserve for those who cannot be employed against a regular wage. But the very fact that the state accepts responsibility for the employment of its citizens (sometimes even as an article of constitution) and that it is held accountable for it, reveals how far the collectivization of care has proceeded: because unemployment has become a matter of concern for the central state, it has been transformed from an individual adversity into a calculated outcome of government policy for which indemnification is due. The problems of unemployment in its modern form can be solved only by a more even distribution of jobs among the population.

5.5 Family wages

It is hardly surprising that family allowances were introduced first and most widely in Catholic countries, where official opinion ruled out family planning. Under these conditions, procreation and pregnancy might be considered a hazard of adult life, not at all undesirable in itself, but causing a financial burden to be covered by some kind of insurance. A moral concern for the survival of the family as an institution inspired the movement for family allowances: the conditions of urban-industrial life were thought to undermine the traditional bonds of marriage and parenthood among the lower classes.

Factory owners preferred married men and fathers for being more staid and reliable workers, and were willing to supplement their wages. On the other hand, this policy might worsen the company's competitive position in relation to that of its rivals. Especially in France, Catholic employers set up amalgamated funds to equalize the costs of family allowances.

Unions and social-democratic parties opposed family wages as they afforded employers undue influence upon the way of life of their workers. They insisted, moreover that wages should be adequate to support a family, without extra allowances.

The state was drawn into these family-allowance schemes in order to equalize burdens more evenly among employers. Its interest was very much activated by a concern with overall birthrates. These tend to decline in the course of industrialization. The aftermath and the renewed threat of war made this a pressing issue in France and also in Nazi Germany.

Entitlement to family allowances is one kind of transfer property, but even more than other transfers, these benefits tend to shade into negative taxes. In fact, in most modern countries, tax deductions are granted according to family size, whereas in many countries wage taxes are collected to finance family benefits under a national scheme. Under contemporary conditions, reproduction is hardly a chance event and only a few children are born per couple. Financial considerations seem to play a minor role in family planning. Family allowances are best considered as a means of distributing taxes more equitably.

6 The beginnings of social security in Western Europe and the United States

6.1 Bismarck's beginning

The first nationwide compulsory insurance scheme against income loss was established in Germany by an authoritarian and activist regime *par excellence*: Bismarck's all-German government. It was imposed against the resistance of the workers' movement[61] and against much opposition in parliament, mainly with the support of the leadership of the Central Association of Industry. Bismarck's personal share in the project has been minimized,[62] the efficacy of his legislation has been doubted – with sounder reasons[63] – but the priority belongs to his regime: the scheme became the model for other countries and in its broad outlines has survived two World Wars, National Socialism and foreign occupation as the foundation of the West German welfare state.[64]

National insurance came about in the Kaiser's Germany under most particular social and political conditions, but this uniqueness does not warrant the treatment of its emergence as an exceptional case without implications for developments elsewhere.[65]

Bismarck's project reveals many essential traits of the social laws which other countries were to adopt in the next half-century. His was an effort at state-building, quite self-consciously designed to strengthen the new German state apparatus[66] and to improve its ties with the industrial working class whose Marxist leaders at the time proclaimed it to be 'without a fatherland'. Bismarck envisaged a class of state pensioners loyal to the government and wary of any change that might threaten their small benefits, people without property and yet with a stake in the political order.[67] His short-term goal was to stem the rapidly swelling tide of the workers' movement by providing a social complement to the repressive *Socialistengesetz* (1878–90), the law against the Socialist Movement.[68] More carefully disguised was the intention to sidetrack the Reichstag, the parliament of the German state, by building a corporatist system of workers' and employers' administrative bodies which was to take over the Reichstag's functions in social and economic legislation.[69] None of these objectives materialized. The Socialist Party grew even more quickly after adoption of the insurance laws, parliamentary influence increased, the corporatist structure was never realized and the positions in the insurance system were manned mostly by labor activists who found shelter there in a society where strike leaders and left-wing agitators were routinely dismissed or even jailed.

National insurance did succeed in creating stronger bonds between the German workers and the new state. It may well have contributed to the Socialist Party's historical decision to collaborate in the war effort in 1914, since by then numerous union and party officials had been integrated into the state's fabric as executives of the national insurance system. And, most important of all, insurance provided the wage-earners with a new, institutional alternative to the private accumulation of property.

But even though Bismarck appeared to ignore the trade unions and bypassed the political parties in the Reichstag as much as he could, he did not simply create national insurance by decree. It was a feat of careful, albeit groping, coalition building and astute exploitation of the opposition's weaknesses.

Gaston Rimlinger[70] and, more recently, Peter Flora[71] and Hans Albers[72] have pointed out that before 1900 compulsory insurance schemes were adopted mainly by authoritarian regimes, and in countries where industrialization had not yet progressed very far, in Germany, Austria, Finland, Sweden and perhaps Italy.[73] Clearly, the authoritarian political elites in this manner attempted to circumvent the parties and to reach out directly to the working masses so as to secure their loyalty. However, Rimlinger's suggestion and Albers's supporting evidence accord with a different interpretation of events. In these authoritarian regimes, primarily in the Kaiser's Germany, not only were industrial workers effectively excluded from government power, as they were at the time in many parliamentary democracies too, but the petty bourgeoisie also had little influence, considerably less than in the democratic polities. The early social legislation of authoritarian regimes contradicts the hypothesis that working-class strength prompted such initiatives, but it does correspond with the view that the weakness of the petty bourgeoisie facilitated them. Small property-owners carried little weight in the politics of Wilhelmine Germany; the rural nobility of the *Junker*, the industrialists and the bureaucrats all the more.[74] As long as rural interests were not threatened by the new legislation, a coalition of the regime and large-scale employers might overcome the opposition of the petty bourgeoisie, divided as it was within the Catholic *Zentrum* Party and the bourgeois liberal groups.[75] The regime could afford to do so, because the defenders of liberalism and small property had failed to gain access to state power after 1848 and remained outsiders thereafter. But this relative independence from middle-class pressures also implied a lack of support which made the regime all the more sensitive to the vindications of another stratum in society, the new industrial proletariat.

The coalition that carried national insurance through the vicissitudes of German politics was one of the three typical alliances that may bring about the scheme: in this case, a coalition between the administrative and political elites on the one hand and large-scale industrial employers on the other. A good deal of the preparatory legislative work was done by leading figures in the *Industrieverein*, and the leaders of this association personally pushed for adoption of the scheme, closely cooperating with Bismarck's civil servants.[76] As is well known, national insurance was adopted in Germany without the support, and even without formal consultation, of workers' organizations. But this did not mean that workers' preferences were not taken into consideration. On the contrary, Bismarck appealed to the workers over the heads of their leaders whom he himself had outlawed.[77] This was as clear-cut a case as ever occurred of Karl Friedrich's 'rule of anticipated preferences': the workers exercised their influence not by direct articulation of their wishes, but because the designers of the scheme anticipated what they might want.

By 1880 the German workers had developed a large, united and politically most articulate movement, and an extended network of sick funds and union insurances. They had by then begun to overcome local and occupational identifications and to develop a broad orientation toward national politics. But both for ideological reasons and because of its repressive policies, the Socialist workers deeply mistrusted the regime in power. Although they did not reject state intervention offhand – August Bebel even advocated it in parliament and after 1890 the Social Democrats were to operate loyally within the existing structures – at the time they could hardly ally themselves with their archenemy Bismarck, nor were they ready to surrender control over their own insurance funds. Thus, the most politicized part of the workers' movement was neutralized through state repression and its own withdrawal into radical positions, while the more reform-oriented part was busy entrenching itself in unions and funds of the workers' own making. But once national insurance was adopted, the Social Democratic elite was quick to perceive and to exploit the opportunities provided by the representative committees that managed the sickness and pension funds and the potential these institutions might have for organizing the working class. On the whole, the Social Democratic leadership keenly gauged the insurance schemes in terms of the power chances they afforded in the class struggle.[78]

The preferences of large-scale industrialists played a much more immediate part in shaping the scheme. In Prussia especially they had been closely allied to the state bureaucracy, both by political alliances and by means of economic regulation. For a long time many companies had operated their own insurance funds under state supervision and large-scale entrepreneurs had little reason to oppose insurance as long as the government protected them against foreign competition with tariffs and maintained the relative advantages among domestic rivals by unitary regulation. Many of them were quite willing to accept part, or even all, of the costs of insurance if this would leave them master on the factory floor and in full control of the funds' management. This counted especially in accident insurance, where safety was an issue that might provoke intervention from outside agencies.[79] On the whole, and especially in the first stages, the *Centralverband* and the regime found themselves in close agreement.[80]

The regime sought ways to domesticate the labor movement and create closer links between workers and the state. It had, therefore, strong interests in controlling the system to be set up, strong enough to be ready to pay a price. It did not shrink back from the task of building an encompassing administrative network to manage the insurance systems; on the contrary, this is what the German state-builders wanted in the first place. It was willing to contribute to the costs, if that was the price of control, and it was even ready to underwrite the actuarial risks of the system. Greater gambles had been accepted by Bismarck's regime in founding the state and expanding its influence in competition with its neighboring nations. National insurance was very much seen as part of the nation-building effort that went with state formation. A strong and nationalist labor force seemed a necessity if Germany was to play its role in the rivalry between states. Inasmuch as this was also an economic rivalry, employers could not be expected to foot the bill entirely, since this would weaken the economic terms of competition with their rivals abroad. But in return for state support by means of legal coercion and financial subsidies (paid in part from protective tariff revenues) employers had to go along with a system that was to be compulsory for them too.

There was, finally, another circumstance that compelled entrepreneurs and the central government to propose reforms: under the old Poor Laws indigent workers had to return to their place of birth for relief, but the rural communities were incapable of supporting them and sent them back to the towns where they had last worked and where they became a burden to the local authorities.[81]

A brief review[82] of the legislation may serve to trace how the preferences of the coalition partners were realized and those of the workers anticipated by the designers.

In the 1880s, three major compulsory insurance laws were passed: on accident insurance, disability and sickness. The first, the *Unfallversicherung*, was also the most controversial and had to be re-submitted twice before it was enacted in 1884. The Employers' Liability Act of 1871 had made employers liable for accidents at work unless the worker's negligence could be proven. Accordingly, insurance contributions were levied from employers, united in *Berufsgenossenschaften* (trade associations) for the management of the insurance and for the promotion of industrial safety under the supervision of an imperial insurance office. Accident victims would receive two-thirds of their wage, or less according to the degree of disablement.

The Sickness Insurance Law was passed in 1883. It was financed by employers' and workers' contributions, for one- and two-thirds respectively, and implemented by a variety of recognized sick funds already in existence or to be established for the purpose. The scheme was managed by committees manned for two-thirds by workers', and for the remaining third by employers', representatives. Benefits consisted of medical care and sickness pay equal to half the wage sum for thirteen weeks at most after a *Carenzzeit* (waiting period) of three days.

Disability insurance, finally, was enacted in 1889. It was financed under a full capitalization system[83] from employers' and workers' contributions in equal parts (in declining proportion to wages earned) and by the state with a fixed yearly addition to each pension disbursed. Administration was the task of semi-autonomous public insurance bodies under elected management in every *Land* of the union. The insurance provided for a pension of two-thirds of the most recently earned wages after at least five years of contribution in cases of complete disablement, workers over the age of seventy qualified for a pension if they had contributed for at least thirty years, surviving widows received 20 per cent of their late husband's former wage. No unemployment insurance was proposed, this remained the province of the trade unions until the law of 1927.

Accident insurance most fully embodied the interests of the regime and the large-scale employers, effectively excluding workers from any say in its workings, but at the same time exempting them from the costs. In the sickness and disability insurance the regime and the employers had to allow for the vested interests of the many funds already in existence. Moreover, they knew that the sums involved in the pensions were bound to expand to astronomic proportions and this too prompted them to opt for combined employers' and workers' contributions under a capitalization system together with state allowances. As a corollary, they accepted workers' representation in the managing bodies. In doing so, the regime laid the foundation for the subsequent tripartite coalition that was to maintain and expand social security in Germany for the next forty years and that was revived after the Second World War to realize the West German welfare state.

With hindsight, it is difficult to grasp the full scope of administrative innovation embodied in the insurance institutions of the Kaiser's Germany. Its principles have remained the guidelines of compulsory national insurance ever since and showed themselves quite compatible with the subsequent extension to new groups of the population and new fields of coverage in Germany and elsewhere.

6.2   The British breakthrough

The next wave of social innovation came almost twenty-five years later, in Britain, where the working class had a longer history and was more numerous and better organized than anywhere else. But here too, the initiative was mostly with an activist regime of politicians out to conquer the working-class vote and administrators eager to try the new techniques of government. In England, however, large-scale employers hardly played a part, while the essential support in passing the pension and insurance laws of 1908 and 1911 came from the workers' organizations.

Capitalist entrepreneurs had played an increasingly important role in English politics at least from the 1830s on. Free enterprise and private accumulation counted as the sole avenues to individual success and national prosperity, while more *étatiste* policies met with fierce opposition. Yet, throughout the nineteenth century the central state had increasingly intervened in education, sanitation and poor relief.[84] Under the Poor Law of 1834 a very differentiated system of local relief had developed, not always as miserly as it has been depicted[85] and with much more central management than appeared.[86] Such state intervention was prompted time and again by the perennial imbalance between local resources for relief and the need for it as determined by broader economic developments. Under the 'New' Poor Law, the threat of the workhouse was intended to keep the poor from applying for relief. But wardens and guardians refusing aid risked indictment by the Poor Law Board for criminal negligence and even murder. Too generous a policy was punished by the local voters who had to pay the poor-rates.

Next to the very intricate relief system, an extensive network of private charitable organizations developed, more and more geared to reeducate the poor into abiding citizens and wage-earners. Mutual societies and union funds constituted a third circuit of maintenance, one that provided not for paupers, but for regularly employed workers, not from rates or donations, but out of their own pooled contributions: here voluntary collective action operated to establish a functional equivalent to the providential functions of private property. The mutual funds constituted voluntarily accumulated and cooperatively managed transfer capital, a transition to the compulsory accumulation under state control. This arrangement at the members' own expense appeared to be an alternative entirely compatible with the Victorian ideal of voluntary accumulation.

Thus, around 1880, a triad of very elaborate and quite viable institutional arrangements operated in Britain; this, together with the political pressure from small property-owners, explains in large part why compulsory insurance was not enacted for another thirty years. These very institutions stood in the way of legislative reform. The ideas and practices prevailing under the Poor Law continued to associate indigence with moral failure and relief with punishment. The encompassing Charity Organization Society insisted that all material aid was to be combined with measures of moral reform. And the mutual societies jealously guarded the autonomy that their members had so sourly conquered. The propertied citizenry which made up the bulk of the electorate did not see why it should sacrifice its earnings for taxes to support those who obviously had not cared to save for themselves.

It took a long series of reports on the conditions of the English working classes to alert the public, and especially the political elites, to the realities of industrial society: the involuntary nature of unemployment and the preponderance of the elderly among the indigent. Social scientists – as they would now be called – were more directly involved in this *prise de conscience* and were more closely associated with policy design than ever before.[87] And throughout the debate Bismarck's legislation served as a point of reference.[88]

More important, the mutual societies found it hard to support their aging members who lived longer than mid-century statistics had predicted and claimed sick pay for the chronic afflictions that now disabled so many of them. In Britain, also, health and disablement benefits functioned as a disguised old-age pension. Only the specter of bankruptcy persuaded the societies in the end to accept a state-pension scheme and this completely altered the political balance on the issue. The unions, who were not themselves involved in pension insurance, had no reason to resist state interference in this field and supported the massive campaign of the National Pension Committee.

The catastrophic defeat of the Conservatives in the elections of 1906[89] brought a Liberal Government to power with a radical wing around Lloyd George in the Treasury and Churchill in the new Board of Trade. They formed the core of an activist regime which by means of a program of social legislation hoped to combine its short-term electoral goal of overcoming the labor vote with the long-term objective of integrating the working classes into the mainstream of British society.[90] Funds were to come from savings on Poor Law relief and from tariffs that favored trade with the overseas possessions and thus promoted integration at the level of the Empire, as social legislation was to foster it at the national level.

An activist regime was in power, while in the country a broad and well-organized base of working-class support for social legislation had emerged. The Pension Act of 1908 was the result of a coalition between regime and workers,[91] as clearly as the Accident Insurance Law of 1884 in Germany had been the product of a coalition of regime and employers. Under the British pension scheme employers were completely excluded from control: the pension was noncontributory, financed from general taxes and paid at the local post office to every citizen over seventy with an income of less than £26 a year.[92] This accorded quite closely with the unions' demands which had served them as a rallying cry for many years.

'It was a pension for the very poor, the very respectable and the very old', writes Pat Thane[93] with hindsight – but it was also an unprecedented breakthrough:[94]

> To the aged poor it seemed unbelievable that one could collect 5s. simply by coming to the post office on Friday. Particularly in the country villages, unsuspecting postmistresses found themselves showered with apples and flowers from pensioners' gardens in gratitude for the simple act of distributing money.

The employers had little to do with the enactment of state pensions. Although the Chambers of Commerce had criticized its costs and the Charity Organization Society had objected to the absence of any attempt to reform the recipients – an effort so central to charitable activities –

many employers had supported it as a contribution to industrial harmony and thus to productivity.[95]

In the next wave of legislation the risks of disease and unemployment were to be provided for. But in the meantime the noncontributory principle had lost adherents, first of all because of its costs, but also because to many it still smacked of the Poor Law dole.[96] More importantly, across the nation and for many years, unemployment and health insurance had been the province of the unions and Friendly Societies. In these fields they had not run up against the same actuarial troubles as in old-age insurance and they now insisted on keeping control of their affairs even if it had to be at a price to their members. They insisted that contributions were levied from workers, as from employers, with the government adding its share. On the other hand – for the health plan much more effectively so than for the unemployment scheme – compulsory state-subsidized insurance did solve the unions' and Friendly Societies' perennial dilemma of having to exclude the poorest workers or to accept increased risks.[97]

Part I of the Bill, dealing with health insurance, was originally intended to provide for survivors' pensions. But here the regime faced the opposition of the Friendly Societies, and, quite suddenly also the rather more formidable forces of commercial industrial insurance with its well-organized army of some 80,000 collectors. These men were in the very profitable business of burial insurance and feared that once widows could count on a pension they would no longer worry about burial costs. The Bill's tortuous history in and out of parliament was very much the result of political conflict on other, unrelated issues; organized employers and employees had little part in it, but the commercial insurance business staged one of the earliest mass campaigns of modern politics. Medical men were to follow their example soon after the bill was passed.

In the end the Act allowed 'approved societies' to manage the scheme: these included both the Friendlies and the commercial companies who had managed to get into the act without ever before having been involved in sickness insurance. Contributions were levied from workers at 4d. a week, from employers at 3d., and the government added 2d. to finance the extra costs of elderly subscribers.[98] This covered sickness pay at 10s. for twenty-six weeks at most and after that disability pay for an indeterminate period of time. It also paid for 'ambulatory' medical care and for medicine from doctors included in the 'panel'.[99] No hospital care was provided, except for tuberculosis, a contagious disease with obvious external effects. The Act was radical in one respect: it covered all workers, even domestic servants – a subject of great outcry: it even compelled ladies to lick stamps for their maids. Dependents remained outside the schemes, except for maternity benefits.

Although the regime around Lloyd George was essential in bringing about the health insurance, it hardly did so in coalition with organized employers or employees: the vested interests of the firmly and widely established Friendly Societies and the rising forces of commercial insurance and medical professional groups came to dominate in the power struggle. Workers and industrialists seem to have accepted the tripartite division of burdens quite passively, without protesting against the regime's concessions to the friendly and commercial insurers.

Workers' and employers' organizations were much more involved in unemployment insurance, and in this instance the regime broadened its base by seeking support from employers also.

Local authorities had shown themselves particularly powerless in relieving unemployment: 'isolated local attempts to give assistance or employment to the unemployed were a hindrance to labour mobility and positively attracted workmen into distressed areas. Moreover, the adequacy of local resources varied inversely with the needs of the local unemployed.'[100]

With the Depressions of 1879 and 1908 it had become increasingly clear to the public that individual cases of unemployment were particular instances of a general phenomenon, associated with the economy as a whole and quite independent of the virtues of the particular workmen affected.[101]

But these insights did not of themselves point to a remedy. As has been pointed out before, unemployment is a cumulative risk and at the time it was even considered 'an uninsurable risk'.[102] The one prior example of compulsory unemployment insurance, an experiment in the Swiss canton of Saint-Gall became a monitory example of failure. Ever since, authorities on the continent had preferred to subsidize voluntary union insurances according to the Ghent system.[103] Bismarck had avoided the matter of compulsory unemployment insurance and in Germany legislation did not come until 1927.

Nevertheless the regime proceeded with a national unemployment insurance, insisting on compulsory membership precisely because of the dilemmas inherent in any voluntary arrangement. Beveridge and Churchill advocated an employers' contribution, because in the long run insurance would improve the quality of the workforce to their advantage, and employers were the ones to hire and fire in the first place. Churchill wrote: 'Unemployment is primarily a question for employers . . . Their responsibility is undoubted, their co-operation indispensable.'[104] The employers, however, were divided on the issue, with leading opinion tending to favor insurance.[105]

The Friendly Societies were scarcely involved in unemployment insurance, commercial companies stayed far from it, but unions had become increasingly active in the field. Their concerns had to be accommodated first. In no case should the unemployed be made to accept work at a wage below standard or forced to cross picket lines. Nor should existing union insurances be taken over by the government.

Under the terms of the act of 1911, employers and workers were to contribute equally, 2½d., the government somewhat less. Unemployed workers would receive 7s. a week against every five weeks of contribution paid for fifteen weeks a year at most. The scheme was limited to some 2.5 million workers in construction and heavy industry and was extended to other trades in later years.[106] A network of some 1,200 Labour Exchange agencies was set up under a new government department in order to bring together labor demand and supply more efficiently (and to test the recipient's readiness to accept employment).[107] Benefits were paid by the exchanges and by the unions to their own members. Disputed cases were to be adjudicated by panels composed of employers nominated by the Board of Trade and by elected workmen's representatives.[108]

Unemployment insurance was essentially a tripartite arrangement with the state in a position of dominance. The coalitional base that supported social legislation after 1908 was broadened to include the employers, although tripartite relations among the partners remained very tenuous. Unemployment insurance did not involve commercial interests as the 'health business' did. As it stood, it covered only the stronger industries, steering clear of economically more precarious branches.

British national insurance began as a government initiative with labor support, bypassing employers as much as possible. It soon grew into a tripartite enterprise, as large-scale employers were persuaded to support legislation. Unemployment insurance had been the most ambitious initiative, but in later years its financial base proved incapable of supporting the burdens of mass unemployment: it turned into a massive open-ended relief system. However, the groundwork for social security had been laid and its shortcomings did not turn opinion against it, but rather served as an added argument for the more extensive and centralized system which was to be established after 1945.

6.3 France: the motor and the brake

In extremely simple form, social insurance began in Germany with a coalition between industrialists and the regime, at first only anticipating workers' preferences and subsequently broadening to include the *Arbeiterkassen*. In England it began with a coalition between the regime and the workers' movement, extending to accomodate the employers on unemployment and the commercial and mutual insurers on health insurance. The late advent of social insurance in France, equally schematized, provides an example of a tripartite coalition of the regime with moderate sections of the workers' movement and large-scale industrialists, seeking to accommodate the *mouvement mutualiste*.

Compulsory insurance came later to France and this very delay made for more retardation. Mutualist and company funds had proliferated in the meantime, constituting so many vested interests against unitary state insurance. Opposing coalitions had ample time to organize political resistance and to set up alternative institutions which they themselves controlled and which, in turn, functioned in the political debate to deny much urgency to any intiative on the part of the state. Something of the kind had occurred in England where the Friendly Societies developed before the nationalization of the insurance system and retarded its advent. In France, employers and *mutualistes* were able to operate with relative autonomy for another twenty years, before, in 1930, a national system came into being.[109]

More clearly than in those other countries, in France a grand alliance of small property owners functioned as the 'brake' on legislation for compulsory state insurance. Its resistance has been described by Henri Hatzfeld, and his analysis of the establishment of social security in France is of wider validity than for that country alone.

The French Third Republic represented the reign of the bourgeoisie and it was as much a reaction against the threats of the Paris commune[110] as against the *étatiste* schemes of Napoleon III.[111] More than elsewhere, social insurance was recognized as an alternative and a threat to private property and it was resisted all the more for it. Small savers feared that enormous investment funds would use the accumulated moneys of national insurance to dominate the capital market. They also protested that compulsory contributions would rob the workers of the last pennies they might save for themselves and their children or invest in an enterprise of their own. Compulsory insurance would thus condemn the worker once and for all to wage-dependency. With hindsight this may look like standing the argument on its head, but to a nineteenth-century property-owner proletarian dependency could still look like a transitory phenomenon which would disappear as the economy grew and wealth increased. This view was not at all incompatible with an ideology of the *patronat* as a patriarchal stewardship which provided for those entrusted to it out of fatherly concern and Christian love. Legal compulsion and state coercion could only be inimical to this bond of care and service, which far transcended the cash nexus.[112] Lay and Catholic teachings of solidarity imposed on all a similar obligation to shoulder one another's burden, not just through spontaneous charity, but in the context of permanent and organized, but always voluntary, institutions such as the *caisses mutuelles*.

Part of the workers' movement, its most intractable wing, shared many of these tenets, but with a difference: The anarcho-syndicalists equally insisted on self-help, but they defined it as a collective effort on the part of the workers themselves. Their ranks were recruited mostly from highly skilled workers in small enterprises which still operated under pre-industrial conditions. Accordingly, their radicalism had a somewhat nostalgic hue.

Against the petty bourgeoisie and the anarchists, the National Confederation of Labor, CGT, was unanimous in insisting on state intervention and noncontributory insurance. Its ranks were divided on the issue of reform versus revolution: should the existing French state, the Third Republic, be entrusted with social insurance, or should it first be overthrown to make way for the dictatorship of the proletariat? Jules Guesde spoke for the radical wing of the movement which opposed each and every measure as a contribution levied from the workers to keep capitalism alive. Jean Jaurès led the reformist tendency and cautiously supported the initiatives of the succeeding regimes, even the meager pension law of 1910.

A figuration of conflict, in which one side is made up of both a conciliatory mainstream and a radical fringe, is often prone to produce compromise. The moderate majority may exploit the presence of radicals by threatening that either the latter will take over the entire movement or they themselves will be incapable of resisting radicalization among the rank and file: better deal with the moderate wing right away than having to cope with the radicals later. Although the two wings may fight each other even more bitterly than the common enemy, their combined dynamics may further compromise, if the threat is successful. Not so in France.[113] The already niggardly Pension Law of 1910 was undone by a court verdict in which the obligation to contribute was declared void. 'The law had been enacted by those who least wanted it';[114] and thus it had been paralyzed from the beginning. As a result the number of pension insurances actually declined in subsequent years.[115]

The field of insurance remained the province of the *sociétés mutuelles* and the company funds. The mutual funds had been outlawed with all workers' organizations in 1791, and persecuted as conspiratory societies under the Restoration. Napoleon III recognized the 'approved' funds, but imposed close supervision by appointed chairmen.[116] Under the Third Republic, however, especially after the law of 1895, the *mouvement mutualiste* was left free to flourish as a network of voluntary associations with government subsidies. This *liberté subsidiée* mostly favored the middle classes who could afford to pay the premiums.[117] After the *échec* of the Pension Law, it remained the major form of insurance against the various risks of income loss with all the shortcomings attendant upon a voluntary system.

As state insurance took so long in coming, company schemes became more important than elsewhere. But, in France too, they developed mainly in the large industries, and especially in the mines, steelworks and railroads. By 1850 Napoleon III had established a compensation fund, the *Caisse Nationale de Retraites*, and many employers had continued to amalgamate their schemes per sector or to reinsure them with commercial companies. It was this plan that was to serve as an example to Bismarck. In 1898 employers were declared liable for industrial accidents, unless there was clear proof of the worker's fault,[118] and this induced them to insure against claims. An attempt to introduce compulsory disability insurance after the German model failed however, as small employers were presumed to be unable to bear the costs.

Company funds sprang up first where demand for labor exceeded supply, especially in those areas where new enterprise was set up:[119]

> The *patrons* are dependent on manual labor, scarce yet necessary, undisciplined, mobile and irregular. The workers know that they are needed and bring competition into play. A single imperative rules the company bosses so as to reverse in their favor this *relation of dependence*: stabilize manual labor, fix it, tie it to the company, 'infeudate' it. The means: make sure that the worker and his family become dependent on the company for their existence.

Ewald goes on to describe the corresponding patriarchial ideology of 'benevolence versus service' as it has been articulated by Fréderic Le Play and the company director Cheysson. Their schemes provided mostly benefits in kind, housing in the first place, because 'the more one pays the worker the less he works.'[120] Favors were carefully bestowed as rewards for 'fidelity'. However, precisely because the company funds tied the worker to his employer by the lifelong strings of promise of a pension which was forfeited upon dismissal or termination, they were greatly resented by union members.[121] The notorious scandals and bankruptcies of some of these company funds in the 1890s also made it increasingly clear that single firms, and even amalgamated funds, were inadequate to guarantee numerous and lifelong obligations.[122] On the other hand, employers welcomed the opportunities for control over their workforce that these schemes afforded them and used the accumulated workers' contributions as venture capital, albeit mortgaged by pressing moral obligations. With time, however, the employers' share in the contributions and their outstanding commitments began to weigh more heavily, especially as disabled and retired workers tended to survive longer than the insurers had been led to expect on the basis of mid-century actuarial statistics, so that the increasing burden put the older companies at a disadvantage with respect to more recently established and less heavily committed competitors. As a result, large-scale and long-established industries were not so much adverse to state insurance and were ready to pay their share if only they were not forced to relinquish control over the schemes, and thus loosen their grip on their work force. French large-scale industry, however, hesitated to break with the small employers on the issue of insurance and this muted their support for a national plan.[123] In the end, even an attempt to introduce limited unemployment insurance, if only to prevent jobless *mutualistes*, unable to pay their contributions from losing their insurance, failed as late as 1925.

If social scientists have been instrumental in bringing about social insurance, they have also helped to defeat it. In France, Jacques Rueff presented impressive statistics on the correlation between unemployment and the level of real wages, contending that both were kept up artificially through union pressure and unemployment benefits.[124] It took another thirty-three years before the regime, in 1958, organized employers and workers could be made to agree upon an unemployment insurance scheme.

Yet barely five years after its failure in 1925, a national, compulsory system for health, disability and pension insurance was enacted, covering all workers in industry and commerce.[125] By then, a tripartite coalition of large-scale employers, moderate unions and the regime had succeeded in designing a scheme of shared control which did not alienate the partners and was acceptable to the mutual societies which dominated the insurance business. The medical profession proved hardest to appease, but for the moment gave its consent.[126] The Communist Party and union opposed the 'Fascist law' as the product of *chicanerie bourgeoisie*. They rallied to the support of social legislation only after 1945.[127]

The *assurance sociale* of 1930 allowed 744 'approved' funds to provide health, maternity and death coverage for their members on a repartition basis, while some eighty funds carried the disability and old-age schemes on the basis of full capitalization.[128] In every department a *caisse* was established to insure those who remained outside the 'primary' funds, because they did not wish to adhere or were rejected.[129] The *caisses départementales* had also been intended to act as premium collectors, reinsurers, compensation-clearance centers and supervisory agencies for the voluntary funds, thus superimposing a strong state structure on the fragmented mutual system. However, in a second version of the law (1930) these administrative and supervisory functions were confided to separate institutions under a *Caisse générale de garantie*. This victory of the mutualist movement over the state's *supercaisses* was partly undone again by the unexpectedly large influx of subscribers to the departmental *caisses* which insured over 60 per cent by 1931.[130] This development was to add arguments for a unitary system in 1945.

In its final reading, the law of 1930 excluded agricultural workers and those covered by other schemes, mainly railroad and government personnel. But before long it insured 10 million wage-earners, with employers and workers each paying 4 per cent of wages and the state contributing from what it saved on the 1910 pensions and public assistance.[131]

The *caisses* were managed by employers' and workers' representatives, except for those founded by the workers themselves, which remained under their sole control – a concession to long-standing union demands.[132] But a centralized administrative superstructure was already in place to manage this manifold and fragmented base, imposing compulsory membership on the workers, exacting contributions from them and their employers, setting standards of coverage and management, compensating for deficits in one branch or region with surpluses taken from others, and auditing all benefits and services. Thus, the stage was set for the further nationalization of social insurance after 1945.

That compulsory insurance came late to France is best explained by the political strength of the small property-owners who formed the great obstacle to be overcome. But why, after so many abortive attempts, did they give in by 1930? There was of course the embarrassing precedent of Alsace-Lorraine, where the Germans had introduced their social legislation, a structure which could not be undone when the region became French again. The 1920s had been a period of relative prosperity, and progressive taxation now yielded considerable resources for the government. There was also an increasing readiness on the part of the social-democratic unions to deal with the regime in power. Large-scale employers had been more ostentatious than obdurate in their opposition: what mattered to them was control more than cost. And all along there had been the experts and the administrators, *les grands commis d l'État* who continued to devise new strategies and new compromises to get social legislation accepted.[133] But, unlike other countries, France produced no statesman who stood for social security the way Bismarck, Churchill and Roosevelt did.

It was above all the gradual erosion of the political privileges that private property conferred, the irresistible increase of wage-earners and of the more privileged *salariés* among them, the growth of large enterprise and big government that finally shifted the balance and allowed a succession of center–right cabinets an opportunity to succeed where earlier governments had failed. Once the mutual movement accepted the principle of state subsidies and state coercion, the central administration began to take over. In this respect, the most inveterate champions of the *liberté mutualiste* were right, more than even they had expected: once the law was in place, it turned out to work quite smoothly and French citizens joined the departmental *caisses*, opted for extension of coverage and membership, without bothering too much about *mutualiste* autonomy, as long as the state made sure that benefits and services were being delivered.

Because the struggle had lasted so long, another alternative to national social security sprang up in the meantime – not an insurance system this time, but a system of allowances, paid to workers in proportion to the size of the family they had to support.[134] These *allocations familiales* were the product of Catholic social activism, a 'third way' between the *laissez-faire* of liberal thought and the state insurance systems preferred by the socialists and the radical workers' movement. Catholic employers started the practice on a voluntary basis, but they soon found that it made family fathers more expensive as employees. To equalize burdens among participating companies, they established amalgamated compensation funds. A law of 1932 (coming shortly after the papal encyclical *Quadragesimo anno*, recalling the fortieth anniversary of the social encyclical *De rerum novarum*), made these family wages compulsory, leaving the management of the *caisses familiales* to the employers until the state took over in 1945.

France was as slow as the United States in welfare legislation, and in the case of France the explanation must be sought in the relative strength of the small property owners, especially in their political strength. The timing of welfare legislation must be explained in connection with the erosion of their political power base. In France the unions certainly were not weak, as in Germany and the United States, but on the issue of social security they were badly divided. In France, as in Germany, large-scale employers were in a strong position, but they were allied less closely to the regime than their German colleagues had been in Bismarck's time and clung more to an alliance with the small entrepreneurs. France was a welfare laggard because of the strength of its petty bourgeoisie, the United States lagged behind on account of the weak organization of the central – i.e. federal – state and the weak position of the labor unions.

6.4   The American big bang

Social security was instituted in the United States as part of the 'New Deal' policies of Franklin D. Roosevelt, with sudden momentum, but not wholly without precedent. By the end of the nineteenth century the United States had been well on the way to becoming a welfare state of sorts: the aftermath of the Civil War had engendered a veterans' pensions system of remarkable generosity and extensiveness. As the years went by the causal connection between war injuries and disability was gradually severed and almost anyone who had fought for the Republic could claim payments for disability or old age, his surviving dependents qualifying for orphans' and widows' pensions. This largess did not flow from legislative design, but from many thousands of personal interventions by politicians on behalf of individual constituents.[135] By 1890 some two-thirds of northern white Americans over sixty-five were receiving federal pensions; blacks found themselves excluded, and so did the immigrants who had entered the country in increasing numbers after 1865.

The ethnic communities in the eastern cities developed their own care arrangements as part of the urban political machine system. Ward bosses organized the newcomers from their country of origin, making sure they voted for the right candidates. Once elected into office, these politicians returned the favor with jobs, contracts, grants and handouts to their ethnic constituency. The machine worked with political persuasion, interest brokerage, appeals to ethnic and religious loyalty, threat and extortion, but also by a finely meshed web of small favors and services to bewildered newcomers, the needy and the aged. In this respect it represented at once an alternative to philanthropic intervention, and like it, a predecessor of subsequent social work and community action.[136] Because of its intimate ties with local government, urban-machine politics represented an embryonic version of a state welfare system, strong on personalized delivery (also of a dismal kind). The machine system, however, may well have lacked legitimacy in the wider community, enmeshed as it was in favoritism and incapable, therefore, of regular and dependable provision.

Immigrants also established mutual societies after the European pattern, which covered the risks of sickness, accident and death.[137] But these funds never knew the popular success they had in Europe. By 1929 750,000 employees were enrolled through their companies in 'mutual benefit associations'.[138] By that time also, about a million workers were covered by industrial group insurance plans against similar risks.[139] Trade unions hardly played a role in insuring their members and commercial insurance was only beginning to enter the field.

Poor relief all along had remained a local matter in the Elizabethan tradition of the almshouse and the poor rates, varying widely from one town to another but without much change throughout the period. Religious charity continued at the parish level, while the new, industrial poor increasingly became the concern of philanthropic societies which adopted the pedagogic principles developed by their British counterparts in the Charity Organization Society.[140]

As a consequence, what welfare existed by 1910 either consisted in archaic poor relief, or in more modern and indigenous arrangements, such as the veterans' scheme and the urban machines, which reached large proportions of the population, but became increasingly associated with electoral handouts and local graft. Public, mutual or commercial insurance, as yet, hardly played a part.

The Progressive Movement for 'good government' which mobilized its reformist energies in an all-out campaign to abolish corruption, favoritism and 'giveaway schemes', not only did away with much local machine politics, without replacing its grants and favors by regular public assistance, but also with the veterans' pension system which might easily have evolved into a permanent, universal retirement plan. 'Honest government' and a 'balanced budget' turned out to be ill-suited tenets for social policy.[141]

As a result, much was undone and little established for the next quarter of a century. By 1930, at most 10 per cent of the aged were drawing any kind of pension, and they mostly received veterans' benefits. Unemployment remained completely uncovered by law or private insurance,[142] and much the same applied to sickness and disability.[143]

Yet Progressive experts were active in promoting social policy reform.[144] They were successful in obtaining revision of industrial liability law, which in the United States, as elsewhere, followed the spread of the factory system. Between 1911 and 1920 forty-five states enacted workmen's compensation laws, albeit with very uneven, and usually minimal, benefits.[145] A majority of states also enacted 'mothers' pensions' for 'worthy widows' with dependent children, leaving both the setting of eligibility requirements and the funding to counties and municipalities.[146]

Apart from these minor reforms, hardly any legislation was enacted by the forty-eight states of the Union until the 1930s. Nor did mutual societies or company funds fill the void. What pressure for social reform there was mostly came from experts in the American Association for Labor Legislation. The major union, the American Federation of Labor under Gompers, although accepting pensions from 1909 on, consistently opposed social legislation until the early thirties. It represented mainly skilled, white workers in craft unions and put its faith in wage bargaining only. The AFL was traditionally hostile to government, out of a general 'American' dislike of public interference which it shared with business circles, and because of a long history of union repression which had inspired an almost socialist view of the state as the instrument of the ruling class. Any reform that might grant the workers benefits over which the union would have no control aroused in it a suspicion of state usurpation. Moreover, the union was afraid of losing the loyalty of its members if they could draw benefits without it.[147] Apparently, in the United States, unions never had much opportunity for learning how to deal routinely with state officials in the course of inspection or committee work, and their leadership appeared less tempted by the career and control possibilities that state regulation might bring. They stuck to 'voluntarism' – the belief that terms of employment should be set by collective bargaining, free from government interference and kept aloof from issues of social insurance.[148]

Employers, if not actually hostile, like the National Association of Manufacturers, were at the least reluctant to support social legislation. In the twenties some progressive companies began to develop stock-sharing schemes and 'human-relations' techniques to promote the loyalty of their workforce. In the same vein, they also introduced pension plans and health insurance. Although such 'fringe benefits' became a major complement to social security for employed workers after World War II, 'during the 1920s, welfare capitalism was pitifully inadequate.'[149]

The 1920s were an era of relative economic prosperity. Succeeding Republican presidencies of a conservative hue restricted their social policy to encouragement of voluntary initiatives at the company level. The 'associative state,' as Herbert Hoover called it, provided minimal protection only to those who were securely employed.

In retrospect, the exceptionally strong position of the propertied classes in America formed the most formidable obstacle to any attempt at enacting social legislation and creating institutions that could provide an alternative to private accumulation: 'industrialization made the nineteenth-century capitalist so powerful that judicial and legislative policies came to reflect, almost directly, the wishes and interests of a single privileged stratum.'[150] Factory workers, immigrants especially, long continued to see their position as transitional: the next generation would move up in society. In America, much more than anywhere else, wage-workers constituted not so much the dispossessed classes as the not-yet-propertied classes. The idea that one should, or indeed could, earn an honest living by the work of one's hands and put something aside for hard times to come, was so paramount that it paralyzed initiatives for collective provision. When the Great Depression destroyed these expectations and temporarily broke the political domination of business interests, social security took only a few years to come.

The American figuration of separate states in a federal union provided this process with a dynamics of its own. Social legislation belonged to the sphere of competence of the states. But the states were in no position to shield their local economy from that of the United States as a whole. European national states could, if they so decided, erect tariff barriers to protect their industry from foreign competition. American states could do nothing to ward off a competition from their neighbors: in this respect their position more resembled local or regional authorities under a European nation-state than that of a central state itself. But in the twentieth century, local government in Europe had lost all competence in social and economic legislation to the center, while the American states remained the primary agents in these matters. 'Unless all states taxed employers in comparable amounts, the employers in lagging states would derive a comparative advantage over their more progressive neighbors . . . Only a federal program of concerted action by all the states could overcome the obstacle.'[151] Accordingly, when experts and industrial unions began to campaign for social reform, they had to approach groups of adjacent states at the same time and meanwhile seek access at the federal level. But once the federal government promised grants-in-aid to their programs, American states hastened to introduce social insurance. In other words, the dynamics of American society with a unitary economy and with separate states and federal legislative authorities explains much of the long delay and sudden breakthrough of social security in that country.[152] The dramatic financial collapse of 1929, and the extraordinary severity and persistence of the economic crisis in the United States contributed to this explosive 'big bang' pattern.[153] But once social security had been established, it gained a momentum of its own, an intrinsic bureaucratic expansionism, and except for health insurance, developed along much the same lines as in other countries.

The Great Depression of 1929 and the subsequent political realignment which brought Roosevelt and the Democratic Party to power in 1932, also created the conditions for the introduction of social security into the

United States. Within three years a nationwide, compulsory system of old-age pensions and unemployment insurance had been instituted.

This time, an activist regime was in power, overwhelmingly supported by organized workers. The AFL had come around to supporting social legislation and had abandoned its non-partisan policies for an alliance with the Democratic Party. And in the meantime, new unions were being organized in the CIO along lines of industry instead of craft, and these squarely favored social security and the Democratic Party.[154]

A tide of mass campaigns for pension insurance rolled over the country, unconnected with either unions or parties, but greatly adding to the pressure for reform. Small farmers, confronted with bankruptcies all around them, also rallied to the support of social security. And with unemployment levels at 25 per cent or higher, 'by 1932, local and state governments were begging the federal government to take over the burden of dealing with their distressed constituents.'[155] Finally, 'business prestige was at an all-time nadir.'[156] Thus, the property owners as the hereditary enemies of social security, were in political disarray, while the states, the archenemies of federal intervention, could no longer do without it. Within this constellation the Roosevelt regime cautiously advanced its proposals.

On the face of it, the Social Security Act of 1935 entailed a federal compulsion for almost every wage-earner to save part of his or her income to accumulate a pension, payable when they reached the age of sixty-five.[157] It seemed a rigorous, individualist capitalization scheme, ruling out any benefits, unless they had been paid for in the past. But behind this austere façade a more complicated and ambiguous, at times even generous, structure evolved. First of all, in the calculation of benefits, a minimum level was guaranteed even to those who had paid contributions only for a short period or over a low wage sum; additional contributions added less to the pension to be disbursed.[158] Second, in order to bridge the period before accumulated pensions became payable, state pension plans were supported by matching federal grants in aid, a *don royal*, which was intended as a temporary measure, but it has remained a major feature of the system ever since.[159] With the main program came other schemes for aid to the blind and to dependent children, all of them means tested and with no specified minimum standards. Southern states rejected any minimum, as it might interfere with their long-standing discriminatory practices toward indigent blacks.[160] Third, the Act of 1935 included an unemployment insurance which allowed employers to deduct from federal taxes their contributions to state unemployment programs satisfying federal standards: 'within two years every state had an unemployment insurance law.'[161] And most states adopted the Wisconsin system of levying lower taxes from employers who refrained from laying off workers.[162]

In a national constellation of unprecedented political radicalization, this much remained of the original concepts of the Wisconsin experts, once Roosevelt had cautiously trimmed them and Congress had reinforced states' rights and employers' liberties. But once in place, the same program was defended and extended step by step with great skill and determination by the moguls of the Social Security Board.[163] Dependents and survivors were included under old-age insurance in 1939, disability benefits were enacted in 1956, health insurance for the elderly (Medicare) and for welfare clients (Medicaid) came in 1965. And although social-security expenditure as a percentage of GNP is still lowest among the capitalist democracies (except for Japan), its share has doubled between 1960 and 1977: a growth rate surpassed only by the Scandinavian countries and the Netherlands.[164]

A national health insurance has never been instituted in the United States. In 1973, three-quarters of the civilian labor force were covered by a patchwork of private insurance for medical expenses.[165] Temporary disability insurance had been adopted by six states, New York and California among them, by 1983, while almost half of the remaining workers in private industry were protected by company plans or labor–management contracts.[166]

Both Heidenheimer and Janowitz have argued that the United States lagged behind the European nations in developing a system of social security, but was ahead in building an educational system: 'Massive support for the expansion of public education, including higher education, in the United States must be seen as a central component of the American notion of welfare – the idea that through public education both personal betterment and national and social and economic development would take place.'[167] Competition between denominations stimulated interest in education, and the accumulation of knowledge at an early stage of life was seen as a sound investment for a future career. Local and state governments could more easily contribute to the collectivization of education than to the collectivization of risk protection, as the former would improve their competitive position in the long run, whereas the latter might worsen it in the short term.

A coalition of a reformist regime and organized workers supported social security in the United States and carried through its major extensions,[168] all the while anticipating and accommodating employers' interests and states' rights. Yet this base was never completely superseded by the tripartite coalition which emerged in other countries, to be institutionalized in the administrative apparatus of social security.[169]

This allowed unions and employers to bargain outside the social-security system for separate company schemes, which then tended to reinforce the general tendency of American social arrangements to treat generously only the stably employed. The same rather narrow political base of social security has allowed special-interest groups such as insurance companies and the medical profession to acquire a virtual veto.

The figuration of states, each with limited political autonomy, competing with one another around a federal government within one national economy, added its particular dynamics. It delayed the advent of social legislation. But once economic depression and political upheaval had shifted the balance and social security had become a fact, the position of the federal government was strengthened at the expense of the individual states. In this manner, developments contributed, as they did elsewhere, to the process of state formation.

6.5 The Netherlands: a long sizzle and a late bang

The history of social security in the Netherlands is one of fragmentary and halting legislation. A Workmen's Compensation Act was passed in 1901, but it took another twelve years before an Invalidity and Old Age pension was introduced by Talma, which did not become operative until 1919. Implementation of a sickness insurance law, also enacted in 1913, was delayed until 1930. Legal regulation of sick funds was finally realized by the German occupation regime in 1941. Compulsory state unemployment insurance was introduced as late as 1952.[170]

And yet, by the late 1970s the share of social expenditure in the national income of the Netherlands had become the highest in the world. Both the relatively slow and niggardly beginnings and the late, but dramatic, expansion of social security in the Netherlands stand in need of explanation.

The early history of social policy in the Low Countries coincides with the beginnings of party organization and the emergence of unions and employers' associations. The social issue proved to be a major organizing focus, all the more so after the franchise was extended in 1897 to include also 'the workman established in his state'.[171] As a conflict about the organization of society, it formed a continuation of the school struggle which was finally resolved by the compromise of 'pacification' in 1917.

Industrialization came later to the Netherlands than to the surrounding countries, accelerating precisely in the period 1895–1914.[172] As a result, the level of organization among both workers and employers was still low by the end of the nineteenth century. Moreover, the issue of public versus denominational education had left its imprint on Dutch society.

As a result, parties, unions and other associations formed along confessional lines. Catholic and Protestant employers hesitated between membership in 'general' or in denominational associations, while activist and socially conscious leaders succeeded in organizing the religious workers in denominational unions. This was part of a more pervasive *verzuiling* or 'pillarization' of Dutch society into denominational 'pillars', supporting one national roof – the level where the elites of each denomination settled their differences. This alignment took shape in the second half of the nineteenth century and lasted well into the 1950s. As a result, social-economic conflict was always somewhat fragmented and dampened on account of the cross-cutting denominational cleavages of a 'pillarized' society.[173]

In this constellation, Protestant and Catholic parties – each with a constituency heterogeneous as to social economic background – came to occupy a pivotal position in parliament from 1901 on. Their coalition ruled almost without interruption to the present day, at times with Liberal–Conservative and, after 1939, also Social Democratic support.[174] In order to maintain this pivotal position and keep their heterogeneous electorate together, Christian politicians from the beginning sought a tripartite, consensual base for a cautious social policy. To them, social security was in the first place an instrument to build corporatist structures in which workers and employers would work together, guided by the tenets of denominational inspiration and organization.[175] In the second half of this century, when industrialization had proceeded much further and confessionalism was losing its hold on political life, the Christian parties were in danger of losing their pivotal position and had to face direct competition from the Social Democrats for the workers' allegiance on social-economic issues.[176] Once the basic structures of social security had been established on a non-partisan tripartite base, this competition accelerated the accumulation of transfer capital, financed with the proceeds from international trade and the yields of domestic natural gas deposits.

In the Netherlands the transition to a parliamentary monarchy was made quite peacefully in the years 1848–68, without the agitation which in other countries mobilized the petty bourgeoisie into political organizations. Moreover, the confessional-party system which grew out of the subsequent school struggle prevented small property owners and the independently employed from articulating their interests clearly and in unison. Before the hold of the rural aristocracy and the urban partriciate in the western provinces had been broken, and the property owners could find a voice of their own, they had already been realigned along denominational lines of cleavage. Their interests were mediated within the Christian and Liberal parties, rather than articulated unequivocally by political organizations of their own. Only the large-scale industrialists, relatively small in number, succeeded in organizing on the basis of social-economic interest and they did so in their opposition to the Workmen's Compensation Act.[177]

The Act of 1901 was passed by the last of the Liberal–Conservative governments and very much inspired by Bismarck's legislation. It was the product of an – in this respect – activist regime which almost succeeded in bypassing both workers and employers and establishing a compulsory, collective insurance on the basis of *risque professionnel*, at employers' cost, and entirely administered by a single government agency, the *Rijks-verzekeringsbank*. Almost, but not quite: the bill provoked unprecedented resistance from employers, who insisted on the freedom to insure themselves or to combine for that purpose on a voluntary basis. They did not so much resist the monopoly of the *Rijksverzekeringsbank* to decide claims and pay benefits, nor did they reject its supervision over their voluntary insurance institutions. The employers had been mobilized by the fear that the Act was to be only the first of a series of social laws.[178] The campaign was effective in its limited purpose, the law was rewritten to allow voluntary 'reinsurance'. It was also successful in the long term since it led to the establishment of a Central Employers Insurance Bank,[179] and, even more important, to the founding of the *Nederlandse Vereniging van Werkgevers* in 1899: the Employers' Association which has remained the leading vehicle of employers' interests to this day. But the very effort of the employers evoked repercussions elsewhere.[180] The Protestant politician Kuyper formulated the Christian principles of social security in his 'great amendment' which, although defeated at the time, became the foundation for all later social legislation. The socialist and radical workers hesitatingly united in a national committee in support of the original bill and in doing so helped the government in getting the law passed with only minor modifications. Opposition from small entre-preneurs played scarcely any role, also because minor employers and less dangerous industries were exempted from the law until its scope was greatly extended in 1921.

Thus, the first social-security law enacted in the Netherlands was the product of an activist regime which had anticipated the preferences of recently enfranchised workers, and counted on employers' support. For lack of strong employers' organizations, it had relied on a state monopoly of administration. But in doing so it inadvertently mobilized the employers against the bill and provoked a political campaign which led to the establishment of a permanent employers' organization and strongly stimulated the workers to counteract with organizational effort.

The law had scarcely been enacted when the political constellation changed radically: the Christian coalition came to power and Kuyper began preparing a series of social laws which were to embody the corporatist tenets of the Catholic 'subsidiarity principle' and the Protestant principle of 'circles of sovereignty'. Workers and employers, organized according to their faith, were to collaborate in trade associations or labor councils together with 'crown appointees', so as to set working conditions and manage social insurance. This concern with the organization of industrial relations was only one aspect of a broader effort to dampen the class struggle by the tight organization of society along denominational lines: *verzuiling* ('pillarization'). In this context, petty-bourgeois mistrust of big government, big business and big unions was not expressed in all-out opposition to social and economic regulation, but rather it was accommodated into a scheme that would restrict these forces, fragment and fetter them in relatively small, relatively autonomous local or sectoral associations – a vision shared in widely varying elaborations with the Socialists, the Fascists, and even the Anarchists of those years. Small entrepreneurs could hope to remain outside of this corporatist order, or, if compelled to join it, bargain on equal terms and accept regulations as the price of protection.

After twelve years of Christian coalition government, Talma succeeded in enacting the foundations of Christian social policy: a labor council law, a sickness law and an old-age-cum-invalidity pension. None of these laws became operative, although – by mistake or by design[181] – an amendment to allow free pensions for persons then over seventy was accepted by the government for immediate implementation by the *Rijksverzekeringsbank*. It took the misery of mass unemployment in the years of neutrality during the First World War and the subsequent brief scare of revolution before the Pension Act was implemented in 1919,[182] but by then its terms had to compensate for the relatively favorable conditions of the provisional pension of 1913.[183] However, Talma's sickness law and the sick-funds law which was to be its complement, met with unexpected delay. Again, the major issue was control over implementation. The Social Democrats tended to favor the 'labor councils' of 1913, putting their faith in local semi-public bodies. The confessional parties preferred the 'trade associations' (which had originated in employers' initiatives, but by then admitted workers' representatives up to parity). In these bodies, workers' and employers' organizations were to collaborate by industry.

As trade unions were becoming more national in orientation, their preference for local bodies declined and by the 1920s they tended to accept the – nationwide and sectoral – trade associations as the executive agencies of insurance. But the unions insisted that the employers should pay the fees. In the end, both types of agencies were allowed under the law and premiums were shared evenly by employers and workers.[184] But by now, medical men were organizing themselves and their resistance resulted in adjournment *sine die* of the sick-funds law. It was finally promulgated by decree of the German occupation authorities in 1941. Premiums were levied from employers who could deduct half the sum from wages.[185] Compulsory unemployment insurance was realized only in 1952. In the preceding period the central government had supplemented voluntary union funds and subsidized municipal relief throughout the worst ten years of the Great Depression.

For lack of studies on the political history of social security in the Netherlands, the causes of retardation can only be guessed at. Parliamentary historians and legal students have proposed a host of reasons and coincidences, but none of these appears very compelling. Strong and persistent pressure for social legislation was lacking throughout most of the period. The political struggle seemed concerned not so much with social security *per se* as with the organization of industrial and wider social relations in the country, that is with the 'ordination of society'.[186] From their pivotal position in Dutch politics the Christian-coalition parties could set the agenda and formulate matters of social policy as issues of social ordination. But their narrow parliamentary majorities did not allow them to actually weave this pattern into the fabric of industrial society. In the course of thirty years they succeeded, however, in establishing a tripartite and quite uncontroversial system of social security which slowly superseded the earlier *étatiste*, Bismarckian structure of the Workmen's Compensation Act and went beyond the pension laws in bringing together the 'industrial partners' in structures which were to mediate between 'state and society'.

No intensive campaigns, no activist cliques or political upheavals operated to cause a legislative breakthrough. As a result, social-security legislation was highly incremental in nature, and after 1900 invariably tripartite in character. There was no broad support for, but no acute articulate opposition against, the laws. And yet a similar figuration of political forces as had made for such slow and piecemeal legislation before the Second World War generated a remarkable expansion of social security under the social and economic conditions that prevailed after that watershed.

First of all, the Netherlands went through a phase of rapid industrialization in the postwar years. The prewar effort at organizing industrial relations paid off in the 1950s in the form of an extremely efficient system of consultation between workers, employers and 'crown

214

members' who could hammer out compromises and process legislation without much opposition. This, in turn, contributed very much to a smoothly operating economy. The political strength of large-scale employers and national unions increased accordingly. Secondly, the independent small middle class, politically never very strong, continued to decrease in numbers after 1945, while the proportion of salaried employees kept on growing.[187] Thirdly, while the Christian parties maintained their pivotal position in parliament, their majority became increasingly precarious and disappeared once and for all after 1967; from 1945 they governed with either Liberal or Social Democratic support. Confessionalism was slowly losing its hold on Dutch politics and a fierce competition between the Catholics and the Socialists ensued, after the new Labor Party began to campaign, from 1946, for a 'breakthrough' into the Catholic workers' vote in the south. Finally, a quite consensual system of social security was already in place. During the war years, the German occupation regime, the Dutch government in exile and the underground political leadership had all been busy elaborating plans for it.

As a result, the activist postwar regime of Social Democrats and the Christian parties, inspired by the main ideas of the Beveridge plan and by a general mood of reconstruction, passed an emergency Pension Law[188] which was succeeded by the General Old Age Law of 1956. This was the first of the 'national insurances' (*volksverzekeringen*) to provide coverage to all citizens, without a means test. An unemployment insurance, implemented by the trade associations and with premiums shared between employers and employees, was enacted in 1949 and became operative in 1952.

In the 1960s two new laws were enacted which made for an explosive growth of income transfers in the Netherlands: the General Assistance Act of 1963 and the Disability Act of 1967.[189] The two had been intended as the concluding acts of the Netherlands social legislation, but their exceptionally generous terms unexpectedly modified the conditions of the labor market in the following period of recession, the first by providing a more or less viable and secure alternative to gainful employment, the other by providing a not entirely uncomfortable exit from it.[190]

The laws were passed without major conflict in parliament or in the country, enacted and extended by Christian–Liberal as well as Christian–Socialist coalition governments. The role of the trade associations diminished in comparison with earlier laws, and that of the central state gained in weight.

On the whole, these laws were the product of coalitions between employers' and workers' organizations with a succession of expansionist regimes in a period when the political resources of the self-employed middle class dwindled increasingly.[191] A sustained period of full employment, favorable trade balances and rich proceeds from domestic natural gas deposits set the mood and provided the financial space for the expansion of social legislation.[192] Finally, the ongoing competition between the Socialists on the one hand, and the denominational parties (the Catholics and the Protestant Anti-Revolutionary Party) for the working-class vote added impetus to social-security reform.[193]

In the Netherlands, as elsewhere, between 1948 and 1970 social legislation worked. The equanimity of the welfare state gradually wiped away the bitter memories of the Great Crisis and inspired a sense of confidence which may have been unparalleled in history. And, throughout this period of social legislation few foresaw that unemployment might once again become a major social problem, as it did from the early seventies on. The level of benefits, fixed in earlier, better days, was multiplied by the increasing number of the jobless to generate an autonomous growth of social-security expenditure and an almost uncontrollably increasing government deficit.

The net effect of this development in the Netherlands has been a marked decrease in the proportion of privately owned wealth in total wealth and a corresponding rise in the share of transfer capital. Not counting transfer property (which is not included in statistics), private wealth has been distributed a little more evenly, but much less so than income. Similar developments have occurred in other advanced capitalist democracies.[194] The increasingly egalitarian distribution of income is due in great part to transfers, and it has been argued that total transfer income varies inversely with total income from capital (rents and profits). The two forms of 'institutional income' together remain constant in proportion to labor income.[195] This finding suggests that transfer capital is in fact formed directly at the expense of private capital and that the worst fears of an earlier generation of property owners have come true, although many of its sons and daughters are among the first beneficiaries.

7 Conclusion

The initial introduction of nationwide social security constituted the most incisive spurt within the collectivizing process in the past century and a new phase in the process of state formation. For the first time, a considerable part of the population, which was to increase without interruption from then on, was brought under a single compulsory and collective scheme to protect it from the adversities of working life.

By the turn of the century, only the state appeared to possess the administrative potential, the scope and the robustness over time to accomplish the task. It alone could overcome the dilemmas of voluntary action by its coercive powers to levy taxes and impose membership.

Compulsory accumulation of transfer capital meant direct interference with the cash nexus between employers and employees and with the spending patterns of individual wage-earners. The state bureaucracy would be present on every shopfloor and in every household. Small independent entrepreneurs resisted this prospect everywhere and all the way. And the stronger their political position, the longer was legislation delayed.

Workers tended to support social security as their organizations became more established and developed a nationwide base with a corresponding orientation to national politics and the central state. Large-scale employers resented the costs of the scheme and the interference from bureaucratic agencies. But they also realized that it would improve industrial relations and relieve them of the responsibility to care for disabled and aging employees and their families. To both large-scale employers and workers, social security increasingly became a matter of cost and control, and in the end, a negotiable issue.

The fourth party in this figuration, the regime in power, represented the one necessary actor. Nothing could be accomplished without it, but in order to overcome petty-bourgeois opposition and to ensure the actual implementation of the scheme, it could not proceed without support from the legislature and the country. The regime might go ahead without the unions, as the Bismarck government did, but only because it was assured of the collaboration of large-scale employers and the tacit acceptance of its plans by the workers. It could also, like the Lloyd George cabinet, enact national insurance while sidestepping the employers, but that required a coalition with the labor unions. In the United States, the Roosevelt regime instituted social security with support from the unions, and left it to state politics to work out specific compromises with unions and employers. In France and the Netherlands, social security was brought about after much delay by precarious tripartite coalitions. In all these countries, resistance to social security died from 'natural' economic causes as the numbers of small entrepreneurs dwindled, while support for it increased with the proportion of wage-earners in the workforce.

7

Conclusion: The Collectivizing Process and its Consequences

The contemporary welfare state has become a vast conglomerate of nationwide, compulsory and collective arrangements to remedy and control the external effects of adversity and deficiency. This collectivizing process occurred in the course of the modern era against the background of state formation and the rise of capitalism in the West. The main impetus for collectivization came from struggles between elites which sought to ward off the threats arising from the presence of the poor among them, and, to exploit the opportunities which the poor also represented. Yet, no matter how powerful or rich, those established in society could not handle these opportunities and dangers on their own: that required collective action. But the prospect that the inactive among the elites might also profit from such efforts was usually enough to discourage others from taking the initiative. The major episodes in the development of poor relief, health care and education may be interpreted as contests among the elites about the ways in which to deal with the indirect effects of destitution, disease and ignorance as it afflicted the poor and powerless strata in society directly. In seeking ways to manage these changing interdependencies, between the rich and the poor and among the elites themselves, collective charitable arrangements were formed, at the parish level first, later at the level of cities and, finally, at the national level. In the absence of a central, coordinating agency, the initial stalemate of mutual suspicion was often overcome through manipulation of mutual expectations or by shared illusions. But once collective action was initiated, it might contribute both to the creation of collective goods and to the formation of a relevant collectivity. In the course of this collectivizing process, new forms of mutual control and dependency developed which helped to enforce the collective enterprise.

In the modern era, as city governments and states succeeded in exerting more effective control, they also began to intervene in conflicts among local elites over the management of the poor. By means of such interventions, collective arrangements were being tied more closely to local and central governments and this in turn contributed to the expansion of the state apparatus.

1 Summing up: state formation and the collectivization of care

As state formation proceeded, production, storage, transport and trade became more secure from robbery and plunder. This generalization of protection went with a dissolution of specific, feudal protective relations, while relations of property and monetary exchange were extended and intensified – that is, secured by law, in the last analysis, by state coercion.

But as the economy expanded, it also became more vulnerable to minor, sudden and passing attacks: domestic pacification had not abolished crime and banditry. And the vagrant poor, excluded from all property, became even more of a threat to expanding crops, growing stocks and lengthening supply-lines. The established strata sought to abate this danger in a collective effort to pacify the dangerous poor – part of the process of residual pacification.

If the poor were not driven away, charity was the means to appease them. Medieval priests, in their role of 'charitable entrepreneurs', promulgated a uniform rule of distribution which could serve as a 'focal point' for coordinating almsgiving. They also manipulated reciprocal expectations among the established families and created a public setting for ostentatious giving and mutual inspection of each one's contributions. Collective charitable action in turn contributed to the emergence of the parish as a collectivity. In the context of this emerging parish community, 'public order' as a collective good acquired increasing social relevance. The parish community also facilitated mutual social control and developed sanctions against those who would not contribute.

Similar dilemmas of collective action repeated themselves in early modern Europe at a higher level of social aggregation. During this phase, relatively autonomous communities found themselves affected by vagrancy and banditry in the region, but were incapable of coordinated action in the absence of effective central authority. Again, they depended upon one another to achieve residual pacification at the level of the region, but could neither trust nor coerce others to cooperate. Every town was ready to pass on its burden of relief-seekers to the next and thus added to the general chaos. No town could afford to remain alone in opening its gates to the needy. This time the dilemmas of collective action were overcome by an illusion: the false expectation that a workhouse would allow the community to control the influx of relief-seekers and make them earn their own upkeep. When disillusion came, many cities had already established a workhouse. Central authorities used their still-limited resources to maintain the regional equilibrium of poor relief by persuading the municipalities to keep their workhouse going and to lock up their share of vagrants (chapter 2).

In a period of expanding markets and extending government bureaucracies, the poor also represented opportunity to entrepreneurs and state officials. The emerging capitalist and administrative elites sought to establish direct links with the population at large and tried to bypass the local nobility and clergy who held the monopoly of mediation between their relatively isolated clientele and the rest of society. Outside the metropolitan area, peasants, craftsmen, and paupers often spoke a distinct regional dialect and did not understand the 'standard language'; even fewer could read or write. This ignorance, hitherto mostly irrelevant to daily pursuits, began to turn into a deficiency as dealings with the central state and national markets became more important. The local elites, fluent in both the regional dialect and the standard language, and also able to read and write, stood to gain from the increased demand for the mediating services they monopolized. Popular ignorance of the national communication codes hindered the metropolitan elites from seeking direct access to the population at large.

A 'floral figuration of languages' prevailed, consisting of a number of relatively disjoint communication networks, mutually isolated by un-intelligibility of speech or, where a common language prevailed, by the impossibility of written communication and the costs of travel. Local elites mediated between their local network and the rest of the nation in the standard language or in writing. They formed the intersections between these relatively disjoint peripheral networks and the metropolitan network where the standard language was spoken, read and written.

Metropolitan officials and entrepreneurs – in the heart of this floral figuration – strove to overcome the local mediation monopolies in a campaign for linguistic unification and mass literacy, a major aspect of the wider process of national mobilization. They supported the establishment of a nationwide system of compulsory elementary education in a standard curriculum of codes for national communication. Local elites resisted the attempt, but competition forced them to set up schools of their own. The same rivalry prompted them next to unite in nationwide educational organizations to resist a state monopoly, and finally to seek state support while yet accepting central regulations. In the end, they found themselves absorbed into an alternative, nationwide educational system, almost equally uniform and coercive, leaving them with only nominal control in most countries (chapter 3).

Industrialization and urbanization brought masses of people closely together in a new state of aggregation: the nineteenth-century industrial city. Under these conditions of physical proximity, the concomitants of poverty – squalor, malnutrition and ill health – produced novel adversities: the epidemics, which hit the poor hardest, but also threatened the established citizens, while paralyzing the city's social and economic life.

The specter of cholera served as a paradigm of this new and threatening urban interdependence. The paradigmatic response was found in the concept of urban sanitation through a 'venous-arterial system' of fresh-water supply and sewerage which would shield city-dwellers from one another by encapsulating domestic life in private homes, while connecting everyone to the grand urban service networks.

In the meantime, citizens who could afford it left for 'better' neighborhoods. The aggregate result of these individual moves was spatial segregation into socially more homogeneous zones. In the new, wealthy areas, this process facilitated collective action among the urban elites to modify and control the external effects of poverty in the wider urban setting: crime, revolt, contagion and 'social contamination'. In this context, permanent police vigilance was instituted and a series of urban service networks established. Sewage disposal and water-supply channels, gas pipes and electricity cables, transport tracks and telephone lines spread over the city. In the late nineteenth century they were often installed first in the wealthier areas, branching out from there, until the city was almost saturated and only the poverty areas were left to be connected, by government coercion and at marginal costs only (chapter 4).

As industrial mass production expanded, people working in regular employment for a money wage became the vast majority of the labor force. Unlike property owners, these wage-workers lacked the resources to fall back on when they found themselves without work because of disability, disease, old age or for lack of jobs. Nor could they make provision for their surviving kin. Wage-workers rarely accumulated private savings, but some did take commercial insurance and many joined mutual funds. These small, relatively autonomous Friendly Societies at one point were the most common collective arrangement against adversity among the working classes. However, what made for their success also constituted their weakness. As they were small in size and operated by the members themselves, they lacked expertise or procedures for inspection, routine adjudication and conflict resolution. Their membership was socially homogeneous to a high degree, which made for solidarity, but also exposed the funds to an accumulation of similar risks. As the mutual funds were autonomous, they were tempted to exclude the workers who were paid least and most at risk; they were even compelled to do so, if competing funds did the same. As so often, a system of small, autonomous arrangements left a lower stratum in society uncovered (chapter 5).

The mutual funds proved increasingly incapable of solving the problem of industrial poverty. And gradually it became accepted as a fact that under urban, industrial conditions, poverty was not so much a reflection of individual moral worth, but that it might hit anyone who found himself without steady employment. The large numbers of paupers were perceived as a menace by the established city dwellers. As workers started to organize, their unions, too, appeared to threaten labor peace and public order. In these circumstances, large-scale employers, moderate workers' leaders, activist administrators and politicians proposed to establish compulsory collective funds on a nationwide scale to provide benefits to workers in compensation for income lost through involuntary unemployment. This collective accumulation of transfer capital formed an alternative to the providential functions of privately accumulated property. Small entrepreneurs and the independently employed resisted these schemes, as large funds might compete with their small holdings on the capital market and compulsory measures interfere with their autonomy. The security it conferred on workers also threatened to undo their precarious social distance from the working class.

Only an activist regime could overcome this political opposition, with the support of either large-scale employers or organized workers or both. The moment and the momentum of social-security legislation was determined by the balance of forces between the petty bourgeoisie and the growing industrial classes of workers and employers, with the political regime in a pivotal position. The scope and nature of transfer-capital arrangements was determined mainly by the composition of the political coalition that brought it about.

Within fifty years after the first social-insurance laws in Germany, nationwide collective and state-controlled arrangements for the accumulation of transfer capital had emerged in all capitalist democracies. On the eve of World War II all the basic institutions for the collectivization of health care, education and income maintenance had been established in Western Europe and the United States. The groundwork had been laid for the high-rise construction of the postwar era: 'The second great revolution of this century in social care, beginning after Dunkirk and quickening into effect after 1945, continued the process.'[1]

2 Collectivization after 1945: the hyperbole of expansion

Since the Second World War, education, health care and income transfers in Europe and the United States have expanded exponentially, and in all dimensions: more people went to school for more years, in smaller, better-equipped classes. The control of the central state over education grew at a pace. More people sought treatment for a quickly extending range of complaints and found much more elaborate facilities and services, equally under increasing control of the central government. Also, the accumulation of transfer capital accelerated rapidly, its provisions extending to almost the entire population, its benefits covering a broadening range of adversities at a more generous level in an absolute and relative sense. State agencies were involved ever more closely in the management of enterprises and in the private lives of workers and claimants.

The expansion occurred in two spurts: from the late forties to the early fifties and from the mid-sixties to the early seventies. Since then, the expansion has levelled off, and in rare cases it was actually reversed.

By the late 1930s the administrative and fiscal innovations for the management of the welfare state had been introduced and tried by all Western governments. State bureaucracies had been proven capable of setting up and running vast educational, health-care, insurance and assistance systems. A broad base of political support for such nationwide, collective and compulsory arrangements had been shown to exist. In principle, the problems of financing seemed manageable. Students, patients, clients, contributors and claimants by the million appeared to be competent participants in these systems. In other words, the proof of viability had been supplied, not by inference from lofty axioms, but through sound induction from everyday experience. In Heclo's words, the 'era of experimentation' had ended and the 'era of consolidation' begun, to be followed by another phase of 'expansion' in the fifties.[2]

The expansibility of the new formulas for state administration had been demonstrated during World War II when governments, in close collaboration with large-scale industry and the unions, carried on a war economy with spectacular results, especially in England and the United States. After the war this 'wartime triangle' was not disbanded.[3]

As a result of mobilization for total warfare, the state apparatus had increased enormously in capacity. Government bureaucracies were now up to the administrative challenges of managing a much enlarged welfare system.[4] The experiences of wartime military administration, production battles, civil protection or evacuation schemes and propaganda campaigns had taught Western governments how to steer the economy, to orchestrate public opinion and to manage the lives of their citizens to a degree that seemed to dwarf the demands of running a welfare state, a task which not long since had still appeared so formidable. This pervasive governmental intervention had been carried out with the apparent support of the vast majority of the public. In England and the United States it had contributed to total military victory. Massive state regulation not only proved to be compatible with democracy, but now seemed a necessary condition for its survival both against external threats and domestic discontent. This domestic brand of compulsory collectivization persuaded even the Dutch, the French and the Germans after their experience with the totalitarian version: after 1945, democratic society everywhere seemed to imply a welfare state.

The lessons of the wartime triangle and the war economy combined with a pressure in the same direction: in the years before and during the war, political elites had been forced to seek the loyalties of the working class as recruits in the international conflict between states and as voters in domestic contests. If Communism, Fascism and National Socialism became a magnetizing influence upon workers and intellectuals, especially in continental Europe, the Soviet system had proven its viability by its military achievements, and domestic Communists had fought in the forefront of resistance against Nazism. The Communist program appeared to offer an alternative to both National Socialist state terrorism and the capitalist crises of the pre-war era. At a time when working people were no longer immediately needed as recruits, and when demobilized soldiers might be in a weak bargaining position on the labor market as peacetime employment was expected to pick up only slowly, it was this threat of a revolutionary working-class movement that loomed large for the politicians of the major democratic parties.[5] Moreover, the demobilized soldiers were voters too, and they had not forgotten the promises of 'a world free of want' made during the war. In the following years, the process of decolonization which involved Britain, France and the Netherlands in a series of limited, but distant, costly and unpopular wars and the American military effort in Korea also prompted governments to seek the support of working-class voters and soldiers through a more generous social and educational policy.

The war economy had reconciled big business with government intervention. The Great Depression and the war economy had disrupted the patterns of production and the political organization of the small middle class of shopkeepers, craftsmen, traders and peasants. The vicissitudes of currency during the period between the wars and the wartime monetary measures seemed to ridicule the virtues of private saving. Small bourgeois right-wing politics was in disarray. The traditional opposition against state social policy was weakened even more when the self-confident proponents of social security began to promote schemes that were to cover the self-employed also. This, of course, tempted many small entrepreneurs who had lived through the years of inflation and austerity.

The American Democratic Party, and the large Christian and Social Democratic parties in Europe, often with the active cooperation of economically conservative 'liberal' parties, launched a program of social security, health services and educational expansion. What they lacked for the moment in financial resources they often made up in legislative zeal which laid the groundwork for later expansion once the means were available. The basis of these policies was highly consensual. A coalition of large unions, big business, and the regime in power agreed upon a program of social spending to be financed by general payroll taxes, in the silent hope of shifting higher wage costs to consumers in a sellers' market. Vulgarized Keynesian notions of increasing consumption by government expenditure stimulated these efforts. But it was the prolonged wave of unexpected and exceptional economic growth that carried the flow of social spending along.[6] As a result, 'welfare state politics could lie in repose while the engine of economic growth did its work.'[7]

This first phase of hyperbolic expansion profoundly affected postwar societies. The vast majority of citizens were enrolled in collective arrangements for health care and income protection. As a first consequence, many voters might well object to collective and public spending and to high taxation in general, but when it came to cutting specific benefits which profited them especially, they tended to oppose such measures much more strenuously than they supported retrenchments in general and in the abstract. In this manner, strongly motivated minorities combined to defend their interests successfully every time they were threatened by a – necessarily less determined and cohesive – opposition.[8]

The second consequence of this expansion was the emergence of a stratum of professional experts and administrators who depended on these collective arrangements for employment and advancement. These 'new' middle classes represented a formidable array of interest groups for the promotion of the expansion of collective arrangements. The professional groups succeeded not only in forming close links with the state apparatus but also in establishing their 'regimes' over increasing sections of the population which accordingly became their clienteles. The establishment of an educational, a medical and, more recently, a relief regime has been a major aspect of the formation of welfare states in this century: the theme will be discussed more fully in section 7.3, with special attention to the medical profession.

The third consequence of the expansion of collective arrangements and of the corresponding emergence of expert regimes was a broad transformation of mentality among the citizenry of contemporary welfare states. This transformation operated at three levels: (1) An increase in the valuation of what these expert regimes and the welfare state have to offer – health, knowledge and the protection from income loss. In other words, people increasingly appreciated these values and accordingly defined the daily events in their lives in terms of the basic concepts of the professions they expected to be provided: a process of 'protoprofessionalization'. (2) A general shift in the direction of greater self-constraint and a stronger orientation toward the future. At this point, the collectivizing process and the civilizing process interacted. (3) An increasing awareness of the generalization of interdependency in modern society, a transition from the perception of events mainly in terms of religion, magic and conspiracy to a consciousness of the dependencies between groups – an awareness of the ways in which the adversities and deficiencies that afflict one group indirectly affect others also: a transition from charity to social consciousness. The transitions in mentality that went with the collectivization of welfare will be discussed at more length in section 7.4.

The consequences of the expansion of the welfare state have contributed to its further expansion. In many respects, the first postwar phase of growth brought about changes in society which then helped to induce subsequent phases of the collectivizing process. Increasingly, the welfare state acquired a momentum of its own. More and more, its collective arrangements began to constitute a strategic environment – a context providing the options for the everyday decisions and non-decisions of its citizens.

The second burst of expansion occurred during the sixties and early seventies.[9] It could only have occurred because of the continued wave of economic growth that set in again in the late fifties. But the surplus might have been used in other ways. The fact that a large part of it was spent on increasing collective benefits and services owed much to a combination of popular agitation for increasing welfare provisions and pressure for expansion from within the service bureaucracies themselves, which by then had grown into powerful and active interest groups. Developments were most explosive where the two combined, where skilled helping professionals were sent out to help organize potential categories of clients and claimants.

However, a succession of spectacular events jolted governments into a readiness to initiate another round of social-policy reform. In the late sixties, race riots in the United States dramatized the problems of poverty, especially among recent black urban immigrants. At the same time student revolts everywhere suddenly highlighted the discontents of higher education, which by then had just become accessible to the children of the working class – the latest turn in the spiral of educational expansion.[10] In Europe, large workers' strikes coincided with student unrest. A new generation of intellectuals, most of them social scientists, provided a suitable political interpretation of the rebellions. The entire sequence of minor revolts, occurring now in one country, then in the next, evoked a sense of urgency and threat which had long been absent. Thus the rebellions of the sixties contributed one more necessary ingredient for welfare reform: concern among the elites.[11]

Governments had long since subsidized health educators to promote hygiene and prevention. In the process, schoolchildren and adults were sped on their way to the doctor's office. Parole officers and social workers had been serving as guides in the bizarre labyrinth of welfare legislation. Partly in reaction to the unrest of the sixties, governments also began to send community-action workers into 'problem areas'. They appointed lawyers to defend the interests of lodgers against landlords and claimants against welfare bureaucracies.[12] Many of these vanguard platoons of the welfare state were sent out with marching orders drafted by academic sociologists.[13] In short, the agencies of the state were sowing the seeds for their own proliferation.

In all these cases, the increasing supply of helping services did much to raise the demand. But this observation, correct in itself, has served to obfuscate the fact that the clients who now for the first time articulated a desire for professional help had suffered ills and complaints all along. 'Outside agitators' may well have been at work, but there also was – as always – internal discontent. The supply of professional experts may have created the manifest demand – it did not create the misery.

The second phase of hyperbolic expansion in the welfare state was made possible by sustained economic growth and shaped by a particular political constellation of strongly motivated minorities demanding spending increases on specific programs and confronting a much less cohesive or intense opposition to increased government spending in general.[14] Within this constellation, expert administrators and helping professionals promoted their particular services and found support within a population which increasingly accepted state intervention as a means to solve 'social problems' and which put a growing value upon professional expertise as a remedy to social and personal ills.

At a point where this collectivizing process appeared to have become self-perpetuating, it nevertheless began to slow down. The hyperbole of expansion was approaching its limit.

By the mid-seventies, the powerful forces toward expansion were checked – mainly by the budgetary deficits they caused. Once the necessary condition of economic growth was no longer fulfilled or the perspective of unlimited and undisturbed growth no longer taken for granted, the expansion of welfare arrangements began to decelerate. The turning-point came with the oil crisis of 1974. But underneath, larger and more enduring facts of international competition had been at work. Social security and health care were mainly financed from payroll taxes and thus increased labor costs in the countries concerned. By then, many non-Western countries had industrialized to a point where they could successfully compete in the market for manufactured goods, because of their much lower wage costs. As social spending continued to increase in the West, while governments, unions and employers were loath to raise payroll taxes, a deficit resulted which had to be compensated either by public borrowing or by inflationary spending: a 'fiscal crisis' ensued. Leftist governments, such as that of Mitterand in France, found themselves incapable of continuing expansionist policies.[15] But right-wing regimes, such as the Reagan presidency in the United States, also proved unable to rescind health, education or social-security expenditures.[16] In multiparty systems, coalition politics even reinforced spending patterns. Where bourgeois and social democratic parties alternated in government,[17] as in the Netherlands and Scandinavia, or in Italy, social expenditure nevertheless continued to increase.[18] What was imposed or achieved in most countries by the mid-eighties, was a policy of limiting growth, of levelling off hyperbolic expansion, until it approached an equilibrium asymptote.[19] Where, in some countries programs were actually cut back in absolute terms, they usually concerned assistance to the poor, especially families (i.e. mothers) with dependent children, or adolescents without employment history – whose numbers were sharply increasing everywhere – and the permanently disabled who had for long, or always, been without work. Those who were least organized and politically weakest were hit hardest by the retrenchments.[20] The aged, on the other hand, proved to be a formidable bastion.

When it came to saving on welfare services, the helping professions which had emerged most recently, were less established in terms of academic prestige and had less access to the political regime, also

228

suffered the heaviest cutbacks: community organizers, psychotherapists, physiotherapists, neighborhood nurses, family assistants, social workers and so forth.[21] The medical profession and the teaching body were able to put up much more effective resistance.

The coalition to maintain the basic arrangements of the welfare state still holds in most countries.[22] Even determined conservative regimes, such as Thatcher's or Reagan's, have not undone the basic tenets of collectivization and transfer-capital accumulation.[23] The 'welfare backlash' has been more of an ideological exercise in verbiage, than an effective or consistent policy.[24] The result, so far, has been not so much a reversal as a declaration of the process. For reasons of their own, the parties in the conflict have resorted to hyperbole of the rhetorical kind. On the left, every attempt at slowing down expansion is decried as the first step toward the demolition of the welfare state. On the right, the hyperbole of expansion serves as a rhetorical device to justify any budget cut as a means of limiting expenditure that has gone out of control.

In fact, the underlying consensus about the basis of the welfare state is still so encompassing that it remains largely unnoticed, a 'silent majority'. The discussion mostly centers upon relatively recent additions which, for their great symbolic value, hardly affect the total amount of expenditure. But of course they matter very much to whoever is directly affected by such measures. Consensus is, however, almost completely lacking when it comes to future elaborations in the collectivization of provisions. For this reason, also, the hyperbole seems to have reached its asymptote and, for the time being, equilibrium appears to have been achieved. Very few people really want to go backward, and even fewer have a clear vision of the direction future policies are to take.[25]

The limits of the welfare state are not necessarily in the financing and managing of the system. The restrictions seem to be in the potential for effective redistribution. The critique may be phrased in terms of redistributive justice and civic morality, or in terms of effective incentives and allocations. But there are also other objections. The contemporary welfare state has become a strategic environment in which people operate as calculating entrepreneurs. This applies to the experts who derive their income from services supplied within a highly collectivized context. It also goes for the claimants who obtain their benefits and services within that setting. Finally, taxpayers, especially wage-earners, contribute up to half their income and more to the financing of provisions from which they themselves may benefit only many years later, or maybe never. The welfare state as an anonymous and mostly 'value-free' system, spawning so many opportunities for gain, imposing so many restrictions and levies in a quite inscrutable way, asks to be exploited and deceived. The rich can afford to hire experts to find the crevices in tax legislation, they may employ lawyers, accountants and even 'subsidiologists'[26] to work full time at seeking legal loopholes. At the same time, bureaucrats are busy stretching the mazes of administrative regulation to fit the needs of their organization. For small, private taxpayers and individual claimants, maximizing their advantages and minimizing their costs remains a one-man enterprise. But everyday conversation helps them to find out the recipes for dealing with taxes and benefits in entrepreneurial fashion. There are not enough inspectors to check up on everyone, to make each pay his due and to ensure that every recipient is really entitled to her or his share. Moreover, attempts at policing constitute further intrusions on behalf of the state into such intimate matters as how one spends one's time (in gainful, but unreported, activities?) and with whom one shares table and bed (with a lover who might help with household costs?). Obviously, welfare arrangements must operate with a considerable amount of 'loss'. But compared to a combustion motor or a light bulb, which waste more than two-thirds of their energy in generating useless heat, social security and social assistance are marvels of efficiency, spending less than one-tenth of funds on administration and losing a comparable amount on evasion and fraud. Of course, machines are not held accountable for their wastefulness, while inefficient machines are driven out by more efficient models. Citizens, on the other hand, not only blame others for their deceptions, they also tend to imitate them out of competitive necessity or out of spite. Dishonest contributors and recipients 'always drive out' honest ones, according to Gresham's law as applied to the welfare state. Worst of all, a welfare state operating with perfect efficiency would be perfectly efficient only as a police state. This, more than anything else, is the coming dilemma of social policy.

The relations between the welfare state and its contributors or beneficiaries are mediated by more or less autonomous experts. These state-related experts have played a major role in shaping the arrangements of collective care. They have also contributed to transformations in the modes of interaction and experience among the citizens of welfare states.

3 The transformation of the middle class and the rise of the expert regimes

The twentieth-century collectivization of care is closely connected with the transformation of the middle strata of society, from mainly independently employed small entrepreneurs into mostly wage-dependent, educated employees of large organizations.[27] Their resources shifted accordingly from private economic capital to cultural capital and a share in the collective transfer capital. Like other wage-earners, the middle cadres, and government employees especially, came to rely on collective transfer arrangements rather than on private savings, but their provisions tended to be far superior to those of manual workers. The more generous insurance schemes for government and company cadres served both to maintain a precarious social distance and to set a standard for social policy in general.[28] The overwhelming preference of these educated wage-dependent cadres for collective provision testifies to their proletarization in comparison to the self-employed. Individually accumulated knowledge distinguished them from manual wage-earners, whose *embourgeoisement* threatened to efface other class distinctions. Their expertise and their collectively accumulated transfer claims had to compensate for the occupational autonomy and the private accumulation that went with the self-employment of the old middle class.[29]

But this transformation of the middle classes was tied to the emerging welfare state in yet another manner: the collectivization of health care, education and income maintenance provided steady employment for untold numbers of trained experts in the management of the new arrangements. In one and the same grand development, the sons and daughters of the small independent bourgeoisie which was being threatened by big business or large-scale industry and the ambitious children of upwardly mobile industrial workers who had found new opportunities for advancement in large organizations were recruited into the expanding service bureaucracies where they were to take care of those who could not, or would not work or who did not yet or no longer had to.[30] The cushion of employment in the service apparatus thus absorbed a good part of bourgeois frustrations and working-class aspirations by admitting younger generations to the 'distribution elites' who managed the expanding 'social clienteles' of the welfare state. There, they allocated scarce resources through bureaucratic procedures in exchange for political loyalty.[31]

Even states are figurations of human beings, each linked to other social groups within their territory, all of them together constituting a 'family of states' in mutual and competitive interdependency. The most visible persons in such state figurations are those at the summit of the hierarchy: the administrators and politicians who are nominally in charge and sometimes in a position to change the actual course of policy. They constitute what has been called the political regime. But from top to bottom, states are made up of human beings. The expansion of the state apparatus implies a corresponding increase in the numbers of people employed in it, earning their living, constituting groups, subgroups and counter-groups within it, defending their personal, collective, professional or departmental interests against others and identifying with the state apparatus as a whole in confronting those outside of it. Moreover, beyond the formal confines of the state bureaucracy, other groups have emerged, tightly bound to it for the legal protection of their position, for subsidies and for political support, contributing in exchange their services, their expertise, authority and loyalty, and all the time striving to improve their position in relation to that of other groups. They are the professional and semi-professional cohorts that function in alliance with the central state, never entirely dependent, never entirely reliable, yet for maintaining and advancing their position completely oriented to it.

All these groups may be studied from a common twofold perspective – considering them in their special relationship to the state, and as the holders of a special resource, expertise. Whether these two conditions make them into a 'class' or a 'social layer', a 'category' or a 'fragment' of something else, is not the issue here. There are significant differences among them and their common characteristics mark them off only gradually from other groupings in society. What matters for our purpose is how these groups emerged in the process of state formation and how they in turn contributed to the collectivization of care.

3.1 Professionalization and the advent of the expert regimes

Educators, doctors and nurses, social workers and administrators all perform expert services for their students, patients and clients. In doing so, they engage in direct encounters with their clientele. These immediate client–expert relations are embedded in a double context: of connections with the profession and with the state.[32] The state and their particular profession provide these experts with the remedies and resources to apply at any given moment. But they also impose often conflicting demands. Thus, for example, social workers are professionally committed to secrecy and required by state agencies to provide information. In resolving such contradictions from one day to another, helping professionals dispose of a considerable, but varying, measure of discretion.

State-related experts function with two constituencies, the profession and the state, and with a third – virtual – constituency formed by their actual and potential clientele. It is typical of the development of modern states that this third constituency has remained largely virtual: the sick, the needy, the ignorant have been constituted by the state, the labor market and the professions into well-defined categories of patients, clients and students, but they have only rarely organized themselves apart from this clientele relation into relatively autonomous constituencies of their own. University students have been most successful in setting up their own organizations and these have indeed confronted the teaching body and the state. Here and there, specific patient groups have organized, but even in the definition of their membership they have reflected the categories of the medical profession and often they have turned out to be supporters' groups for the claims these professionals make upon the state. This applies to parents' associations and teachers, patient organizations and doctors, neighborhood groups and community organizers. Social-security and welfare clients have been notoriously passive in making themselves heard and depend almost entirely on unions and political parties to articulate their demands, aggregated within much more general programs.[33] Thus, the clientele of the state-related experts has remained mostly a virtual constituency, defined by professionals, bureaucrats and politicians, evoked by them as part of their advocacy, but almost always quoted, rarely speaking directly, a class not 'for itself' but 'for others'.

In this manner, the clients' needs and interests have been defined for them; curricula, therapies and programs have been scheduled before-hand by the organized professions and the state, leaving it to the state-related experts to fit them into such schemes with a due measure of discretion and flexibility. That is their management task.

In the course of the past century, teaching, healing and helping have become almost exclusively the province of highly organized groups within the state and at its periphery. The avenue into their ranks is through formal education, by means of cultural capital accumulated during a long march through the teaching institutions which originated in an earlier wave of collectivization and state regulation. The resources of these experts consist in formally recognized knowledge, made certifiable and interchangeable through diplomas.

Early in the nineteenth century, at a time that central governments were intervening to dissolve guilds and disband 'coalitions' of craftsmen, traders and, especially, workers, a new state-related group monopoly was being created: in elementary education – a field which hitherto had been almost exclusively the province of the church. The struggle of metropolitan circles of entrepreneurs and officials against the regional elites of aristocracy and church had gradually drawn the state into the field of elementary schooling. Before too long, this resulted in the central imposition of standards for the curriculum, the schools and the teachers.

Having set the norms, the state was held to enforce them and this compelled it to provide the resources to implement its own standards. By requiring certification of teachers, the central government was drawn into setting up normal schools and then setting salaries such that the alumni would actually choose a teaching career, and, next, making sure that school boards could afford to pay them. The complement of this policy was the exclusion of unqualified teachers from the schools. This, in turn, meant pressuring school boards to reject or to fire incapable employees which they had hoped to keep off the poor rolls by providing them with a living as schoolteachers. This interference, too, had to be paid for: in grants.

The result was the formation of a teaching body of quite homogeneous social extraction, education and, insofar as they served in the public-school system, similar outlook. In those countries where denominational school systems developed, parallel teachers' battalions were drafted, quite similar in social background and in training, but with a clearly distinct worldview. But all teachers shared a pedagogic sense of mission and an educational *esprit de corps*. As the century progressed more and more of them came into the direct or indirect pay of the state.

School teaching had been a lowly occupation, but the great struggles over education did much to raise the prestige of the schools and the teachers, while the ensuing involvement of the state greatly improved material conditions. As a result, by mid-century a teaching career had become an attractive prospect for many clever working-class children and at least a palatable alternative for the sons of the independent petty bourgeoisie.[34] Equally important, with the material improvement of education and the rise in its standing, school teaching became an honorable occupation for middle-class girls, for some time almost the only one, until similar developments in hospitals and philanthropic institutions also paved the way for women to earn a dignified living as nurses and visitors to the poor.

One major effect of the struggles over education was a constant and pervasive campaign to persuade children to attend, mothers to send them to school, fathers to relieve them from productive chores and employers to let them go to school. As school attendance increased, the prevalent notions of competence began to change, from something acquired and proven in the tasks and pleasures of everyday domestic and working life to something to be mastered only in special institutions under specialist guidance and certified through a formal document. Having persuaded so many of the desirability of schooling, the schoolmen finally succeeded in making it indispensable for everyone: the emergence of illiteracy as a new category of deficiency, as a residue of ignorance, signified the final victory of literacy. Universal elementary education created residual problem categories of 'unteachables', 'unreachables', and 'school leavers' which in this century became the object of intervention by specialized pedagogic experts.

Thus, the educationalist movement, aided by the state and with the teachers as its infantry, 'established an *educational regime* over the population. No one could do without education anymore – it alone could provide valid, that is certified and recognized, knowledge. The better part of childhood and adolescence were to be spent under the direct control of the school, while domestic life had to adapt to its daily and seasonal schedules and standards of cleanliness, dress and speech.

Only in one respect were the teachers less than successful: in gaining autonomy of control over teaching practice, the curriculum and admission to the occupation. They never achieved the relative autonomy of such professions as law and medicine. The reasons are threefold: their expertise did not appear sufficiently esoteric – it was precisely the common denominator that all the elites had mastered. Second, teachers as an occupational group had no alternative to employment in the school system: whatever private practice existed quickly disappeared with the advent of state-aided education. They could never threaten, as doctors could, to desert institutional employment for independent practice in a free market. Finally, the school system in its entirety is a hierarchy from nursery to university and schoolmasters could rise in it individually, rather than having to close ranks as an occupation and strive for collective status improvement.

An academic pedagogic profession does exist, but teachers are not the practicians, but its students and clients. In the interstices between the canons of pedagogy and the official curriculum, teachers may find a measure of individual discretion. Accordingly, activist teachers strive to increase their prestige and autonomy by pitching the precepts of progressive pedagogy against the demands of the formal program.

Teachers from early on, and by sheer force of numbers, have constituted the basis of the new salariat.[35] Moreover, they gained control of the routine allocation of cultural capital on which the new middle classes depended for social advancement.

Formal education increasingly provided access to careers within the expanding state apparatus itself. Civil servants became another major formation within the wage-dependent middle classes. Both local and central government administration have grown enormously in the past 150 years,[36] providing succeeding cohorts with the opportunity of a civil-service career, which for the rank and file meant above all security, some prestige and a chance of promotion.[37] Nineteenth-century government has been called 'the poor relief of the aristocracy', but in one country after another, inherited rank or political favor were abandoned for meritocratic employment and advancement systems.[38] As a result, young men from the ranks of the old middle classes who had passed their exams could find stable and honorable employment with the civil service and enter the new middle class as state-related experts.

Although employees in the state bureaucracy formally possess little discretion, some expert groups developed a high degree of autonomy within the government hierarchy: the corps of engineers, for example, or the budgetary and accounting agencies, all of them staffed with specialists who brought a sense of professionalism and *esprit de corps* to their office. Conflicts of interest or opinion, however, are usually fought out outside the public arena and the semblance of hierarchical decision-making is carefully kept up for the outside world. But, of course, all civil servants operate as entrepreneurs within their bureaucratic context, managing to maintain a measure of discretion and to extend it beyond the formal confines of their office, while their superiors, in turn, will strive to increase the autonomy of the department consigned to them. These pressures within the administration for discretion and autonomy, and for increase in size, on the one hand make for a dynamics of overall expansion and on the other hand reduce the manageability of the state apparatus for the political regime which is nominally in control.

Unlike the relations between the teaching body and its pupils, direct encounters between the central state administration and the public are mostly brief, formal and restricted to specific government agencies. The police, being the most present and visible in everyday life, may have equalled the teaching body as a formative agency during some periods and for some social strata, especially the nineteenth-century urban poor. A police regimen of varying density extends over the population, lightly and hardly perceived in ordinary life, quite intense in the regulation of crowds or modern traffic, and turning into a total regime for convicted transgressors or for the citizens of a police state.

In countries with a conscript army, the military exert a comparable influence, more briefly and more intensely, over adolescent males during their years of service under a total 'military regime'. Maybe the most pervasive official presence in adult, middle-class life by now is the revenue service, not so much on account of the taxes it imposes, but through the constant self-monitoring it requires from the taxpayer who is to create a paper shadow of all his transactions so as to reinterpret them for deduction intended or unintended by fiscal law.[39]

For present purposes the administration of social security and assistance is of special interest. The collection of millions of contributions every week or month, and the management of funds comprising billions of dollars and of liabilities running into hundreds of billions, has become a quite straightforward and routine affair for modern bureaucracy, requiring relatively little personnel and causing surprisingly little conflict or corruption.[40] Social-security dues are usually levied as payroll taxes, without the contribuant having to do, or even to understand, anything about it. Management of the funds is a highly technical matter carried on entirely by specialists.

The day-to-day contacts with welfare claimants and social-security beneficiaries are relegated to separate services, and appeal from their decisions is again entrusted to specialist agencies. It is through such encounters that the welfare state manifests itself in the lives of its citizens, and it is there that its formative effect is directly being realized. At these intersections between the sphere of the state and the lives of individual citizens, expert groups have come to occupy monopolistic mediating positions.[41] When no completely unambiguous and certifiable fact is sufficient condition for disbursement, bureaucracies must face contention and claimants find themselves pressed to present their case as convincingly as possible: the interaction transcends the limits (or rather the ideals) of administration and enters the sphere of negotiation. Once reliable birth records were kept, old-age insurance was blessedly free of the demand to establish entitlement, proof of age being sufficient. Survivors' pension schemes have also relied on public records alone. But all other benefits require more subtle proof of eligibility and in due time entitlement must be re-established. This is the task of the social workers and public-relief officials, experts on indigence, who mediate between disbursing agencies and their clients. When benefits are means tested, and even more so when they impose some standard of proper comportment, clients are under scrutiny and pressure to ensure their continuing entitlement. In other cases, or even at the same time, welfare workers are involved in reforming their clients' behavior, helping them to qualify for benefits and advocating their claims. All these interventions together constitute the welfare regime, which affects the beneficiaries of the welfare state in varying degrees and imperceptibly shades off into the total regimes of rehabilitational and custodial institutions – in older terms: from 'outdoor relief' to 'indoor relief'.

From early on, doctors and lawyers were involved in this welfare regime: accident-compensation suits required medical men to offer testimony as to the cause, nature and prognosis of the injury, and lawyers were to carry on the often tortuous suits, which were finally decided by judges. Although, subsequently, disability-insurance law abolished the requirement to establish legal guilt, the need for medical expertise increased as the grounds for disbursement were widened. Health insurance next drew doctors into mediating positions tooth and nail. Jurists remained out of the front line, limiting themselves to designing the regulations beforehand and dealing with particular cases only on appeal. But whenever the claimant's physical condition, and more and more his mental state also, was even remotely at issue, doctors were called upon to decide. And increasingly they set the terms for allocation of benefits in the modern welfare state.

In order to trace more precisely the figuration in which these professionals have mediated between the state and its clients, it is useful to analyze in some detail the struggle for establishment carried on by doctors in the course of the formation of the welfare state.

3.2   The reluctant imperialism of the medical profession

The medical profession owes its position in contemporary society to its struggle for establishment and to three related developments: the emergence of medical hospitals as scientific training and treatment institutions out of the asylums and poorhouses of the past; the establishment of public-health services for the prevention and treatment of contagious diseases and other afflictions associated with urban poverty; and, finally, the emergence of a mass market for medical services financed by transfer capital in the form of social security, social assistance and health insurance. These processes created the conditions for a vast expansion of medical practice and research. But even before the great discoveries in medicine had been made, and before social insurance and sanitary services had been established, medical doctors had begun to organize. By the middle nineteenth century leading practitioners and university professors were seeking to regulate access into the profession, to exclude unqualified practitioners, to set tariffs and to seek state legislation to enforce their regulations.[42] The universities and the teaching hospitals formed the center of this movement, and the referral system among bona-fide colleagues represented a powerful mechanism for maintaining unity in the ranks. The prestige of medicine was enormously increased by the advances in medical knowledge that began during the last quarter of the nineteenth century. The new remedies afforded the doctors additional possibilities of treatment, especially in individual practice. As a result an earlier orientation towards collective arrangements of prevention and sanitary inspection shifted back toward a preference for independent curative practice in a free market.[43] But doctors remained divided and ambivalent about these options. Collectivization of health care represented on the whole a low-risk, low-profit strategy: employment and a steady demand for medical services seemed assured under a national-health scheme, but incomes would be limited and professional autonomy was likely to be restricted. A free market of medical services, on the other hand, might well yield high profits for a few prestigious practitioners, but it might also leave the less successful with a meager income from a back alley or country practice.[44] Independent practice would allow greater autonomy and a fuller realization of professional ideals, except one: equal treatment of the indigent, which seemed better assured by collective arrangements.

The medical profession was thus confronted with a dilemma which individual doctors solved in their own way, as did organized groups in different periods and in different societies. Much depended on the actual conditions of the market for medical services, the supply of young doctors, the effective demand among the public, and much depended on earlier experiences with collective arrangements such as mutual societies and clubs for the sick.[45]

The position of the profession was very much shaped by the elites that dominated organized medicine: leading practitioners tended to favor self-employment in a free market, while the supporters of collective arrangements could be found among university professors and the administrators of public hospitals or public-health services. Of course, political persuasion played a major role, although it may often have correlated with a doctor's position in society.[46]

As a result, the position of the medical profession within the welfare state varies from country to country, and variation among national systems in this respect is greater than in almost any other.[47] Yet the influence of professional medicine was enormously extended everywhere, and along similar lines. Everywhere, also, the medical profession achieved a degree of autonomy unparalleled by any other occupational group.[48]

One might construct a continuum of increasingly collectivized medicine. The United States system of health care would be at one end. Even there, Medicare and Medicaid represent huge and expanding nationwide collective arrangements under state control and the Blue Cross and Blue Shield schemes are voluntary, 'semi-public' arrangements, carried by a coalition of professional organizations and state administrations.[49] Company and union medical insurance provide a third form of collective coverage, which, while being nominally private, is also only nominally voluntary.

Next on this continuum would appear the French system, with its sacrosanct *entente directe*: the unmediated agreement between doctor and patient. In fact, a system of national-health insurance and voluntary additional coverage in 'mutual societies' has introduced strong third-party control and an overriding role for the government. In Germany and the Netherlands, doctors are nominally self-employed and independent, but the system of contracting with government-controlled sick funds has eroded much of this autonomy in exchange for greater economic security. Britain, finally, with its encompassing national-health system would represent the most collectivized health-care system, but even there, doctors do not receive fixed salaries or maintain nominal independence. Only in socialist countries is the health-care system run as direct government bureaucracy.

The medicalization of society was not just an automatic outcome of the growth of scientific medical knowledge. Other mechanisms were at work. Medical doctors increasingly became involved in a specific brand of conflict resolution.[50] They succeeded in gaining power of definition and power of allocation: the power to assign categorical status and scarce resources to individuals involved in contested situations.

To this day, individual doctors strive to increase their social chances of income, prestige and the realization of occupational ideals. In this respect they are no different from others, although the realization of occupational ideals is reserved to the highly skilled and relatively autonomous occupations.

Doctors, on their own or in specialized groups, are continually trying out new remedies, devising new definitions of sickness and advancing new ideals of medical care.[51] In doing so, they sometimes succeed in devising a medical definition for a condition which has hitherto been perceived in terms of moral, or rather social, conflict and handled accordingly.[52] Thus, by the turn of the century, sexual nonconformity had been redefined by medical men as a suitable case for treatment. Women's troubles in the family were approached as medical problems of the reproductive organs, or as another kind of disease, 'hysteria'. The lingering complaints of accident or war victims were no longer always treated as cases of simulation, but sometimes as 'post-traumatic neurosis'. But in all these cases there was explicit or implicit social conflict: a clash between sexual preference and moral or legal norms, a wife's failure to perform according to her husband's expectations, a worker failing to satisfy his employer's demands. Doctors, moreover, confronted highly contested issues such as prostitution in terms of the prevention of venereal disease, and rephrased the equally controversial questions of birth-control and abortion in medical terms of maternal health and the viability of the foetus.

Conclusion

With the advent of health insurance and sick pay especially, it fell upon doctors to decide in which cases absence from work was justified. This meant an extension of medical intervention into the day-to-day relations between workers and management, in which very many conflicts about labor discipline would be carefully couched in medical terms. The most widespread form of the medicalization of discontent was the permitted absence from work in the guise of sick leave.

Medical experts – and psychologists who emulated the medical model – became instrumental in screening candidates for jobs, in deciding who was to be drafted for military service and who would go free, or whether a suspect should stand trial, and whether a convict should go to jail or ought to be sentenced to psychiatric treatment. Doctors, again, decided who was to be admitted to accident, life and mortgage insurance, and on what terms. As the state was increasingly drawn into the distribution of scarce goods, 'medical advice' qualified a citizen for priority in housing, for special provisions, even for private parking spots. Often, social workers prepared the case, referring controversial clients for medical advice, which usually turned out to be decisive, unless it came to administrative appeal and legal proceedings, and even then medical testimony might decide.

The assignment of categorical status and the allocation of scarce goods by doctors using a vocabulary of medical justification is a form of conflict resolution – a major, but latent, function of medicine in modern societies.[53] These interventions have not been simply imposed upon people by the state apparatus or the ruling class, nor did the medical profession just arrogate this function to itself.[54] Doctors may have taken the initiative sometimes, but they have always operated in tacit collusion with the parties in the conflict. The weakest party, say an individual worker, stood to gain by having his or her demands redefined as medical necessities. In this manner, the claims were objectified, but at the same time individualized, reduced to the specific and well-demarcated problem of this specific employee. This limitation of the dispute might prompt the strongest party, e.g. management, to accept a medical resolution of the conflict, so as to guarantee its social isolation.[55] Medicalization of the contested issue automatically resulted in a state of exception. Even if the exception concerned hundreds of thousands, or even millions, medicalization ensured that they all remained separate cases, never combining to constitute a party in a wider social conflict. Even when 5 per cent, or 10 per cent of the working force was medically defined as disabled, this did not reflect upon prevailing working conditions, but referred to individual deficiencies only. Medical diagnoses, no matter how many, never added up to a social critique. The gain for the third in this league, the doctor, came from the chances for prestige, income and the realization of occupational ideals.

Parties involved in conflict often sought a medical solution to their predicament. The successful reformulation of their dispute in technical-scientific terms already presupposed a certain measure of familiarity on their part with the basic notions and fundamental stances of the medical profession: a certain degree of proto-professionalization, which was itself an external effect of the professionalization of medicine upon widening circles of laymen.[56]

All these triangular collusions between opposing parties and doctors occurred in separate episodes, without those involved being aware of the effect of their strategies of conflict control in the long term and in a broader context. In due time, however, the academic and organizational elites in the medical profession were confronted with the accumulated effects of incidental medical intervention. What had gradually become the generally known and accepted practice of individual doctors and separate groupings of doctors in the end required the articulation of a general policy for the profession. But once these socially contested issues became a topic for discussion within the medical profession, almost inevitably problems of legitimation occurred. Whenever the emerging practices could not be fully justified in terms of a consensus of medical knowledge, as many different opinions would appear within the bosom of the profession as existed within the population at large. Such conflicts within the medical profession sprang up about the issues of abortion, birth control, prostitution and homosexuality. They also occurred when the long-term consequences of industrial accidents or of war injuries were at issue, or when some doctors engaged in health screening for insurance and job recruitment, or when others became involved in the prescription of addictive drugs or the treatment of addicts, in the guidance of suicides or the euthanasia of terminal patients. The very social conflicts that had been veiled by medicalization threatened to burst into the open within the medical profession itself. But the power base of the profession rested upon consensus within the ranks, its authority was grounded in unanimity about the canons of scientific medicine. When the medical regime expanded into aspects of life where medical expertise was insufficient to justify its precepts, opposing worldviews within the profession risked coming into open conflict. This division would erode the bargaining position of the medical elites in their dealings with the state and state-related agencies. The extension of the medical regime beyond the confines of its scientific legitimacy also affected the authority of the medical corps towards outsiders. It exposed their exercise of medical competence to public scrutiny and political debate, precisely on those issues wherein the profession was vulnerable by definition, as its policies could not be fully justified on the grounds of medical expertise, the only base of legitimacy for its exercise of power.

In fact, the profession in its entirety has often been hesitant to expand its empire when opportunity seemed to beckon. It is at this aggregate level that problems of maintaining consensus and authority arise, threatening the medical profession as a whole. This concern with their legitimation explains the reluctance of the managerial and academic elites to extend the medical regime into ever further fields.[57] The fact that it did nevertheless expand was in part the unintended and combined result of a series of interventions by individual doctors in social conflicts in tacit collusion with the parties involved. Company and insurance doctors, general practitioners and psychiatrists were mostly heavily involved in the manifold forms of medical conflict resolution, and they were among the least prestigious in the medical profession. Yet, through their efforts mostly, the medical regime has been extended far beyond the limits of nineteenth-century practice.

Other causes, more intrinsic to scientific medicine, have also operated to expand the medical regime in contemporary societies. The practice of mass screenings for contagious disease confronted all citizens with medical procedures. The development of increasingly refined techniques for the detection of early-warning signs of disease brought growing numbers of people – healthy to all appearances – to the consulting room. By now there remain only patients and those not yet patients. They all try to heed the doctor's advice to slim and stay fit, refrain from smoking and choose their diet from a dwindling medically approved menu. And again, enterprising doctors go far beyond the professional consensus in prescribing proper ways of life, diets and regimens for docile proto-patients.[58]

If the medical regime in its light and extended form has become the most important source of guidance in contemporary everyday life, the total institutional form has equally expanded: chronic and degenerative diseases require extended hospitalization, while an aging population supplies a growing number of inmates for nursing homes. The collectivization of sickness and old-age provision has facilitated the financing of these forms of institutional care, and the institutionalization of disability and old age has again reinforced the expansion of the medical regime. In many respects doctors have become the arbitrators of social conflict, the arbiters of social standards in a society in which other sources of moral consensus have largely disappeared.[59] Other professions have tried to emulate this medical model, but even they must accept the competence of the medical profession to decide the limits of their competence.

The medical regime in the first place, the educational, welfare, and even the police, military and fiscal regimes constitute a social context in which people articulate their experiences and manage their interactions with one another. It is in this sense that the expert regimes are formative for the mentality of citizens in the welfare state.

4 The collectivizing and the civilizing process

The collectivization of the arrangements for coping with adversity and deficiency has altered the conditions of everyday existence. In the context of this collectivizing process, the emergence of expert regimes has affected the basic stances and concepts with which people handle their day-to-day interaction and experience. These changes may be approached at three different levels: (1) the cognitive impact of professionalization upon lay outsiders: protoprofessionalization; (2) the civilizing effect of the collectivization of care upon the management of affect; (3) the transition from charitable feeling to social consciousness.

4.1 Professionalization and protoprofessionalization

Doctors, social workers, lawyers, psychologists and their like are engaged in a continuous formative and informative practice. They provide their patients and clients with facts, explanation and advice. Some of them also write books for a general audience, publish in popular journals or newspapers, or appear on radio and television. The gist of their message – picked up in the privacy of the consulting room or from publicity in the media – is repeated and elaborated upon in private conversations among lay people and processed into an unwritten user's manual for the helping professions. Patients and clients are the first to absorb professional notions and attitudes and to pass them on among their relatives and friends. Formal education, often implictly, as part of the 'hidden curriculum', conveys a general notion of the division of labor among the professions, of their fundamental ideas and practices.

In these ways, a simplified and censored version of professional knowledge is transmitted to clients, patients, schoolchildren and the mass audience. In the process, the citizens of the welfare state are being taught the essentials of hygiene and a limited repertory of diseases, their symptomatology and cure. They learn the essentials of taxes and benefits. They pick up some notions of criminal and civil law and of legal procedure. They adopt the notion that people may have hidden motives, even hidden to themselves and that these may be a cause of mental problems. It is this *éducation permanente* in the arts of modern citizenship that transforms people into more or less 'competent members' of contemporary society.[60] But by the same token, such knowledge is devalued by its universal availability.[61] As a result, the science of medicine and the medical profession have risen in esteem and the demand for medical services has increased accordingly.

This more calculating, more foresighted stance towards the body has its counterpart in similar stances toward the psyche, as an object that must be cared for, if need be by specialists, by psychologists, psychotherapists and psychiatrists. And a comparable attitude emerges with respect to the relations between human beings. Here too, legal and psychological expertise concur in conveying a more detached approach. Rather than throwing themselves into a conflict and fighting it out, people increasingly tend to look at it with some mental distance. They tend to define their own and their opponents' position in general, formal terms and refer to abstract rules of more encompassing validity. Not only will they try to control their passions, they may even abstract from what they themselves consider right or wrong in order to find the practical rules with which to manage the controversy. In seeking these more detached stances towards their own body, their affects or to other human beings, they tend to apply – implicitly or explicitly – the basic stances and notions they ascribe to the relevant professions.

In all these respects people increasingly orient themselves in everyday life to the fundamental notions and stances of the professions and they adopt corresponding standards of behavior. They do not themselves become professionals, but rather professionals *in nuce*: protoprofessionals. This protoprofessionalization, as the process of medicalization, psychologization, juridicalization, and fiscalization of everyday life may be called, is the external effect of the process of professionalization. It extends to ever-widening circles of laymen; it is transferred by the clients of the professions, in the 'hidden curriculum' of formal education, and increasingly through the mass media which adopt the professional division of labor as an editorial categorization of human affairs.

No doubt, the degree of protoprofessionalization which prevails in someone's personal network facilitates his or her access to professional services. Well-informed lay persons will articulate their troubles as problems for professional treatment and seek corresponding professional service for the problems so defined.[62] Professional helpers, in turn, will

245

be more inclined to accept the clients who in their perception clearly present problems for which they feel competent.

This conceptualization helps to avoid some obvious pitfalls. First of all, professionals do not simply force themselves upon innocent and unknowing clients or 'client-systems' – such persons or families usually have long since learned to define what bothers them in terms of some available protoprofessional vocabulary. Second, the supply of professional services does increase the demand for them, since obviously the smaller the social distance from such professional help, the more people will tend to define what troubles them in the relevant protoprofessional terms. And, as has been argued before, the supply of expert services may increase the manifest and articulate demand, but it does not create the suffering. Things went wrong before there were expert helpers – since their advent they go wrong differently. People redefine their own troubles in terms they have borrowed from the professional vocabulary, while at the same time retaining all sorts of other vocabularies current in society. Professional assistance is just one option which they may pursue among the many strategies their environment affords them.

Protoprofessionalization is an aspect and a phase of the rationalization of everyday life. In this respect it is very much related to a more general development, that of the civilizing process.

4.2   The collectivizing and the civilizing process

The collectivization of arrangements for coping with adversity and deficiency has changed the ways in which people manage their emotions and handle their relations with others. On the whole, these changes have gone in the direction of greater, and also more subtle and flexible, emotional controls and an increasing consideration of the consequences of one's actions for others and for one's own future.

In this respect, the collectivization in education, health care and income maintenance has affected workers, peasants and poor people more than the higher strata in society, who may have helped initiate these arrangements, but have alternative resources to rely on for coping with the adversities and deficiencies in their own existence.

Accordingly, changes in affect management and modes of conduct which had come about in earlier stages of history among the aristocratic and bourgeois strata of society have occurred in the past century along similar lines among the working class. The collectivizing process has extended the civilizing process to the lower strata of society.

The process of civilization has been analyzed by Norbert Elias for European society since the late Middle Ages.[63] His foremost concern was with the feudal elites, the courtly society and the 'professional bourgeoisie'. In his view, competition among social groups within increasingly dense and complex networks of interdependence compelled their members to adopt stricter standards of affect control, also in order to withstand 'the pressure from below'.[64] In his 'synopsis' of the theory of the civilizing process, Elias comments on the developments in the lower strata of society:[65]

> To an increasing degree, the complex functioning of Western societies, with their high division of labour, depends on the lower agrarian and urban strata controlling their conduct increasingly through insight into its more long-term and more remote connections. These strata cease to be merely 'lower' social strata. The highly differentiated social apparatus becomes so complex, and in some respects so vulnerable, that disturbances at one point of the interdependency chains which pass through all social positions inevitably affect many others, thus threatening the whole social tissue.

Clearly, the civilizing process, like the collectivizing process, is immediately connected to the growing interdependence of human beings, or to the extending and intensifying 'external effects' of their actions upon others. And in its most recent phase, the civilizing process increasingly affects the working classes also.[66]

What Elias calls 'the pressures for foresight and self-constraint' is reminiscent of the ideals of 'providence' and 'decency' which the nineteenth-century philanthropists wished to impress upon the poor and working classes in their society. It is 'usually under heavy social pressure' that members of the lower classes come to restrain their momentary affects and to discipline their conduct. It is not just willing acceptance of the pressure exerted consciously by priests, or later by philanthropists and finally by social administrators that brings about these changes, as an earlier and 'naïve' generation of historians and students of social policy would have it.[67] Nor can these lower-class clients be considered the dupes of a bureaucratic-professional conspiracy to rob them of their independent capacity to deal with their own lives, as later cohorts of sociologists and social historians have contended. A more self-conscious and critical generation of authors in the wake of Illich and Lasch, Foucault and Donzelot, has described changes in working-class mentality as the outcome of external imposition upon formerly private lives, of an alien intrusion in what was once a personal sphere.[68] Institutional care and professional service were unmasked as 'social control' and 'disciplining', as if these clients, patients, students, claimants were objects only and had themselves no active part in the process.[69] If they were not regarded as the outright victims of an inhumane bureaucracy, they were considered to be dupes who failed to see that under the guise of their 'best interests' they were being made to conform to a 'hidden agenda', stealthily robbed of their autonomous competence in their own, everyday environment.

In fact, the process is much better understood as one of interaction, of contest and collaboration, collusion and duplicity, between bureaucrats and experts on one (not always the same) side, and their clients on the other hand. Lower-class clients, schoolchildren or patients were engaged in the process as actively as their professional counterparts and neither foresaw nor controlled the outcome. And, for the lower classes, the balance of satisfaction and discontent in the civilizing process is as hard to assess as it is for the other strata of society that went through it.

The constraints upon affective and impulsive behavior were not just imposed from the outside, but also adopted. In Norbert Elias's term they became social constraints to self-constraint and finally self-constraints experienced as *ich-gerecht*, egosyntonic, experienced as part and parcel of one's person.

From very early on alms were given on condition that the poor comported themselves decently, but there were few controls upon their day-to-day behavior. In the early modern poorhouses such attempts were first made in systematic fashion and even there the regime was too punitive and too irregular to exact much more than token compliance from the inmates.

Mass elementary education, for the first time, provided a setting in which children were exposed to the pressures toward self-constraint and foresight for a prolonged time and within a tightly controlled environment. The very effort of imparting and mastering a standardized version of the language, of reading and writing, implies an attempt to rule out deviant, local, idiosyncratic habits and turns of speech. Probably, the complete schoolchild was the one who succeeded in shifting subtly from family and village codes of behavior and speech to school and national modes, whenever he or she believed that the situation required one or the other, i.e. whenever he or she believed one or the other to be the most suitable. None of these exacting skills was immediately gratifying to young children; they all demanded an orientation to a remote future in which they might one day turn out to be of use. The school was, as its proponents contended, a civilizing institution *par excellence*. And it performed its function as much through its manifest teachings as through the 'hidden curriculum' which imposed strict control of movement and bodily functions,[70] the mastery of precise forms of pronunciation and meticulous hand movements in writing, the submission to a rigid time schedule, and the orientation towards a future that must have seemed very remote indeed. Factory discipline for adult workers must have seemed less exacting in comparison. Moreover, children were not simply forced to go to school, they were also pressured into wanting to attend and they gradually learned how to bargain with adults in a position of authority about the small margins of acceptable deviance. And all the time, they also stood to gain from the experience. Gradually, the external constraints toward self-constraint turned into self-imposed constraints – a 'second nature'.

The nineteenth-century campaigns for urban sanitation and the large-scale construction of working-class housing compelled workers to conform to more exacting standards of cleanliness and appearance, while permitting them a relatively shielded space in which to create the intimacy of domestic life. Family scenes could be hidden from outsiders and staged for visitors. Bodily grooming or defecation occurred in solitude behind walls, and walls hid parental intimacy from children.[71] As social constraints imposed standards of intimacy and privacy, social policies helped working-class parents and children to maintain those standards in domestic life and internalize them in their personality formation.

Elias writes:[72] 'No less characteristic of a civilizing process than "rationalization" is the peculiar molding of the drive economy that we call "shame" and "repugnance" or "embarrassment".' Nineteenth-century urban policies have contributed to the material conditions for this 'lowering of the shame threshold' among the working class.

Nowhere was the interplay between social constraints toward self-constraint more visible than in the reciprocal pressures that the members of workers' mutual societies exerted upon one another and upon themselves. In these Friendly Societies, the more exacting standards of conduct functioned not only to assimilate their members to the next higher strata in society, such as independent craftsmen and shopkeepers, but also to maintain a social distance toward the lower ranks. They served to ward off the 'pressures from below' exerted by the casual workers and paupers who all too often refused to acknowledge any difference in standing which might anyway be undone with a few weeks of unemployment. The actuarial calculus which prompted the Friendly Societies to seek the membership of the better off and to exclude the worse off, closely paralleled a status calculus which made their members emulate the standards of their 'betters' and increase the distance from their 'inferiors'.

But the main function of these mutual funds was to provide a collective alternative to private saving. The propensity to save epitomizes the tendency to 'subordinate momentary affects to more distant goals', the orientation to a more distant future, constant self-constraint and the deferral of gratification. It was the paramount virtue of the 'professional bourgeoisie'. And in the Friendly Societies workers compelled one another to restrain their spending, just as bourgeois families had compelled their members from early childhood on to save for the future. The difference was that these workers did not rely on family resources, but on peer solidarity.

For a number of reasons, discussed in previous chapters, these mutual societies were inadequate to protect the working classes and the jobless poor against income loss. Compulsory, nationwide accumulation of transfer capital under state control became the functional alternative to private and collective saving. Social-security contributions were levied in the form of payroll taxes, under external constraint. In this respect, social compulsion has not been superseded by more internalized controls. On the contrary, an increasing range of arrangements to provide for future adversity have been imposed with state compulsion. Such arrangements have come to include the wage-earning middle cadre, compelling them to accumulate collectively, where the self-employed middle classes had accumulated individually under self-constraint.

Two related developments appear to be interacting at this point. On the other hand, this financial orientation towards the future is imposed by compulsory insurance schemes. On the other hand, modern citizens display an increased 'risk aversion': they are increasingly willing to forgo present income so as to avoid the risk of adversity in the future.

This gradual increase in the desire for financial security occurred also among workers who in earlier periods were believed to be improvident and not to care for their future. An invisible insurance had existed all along among the workers and paupers of pre-industrial society. Kin and neighborly obligations or peer solidarity helped to relieve some of the most pressing needs, even if they could rarely be counted upon. Charity and the dole, most often in kind, rescued many in times of utmost hardship. Common grounds or small vegetable plots had yielded a little food on the side. Industrialization, urbanization and a series of government measures cut off these escapes from the money economy, one after the other. Claus Offe has characterized the entire history of social policy as 'a transformation of non-wage workers (*nicht-Lohnarbeiter*) into wage-workers'; a process of 'active proletarization' which forced the expropriated, or 'passive' proletarians to offer their labor force for a wage and thus to contribute to the accumulation of surplus value.[73] It was in the course of this process that workers became entirely dependent on the money economy, on the labor market and thus on wages and also on monetary insurance. It was only then that their risk aversion was to become visible to economic historians.

Workers adopted a lifestyle and a pattern of consumption that rendered adaptation to a lower standard of life more difficult also in another sense. Backsliding of this kind began to be considered more shameful and degrading than before, whereas at one time it had been considered an unavoidable part of the vicissitudes of life. Moreover, property, especially real estate, does not fetch its true price when sold under the pressure of financial distress, much less so when the market is flooded by sellers in similar circumstances. In this manner home ownership also inspired risk aversion, and a certain *embourgeoisement* with it.

Finally, at least from marginal-utility theory, it is to be expected that poor people in general, once absorbed into the money market, should show greater risk aversion than the rich: to them adversity makes the difference between austerity and starvation, whereas for the wealthy with some property to fall back on the difference is only between comfort and austerity at worst. For all these reasons, as the money economy pervaded the whole of society, financial risk aversion increased and the demand for insurance grew also among the working class.

Risk aversion implies a subordination of momentary affects for the sake of more distant goals, as Elias would express it. Apparently, most people have come to accept this deferred gratification, without relying entirely on their capacity for self-constraint to restrain spending. Compulsory insurance thus acts as an external reinforcement of a capacity for self-constraint which is as yet not wholly taken for granted.

Social security has levelled the peaks and depths of material existence, taking away part of disposable income and adding to it in times of income loss. Momentary impulse and peer pressure to spend whatever one had whenever one had it have declined. Poor men's feasts and beggars' banquets have disappeared from modern societies, and so has fasting, self-enforced or imposed for lack of food. With the despair of starvation, the ecstasy of abundance has vanished. As the peaks and depths of material existence levelled off, emotional highs and lows were also evened out. Just as the seasonal rhythm of dishes has vanished with a constant supply of meats and greens in an era of industrialized agriculture and internationalized food trade, the succession of enforced toil and equally enforced idleness among farmhands and casual workers is making way for a perfectly predictable scheme of workdays, holidays and vacations. This equalization of life's events goes with a levelling of contrasts in the mood and behavior of individuals. Within the same process, contrasts in conduct between higher and lower groups in society are also diminishing – another dimension of the civilizing process, according to Elias. Whereas in earlier times leisure was reserved for the upper classes and work was an attribute of the lower classes, in contemporary societies every able person is expected to earn his living through regular work.[74] At present, social and labor legislation also guarantee the working classes their measured share of leisure time.

In all these respects, the collectivizing process and the civilizing process have worked in parallel, in mutually interacting ways, to shape the standards of conduct and the modes of affect-management among the working and the employed middle classes.

4.3 From charity to social consciousness

In the course of the modern era the vocabulary for discussing the issues of ignorance, poverty and disease has gradually shifted from a religious to a social idiom. No doubt, the emergence of 'scientific philanthropy' marked a turning-point in the discourse on poverty and its concomitant evils. But long before the nineteenth century, a shift occurred from religious concerns with the eternal salvation of the giver's soul to more wordly considerations of helping the needy to help themselves in this life. And all along, this changing discourse on poverty was structured by the anxieties and expectations aroused by the poor among the more established ranks of society.

In earlier times the discourse on poverty was inspired more by fear of the vagrant, alien poor, than by consideration of their potential usefulness as farmhands or servants. After all, only so many could be employed, the others had to be chased away or sent on with some alms to appease them – a matter of residual pacification. To this day, young, unemployed men are feared as potential criminals or rebels. Con-temporary social scientists, by explaining 'social problems' such as crime, vandalism or drug abuse in terms of the underlying economic and social deprivation, implicitly continue a tradition of warning the established that the poor may threaten their security, *if* conditions are not improved. The warning is delivered, not with religious invocation or moral exhortation, but with the 'rhetoric of induction'[75] which characterizes the genre. In the present era, in which 'full employment' did prevail for a long time and employment for every able person is still conceivable, the valid poor are considered to be useful in principle, if not in fact, and their idleness to be social waste. Thus, these 'marginal groups' represent not only danger, but also opportunity, and more so than in earlier times: not only as a reserve army of workers, but also as a 'segment of the consumer market', a cohort to be recruited, and a 'vote' to be wooed.

The discourse on poverty has been transformed in another respect also. Notwithstanding Christian teaching about the equality of all men, this notion remained mostly a spiritual insight: 'There but for the grace of God, go I'. The difference between paupers on the one hand and established farmers or citizens, let alone noblemen, was felt to be enormous, as if different species were concerned. Gradually, the idea has taken hold that people are shaped by social circumstance and that the poor under more favorable conditions would have been much similar to the better off. 'There, but for the grace of class reproduction and vertical mobility, go I.'

But the scope of the discourse has changed most of all. Medieval charitable teaching was concerned with the immediate encounter between a Christian believer and a poor soul. In the course of time, people began to think of the poor as a more general and remote category. They came to be concerned about conditions that prevailed not just under their very eyes, but also elsewhere, in another part of town, in a distant region of the nation or even far away in the periphery of the modern world.

These shifts in the discourse and in attitudes about the poor may be explained by the 'generalization of interdependence' in society. With the lengthening and strengthening of the chains of interdependence went an increasing awareness of these interdependencies among the people who were so linked together. The learning process occurred through wars, epidemics, famines, revolutions and economic crises. But there were also the more gradual lessons to be learned from the workings of the market and the division of labor or from the functioning of the state and its network of agents. The moral economists and social thinkers who succeeded them interpreted events in terms of chains of human action and thus helped to provide means of orientation in terms of social interdependencies.

This awareness of the increasingly intensive and extensive chains of interdependence, coupled to a willingness to contribute to remedies for the adversities and deficiencies that affect others, may be called 'social consciousness'. It is, in the first place, a cognitive state. It implies an understanding of remote and long-term social consequences. It entails a sense of generalized responsibility, and the term therefore also refers to a moral stance.[76]

In his essay on 'Capitalism and the origins of the humanitarian sensibility', Thomas Haskell rejects an explanation of the anti-slavery movement in terms of the 'interests' of its adherents: 'Whatever influence the rise of capitalism may have had generally on ideas and values through the medium of class interest, it had a more telling influence on the origins of humanitarianism through changes the market wrought on *perception* or *cognitive style*.'[77] The 'market-oriented form of life', Haskell argues, rewarded and thus promoted 'a certain calculating, moderately assertive style of conduct', it also 'taught people to keep their promises' and 'to attend to the remote consequences of their actions'.[78] Haskell considers this development a stage in the civilizing process and his approach in fact 'converges with that of Elias.'[79] Norbert Elias stresses the monopolization of violence in the process of state formation and the restraints this pacification imposed upon people: only when society had been pacified to a degree that economic transactions could proceed relatively undisturbed by violent actions could a 'market-oriented form of life' develop, and Elias leaves its civilizing effects mostly implicit.

Haskell stresses the orientation to market relations, as it 'gave rise to new habits of causal attribution that set the stage for humanitarianism.'[80] It did so by convincing people that they were in fact causally involved in the suffering of indigent strangers by drawing their attention to the remote consequences of their own acts for others. Through this form of life, moreover, people had the chance of obtaining 'recipe knowledge', i.e. practical insights toward intervention. They acquired 'recipes of sufficient ordinariness, familiarity, *certainly of effect*, and facility to operate'.[81]

Accordingly, orientation towards the market increased the sense of causal involvement, of practical competence and trust in the efficacy of action. It was the cultural practice of promise-keeping, emerging with the spread of market relations, that strengthened the force of conscience in human beings, says Haskell, by 'encouraging new levels of scrupulosity in the fulfillment of ethical maxims'.[82]

Haskell's argument does explain the rise of philanthropy, of personal commitment to organized action for remedying the deficiencies and adversities of others, often remote and unknown. Notwithstanding its momentous consequences, humanitarian sensibility remained the state of mind of a – predominantly bourgeois – minority. In a subsequent phase, workers in great numbers became involved in a labor-market-oriented form of life and along similar lines to those suggested by Elias and Haskell, they developed a 'proletarian sensibility': a 'solidarity' which included their unknown and remote fellow workers.

It has been stressed before that the working classes relied more strongly on collective arrangements than the petty bourgeoisie did, but their collectivism often went together with a strong personal commitment. As voluntary organizations and voluntary funds were replaced by compulsory arrangements on a nationwide scale and under state control, this personal involvement was increasingly superseded by institutional interventions on the part of full-time administrative and professional experts.

Humanitarian and proletarian sensibilities have increasingly made way for a social consciousness: an awareness of interdependency and a sense of responsibility for the plight of others is combined with the conviction that these others ought to be helped, but not anymore by anyone in particular: 'Something ought to be done about it.' If there is misery, 'it must be taken care of' – not by the beholder, but by something else, by 'it', by the hidden subject of all these phrases in the passive mode: the state. The state is the abstract, universal and anonymous caretaker of all members of society. No one is under any immediate obligation to the stranger who may implore his aid. The modern concern for the sick and the poor beyond one's intimate circle can be more intense, because it is certain not to cost anyone too much in particular – at most a small increase in fees and taxes. And once they could afford this infinitesimal share of the collective burden, people allowed themselves to be more easily moved by the sight of suffering. The price of empathy has gone down so much that even common people can afford it.

It would be wrong to disparage this 'social consciousness' just because it is diffuse and abstract and does not impel toward direct, personal intervention, for it is not at all gratuitous. It implies the silent consent to a considerable tax-burden and to a redistribution of income which affects the vertical differences of income only slightly, but those between generations, between sexes and between the active and the non-active significantly. This social consciousness also provides a permanent and pervasive legitimation for claims for indemnification, reimbursement and assistance, the more so where the apparatus and the resources appear to be effective and available.[83]

In short, social consciousness relates to charity as transfer capital to alms and as industrial production to craftsmanship.

'The major alterations of sensibility are consequences of shifts in the conventional boundaries of responsibility', writes Haskell.[84] The most incisive shift at the present time concerns the sense of involvement with the suffering of people in 'Third World' countries: the plight of the victims of famine, war and state terrorism. Television coverage, especially, seems to have increased the awareness of their lot among Western audiences. Mass tourism has greatly contributed to it. At the

255

same time, popularized versions of social-science theories about economic imperialism and the international terms of trade have fostered among the Western public a sense of causal involvement and of the responsibility of states and corporations in the West. However, there appears to be no familiar recipe for remedying this suffering with any certainty of effect. This is what causes the sense of tragedy and impotence so widespread in the Western discourse on poverty in the world periphery.

Poor as they are, the indigent of these faraway countries seem to represent neither danger nor opportunity. Only the somewhat richer nations in the Third World can afford the military resources for limited war or international terrorism. And those are also the nations that provide most opportunity for trade and investment. Terrorism is the weapon of the weaker in the family of states, but not of the weakest. Nor is it used to instill fear of the poor or to persuade the richest nations to improve the lot of the poorest. The small elites who wield these weapons have interests of state and of their own group to defend, and these do not necessarily coincide with those of the neediest in their society.

But the technology of mass communication and air travel works both ways: people in the Third World learn about life in the West through their media and they, too, can travel. A growing stream of immigrants comes from the periphery of the modern world to the metropolises in the core regions. The rich nations may try to exclude them, but are often unable to stem the tide. They cannot permanently guard the full stretch of their frontiers. Sometimes the migrants' home governments promote their departure in hopes that it will reduce domestic unemployment and bring in hard currency from workers abroad. On the other side, in the economies of the world's core, immigrants form a pool of cheap – and often illegal – labor. While their presence is decried as a threat to public order and public funds, they are silently and readily employed in the least attractive niches of the economy.

The stream of migrants from the poorer regions to the richer does create a clear interest on the part of the core countries to try to improve living conditions in the periphery. Western states have tried at times to promote employment in the home countries of immigrants and they may continue to increase their efforts, especially if the immigrant flow is clearly bilateral and the problem of other wealthy nations profiting from the effort is minimal. But once more, this time at global level, the dilemmas of collective action appear, and once again, the problem is one of coordination among the rich.

At present, there are transnational organizations which can act to some degree as central coordinating agencies, but they dispose of even fewer resources and less authority than the absolutist states of the seventeenth century. Even though the dynamics of interdepency between rich and poor and the dilemmas of collective action among the established repeat themselves on a world scale, there is no historical necessity for the collectivizing process to proceed at a global level.

Notes

Chapter 1   Introduction

1 Cf. Elias, 1978b, pp. 128–33; Goudsblom, 1977, pp. 6–8, 126–37.
2 This is the predicament that Mancur Olson has again brought to the attention of social scientists.
3 Cf. on this theme, Esser, esp. pp. 685–6.
4 Cf. De Swaan, 1978a.
5 Cf. Baumol, p. 25: 'An externality consists of the interdependence together with the lack of accompanying compensation.' The present usage is wider than in economics: it refers to the effects not only of economic transactions, but also of other human interactions or of 'acts of nature'.
6 See, e.g., his discussion of classes, 1985, pp. 318ff., especially pp. 342–4.

Chapter 2   Local charity, regional vagrancy and national assistance

1 Sahlins, p. 37.
2 Ibid, pp. 95ff.
3 Mollat, p. 42.
4 Cf. Furet; De Pauw; Gutton, 1971.
5 Cf. title essay in De Swaan, 1982.
6 Cf. Gouldner, 1973, p. 242: 'a norm of reciprocity, in its universal form, makes two interrelated, minimal demands: (1) people should help those who have helped them, and (2) people should not injure those who have helped them.' The second condition in particular is germane here.
7 Respectively Bonenfant, p. 117, 156ff; Stekl, p. 24; Dorwart, pp. 96–7; Geremek 1974, p. 351.
8 Briod, p. 15.

9 Ibid.
10 Geremek, 1974, p. 351.
11 Geremek, 1976, p. 209; Gutton, 1971, p. 23.
12 Geremek, 1976, p. 212; Garraty, p. 28.
13 Geremek, 1976, p. 221.
14 Abbiateci; Hufton, p. 206; E. Weber, p. 16; Geremek, 1976, p. 215.
15 Beier, p. 14.
16 Küther, p. 16; cf. Hufton, pp. 202ff.
17 They had to be 'Rufflers' and 'Upright Men' as Thomas Hardon's highest orders of rogues were called; quoted in Aydelotte, p. 27.
18 Cf. Salgado, p. 91: 'For an old woman living by herself in an Elizabethan village the difference between bare survival and barely tolerable misery may only have been a handful of peas, a bag of corn, or a few eggs. A reputation for witchcraft might, within limits, be a useful way of ensuring that her neighbours did not let her go without too often.'
19 Cf. ibid., p. 87: 'The fact that they were women is only to be expected because old women and childless widows were economically and socially the most vulnerable members of a small community.'
20 Le Goff, 1964, p. 297.
21 Küther 38; for other estimates cf. Endres, pp. 223–5, Sachsse and Tennstedt, p. 102; for France: Geremek, 1974, p. 358.
22 Lis and Soly, p. 115.
23 Aydelotte; Geremek, 1976; Mollat, pp. 198–202; Salgado.
24 Sahlins, pp. 88, 194.
25 Exod. 20:17; Deut. 5:21 adds 'his field'. By then, the Jews had settled down to working the land.
26 Beier estimates that Elizabethan vagabonds walked only a few miles a day, covering an 'area' in the course of time, but never straying far from their place of origin.
27 This is the classic Marxist view, often phrased in functionalist terms.
28 See Blum for a general description of village communities in Europe after the Middle Ages, e.g. p. 541: 'The village community as a corporate body managing communal resources, directing the economic activities, and supervising the communal life of its residents first emerged in Europe during the later part of the Middle Ages and spread across the Continent in the succeeding centuries.' And p. 546: 'The community also provided welfare services for its members . . . It took care of the indigent, the sick, and orphans and sometimes appointed guardians for minors.'
29 Monasteries and seigniorial houses assembled a fixed number of the poor around them, often privileged by a relatively comfortable charity; Goglin, p. 54; Mollat, pp. 165–9.
30 St Chrysostom ordered the richest 10 per cent to care for the poorest tenth; Goglin, p. 30.
31 Mollat, p. 64; C. Bloch, pp. 125–6; Gonthier, pp. 141ff.
32 Bonenfant, p. 26; Mollat, pp. 57, 221; Goglin, p. 167.
33 Goglin, p. 33; Mollat, pp. 55, 66.

34 One-half for the clergy, a quarter for buildings and a fourth for the poor; Goglin, p. 31. But the peasants usually suspected that the tithe would enrich the high clergy most and resented it accordingly; Le Goff, p. 226; and this continued up to the Revolution: C. Jones, p. 39.

35 Troeltsch, pp. 134ff.

36 Cf. Fischer; Gutton, 1974; Gonthier; Bonenfant; Kossmann-Putto.

37 Gonthier, p. 152.

38 Fischer, p. 314 (this quotation and all others from sources not in English have been translated by the author); cf. also Sachsse and Tennstedt, pp. 63ff.

39 Fischer, p. 265.

40 Bonenfant, pp. 117, 150ff.

41 Cf. especially Axelrod. It is of interest in the present context to note that all solutions to the problem, even though staunchly reductionist, begin by defining it in terms of process, whether 'natural selection' or 'iterated games' (M. Taylor) or the spread of a particular strategy (e.g. 'tit for tat') through a population on account of its competitive advantage (Axelrod).

42 An interesting, but mostly unsuccessful, attempt along neo-Darwinian lines has been made by Boorman and Levitt.

43 See Elster, 1979, for the incompatibility of theories in terms of 'selection' and theories in terms of 'action' and 'intention'.

44 Merton, pp. 475ff.

45 For a model using expectations about the collaboration of others as a variable, cf. Bowman.

46 On village ostracism, cf. Blum, pp. 551–2.

47 Le Goff, p. 85, following W. Arthur Lewis, places the end of the European 'frontier' at the beginning of the fourteenth century.

48 Geremek, 1974, pp. 366–7; Gutton, 1974, p. 41.

49 Thus, in 1459 for the first time, the towns of Brabant, plagued by bands of discarded soldiers and tired of chasing them away to the next town, came together to petition the States of Brabant to enact an ordinance against vagrancy: the regional government consented, but proved incapable of enforcing the law; Blockmans en Prevenier, p. 533.

50 Gutton, 1974, p. 38: at times alms were distributed to poor strangers at the city gates which were then closed on them.

51 For Amsterdam, cf. Oldewelt.

52 Foucault, 1972, pp. 56ff.

53 Cf. Oxley. On private philanthropy, see Jordan; on the effects of the law in one village, cf. Wrighton and Levine, pp. 173ff.

54 Quoted in Tate, p. 163.

55 Quoted ibid. from the Preamble of the Law of 1662.

56 Oxley, p. 15.

57 Geremek, 1974, p. 365.

58 e.g. Van den Eerenbeemt, 1977, p. 149.

59 Cf. Rothman, Trattner.

60 Rothman, p. 50; Coll, p. 132.

61 Rothman, p. 50.

62 Cf. Endres, pp. 230–1; Küther, p. 15.
63 Van den Eerenbeemt, 1968, pp. 117–19; cf. also Van Loo, pp. 26ff.
64 Trattner, p. 22; cf. also Gutton, 1974, pp. 122ff.
65 Foucault, 1972, p. 70; cf. also Kingdon, p. 51, on the 'laicization and rationalization' of poor relief in Calvin's Geneva and elsewhere.
66 Martin, p. 31.
67 Cf. T. C. Schelling's discussion of 'focal-point solutions'.
68 Cf. Gutton, 1971, p. 458.
69 Cf. Martin.
70 See, e.g., Gutton's account of the vicissitudes of royal intervention in Lyons (1971) pp. 455ff, 486; cf. also C. Bloch on the *ancien régime* in France; Dorwart, pp. 94–111, on Prussia; Midwinter (1972) on early British Victorian reform; Schama, 1977, on the *Bataafse Republiek* in the Netherlands; Melief for the period 1795–1854 in that country; for America: Trattner, p. 98: 'towns that did subsist the state poor were reimbursed by colonial treasury'; cf. also pp. 38–9 on local intervention by state governments in the independent US.
71 Dupeux, p. 67.
72 Trattner, p. 22.
73 Abel, pp. 46–54.
74 Cf. Katz, 1986, p. 21, on the US in the early nineteenth century: 'Towns often spent more money ridding themselves of paupers than they would have spent supporting them. Aside from the trouble and the expense for endless litigation, the system was often cruel, for old and sick paupers were shipped from town to town, even in the middle of winter.'
75 Cf. the almost farcical account of ineptitude and opposition among local authorities in Brabant by Van den Eerenbeemt, 1968, pp. 106ff. The city of Den Bosch refused to finance measures since these might benefit the countryside also.
76 Gutton, 1971, p. 458.
77 Cf. Beloff, pp. 107, 116ff; Burg.
78 'In effect, this balance of power can be preserved only by invoking the Kantian categorical imperative: act in such a way that if everyone acted in this manner it would be in your interest.' Rapoport, p. 306. Compare, however, the present argument.
79 Olson, p. 46.
80 Ibid., p. 29.
81 Ch. Tilly, p. 440.
82 Martin, p. 32: The 'offer of the House'; cf. J. Taylor, p. 60, quoting from the Workhouse Test Act of 1723: the poor who refused to enter 'shall not be entitled to ask or receive collection or relief . . .'; cf. also Foucault, 1972, pp. 71–4.
83 Gutton, 1971, p. 435.
84 Cf. L. Koch, p. 431; Foucault, 1972, pp. 80ff; Lis and Soly, pp. 123ff; Sachsse and Tennstedt, p. 116, aptly qualify these multiple purposes as 'a functional overloading'.

85 e.g. the workhouse at Gouda (in the Netherlands) in 1854 abolished hot meals to stem the influx of valid poor (cf. Van den Eerenbeemt, 1977).
86 e.g. Charles Dickens's *Oliver Twist*, or *Little Dorritt*, Arnold Bennett's *Clayhanger*.
87 e.g. Geremek, 1974, p. 356.
88 Cf. Küther, p. 142; cf. Stekl for Austria; Ignatieff for the dismally punitive character of workhouses in mid-nineteenth-century England.
89 e.g. the 'almshouses' in the United States; cf. Coll, p. 135.
90 Cf. Oxley, p. 32; J. Taylor, p. 70.
91 Oxley, p. 85; cf. Van den Eerenbeemt, 1977, pp. 34ff. Katz, 1986, p. 24: 'Poorhouse advocates even exuded optimism about paupers' ability to produce their own food and do other useful work ... The optimism of early almshouse sponsors and administrators contradicts most reports made only a few years later.'
92 Cf. J. Taylor, p. 63.
93 Cf. ibid., p. 66.
94 Gutton, 1971, pp. 466–7.
95 Lenhardt and Offe, p. 101.
96 Rusche and Kirchheimer, p. 7; 'The houses of correction grew out of a social situation, in which the conditions of the labor market were favorable to the lower classes.'
97 However, Lis and Soly have argued that in France workhouses did serve to recruit cheap labor at a time of high demand, at least until the 1630s; for the subsequent period of slack, however, the authors consider disciplining the poor the major function of the workhouse. Lis also shows that poor relief in nineteenth-century Antwerp was reformed so as to recruit workers for the textile industry.
98 Piven and Cloward, 1972, p. 3.
99 Cf. Gutton, 1971, pp. 458ff.
100 e.g. Depauw, p. 403: the exiled poor used to hide among the Paris crowds; cf. Kaplow, pp. 129ff; cf. Dorwart, p. 111, on Prussia.
101 Foucault, 1972, p. 75. Cf. K. Koch, p. 347. Sachsse and Tennstedt, 1980, argue that – at least in Germany – workhouses were too few to regulate the labor market – they served the purpose of discipline and deterrence.
102 e.g. Coll, p. 134.
103 Wallerstein, p. 254. Cf. J. S. Taylor, p. 60: 'Proselytization came by successful example; if one enterprising parish in a region established a workhouse that reduced poor rates and relief applicants, neighbouring parishes followed suit . . .'
104 Foucault, 1975, pp. 123–30.
105 Cf. Stekl, p. 54; Lis and Soly, pp. 118ff.
106 Cf. Geremek, 1974, p. 363.
107 Cf. Küther, p. 143; Van den Eerenbeemt, 1972, pp. 51ff. Kingdon, pp. 67ff, argues for the opposite direction of diffusion.
108 Cf. Foucault, 1972, pp. 82ff; Ignatieff, *passim*.
109 'The old poor law workhouses can be seen as the ancestor of most of the

institutions which form part of the modern social services.' Oxley, p. 79.
110 Midwinter, p. 194.
111 e.g. Gutton, 1971, pp. 454ff; C. Jones, pp. 131ff.
112 Elias, 1978a, pp. 91ff, esp. p. 114.

Chapter 3 The elementary curriculum as a national communication code

1 By 1980 all over the world 74 per cent of children aged six through eleven were enrolled in schools, against 62 per cent in 1962, according to official statistics as collected in the UNESCO *Statistical Yearbook* for 1984. In North America enrollment is 100 per cent, in Europe and in other 'developed countries' over 90 per cent; in Africa percentages went up from 32 in 1960 to 63 in 1980. Enrollment figures for girls are consistently lower.

2 The term is Bernstein's.

3 Kaestle (1976, p. 81) writes about England: 'By 1825 the opponents of mass schooling, not the advocates, were on the defensive.' Cf. Graff, p. 22: 'By the end of the first third of the nineteenth century, opposition to the universal institutional schooling of the masses had largely vanished in Anglo-America and much of western Europe. Though the nature of the opposition had differed from place to place, from Great Britain to the Canadian provinces and the American republic, the educational solutions reached early in the century were similar in goals and content, if not always in structural forms.'

4 For rural France, cf. E. Weber, pp. 30ff.

5 Parisians considered the *campagne* as 'a country of savages', ibid. pp. 3–22.

6 Cf. Mandeville, *Fable of the Bees*, 1724, I. 328–9: 'To make the society happy and people easy under the meanest circumstances, it is requisite that great numbers of them should be ignorant as well as poor. Knowledge both enlarges and multiplies our desires . . . Reading, writing, and arithmetic are very necessary to those whose business requires such qualifications, but where people's livelihood has no dependence on these arts, they are very pernicious to the poor, who are forced to get their daily bread by their daily labour.'

7 'Between 1680 and 1780 there was a marked slowing down of growth in basic literacy due to fear among the upper classes that popular education was a contributory factor in causing the revolutionary activity of the 1640s and '50s', L. Stone, 1969, p. 136.

8 Chisick, pp. 261, 263.

9 Ibid., p. 270; the best one could do was 'to soften the peasants' condition, without ever helping them to leave it', says Rousseau in *Julie ou la Nouvelle Héloïse* (quoted by Chisick, in French, p. 269). And so Voltaire: 'It seems essential to me that there should be ignorant beggars' and: 'it is fitting that the people be guided, not that it be instructed, it does not deserve it' (quoted, in French, by Ariès, p. 925).

10 Chs I and II of *The Wealth of Nations* (pp. 109–21). Cf. also Maynes, 1985,

p. 123: 'the early industrialization process, and the urban growth that went with it, had an initial negative effect upon levels of popular literacy.'

11 Quoted from M. Tylecote (1851) in Simon, p. 153.

12 Schama, 1970, p. 593.

13 Cf. Van der Giezen, p. 24.

14 Cf. Heinemann.

15 H. Silver, 1977, p. 206.

16 Cf. Aumüller, p. 63; cf. also Tyack, p. 14, referring to conditions in rural America around 1900.

17 Cf. W. E. Tate, p. 31.

18 J. S. Taylor, p. 70; also vagrants and discarded veterans, sometimes holding a concession to serve liquor so as to add to their income: Aumüller, pp. 59–60, 63.

19 Cf. Chartier et al. for eighteenth-century France, pp. 41–4.

20 The technical branches of the military may have been among the first exceptions. The eighteenth-century French artillery schools admitted commoners and prepared them for high office, regardless of family rank and wealth. The weapon of the artillery in its entirety was therefore looked down upon until it proved its formidable powers and caused the demise of the most aristocratic cavalry. Cf. McNeill, 1982, pp. 166–73.

21 Drucker, p. 15, cf. p. 18. By the twentieth century this had changed: 'We are undergoing the educational revolution because the work of knowledge is no longer unproductive in terms of goods and services. In the new organization it becomes the specifically productive work.'

22 Cf. Tyack, p. 16.

23 Cf. Strauss, p. 96, on Germany in the 1530s: 'Bible reading was coming under suspicion for nourishing the seeds of an uncontrollable sectarianism.' Three centuries later literacy still held the seeds of rebellion: 'literate slaves sooner or later came upon the writings of the abolitionists and literate working people sooner or later came upon the writings of union organizers.' (Cremin, 1980; p. 493).

24 Cf. Gontard, p. 8.

25 'Thus all the evidence suggests firstly that one of the main causes for the growth of popular education in the west has been the struggle between the various Christian religious groups for thought control over the poor; and secondly that the Protestants were the first to see the potential value of the school and the printing press as weapons in this battle.' Stone, 1969, p. 83.

26 Barker (pp. 67–8) contends that the transference of educational facilities from the church to the state was more rapid in Protestant countries 'because the secularization of religious endowments which accompanied the Reformation so much diminished the resources of the Church that Protestant States were necessarily compelled to assume some of the old functions.' This seems to contradict the finding that elementary schools were more frequent wherever comunities had common property at their disposal to meet the expense of education; cf. Maynes (1979).

27 On literacy rates in England and the US, cf. Cressy, Lockridge, Schofield

(all reprinted in Graff, ed.), L. Stone, 1969; for France: Furet and Ozouf; LeRoy Ladurie (who finds a close, but spurious, correlation between literacy and body length: both being related to regional wealth). For comparative time-series, cf. Chartier et al., pp. 87–109; Maynes, 1985, p. 14.

28 Cf. Chisick.

29 Cf. Heinemann.

30 Advocacy of mass schooling was the virtually unopposed mainstream view in America, even among the elites, but among the English upper classes the two contrary attitudes existed as elsewhere in Europe; cf. Kaestle, 1976.

31 The issue of education for girls was an entirely different matter, even more dominated by moral concerns; cf. Maynes, 1985, pp. 97–102 (with references).

32 Cf. Aumüller.

33 Cf. for the role of such middlemen in fourteenth-century rural France, Duby, II. 248ff. The notary public united in his person all the liaison activities that the village fulfilled for the twenty or so hamlets surrounding it (p. 254). In modern Europe, cf. Maynes, 1985, p. 13: 'Even though there were many illiterate backwaters – regions where the population was illiterate almost to a man and a woman – even in these regions, the people of the towns and the cities were often adept at reading and writing, and their frequent contacts with rural residents must have kept the latter, too, in touch with the content of written culture.'

34 'A simple narrative of the triumph of benevolence and democracy no longer can be offered seriously by any scholar even marginally aware of educational historiography during the last fifteen years.' Katz, 1976, p. 382.

35 Parsons, 1961, p. 434.

36 Vaughan and Archer, 1971, p. 5.

37 Recently, the debate on these issues was revived by a polemic between Elster, 1982, and others.

38 e.g. the contributions to Hartmann, Nyssen and Waldeyer; cf. also Bowles and Gintis. Cremin (1977, p. 55) criticizes this argument from analogy to function to explanation in Bowles and Gintis: 'Once again, the correspondence tends to be asserted rather than demonstrated, and, apart from the similarity nothing of its nature is elucidated.' For a brief review of the discussion in England, cf. Digby and Searby, pp. 24–5.

39 Cf. Vaughan and Archer, 1971; cf. also L. Stone, 1969, p. 95: 'the rise of literacy in marriage records of Englishmen after about 1780 predicates an improvement of educational facilities some fifteen years before, which is well before the industrial revolution had seriously begun.' Schofield concludes his research into literacy rates in England 1750–1850 with the remark (p. 453): 'Nor does the static nature of male illiteracy, both nationally until the decade 1805–1815, and in several occupational groups until the mid-nineteenth century, lend much support to the notion that an improvement in literacy necessarily precedes or accompanies economic growth.' Graff finds that in nineteenth-century Ontario literacy made no clear differences for earnings or carriers (p. 198 and *passim*) and concludes that, in general, 'In

much of North America, moreover, education *preceded* industrialism' (p. 231, *his italics*). Lundgreen's quantitative study of enrollment figures and national (labor) income ends with the conclusion 'that in Germany in the nineteenth century, as in the postwar period 1950–62, very little of the impressive rate of growth of output appears directly attributable to the growth of education' (p. 47).

40 Katz, 1976, explains the emergence of mass elementary education in the context of the transition to capitalism, without resorting to 'systemic requirements'. Rural upheaval, immigration and urbanization, and the rise of a class of dispossessed wage-workers inspired great anxiety among the established bourgeoisie who tried to control these masses with various novel institutions, the schools among them. This allows for the cultural and political aspects of the process and also deals more adequately with the problem of timing. Yet the 'metropolitan' bourgeoisie had more than just reactive motives to propagate a national code of communication.

41 Vaughan and Archer, 1971, p. 16.

42 Ibid., p. 217; Laqueur, 1973, objects that neither did the established church control education so completely (there were in fact many private schools), nor were the middle classes ever as homogeneous as that.

43 The notions of national and regional communication networks are related to Karl Deutsch's ideas (1953) of (imaginary) 'maps of *speech communities*, on which each speech contact would be represented by a single line, so as to show the relative *densities of speech traffics*', p. 41.

44 Cf. Glück, pp. 67–90, for a discussion of the problems in defining these terms and assessing the actual degree of mutual intelligibility, especially in historical-sociological studies.

45 In actual fact, languages within a language figuration tend to resemble one another to a greater or lesser degree. An index of mutual intelligibility between languages could easily be incorporated into the model. There are, however, no systematic data on the similarities between languages that are suitable for the construction of such a revised model.

46 A combination is a subset of S; from a set of elements, $n!/k!(n - k)!$ different combinations of k elements may be formed.

47 A variation is an ordered combination, i.e. a subset of S with a specific sequence of elements. For every combination of k elements, there exist k! variations.

48 Greenberg's main interest was in a general characterization of *language systems* with respect to their diversity (Greenberg's A) or potential for communication (Greenberg's H). Greenberg's A corresponds to indices of fragmentation (e.g. for a voting population); Expression (1) below is formally identical to Greenberg's H. For a further elaboration of Greenberg's indices see also Lieberson, 1981.

49 Marc Raeff describes the early eighteenth-century court bureaucracy in Prussia in very similar terms: 'By intervening in the daily activities of its subjects and by fostering the maximum utilization of all resources and creative energies, the absolutist state undermined the estate structure, on

which it often relied in practice and promoted the dynamics of modernization and the formation of classes' (p. 1228). For a historical discussion of the functions of literacy in state formation, cf. Goody.

50 One occupational category had a very immediate interest in literacy: publishers, and most of all, the producers of newspapers and textbooks. American authors, especially, have stressed the importance of their alliance with educationalists in promoting universal elementary education, e.g. Tyack, p. 95; Soltow and Steven, pp. 58–88; Cremin, 1980, pp. 298–334.

51 e.g. Magraw's account of mid-nineteenth-century opposition to public education by rural *notables* and clergy.

52 Sometimes, these monopolistic mediation advantages may be taken quite literally. In the seventeenth century the master scribes and their corporations were angered by the competition from the *petites écoles* and sued them time and again, without success (Ariès, p. 911). These scribes were at the same time writers, translators, calculators and bookkeepers.

53 Cf. Maynes, 1985, p. 37: 'But, by and large, village affairs throughout Europe were run by the better-off landholders – in some cases petty, in others aristocratic. In the towns, the notables included property-owners, *rentiers*, merchants, professionals, officials, and the like, who by the late *ancien régime* had secured control over town politics and exercised oligarchic power. In towns where the new industries were established, entrepreneurs were a critical force.'

The position in the model of these local petty bourgeois as lingua-franca speakers, with a mediating monopoly for a regional clientele, makes this category different from that of the metropolitan bourgeoisie of officials and entrepreneurs. Here class, regional and network position do not make for coinciding interests.

54 M. Bloch, pp. 121–2.

55 Eisenstein, p. 61.

56 Laslett, p. 193.

57 Cf. Cohen, esp. p. 81; repr. in Deutsch, p. 42.

58 On the recent situation, cf. Siguan.

59 For a survey of surviving regional languages in contemporary Europe, cf. Stephens.

60 Cf. Hechter.

61 Ibid., pp. 110ff.

62 Cf. Withrington.

63 Cf. Marsden; David Williams, pp. 246ff.

64 Cf. K. Morgan, pp. 242ff.

65 E. Weber, pp. 70ff.

66 Ibid., p. 71. Chartier et al., p. 107, write about the eighteenth century: 'Occitan bilingualism consists in the coexistence of, on the one hand, an elite for whom the conquest and mastery of French and the refusal of dialect are the very conditions of their integration in the national community and, on the other hand, the common people who can neither read nor write their language.'

67 Cf. Cruzon, p. 40.
68 E. Weber, p. 86.
69 Cf. Van der Plank, pp. 241–7.
70 Engel, p. 75.
71 Glück, pp. 196–236.
72 Ibid., pp. 297ff.
73 Goudsblom, 1970, pp. 109–10.
74 Van der Plank, p. 68.
75 Thernstrom (ed.), p. 619. Contemporary Hispanics in the US, mostly Mexicans and Puerto Ricans, may prove the exception to this pattern, if they are willing to pay for the official privilege of speaking and writing Spanish with a lasting second-class position.
76 Dorian, pp. 37, 40; Van der Plank, p. 114, observes that the lower strata within a linguistic majority may oppose this assimilation to the dominant language by a heteroglottic minority out of fear of increased competition.
77 A pair of speakers, h and i, communicating in some shared language(s) L, may be extended with a 'bothersome third', j, who shares with the first speaker all the languages the first shares with the second. The bothersome third may be excluded from the communication between h and i only if there exists an 'exclusive' language L which they both speak and which the third, j, does *not* understand, i.e., if there is an L such that, $L \in c_h$ *and* $L \in c_i$ *and* $L \notin c_j$. The odds u_h' for speaker h, of finding a speaker i with whom he shares a language L and of excluding a speaker j who does not know L are: $u_h' = \Sigma_i \Sigma_j (f_i.f_j)$, for $L \in c_h$ *and* $L \in c_i$ *and* $L \notin c_j$. This condition is never satisfied for speakers of the general language only: for such speakers $u_h' = 0$. But speakers of the general language *and* of some exclusive language L may indeed be part of a triad that satisfies the condition, such that $u_h' > 0$, and this expresses the advantages of speaking an exclusive language.
78 Van der Plank.
79 Cf., Stephens, *passim*, esp. on Occitan, p. 297.
80 Cf. Dorian, for an example of a detailed study of actual speech practices in the case of contemporary Highland Scots.
81 'He's English, Buck Mulligan said, and he thinks we ought to speak Irish in Ireland. – Sure we ought to, the old woman said, and I'm ashamed I don't speak the language. I'm told it's a grand language by them that knows', James Joyce, *Ulysses*, pp. 12–13. See also Cf. Hobsbawm and Ranger (eds), especially P. Morgan's contribution.
82 Cf. Wallerstein, p. 152: 'it seems to be true in general that any complex system of ideas can be manipulated to serve any particular social or political objective. Surely Catholic theology, too, has proved its capacity to be adaptable to its social milieu.' Thus, in the eighteenth century, the Catholic hierarchy in Latin America supported the Castilianization of Quechua- and Aymara-speaking Indians, cf. Heath and Laprade in Cooper.
83 The term is Cremin's (e.g. 1980, p. ix), who stresses the uniquely American contribution to the development of 'an authentic vernacular' in education, 'compounding evangelical pieties, democratic hopes and utilitarian strivings'

and helping to create a unified (American) society. No doubt, the effort was most monumental in the US, but similar efforts were made by the Dutch *Nut* in the Batavian Republic, and similar hopes were entertained by many educationalists in other countries.

84 Butts (p. 206) traces this dual development further back: 'In general, the effect of the Reformation was to crystallize the distinction between a vernacular elementary education for the lower classes and a classical secondary education for the upper classes.' Cf. Mialaret and Vial for France.

85 Cf. Digby and Searby (pp. 36–40) on the revival of the classics in nineteenth-century England.

86 Cf. for the Netherlands, Röling, p. 72; for stratification and education in the eighteenth-century Netherlands, see Frijhoff.

87 Bernstein, p. 79; the author continues: 'Access to an elaborated code will not depend on psychological factors but on access to specialized positions within the social structure, by virtue of which a particular type of speech model is made available. Normally, but not inevitably, these positions will coincide with a stratum seeking, or already possessing, access to the major decision-making area of the social structure.' And, more explicitly (in italics, p. 176): 'One of the functions of the class system is to limit access to elaborated codes.'

88 Heinemann, p. 23.

89 In *De la littérature allemande* (1780) quoted (in German) by Heinemann, p. 60. Another 'metropolitan' metaphor: 'Just as money has come to circulate widely, so should culture' (ibid., p. 61).

90 Ibid., p. 38.

91 Ibid., pp. 58–9.

92 Ibid., pp. 111ff. Yet one of them, Von Rochow, carried out radical reforms on his estate, abolishing the commons, and founding schools for all his tenants. 'Children belong to the state, the state wants them to be educated, in the schools' (quoted in German, by Heinemann, p. 149). He published widely on the subject of educational reform and became one of Federick's closest advisers, but his projects were not imitated on other estates.

93 Van den Eerenbeemt, 1977, p. 47.

94 Quoted in Tate, p. 169.

95 Heinemann, pp. 60ff; cf. Müller, *passim*.

96 Heinemann, p. 136; Roessler, p. 319, quotes a peasant who cried out: 'Rather my head off, than new books in the hands of my child.'

97 Maynes, 1979, p. 613. But 'where economic opportunity intervened to disrupt rural routing, the peasants quickly gave support to the schools.' E. N. Anderson, p. 268.

98 Heinemann, p. 135.

99 Dorwart, p. 173.

100 'The principle and to a limited extent the practice of compulsory elementary education owe their introduction into Prussia to the Hohenzollern rulers of the eighteenth century.' E. N. Anderson, p. 261.

101 Dorwart, p. 179. There was, however, a third lingua franca, French, the court language.

102 Aumüller interprets these schemes, which were realized in the poorhouses and the regimental schools, in terms of the pressing need for skilled labor under the conditions of emergent capitalism. But they appear to have been inspired more by a desire to shape unruly paupers into virtuous citizens than by a pragmatic sense of training workers for the factories of those days. In other words, it was more a matter of 'police' than of 'economy', as is true of the poorhouse policy as a whole, cf. also Roessler, pp. 303–5.

103 Cf. on the social consequences of the Landrecht, Kosselleck, 1967.

104 E. N. Anderson, p. 276.

105 Busshoff, p. 392; the king warned against 'das Übel der Überbildung', the evil of overeducation for teachers and their pupils.

106 By the end of the century there were about 7,300 Catholic schools in Germany, as against 22,000 Protestant schools in a total of 36,000 (cf. E. N. Anderson, p. 276). The position of the Catholic Church during the first half of the century was that of a minority denomination with strong local power bases in the south and east (cf. also Glück, pp. 178–95). As long as its monopoly at the local level was respected and its religious teaching not interfered with, it found itself comfortable with its liberalist stance of equal support for every denomination, while accepting the preferential treatment of the Lutheran-State Church. As a consequence it was staunchly regionalist. Only after the foundation of the Reich in 1871 did a serious *Kulturkampf* ensue.

107 Cf. E. N. Anderson, p. 276.

108 On the whole, the *Volksschule* teachers during the nineteenth century performed a 'platform function', writes Busshoff, p. 396.

109 Aumüller, p. 53.

110 Hartmann, p. 180.

111 Cf. Müller, *passim*; Waldeyer, esp. pp. 161ff.

112 Gontard, p. 15; see also Chartier et al. on education in France under the *ancien régime*.

113 By 1698 Louis XIV had prohibited child labor until the age of fourteen and made school attendance compulsory; the *intendants* had to see that schools were established and that the children of the poor would receive free instruction, subsidized by local authority: the 'policing of the schools increasingly became part ecclesiastic, part secular', writes Poutet, p. 110.

114 Gontard, p. 14.

115 Allain, p. 33.

116 Gontard, p. 187.

117 A French *instituteur* was to be dispatched to every dialect-speaking community, cf. Allain, p. 37.

118 Gontard, p. 187, on the Convention of 1793. These ideas went back to the proposals of La Chalotais, in his *Essai d'éducation nationale* (1763): 'I insist on demanding for the nation an education which depends solely on the state, since to the state it belongs in essence, because every nation has an

unalienable and imprescriptible right to instruct its members.' (Quoted in French by Ariès, p. 919).

119 E. Weber, p. 72.

120 Gontard, p. 122; but the teachers did not show up or the municipalities failed to provide facilities or the parents refused to send their children to class; cf. Gontard, pp. 129–30f.

121 Cf. Godechot, p. 461: 'Thus, the conservative bourgeois of the *Directorat* did not bother much with education, except to make sure their sons would be assured of instruction so as to make certain that the bourgeoisie would hold its position of power'.

122 A first *rapprochement* had already begun under the Consulate, cf. Gontard, pp. 192–3; on nineteenth century relations in education between church and state, see also Gerbod.

123 Godechot, p. 648, quotes a decree from 1811: 'the inspectors of the Academy will see to it (surveilleront) that the teachers will not go beyond instruction in reading, writing, and arithmetic . . .'

124 Ibid., p. 252.

125 Cf. ibid., pp. 273–96: 'Truly, the method was the revelation of this quarter of the century. With it, the struggle for popular education was won' (p. 296).

126 Ibid., p. 312.

127 Deputy Cuvier, quoted by Gontard, p. 357.

128 Cf. ibid., p. 419. Yet 'in 1832 half the conscripts were illiterate.' There remained distinct geographical variations: 'A line drawn from the bay of St. Michel to the Lake of Geneva separates a surprisingly highly-educated north-east from a relatively ignorant south . . . Possibly the relatively different speeds of economic development may provide some explanation, or possibly the existence of dialects in the south which only resembled French to a greater or lesser degree.' Dupeux, p. 116; cf. Post, pp. 104–8.

129 Cf. also R. D. Anderson, 1975, pp. 18–19.

130 Gontard, p. 453, conveying the triumphant mood of the bourgeoisie.

131 Cf. Vaughan and Archer, pp. 127–8

132 For boys, that is; girls were mostly ignored, cf. Gontard, p. 533. Cf. Mayeur, *passim*; Post, p. 102.

133 Cf. Gontard, pp. 493–536.

134 Cf. Gontard, p. 538

135 Magraw, p. 198.

136 Ibid., p. 196.

137 R. D. Anderson, 1975, p. 38; cf. Ariès, p. 949.

138 Magraw, p. 209; the greater the percentage of large landholdings, the greater the proportion of legitimist *notables*; cf. Prost, p. 177: the lay and clerical parties made a pair of inseparable partners who constituted and reinforced one another mutually, Catholics being forced to oppose 'reason' against laymen compelled to reject 'religion', as each side feared that acceptance of either would rule out the other and defined it accordingly for its opponent. Zeldin, p. 228: the actual curriculum was not so very different.

139 Cf. Harrigan.
140 Cf. Ariès, pp. 925–930; Gontard, p. 272. Thus, the recently created schools for vocational training which provided continued instruction after the completion of popular elementary schooling, should by no means even appear to connect to the secondary-school system. Even Durkheim insisted: 'It is of the utmost importance to distinguish them.' Mialaret and Vial, p. 109.
141 R. D. Anderson, 1970, p. 69.
142 Prost, pp. 192–220.
143 For the history (in English) of the Dutch under French rule, cf. Schama, 1977, Kossmann, R. R. Palmer.
144 'The Society exploited any opportunities arising from local political conflict to its own advantage', e.g. siding with the Catholic population of Brabant against the entrenched privileges of the reformed *heren* and encouraging them to send their children to the Society's schools rather than to those of the reformed church (Schama, 1970, p. 597).
145 Ibid., p. 596.
146 Ibid., p. 609.
147 Ibid., p. 599.
148 Frisian and the dialects of Brabant, Groningen and Limburg are often unintelligible to the unaccustomed ear of Dutchmen from other regions. Even to this day, older dialect speakers find it hard to speak the standard ABN, even though they all understand, read and write it.
149 It is estimated at 75 per cent for males around 1800, second only to Scotland (88 per cent); cf. Knippenberg, p. 35; Frijhoff, pp. 15–17.
150 Ibid.; cf. also Schama, 1977, p. 534: 'The Republic needed the "Nut" to supply its first corps of officials and to sustain the momentum of propaganda for reform. The "Nut" needed the state to lay down authorised minimum standards' – and also to subsidize teachers' salaries.
151 Cf. Van der Giezen, who stresses the strength of anti-unitarian opposition.
152 Cf. Dodde, p. 8.
153 The Education Act of 1806 'was really put into operation and provided an excellent basis for building up a system of public primary schools.' Kossman, p. 96. 'The only serious difficulties arose in 1812 when (unsuccessful) efforts were made to persuade the Dutch to introduce French as a first language in the primary schools' and when, moreover, French financial chaos threatened the teachers' pay; Schama, 1977, p. 540.
154 Cf. Van Tijn.
155 Cf. Knippenberg, p. 90; Röling, pp. 75–84. After financial equality was brought about it slowly increased to 73 per cent in 1970. Cf. also Verberne, p. 219; Dasberg and Jansing, 1978, pp. 56ff.
156 Cf. Röling, p. 85.
157 Cf. Lijphart, who has called the Dutch model 'consociationalist'. Cf. also Stuurman.
158 Cf. Barnard, 1947; pp. 42–50; H. Silver, 1975; pp. 1–5.
159 Cf. Laqueur, 1976.

160 Quoted from the Hansard in Hurt, 1972, p. 20.

161 The introduction of the penny post in 1840 was called 'a most powerful incident to education', as it would increase correspondence and thus literacy; cf. H. Silver, 1975, p. 96. It is, of course, a prime example of facilitating communication in the national network.

162 By 1834 The National Society received postal privileges; the British Society received no help at all, cf. Hurt, 1972, p. 27.

163 L. Stone, 1969, p. 81; cf. also Hurt, 1972, pp. 21ff.

164 Cf. Johnson, p. 98: 'Those who spoke, wrote and preached so much about education, were no doubt an articulate minority. The majority voted more silently with their pockets and were forced, at length, to pay by rates.'

165 Vaughan and Archer, p. 37.

166 Cf. Digby and Searby, pp. 7–8. The Education Department imposed teachers' certifications and a system of payment according to the numbers of children who passed their exams. The policy 'was centralization by stealth, accomplished by regulation not statute, and so largely inaccessible to parliamentary scrutiny. The Minutes also contained a sort of built-in multiplier for the government bureaucracy: as more pupil teachers were engaged, more assistants were certificated and more schools became eligible for grants, so the number of inspectors and clerks to monitor and process the flow of cash increased' (ibid.).

167 On the role of the inspectors in helping to bring about the institutions from which grew the British welfare state, cf. Roberts, *passim*: 'Their industry was prodigious – and their integrity apparently incorruptible.' On school inspectors, cf. pp. 185–202. Cf. also Johnson.

168 Local clergymen, used to settling their affairs through informal social contact, were entirely unaccustomed to dealing with a central bureaucracy, such as the Ministry, and did not know how to go about writing a grant application. Cf. Hurt, 1972, pp. 47–8.

169 On the ambiguity of middle-class policy, with the working masses against church and gentry, against those masses for the protection of its own advantages, cf. Simon, pp. 126ff. Thus, 'fundamentally the utilitarians saw the education of the working class as a necessary means to the emancipation of capital – of the middle class, not of labour, of the working class itself (p. 128).

170 Vaughan and Archer, p. 40.

171 Cf. Simon, p. 152 (p. 173). As elsewhere, there was also opposition from indigent parents who were reluctant to send their children to school: 'They had not only to find the money for the school fees but they also had to forgo the child's earnings.' Hurt, 1979, p. 34.

172 Cf. also Simon, p. 277, on the emerging independent role of the Chartist movement as a workers' party, siding with the Radicals for parliamentary reform, with the Tories for factory legislation.

173 Vaughan and Archer, pp. 40–2.

174 Sutherland, p. 15. For this reason, H. Silver, 1977, p. xi, calls the story of popular education in the nineteenth century 'a kind of military history'. Cf.

also Digby and Searby, p. 10; Glass, pp. 392ff.

175 The voluntary societies were unsuccessful in reaching the most deprived social groups, especially in the cities. Cf. Mars.

176 Cf. Simon, p. 183; cf. also Laqueur, 1976, p. 242: 'Working class radicalism was predicated on literacy . . . The Sunday schools may have begun as attempts at control and indoctrination, they were never imposed upon the working class, which shared many of the middle class values, differentiated itself from the rough and unruly, and took from religious instruction its radical political visions, from literacy its rhetorical and organizing skills.'

177 Vaughan and Archer, pp. 127–8.

178 Simon, p. 166.

179 Ibid., p. 126; cf. also Hurt, 1972, pp. 111ff.

180 e.g. the Tractarian Party in the 1860s. The Congregationalists took the same view and left the British and Foreign Society; Hurt, 1972, pp. 45–6.

181 Wardle, p. 67.

182 Cf. Lawson and Silver, pp. 314ff.

183 Cf. Sutherland, p. 3; Musgrave, p. 63. Wardle, p. 73, quotes a contemporary comparison to the railways: 'The public schools comprised the first class, grammar schools and private schools comprised the second class, while elementary schools made up the third class. Each class of school served a different social class and prepared its pupils for different occupational levels.'

184 Hurt, 1979, p. 95.

185 Musgrave, p. 44.

186 Marsden, p. 187.

187 'England, the richest state of all, was exceptionally slow to act.' L. Stone, 1969, p. 96.

188 Cf. R. D. Anderson, 1975, pp. 6–7.

189 Cf. Jefferson, esp. pp. 362–3.

190 Cremin, 1977, p. 51.

191 R. Collins, p. 107.

192 Cf. Bailyn, pp. 45–6: After the Revolution 'most of the major statesmen had sweeping schemes for national systems of education . . . But the efforts to realize these plans came to nothing . . . Wherever schemes for state systems of education threatened the influence of sectarian groups they were defeated or fell under the control of the denominations.'

193 Cf. Kaestle, 1973, pp. 80ff.

194 Cremin, 1980, p. 174.

195 Ibid.

196 Tyack.

197 Cremin, 1980, p. 70.

198 Kaestle, 1973, p. 166.

199 Cf. Cremin, 1980, pp. 166–70. When it appeared that Catholics might succeed in obtaining state support, the other churches demanded equal

support for schools of their denomination. This may have kept the authorities from giving in to Catholic demands.

200 Cremin, 1977, pp. 49–53.

201 For a brief discussion of the establishment of public-school systems in the various states, see Cremin, 1980, pp. 148–85. But the author warns: 'variegation was the rule' (p. 149).

202 Cf. Baylin, p. 102; cf. also Kaestle, 1973, pp. 20–1: in the eighteenth century, at least: 'The pressure to conform in language or religion came from self-interest, not societal regulation.'

203 Thernstrom, pp. 307–8; Tyack, pp. 104–9; however, some influential immigrant groups did not insist on having their language taught, since this might lead to fragmentation of the educational system, and some small groups opposed foreign-language instruction since theirs would not be taught anyway: an example of the mutual indifference, or even hostility, among different groups of 'peripherals' in the floral figuration.

204 Katz, 1976, p. 397.

205 Cf. Katz, 1976, p. 394: 'In short, the anxiety about cultural heterogeneity propelled the establishment of systems of public education; from the very beginning public schools became agents of cultural standardization.'

206 Tyack, pp. 69ff; Katz, 1968, pp. 163ff; Kaestle, pp. 126–37.

207 Urban school reform in the nineteenth century has been the subject of intense polemics. On the one hand, e.g. Katz, 1971: 'public education originated from impulses that were conservative, racist, and bureaucratic' (p. 3). On the other hand, more positive evaluations, e.g. by Kaestle and Cremin, 1977, 1980.

208 Cf. Monroe, p. 196; moreover, 'until the period of the Civil War the national government did nothing more for the encouragement or support of education', p. 198.

209 R. Collins, p. 108.

210 Cremin, 1980, p. 177.

211 Bowles and Gintis, pp. 176–7: 'John D. Rockefeller and other major financial figures had begun to sense the importance of Southern agricultural productivity and of black labor in the continued profitability of capitalist enterprises.' They were, however, unable to introduce blacks into the system and on this point had to concede to the local mediation monopolies: schooling for blacks remained separate and became increasingly unequal.

212 Cf. Tyack, pp. 109–25; Cremin, 1980, 218–45.

213 This account follows Lieberson, 1980, pp. 137–45.

214 Ibid., p. 167.

215 Ibid., p. 239.

216 'Education was nowhere mentioned in the federal Constitution . . . The several states therefore felt free by tradition and by law to go their own particular ways in education, though from the very beginning they taught one another and borrowed freely back and forth.' Cremin, 1980; pp. 159–60.

217 Machine politics and ethnic-ward leadership, however, may be interpreted as strategies to capture just such middle-men positions of mediation between a relatively isolated ethnic clientele and the outside world of commerce and politics. The American seaboard cities with their multilingual immigrant communities formed floral figurations of their own. The machine politicians could successfully exploit their mediation monopoly for the time it took new generations to learn at school the skills of independent participation in the larger communication network.

218 O. Handlin, 1982, p. 6, points out that immigrants who had belonged to minorities in their countries of origin – e.g. Jews, Turkish Greeks and Armenians – had a tradition of organizing their own schools there and in this respect were at an advantage in the US.

219 Around 1900 on the predominantly Jewish Lower East Side in New York teachers patrolled the schoolyards to catch any scholar speaking Yiddish, writes Berrol, p. 37.

Chapter 4   Medical police, public works and urban health

1 Cf. Lampard, p. 5, for the annual rate of urban concentration in cities of 10,000 and over. In the first half of the century, urbanization was most pronounced in Britain, but after 1850 Prussia, the US and France caught up with a vengeance; the Netherlands, which had been most urbanized around 1800, lagged until mid-century. Cf. also Schmal (ed.).

2 Cf. Lampard; also Verdoorn, p. 31, for Amsterdam.

3 By the close of the nineteenth century, London, New York, Paris and Berlin, in that order, were the world's largest agglomerations and were still growing at a rate that doubled their population about every thirty years; cf. Lampard, p. 9.

4 Cf. Banks for Britain, p. 112.

5 Dyos, p. 5.

6 Ariès, p. 129, describes Paris before 1850 in these terms: 'Overcrowding prevents any social specialization. There is no working-class neighborhood, only a single, teeming, human mass in which all conditions are heaped together indiscriminately. One and the same building may contain in back of a peaceful and provincial courtyard an aristocratic dwelling where life goes on in noble fashion, and on the loud and dirty frontside obscure shops, or tenement flats, some in bourgeois style, others poor, even miserable, often under attic roofs.' Quoted in Butler and Noisette, p. 55.

7 There were the *Griasler* in Vienna, who lived in the city's sewers, cf. Bergmann, and the 'scavengers' and 'rag-pickers' who went through the waste piles and in later years would vehemently resist regular waste and garbage removal, cf. La Berge, p. 224, on Paris.

8 Cf. Elias and Scotson, esp. Elias's Introduction to the Dutch edition of 1976.

9 Cf. O. Handlin, 1979, pp. 65–9.

10 Chevalier, p. 517 *et passim.*

11 Cf. G. S. Jones, p. 146. All the more so, as the urban poor were thought to be 'degenerate' in comparison to the 'healthier' and maybe more compliant rural folk; cf. pp. 127ff.

12 For an unsuccessful attempt in Paris around 1800, cf. Cobb, pp. 241–2; a more recent and sophisticated scheme was the removal of 'antisocial' or 'unacceptable' families to designated areas where they lived under close supervision; cf. De Regt, pp. 199–239.

13 Many governments in rapidly urbanizing countries have attempted to check the desertion of the countryside, but only in the course of the twentieth century have totalitarian techniques of administration developed, allowing them to do so, e.g. in the Soviet Union and China.

14 Recent research does not confirm these nineteenth-century fears and stereotypes. On the contrary, M. Anderson finds that more than half of the mid-nineteenth-century urban population in Britain was born elsewhere than in the town of residence, and 'most migrants from within Britain had enough skills, resources and contacts to cope with living in the towns' (p. 89). The Irish, however, did suffer disadvantages and encounter discrimination.

15 This follows Lofland's ideas on the historical transformation of urban public order, conveniently summed up by her chapter headings: 'The preindustrial city: appearential ordering'; 'The early industrial city: confusion and the dynamics of change'; 'The modern city: spatial ordering'.

16 Cf. Burnett, p. 65: '. . . in general, tenements were found in existing, often old, houses which had once accommodated families of substance, if not affluence, but which had now sunk to rooming-houses of an infinite variety of respectability and disreputableness. They were part of the process of town decay in which, from the late eighteenth century onwards, the better-off classes had begun to desert the noise, dirt and smell of overcrowded city centers for the peace and social homogeneity of the suburbs, leaving behind a vacuum that was quickly filled to overflowing by waves of fresh migrants.' See for the US, O. Handlin, 1982, pp. 366–72; for Berlin, Geist.

17 Cf. Burnett, pp. 58ff; for Amsterdam, see Verdoorn, pp. 226–40.

18 Cf. Wouters.

19 Cf. Lofland, pp. 61–5.

20 Early nineteenth-century Paris may have been the worst; cf. Cobb, Chevalier.

21 For the US, cf. Boyer, for England Wohl, for France (Paris) Chevalier.

22 Prostitution was more conspicuous and more widely spread in the towns; it was also often a sideline for young working women and immigrant girls; cf. Cobb, pp. 234–9. This tended to blur the visible distinctions between 'improper' and 'decent' women; cf. also Trudgill.

23 Cf. De Swaan, 1981.

24 Cf. Van Daalan, 1987, who has studied complaints from aggravated passengers to the Amsterdam Tramway Company around 1900. She also investigated citizens' complaints to the authorities on the vexations caused by their neighbors, which may well have stimulated the city government to sanitary action and to set up health services.

25 McNeill, 1976, p. 261.
26 La Berge, p. 116.
27 Finer, p. 333; Coleman, p. 172.
28 Finer, ibid.
29 From the preamble to the Cholera Act of 1832, quoted in Checkland, p. 3.
30 Frevert writes: 'The history of cholera – as yet unwritten for Germany – is in large part also a history of the class relations in bourgeois society, in which the propertied strata felt increasingly threatened by the dispossessed "diseased" layers of the population' (p. 128). And (p. 125): 'The problem of pauperism – the presence of the poor in the city – was itself considered as an alien body [*Fremdkörper*] that had to be "cured away" as a social disease. Pauperism – as a twofold pathological phenomenon – became a social danger of the first order.' For the class meanings of cholera in Paris, 1832, see also Delaporte.
31 Cf. Finer, p. 349: 'The slum population was fast losing its head, some even believing that the doctors were poisoning the wells to thin off the population and that the inspectors were there mainly to see that the victims were not chosen too wantonly.' People in Glasgow protested against the burning of rags from affected districts (Checkland, p. 2). The English poor considered the cholera scare of 1832 mostly 'humbug' spread by doctors to fatten their purse; cf. Morris, pp. 96–101 (see pp. 108–14 on popular riots during the epidemics). In Germany also, Frevert reports (pp. 130–2), doctors were suspected of having spread the disease to make money and they were threatened and even attacked: the poor had suffered from so many diseases for so long, without the authorities bothering about it, that they took a fatalistic attitude towards this new disease and resented the prohibition on assemblies and markets, which anyway hit them most. It was the same in the US, writes Rosenberg (p. 33): 'Physicians and city officials were attacked and brutally beaten.' Chevalier, p. xxi, on Paris in the 1830s: 'Luckless passersby, judged guilty by their evil looks of propagating the disease and poisoning food and wells, are killed on streetcorners and in the squares or thrown into the Seine.'
32 Frevert speaks of a *selbstschuld Paradigma*, cf. pp. 137–8. Cf. also Risenberg, p. 150: 'To many Americans . . . it was the slum dweller who was responsible for the filth in which he lived.'
33 A flourishing 'cholera industry' sprang up offering all sorts of quackeries (Frevert, p. 130). By mid-century the treatment of choice had become the administration of *constipantia*, a remedy which compensated for its harmful effects only because less frequent defecation limited the patient's odds of reinfection, cf. Finer, p. 343.
34 Cf. the contributions to L. Tilly and Ch. Tilly, 1975, and Tilly et al. 1981, on such 'contentious gatherings'.
35 Cf. Frevert on 'medizinische Polizei', pp. 66ff; Rosen, pp. 142–58.
36 The Metropolitan Police Force for London was created in 1829, cf. Richter, pp. 4ff; cf. also David Jones, pp. 107–13; A. Silver; P. Smith, pp. 15–27; and for Paris, Cobb. For a comparative historical essay, see Bayley.

37 The originally very broad meanings of the term became more and more limited to the control of epidemic disease and supervision of sanitation. In this restricted sense the term was employed in Britain and the US during the nineteenth century. Cf. Rosen, p.153. Wohl, 1977, p. 111, mentions that by mid-century the 'sanitary inspectors' working under the medical officers of health were 'sometimes derisively called "medical police".'

38 The medical officers' 'visitations rendered the home no more sacred or private, in a sense, than a workshop, and their influence, therefore, upon the changing concepts of the rights and duties of property is hard to exaggerate.' Wohl, 1977, p. 116. Kalff has shown how from 1848 on in Paris 'hygiene-commissions' made up of respectable citizens, *notables* and professional men, were entrusted with the task of sanitary inspection; their civic prestige served to persuade home-owners to comply with hygienic measures which the city government, for lack of authority, could not yet impose directly.

39 Thus, coastal towns (e.g. New York) or cities with a tidal river, like Liverpool, were in a better position to dispose of their sewage than inland towns such as Manchester; cf. Daunton, p. 255. In Amsterdam the canals served to carry out the waste to the tidal inner Zuiderzee, but the Jordaan, the core slum area, stood on lower ground and could not be drained at all, cf. Carasso; Van Zon. The hilly character of Paris presented special problems, since all waste water had to pass through the lower neighborhoods, cf. Dupuy and Knaebel. But the main problem everywhere was the fact that the boundaries of political units did not correspond to the hydrological and demographic entities that determined the material requirements of the sanitary system.

40 Matthew Arnold, 1869, quoted in G. S. Jones, p. 221.

41 'In its arbitrary and unplanned way demolition and commercial transformation in nineteenth century London must have involved a greater displacement of population than the rebuilding of Paris under Haussman.' G. S. Jones, p. 159. Dupuy and Knaebel, p. 36, comment on the mid-century reconstruction of central Paris: 'In fact, at the same time that the center was being renovated, the poor and proletarian classes were being forced to emigrate to the outskirts, since they could not afford the heavy costs imposed by the owners of the new buildings. Speculation ran wild, but so did the sudden segregation of habitat according to income.' Cf. Lis, pp. 64–73, on slum conditions and demolition in Antwerp.

42 Daunton, p. 12 (author's italics). This 'encapsulation' both necessitated and facilitated the connection to urban networks for water supply, sewage removal, etc.

43 Cf. Olsen.

44 Wagenaar describes this development from 'mixed' to 'segmented' areas for Amsterdam in the 1870s: at the Golden Bend of the seigniorial Herengracht the stench from the canal had become unbearable, the slums were outrageously overpopulated and the working people became increasingly rebellious. The merchant mansions around the new Vondelpark offered pleasant surroundings and were provided with sewerage connections.

Nevertheless, Bruin and Schijf have been unable to find indications that 'increasing vulgarization' of the city core was the motive for moving to the new park area, although they agree that its streets did become respectable.

45 Workers in London felt that the police ignored their neighborhoods and kept a close watch on slum areas only to protect adjacent residential districts; Miller, p. 92. On English working-class resentment of, and resistance to, police interference with their domestic life and leisure activities, see Storch.

46 Cf. G. S. Jones, p. 247; in mid-nineteenth-century London there was much resentment against 'the "desertion" of the wealthy classes from the poorer districts'.

47 McKeown, p. 125.

48 McKeown adds, p. 153: 'The fall of mortality was not influenced substantially by immunization or therapy before 1935 when sulphonamides became available.'

49 See for a discussion of the medical debate in England, Pelling; in France, Delaporte.

50 Around 1800 Noah Webster, for example, rejected the reports that Irish immigrants had brought yellow fever to New York as 'vulgar tales that disgrace this age of science and philosophy . . . what I would severely reprobate is, the disposition of men to trace all evils of life to a foreign source, when the sources are in their own country, their own homes, their own bosoms.' (Quoted in Rosenkrantz, p. 3). In France, the Spanish policy of *cordons sanitaires* along the common frontier, as a protection against yellow fever had created great resentment. Cf. La Berge.

51 Cf., e.g., Coleman on the pioneering work of Villermé.

52 Murard and Zylberman, p. 63. The authors show the tight links between the French 'hygienist movement' and early ideas of social engineering in medicine (Pasteur), sociology (Durkheim) and political thought (Saint-Simon): 'To reduce all political questions to matters of hygiene.' The discovery of the mechanism of contagion put an end to these almost unlimited ambitions, as priority shifted from public health to personal hygiene and from urban engineering to individualistic medicine. Cf. also Starr, p. 100: 'Much of the history of public health is a record of struggles over the limits of its mandate.' And, p. 196 (quoted from Rosenkranz): 'the "dividing line" between the old and the new ideologies of public health was "an explicit denial of responsibility for social reform".' Also: 'Perhaps nothing better illustrates the movement of public health from the environment to the individual than the growing emphasis on individual health examinations' (p. 192); cf. also Rosenkrantz, p. 73.

53 This 'historical irony', however, is mostly apparent – the actual positions in the scientific debate were much more complicated, as Pelling has shown, p. 299 *et passim*.

54 A constant supply of water under pressure was also required for efficient fire fighting. Moreover, there was no danger of the pipes being stolen even in the poorer areas, as water under high pressure acted as 'a police on the pipe'. Binnie, p. 1.

55 In 1854 the British physician John Snow demonstrated his theory that cholera was transmitted by a water-borne agent, by tracing the incidence of the disease to organic contamination of the local water supply, the notorious Broad Street pump. 'The achievement of the 1850s was to narrow down Chadwick's large indictment of all filth to one kind in particular: that produced by human beings.' Pelling, p. 245. But the controversy continued until Koch identified the specific agent *Vibrio cholerae* (which had already been discovered by Pacini in 1854; cf. Pelling, p. 3).

56 As late as the 1880s in the US, 'the accepted theory of water purification held that water cleansed itself when the sewage was diluted and the stream flowed at a sufficient distance.' Rosenkrantz, p. 81.

57 Cf. Kalff.

58 Gleichmann, 1979a; cf. also 1979b.

59 Finer, pp. 212–13, writes: 'The suddenness with which the people of England appeared for the first time to acquire a sense of sight and smell and realize that they lived on a dung heap was due to the impact of industrial change.'

60 Corbin, p. 169.

61 Elias, 1982, pp. 292–9.

62 Some seventy years later, in *The Road to Wigan Pier*, George Orwell mentions the expression, again with some embarrassment, this time about the nagging sense of distinction his parents had instilled in him in childhood.

63 Liernur's proposals for a sewerage system in Amsterdam provoked a struggle, 'as if he had intended to undermine the very foundations of society'. Knuttel, quoted in Koot. As many did before him, Liernur opposed the combined removal of human faeces and other solid waste together with waste water or rainwater, for sanitary and economic reasons. He proposed to have solid waste removed through air pressure in a system of pipes communicating with a central reservoir for every 100 homes, from which point a 'locomobile' would pump it away to be deposited after drying on the surrounding lands in the form of fertilizer pellets ('poudrette'). The system was adopted on a large scale only in Amsterdam (100,000 homes by 1890), but most of the waste was simply dumped in open water. After 1900 water closets and a combined water-carried sewerage system prevailed; Van Zon, pp. 101–29. The last canal mansions were connected to the city sewer system as late as 1987.

64 'The poor are displaced, but they are not removed. They are shovelled out of one side of the parish, only to render more overcrowded the stifling apartments in another . . .' *The Times*, 1861, quoted in Wohl, 1977, p. 31.

65 Private security services, too, may generate interesting, and even perverse, external effects: as more people in an area subscribe to them, by doing so they expose those neighbors who remain without protection to increasing criminal attention, almost compelling them to subscribe in turn: again, what began as an option for some tends to become a necessity for all.

66 The contents of cesspools seeped into the soil, polluting the grounds. When privy-pans were being collected and hauled over stairs and pavements, their contents leaked onto the floors and gave off bad smells.

67 Although coal stoves used to produce ashes and smoke, while gas burns much cleaner.

68 'A cheap and hygienic water closet for working-class housing did not develop until the last quarter of the nineteenth century.' Daunton, p. 256, where a technical description of succeeding designs may be found; cf. Roy Palmer; see also D. P. Handlin for the US, pp. 455–71; Wright, *passim.*

69 For innovations and failures in water engineering in the US, cf. Armstrong (ed.); for Britain, cf. Binnie. Thus, Roe's invention of the egg-shaped pipe greatly reduced the costs and increased the efficiency of sewerage networks, since even with falling levels the water flowing in the narrower lower half maintains its speed and carrying capacity, while the wider upper part may accommodate larger quantities when necessary; cf. Binnie, p. 5. Glazed-clay sewers and cast-iron water pipes limited leakage and resisted decay much better than earlier brick vaults and bored-log pipes, cf. Armstrong (ed.), pp. 232–3, 401.

70 p. 57; cf. Gauldie, p. 75: 'Water was not a free commodity.' See also pp. 75–81 on the lagging provision of water and sewerage connections in the poorer urban areas in Britain; cf. also Wohl, 1983, pp. 61ff. Cf. Armstrong (ed.), pp. 217–32, for a brief historical review of water supply in major US cities; cf. also Blake. See Verdoorn, pp. 208–15, on water supply and sanitation in nineteenth-century Amsterdam. For Paris see Dupuy and Knaebel; also Goubert, forthcoming. For Berlin, cf. Spree, pp. 118–28. See also Bullock and Read, pp. 87–109 for Germany, pp. 342–56 for France.

71 Cf. Wohl, 1983, pp. 110–16 on English towns.

Chapter 5 Workers' mutualism: an interlude on self-management

1 One important difference between the ancient guilds and the workers' mutual societies is compulsory, voluntary, membership, with all the dilemmas of collective action that go with the latter. For a discussion of continuity and innovation from the *ancien régime* to the mutual-aid societies of the Republican era in France, see Sewell, esp. pp. 55–8; cf. Fröhlich for a systematic comparison of guilds and social-security institutions in Germany.

2 The support networks for tramping artisans in England and the similar *compagnonnages* in France represented another early arrangement for mutual aid: the local chapter sent craftsmen on a tour of the country to seek with a letter of recommendation which entitled them to a night's lodging and a meal at every stop; cf. Hobsbawm, pp. 34–63.

3 Fraternal societies sometimes established 'sick clubs', paid for by weekly subscriptions and entitling the members to treatment by a doctor belonging to the club's 'panel'. Competitive conditions in mid-nineteenth century medicine were such that many medical men eagerly sought appointment by a club, but the resulting lay dominance of medical practice later came to be resented and explains much of the resistance to health insurance among

medical men in the early twentieth century; cf. Peterson, pp. 114–18 and Hodgkinson, pp. 215–49 for 'clubs' and 'dispensaries' in England; Starr on 'lodge practice' in the US, especially among immigrant communities, pp. 206–9, 241–2; Saint-Jours, pp. 228ff, on the *mutualité* in France.

4 Supple, p. 215: 'in 1851 the male population aged 15 or over was about 5.7 mln.'

5 A. Weber, p. 29. Cottereau, p. 143, quotes some membership estimates: 800,000 members by 1870, 'of whom workers accounted for a large share'. Later, the workers' share declined. 'There is no thorough recent study of mutual aid societies.'

6 Tennstedt, p. 113.

7 Starr, pp. 206–9. Furniss and Tilton, p. 238, write on the US: 'There were literally hundreds of these societies, many with capital in the millions of dollars.' They add: 'these societies have been largely unexplored.' Schmidt provides an encyclopedic inventory of 'fraternal organizations', many of which once functioned also or even mainly as mutual insurances, and (p. 3) quotes an estimate of 30 million members by 1920, i.e. 50 per cent of the entire population, but only an – unknown – proportion participated in mutual-insurance schemes.

8 Verdoorn, p. 169.

9 Cf. D. Collins, p. 252, on contemporary authors' pessimistic evaluations of the friendly societies' coverage and solvency.

10 In France, the *mutualité* has survived the advent of social insurance and turned into a federation of cooperative and voluntary insurance schemes for supplementary benefits (among other provisions), steadily growing in numbers to 13 million in 1964 and more than 20 million in 1975, cf. Lavielle; Saint-Jours, p. 259.

11 Thompson, pp. 457, 458.

12 The expression is Norbert Elias's, cf. 1982, pp. 229–46.

13 See, e.g., the byelaws of apprentices' guilds (*Knechtsbossen*) in the appendices to Timmer.

14 In France, many mutual societies used to lavish the money that remained by the end of the year on a great banquet for the members, Hatzfeld, 1971, p. 200. Cf. also Thane, p. 30, on the 'dividing up' clubs, 'slate clubs' or 'tontines' among the poorer English workers: 'the sum remaining in the fund was divided among all members at Christmas.'

15 e.g. Gilbert, 1965, pp. 553–8.

16 Popkin, in his account of insurance and mutual aid in Vietnamese peasant societies, arrives at very similar conclusions by using related notions of collective action. Among traditional peasants mutual suspicion was too great for them to trust anyone with the communal money and as a result provisions were mostly in kind or consisted in labor services in times of need. 'From political economy assumptions it follows that village-wide insurance schemes will be highly specific and limited due to problems of trust and consensus, and that welfare schemes will be greatly restrictive' (p. 47).

17 Cf. Smelser, pp. 360–1. Subscriptions were often picked up by a collector

working on a fee basis and this also led to frequent abuse, cf. Gilbert, 1966, p. 308. Cf. also Shefter for the US.

18 e.g. Starr, p. 207: 'The Lower East Side of New York City was teeming with small benefit societies providing prepaid medical care for Jews who came from the same town or region in Eastern Europe.' Starr and also Katz (1986, pp. 62–3) mention many other examples of Friendly Societies based on ethnic and occupational membership.

19 Cf. Hatzfeld, 1971, p. 200: the fund's chest was often kept in the local 'cabaret'. Gilbert, 1966, p. 308: 'Medical clubs were sometimes organized by the workers in a particular factory or mill . . . But too often a medical club was the adjunct of a casually-run benefit society, more frequently called a "slate club", organized by the clientele of a public house. At worst it was promoted by the doctor himself.'

20 e.g. Treble, pp. 268–9; De Regt, p. 243.

21 The sick funds of the German trade unions for ideological reasons did extend to union members who had not passed 'the narrow gate' of the medical test for the 'free' sick funds; cf. Schönhoven, p. 181.

22 Cf. for the English Friendly Societies' Act of 1875, Gosden, pp. 77ff.

23 Official intervention was not only motivated by a concern with the sound operation of mutual insurance: authorities, especially in France, feared that these working men's associations might become seedbeds of proletarian conspiracy and sedition, not always entirely without reason. Initially all working men's associations were prohibited. Under the Second Empire, legislation provided for government-appointed chairmen and close financial inspection, while established citizens were encouraged to join as honorary members. A central equalization fund was set up to guarantee the solvency of the mutual societies, but it remained mostly ineffective. As workers lost control of the funds, the unions gradually turned against the *mutualiste* movement. Cf. Hatzfeld, 1971, pp. 195–213; Saint-Jours, pp. 195–210.

24 Cf. Supple, pp. 233–5.

25 Cf. Smelser, p. 369.

26 Cf. Gauldie, pp. 196–207.

27 Hodgkinson, p. 236, writing on sick clubs in mid-nineteenth-century England concludes: 'The submerged class was forced, therefore, to depend on better paid and stronger grades of workers. This meant that they had to await the growth of class solidarity before they could provide relief for themselves.' The very poor fell back upon medical relief from dispensaries under the Poor Law.

28 Some Friendly Societies, such as the Ancient Order of Foresters, were transformed into charitable associations after they had lost their providential functions to state social security. Cf. on the Dutch 'courts' of the order Hulsink and De Grefte.

29 Cf. for England, Yeo, pp. 58ff.

30 Especially in England, the Friendly Societies, often of a conservative hue, tended to oppose social insurance and pension legislation out of fear of becoming superfluous: 'Their basic pre-occupation had always been to

safeguard their own well-being,' writes Treble, p. 268, cf. also Gilbert, 1965; D. Collins, p. 254. Lavielle paints a very rosy picture of the collaboration between the *mutualité* and state insurance in his more than sympathetic account of the *mutualiste* movement. Fröhlich, p. 268, suggests that social insurance came to Germany so early precisely because the strong and lasting guild tradition of mutual aid made for an 'almost invisible transition'.
31 Cf. De Swaan, 1986b.

Chapter 6   Social security as the accumulation of transfer capital

1 Heclo, 1974, p. 1.
2 For figures on factual knowledge of social security in the US, see Light, pp. 61ff., who concludes: 'People did know a great deal about benefits.'
3 Van Stolk and Wouters.
4 Cf. Feldstein, 1975.
5 Cf. Atkinson and Harrison, 1978, p. 6: 'non marketable assets'.
6 A. Atkinson follows the British Royal Commission in speaking of 'social property': 'the right to benefits from the state'; this, however, also includes rights of access to schools, hospitals, etc. Wilterdink, p. 45, has coined the term 'semi-private wealth' for 'non-marketable personal rights to periodic revenues from collective funds'. The present term 'transfer property' is reserved for legally enforceable claims to income transfers from the state or from public agencies. It excludes both private insurance and rights of access or rights to benefits in kind.
7 Cf. Feldstein, 1975, p. 78: 'The government's power to tax is its power to meet the obligations of social security to future beneficiaries. *As long as the voters support the social security system, it will be able to pay the benefits that it promises*' (italics in the original). This holds true, not only for 'pay-as-you-go', or 'revolving fund' schemes, but also for accumulated funds, as these will remain reserved for social security only as long as the government (or the voters) do not use them for other purposes, such as decreasing the national debt.
8 Knowledge of the exact conditions of payments and benefits may well be defective; cf. Furniss and Tilton, p. 175. What matters is the overall awareness. Comparative research on this issue is not available.
9 Hatzfeld, 1971, p. 321. But many comparative students hold the opposite view: Cf. Kudrle, p. 112: 'The striking fact about the development of the welfare state in Western Europe and the United States is its diversity.' Cf. also Higgins, p. 47: 'an enormous variety of responses to what, on the face of it, appear to be similar states of need . . .'
10 The one major exception being the absence of national health insurance in the US.
11 The terms moteur and frein are Hatzfeld's (1971).
12 Strictly speaking, some fully funded pensions schemes (e.g. in the US in

1935) were not collective in this sense, as benefits received by an individual were to be a function of contributions paid by the same person. This, however, was more a matter of rhetoric than of actual implementation.

13 Harris, p. 50.

14 Cf. Hatzfeld, 1971, pp. 87–8.

15 Report of the *Comité du Travail* to the French National Assembly, 1849, quoted by Ewald, 1986, p. 213.

16 The inquiries into the conditions of the working class undertaken by government commissions and expert investigators by the end of the nineteenth century destroyed an earlier hope that sanitation alone would be enough to abolish destitution and disease. Cf. Harris's discussion of British social research of the time, especially p. 41.

17 Workmen spent too much on such 'luxuries', their contemporaries believed. Cf. George Orwell, *The Road to Wigan Pier*, on the priority given to minor frills of consumption in the 1920s. Orwell noted that miners would purchase on payday what were to them luxury items, because if they did not buy them right away when they had the money in hand, they might never have an opportunity to enjoy them. More recent is the cliché that poor people will buy a colour TV before anything else: they can hardly be expected to buy one *after* everything else.

18 Quoted in Ewald, p. 331.

19 Cf. Elias, 1982, pp. 229ff.

20 Cf. De Regt.

21 They took up the old battle-cry of the French Revolution: 'put society in charge of the children, the elderly and the disabled.' Cf. Hatzfeld, 1971, p. 190.

22 Quoted by Harris, p. 365.

23 There are minor exceptions, e.g. when people are allowed to buy themselves into a retirement scheme with a lump sum, or when foreign workers receive a one-time grant upon departure to compensate for a loss of rights under a social-security scheme to which they have contributed. Some social-security benefits, disability and old-age pensions mainly, include provisions for dependent survivors and are therefore in a very limited sense 'inheritable'.

24 Cf. Feldstein, 1974.

25 Cf. Hatzfeld, 1971, for France; Maier and also the contributions to Crossick and Haupt on Britain, France and Germany; Wiebe on the US.

26 The notion that the 'right', and more specifically the small independent bourgeoisie, formed the major obstacle to social security has been carefully documented for France by Hatzfeld. Independently of that study, it has been systematically explored in comparative studies by Castles, e.g. Castles and McKinlay, 1979, p. 166: 'We propose a very simple model in which the dependent variable is our composite index of public welfare and the independent variable is vote for the major party of the Right.' Cf. also Castles, 1982, p. 71: 'Both the parliamentary and governmental strength of the major party of the Right are strongly associated with one or more aspects

of each category of public expenditure and each component of welfare, as well as having a significant relationship with the major dimensions of change during the period.' The sometimes quite crude research methods, however, obscure the fact that large-scale industrialists – usually organized in parties of the right also – often supported social-security legislation.

27 Cf. De Swaan, 1988.
28 In mid-nineteenth-century France, especially, the mutual societies were suspected of serving as a cover for workers' agitation, and they often were centers of resistance; cf. Hatzfeld, 1971, p. 195. This was one reason why in France *notables*, employers among them, were ready to become honorary contributing members of the *sociétés mutuelles*, adding to the fund's means while keeping an eye on its affairs.
29 Foundries also from very early on, as workers were wont to walk out and abandon the furnaces.
30 The dismissal of workers just before their retirement by the Aniche Company in 1872 or the bankruptcy of the Terrenoire Mining Company in Bessège in 1888 were traumatic events, as employees lost the pensions they had saved for so assiduously, cf. Trempé, p. 106.
31 Such as the failure in 1869 of *La Fraternelle*, a mutual insurance company which supplemented company benefits; cf. Trempé, p. 108.
32 Cf. Heclo, 1974, pp. 157ff.
33 Cf. ch. 3, section 4.
34 Especially in France, where the memory of the Paris commune lingered on.
35 This desire for independent control of working-class institutions also dominated the American Federation of Labor under Gompers until 1920 and beyond.
36 Crouch applies Olson's argument specifically to trade unions. In the US especially, selective benefits and 'fringe benefits' restricted to union members have been important. Unions feared that governmental social policy might remove incentives for workers to join and readily accepted pension legislation only because they did not need the elderly; cf. Derthick, p. 119; Furniss and Tilton, pp. 160–1.
37 Crouch, p. 175, points out that the rank and file of union membership is primarily interested in wage increases, rather than in procedural goals, whereas 'the leadership, as an organization, *does* gain directly from pursuing participation goals, for these activities extend its role and scope.'
38 Cf. Tennstedt, pp. 223ff.
39 Wilterdink has carefully traced the patterns of growth of such 'semi-private wealth' (transfer capital and life insurance) for the Netherlands: between 1920 and 1980 its share in the national wealth grew from 4 to 15 per cent and surpassed the size of privately owned wealth by 1974 (p. 119). Viscusi, p. 95, mentions that by 1974 in the US 'the anticipated value of Social Security annuities was $2,4 trillion' as compared to a total estimated value of all other household assets of $3,3 trillion. Only some 2 per cent of outstanding social-security obligations were actually covered by trust funds; Feldstein, 1975, p. 77.

40 Cf. Hatzfeld, 1971; Stearns, p. 53: on France: 'with the 1911 law, workers compelled their leaders to accept any crumbs the state would offer.'

41 Cf. Crouch, pp. 68ff.

42 After a period of quantitative comparative studies which explained the growth of social security in terms of ecological and socioeconomic variables, interest in the political role of politicians and experts has been revived: 'politics matter'. Cf. Castles; also Skocpol, and Heclo's 'small band of self-styled social reformers in and out of government' (1974, p. 155) or Hatzfeld's 'grands commis de l'État' (1971, p. 269).

43 Cf. Thane, p. 60; Titmuss, p. 80.

44 Skocpol and Ikenberry.

45 Rosanvallon, p. 165.

46 Marshall, 1965, pp. 82ff.

47 O'Connor, p. 100, suggests an intimate connection in the Marxist tradition: 'The welfare state tends to expand because of the growth of surplus population which has relatively little purchasing power of its own, and the warfare state tends to grow because of the expansion of surplus capital which cannot be disposed of at home (in part, because of the growth of the surplus population).'

48 In the sense of Friedrichs's 'rule of anticipated reactions', pp. 199ff.

49 These protracted lawsuits were, of course, a source of income for lawyers. Yet in each case it served the purpose of the claimant's lawyer to denounce the law as it stood and thus undermine a practice that in the long run profited the profession as a whole. Moreover, the law is not made by practicing lawyers, but by professors of law, judges, and legislators for whom the calculus of practice counts much less. This explains why a state of affairs that profited the legal profession was in the end abolished, in part through the efforts of men of law themselves. Similar reforms have occurred in the medical profession.

50 Employers had an added interest in supporting reform: they resented 'the defamatory character of the law' (Ewald, p. 247) which required that their negligence be established in court.

51 Cf. Stearns; Guillemard (Introduction). Alan Walker, p. 144, sets out 'to argue that the "dependency" of many elderly and its severity consist of a structurally enforced inferior social and economic status in relation to the working population, and secondly, that social policies sponsored directly or indirectly, by the state, occupy a central role in the creation and management of that dependency.' This approach, although partially valid, is marred by its lack of historical perspective: the exclusion of the elderly from the land and from other means of existence and their neglect by younger generations has been a pervasive feature of European pre-capitalist society.

52 Cf. Stearns, p. 21 '. . . such mundane matters as the loss of teeth by age 45. This meant that someone, typically the youngest daughter who might not marry among other things because of a decade or more of care of an aging parent, had to chop up food and spoon it down the elderly gullet. False teeth became a common purchase among the lower classes only after 1850.'

53 And governments incidentally also failed to make good on their bonds or manipulated the terms by allowing inflation, as happened in France and Germany after the First World War.

54 Accordingly, the degree of political commitment to collaboration with small employers played a large role.

55 In fact, in modern nations sickness insurance is well on its way to become a supplementary old-age scheme: in the Netherlands medical costs of children are half those of the middle-aged (45–65 years of age), those of the aged (over 65) almost double and those of the very old (over 75) almost four times as high. Eliminating the costs of treatment for accidents at home, at work and on the road would result in even sharper differences. Cf. *Nota 2000*.

56 e.g. Medicare for the elderly in the US (1965), or the General Disability Act and the General Extraordinary Disease Costs Act in the Netherlands.

57 Only in the US has health insurance remained in large part private and competitive; sick pay for lost earnings was, and is, usually covered by company contracts, casual workers and the employees of financially weak enterprises remaining largely unprotected. Rather than establish a national insurance system, the government in this case also opted for a special plan to cover the excluded population: Medicaid (1965).

58 On late-nineteenth-century attitudes towards unemployment, cf. Garraty, Harris.

59 See Vanthemsche.

60 For a careful study of unemployment policies in Amsterdam and the Netherlands, cf. De Rooy.

61 Strasser, p. 29, discusses the episode under the heading 'The welfare state, the historical achievement of Social Democracy' and, after an ample review of Marx and Hegel, finds himself forced to relegate the founding of social security by the Bismarck regime to a single subordinate clause.

62 Cf. Tampke; compare however the critique by Ritter, p. 42.

63 e.g. pp. 21–9 in Hentschel: 'The provisions were meant as an addition, but an addition to what?', p. 25. Compare, however, Zöllner, p. 97: 'In quantitative and qualitative respects, progress was undeniably great compared to preceding conditions.'

64 e.g. Hentschel, pp. 55–6: 'Ignoring some minor corrections and reforms, the system of social insurance established and elaborated under the Empire was barely kept alive under the Weimar Republic, abused to serve National Socialist ends in the Third Reich and substantially extended only in the Federal Republic and the GDR.'

65 A number of studies are devoted to the influence of Bismarck's legislation on the social policy of other countries; cf. the contributions by Hennock and by Hay in Mommsen (ed.). For a comparative historical study of Britain and Germany, cf. Ritter.

66 Cf. Rothfels, 1938, 1962.

67 Bismarck believed he was emulating the example of Napoleon III in this respect; Ritter, pp. 28; cf. Rimlinger, p. 121; Wehler, p. 136.

68 Cf. Hentschel, pp. 33–9.

69 e.g. Rimlinger, p. 339; Zöllner, p. 88.
70 Cf. Rimlinger, pp. 112–22, 339: 'The loyalty of the industrial masses to the monarchy – the summit of the existing order – was Bismarck's avowed goal.'
71 Flora (ed.), 1983, vol. 1 (Introduction).
72 Alber, 1982, pp. 131–4.
73 Alber, 1982, hesitates whether to classify Italy as a 'parliamentary democracy' or as a 'constitutional dualistic monarchy' (the choice of terms is unfortunate – most parliamentary democratic monarchies have a dualistic constitution). But there can be little doubt as to the authoritarian character of the regime, cf. Ferrera, p. 30, who concludes that Italy was among the countries that took the 'German road' to the welfare state, 'initiating social insurance ahead of the politically and economically more advanced democracies, such as France or England, and doing so for purposes of integration and social control.'
74 Cf. Gillis, pp. 108, 116; Ritter, pp. 19–20; Rimlinger, p. 110.
75 Ullman, p. 148: 'The opponents of workers' insurance were the owners of mostly small and medium-sized companies' (pp. 148–51). Wehler, pp. 134–5, argues that as the German middle class, from 1848 on, suffered a succession of defeats in its 'upward struggle' against the aristocracy and the feudal state, it turned increasingly against 'the threat from below', directing its hatred and aggression toward the organized left.
76 For a discussion of the drafting of the accident insurance bill, see Junius and Neuloh.
77 Rimlinger, p. 121.
78 For a discussion of Socialist positions cf. Rimlinger, pp. 122–30; Ritter, pp. 49–52.
79 For a discussion of employers' positions cf. Ullmann, esp. p. 154: employers wanted workers to contribute to the scheme, but were ready to grant them representation in the managing committees; Bismarck, on his part, proposed that the state contribute.
80 Ullmann: the coalition weakened with later laws, since the employers feared that the *Centralverband* would be undermined by the new *Berufsgenossenschaften.*
81 Tampke, p. 82.
82 This account relies mostly on Zöllner, pp. 92–100.
83 Which turned out to yield a considerable surplus: ten times the yearly disbursements by 1900; Zöllner, p. 100, cf. p. 10.
84 Cf. Roberts.
85 Cf. Fraser, 1981; Thane, 1982.
86 e.g. Roberts, pp. 70, 110. However, Fraser, 1973, pp. 45–50, stresses the independence of the local Poor Boards with respect to the central Commission.
87 e.g. Sidney and Beatrice Webb acted as intimate advisors to Churchill; William Beveridge alternated between a journalistic and an administrative career.
   'By the time of the main Liberal welfare legislation, in particular the innovations of the National Insurance Act in 1911, scholarly definitions

about social stratification and the political response of the working class had turned into commonplaces of parliamentary discussion.' Middlemas, p. 34.

88 Lloyd George made a visit to Germany to learn about social insurance there, and so did union delegations; cf. Hennock; Roy.

89 The Conservatives – the traditional party of the propertied middle classes and farmers – declined from almost 50 per cent in 1900 to less than 20 per cent, the Liberal Party went up from 27.5 per cent to almost 60 per cent, while the Labour Party increased its vote from 0.3 per cent to 4.3 per cent; Flora (ed.), 1983, vol. 1, p. 188.

90 'Some historians have seen the programme of the Liberal Radicals as an attempt to outbid the socialist wing of the Labour Party and the Independent Labour Party, whilst bestowing economic and social security on the working class, via the trade union movement. Others have argued that they were forced, by the tactics and by-election successes of the Tory opposition, continually to run ahead.' Meanwhile, 'their reforms, such as employers' liability and unemployment benefit, damaged Liberal unity during their long parliamentary gestation and antagonized ancient sources of support.' Middlemas, p. 41.

91 'The demand for a "national policy" came primarily from three sources; from radical groups within the Liberal party, from the organized labour movement, and finally and most emphatically from the Royal Commission on the Poor Laws and Relief of Distress.' Harris, p. 211; cf. also Heclo, 1974, p. 84.

92 Gilbert, 1966, p. 223. In the final reading, the maximum income for a full pension of 5s. a week was set at £21, with a sliding scale for higher wages up to £31. Committees appointed by local authorities were to decide on eligibility; moreover, recipients of Poor Law benefits were excluded and receipts from Friendly Societies were counted as income. By 1911 the restrictions of the law had already been 'considerably relaxed' by Lloyd George; cf. Fraser, 1973, p. 143.

93 Thane, p. 83.

94 Gilbert, 1966, p. 226. Cf. D. Collins, 259: the Act 'firmly hedged the Victorian, moralistic attitude to the poor', but on the other hand it abolished once and for all the deprivation of civil rights that had been attended upon receipt of Poor Law benefits.

It tends to be overlooked that social legislation presupposes a highly developed civil administration, as Gilbert's account (pp. 227–8) of pension payment in Ireland testifies: 'there had been no official registration of births in Ireland prior to 1865 . . . As a result pensions frequently had to be granted on the sketchiest evidence.' There were more recipients than there could possibly have been persons over seventy.

95 Hay, p. 444, quotes from the Journal of the Birmingham Chamber of Commerce in 1905: 'These men are assets of the nation, and it devolves on the nation to see that they are not allowed to become pauperized.' Apart from the loosely associated Chambers of Commerce, other entrepreneurs were active, mostly behind the scenes, cf. Middlemas, p. 47: 'In close association,

engineering employers, coalowners, railway companies, shipowners and shipbuilders turned from open action to lobbying Ministers with the aid of a group of well-organized, sympathetic MPs . . .'

96 On the Labour Party's enduring 'hostility to any sort of "dole" to which prior entitlement had not been secured' see Marwick, p. 401.

97 According to one contemporary source, voluntary insurance was unfair 'because the thrifty workman paid twice – through insurance for himself and through rates and taxes for other distressed workmen'; cf. Harris, p. 301.

98 Cf. Gilbert, 1966, p. 349; Bruce, p. 218. Workers earning less than 2s. a week were exempt from contribution.

99 The Friendly Societies had always insisted on keeping the doctors 'on contract', i.e. in their employment, so that they would not identify too closely with the patient's interest and be too cooperative in extending his sick pay. This dependence created great resentment among medical men who more and more began to insist on their autonomy: 'free choice for the patient'. The 'panel' was a list of participating doctors for the patient to choose from. Cf. Gilbert, 1966, pp. 309–11 and pp. 400ff.

100 Harris, p. 211. These unintended adverse external effects of a comparatively active or generous local-relief policy were associated with 'Poplarism', named after the borough of Poplar where the guardians were more generous to the unemployed than elsewhere – they gave outdoor relief for an indefinite period to the dependents of workmen who had entered the workhouse – and were accused by the ratepayers of 'encouraging men to abstain from work . . . and attracting the undesirable and unemployable to Poplar.' Quoted in Harris p. 266.

101 This is an instance of what Anthony Giddens has called the 'sociologization' of society: the penetration of everyday discourse and practice with ideas from the social sciences (cf. pp. 348–54). In this case, the redefinition subsequently changed the realities of unemployment. Thus, conceptual innovation in the social sciences almost imperceptibly affects social institutions and the novelty of the concepts is 'lost' in the process of societal transformation.

102 Harris, p. 302. Consultant actuaries also found the risk impossible to calculate for lack of reliable data about the age distribution of the unemployed.

103 Cf. Harris, pp. 299–303; Garraty, pp. 131–2.

104 Quoted in Harris, pp. 303–4.

105 'Many leading employers . . . seem to have supported the principle, if not the details, of social legislation. Rank and file members of the organization on the other hand, unaware perhaps of the preceding debates and discussions, seem to have been more concerned that short-run costs would outrun potential advantages. It was this groundswell of backwoods opinion which caused some reconsideration on the part of the leaders, and which provided support for organizations like Sir Charles Macara's Employers' Parliamentary Association which opposed social reform.' Hay,

1977, p. 440. Cf. Middlemas, p. 47, for a description of employers' political organizations.

106 In later years workers in many branches resisted inclusion in the scheme.

107 Churchill had introduced these institutions in his law of 1909, cf. Harris, pp. 287–95. On the subsequent fate of unemployment insurance – 'the boldest experiment in social legislation of the entire period of the New Liberalism' – see Gilbert, 1970, pp. 52ff.

108 Harris, pp. 333–4. Bruce, pp. 196–200.

109 Cf. Doublet, p. 27.

110 Cf. Donzelot for the commune and its aftermath.

111 Napoleon created the *Caisse Impériale* which in his time inspired Bismarck in his even more grandiose schemes.

112 Cf. the excellent pages Ewald devotes to the mentality of these patriarchal entrepreneurs.

113 A similar mechanism operated with different results; cf. Hatzfeld, p. 249: 'if liberal conservatism had to make itself appear justified by pointing to revolutionary radicalism, the latter in turn justified itself by referring to the all too "humble reforms" of the bourgeois republic.'

114 Cf. Hatzfeld, 1971, p. 230; cf. Rosanvallon, p. 154.

115 Cf. Hatzfeld, 1971, p. 143.

116 Doublet, pp. 22, 29; Saint-Jours, p. 204.

117 Cf. Saint-Jours, p. 209.

118 François Ewald takes this legal transition from civil liability to *risque professionelle* as the paramount event that generated the transformation of individualist bourgeois society into the *État providence*. In fact, such laws were adopted everywhere at the end of the nineteenth century (for Prussian railroads by 1838) and did not produce compulsory insurance, least of all in France. The requirement to bring civil suit was greatly resented since it compelled accident victims to litigate for years, but as Ewald, pp. 247–8, points out, the legal procedures, requiring proof of their negligence, also were necessarily 'defamatory' to the employers.

119 Ibid., p. 119.

120 Ibid., p. 130. This refers, of course, to early-industrial workers who tended to quit the job when they had earned 'enough' for some time to come and came back only when their money was gone.

121 Strikers demanded a say in their management wherever such company schemes operated; Hatzfeld, 1971, p. 264.

122 Cf. Saint-Jours, p. 223; Hatzfeld, pp. 134–5.

123 Hatzfeld, 1971, p. 161: 'When it finds it necessary, the *patronat* is by no means above seeking help from the state, but as soon as it considers such intervention superfluous it regains its liberal voice.'

124 Cf. Hatzfeld, 1971, pp. 47–55, for a review of the debate and references.

125 A first law was voted in 1928, but before it became operative, it was superseded by the law of 1930.

126 It got its way on the freedom of choice of doctors and therapies, and some autonomy in setting fees, but a long series of conflicts ensued over tariffs

and their payment. Cf. Hatzfeld, 1971, pp. 289–94; Galant, pp. 14–18.
127 Galant, p. 14.
128 Cf. Galant, p. 22.
129 Since the original mutual societies were established as local, occupational, company or religious groupings, they remained at liberty to refuse candidates, except for reasons of age. Pending legislation, all sorts of organizations founded a great number of *néomutuelles* to qualify under the new law; Hatzfeld, 1971, p. 149. An illustration of the 'sociological regularity' proposed in ch. 5, section 3.
130 They had been counted upon to attract only the bad risks, and their benefits, although inferior, were expected to exhaust their resources soon; cf. Galant, p. 20, for regional statistics also.
131 Galant, p. 22.
132 Hatzfeld, 1971, pp. 148, 150.
133 Hatzfeld, 1971, pp. 269–70.
134 Whether childbirth constitutes a 'risk' or is the outcome of 'planned parenthood', of course very much depends on prevailing sexual practices and morality. In the Catholic view it may be characterized as a 'fortunate risk'. In his Introduction, Ewald points out that all 'risks' are socially defined as such.
135 Every pension required a separate Congressional bill, in pre-election sessions the number increased markedly; cf. Skocpol and Ikenberry.
136 This aspect of urban-machine politics – and of urban organized crime also – might help to explain why such machines, just like rural guerilla movements, are so hard to eradicate.
137 'There were literally hundreds of these societies many with a capital in the millions of dollars.' Furniss and Tilton, p. 155, who add in a note: 'these societies have been largely unexplored.'
138 Rimlinger, p. 196; Orloff and Skocpol, p. 734, quote Stevens (1907) for an estimate that various voluntary benefit societies may have enrolled up to one-third of the voting population (i.e. adult males minus most southern blacks).
139 Rimlinger, ibid.
140 The American societies opposed proposals for state pensions as fiercely as the British. These would maintain the needy materially without morally elevating them.
141 Cf. Skocpol and Ikenberry, pp. 102–13.
142 For these data see Rimlinger, pp. 195–6.
143 As of 1929 almost 90 per cent of health-care expenditure was paid individually, 9 per cent from public funds, commercial insurance hardly mattered until the fifties; Furniss and Tilton, p. 175.
144 Especially in the American Association for Labor Legislation, which, from 1913 on, kept pressing for social-policy reform according to the ideas of J. R. Commons, I. Fisher, I. M. Rubinov and others.
145 Skocpol and Ikenberry, p. 107: Employers were compelled to ensure against accidents, but generally free in their choice of insurance – 'private

companies continued to hold sway.' The laws were adopted with a 'remarkably consensual cross-class support' ranging from the AFL to business circles. The injured still carried between 50 and 80 per cent of the burden of industrial accidents; cf. Rimlinger, p. 196.

146 Orloff and Skocpol, p. 745. Both injured workmen and indigent mothers were caught up in court procedures which were often felt to produce highly unsatisfactory results, also by judges and other legal experts, many of whom became advocates of reform.

147 'AFL officials were particularly opposed to programs that might have allowed the government to compete for their members' loyalties such as protection for collective bargaining, medical insurance . . . and unemployment insurance. This last program, for example, threatened to make union activities like collective bargaining seem less vital.' Greenstone, p. 26. And after 1906 'the federation approved of old-age pensions, even if unenthusiastically, because retaining the loyalty of retirees was not a serious worry' (p. 27).

148 Derthick, p. 111. On the functions of 'voluntarism' in the internal power struggles with the affiliated unions, see Rogin.

149 '. . . "welfare capitalism" – the notion that private corporations might meet the social security needs of their own loyal employees – buttressed by "the associative state" – Herbert Hoover's ideal of the federal government as organizer of voluntary cooperation among business, experts, and, local governments.' Skocpol, 1984–5, p. 12. It involved only a handful of companies, and 'exactly the workers least in need of help'. The notion of welfare capitalism served, however, a major ideological function during the Hoover era and after; cf. Skocpol and Ikenberry, p. 115.

150 Greenstone, p. 75.

151 Rimlinger, p. 216.

152 On this 'inter-state balkanization' of unemployment insurance, cf. also Skocpol and Ikenberry, p. 128. Kudrle finds great similarity between the US and Canada, where the nine provinces are also quite autonomous.

153 The expression is Leman's, quoted in Skocpol, 1984–5.

154 'The economic organization of industrial workers only took place [in the CIO] after they had achieved political unity as overwhelming supporters of the Democratic party.' But by the 1920s labor voters were beginning to align themselves with the Democratic Party; Greenstone, p. 37. The author stresses the close collaboration between unions and Democrats and its significance for social-security legislation; cf. also Derthick, p. 110. According to Rimlinger, p. 223, 'Organized labor, which had shown little interest initially . . . finally went to work . . . to help with the passage of the bill.' Skocpol tends to minimize the importance of union support, because of the vehement conflicts that divided AFL and CIO.

155 Skocpol and Weir, p. 43.

156 Ibid. p. 8.

157 Contributors were paid in equal amounts by employers and workers. Separate schemes existed for government employees; farm and domestic

workers were excluded, as were workers in small establishments (up to eight employees). The self-employed were included later, on quite favorable terms. Rimlinger, p. 224.

158 i.e. lifetime earnings were aggregated; contributions over the first $3,000 (later $2,000) entitled to a pension of $15 monthly (0.5 per cent), while additional contributions (over added life income up to $24,000) entitled the subscriber to an extra monthly benefit of 0.083 per cent of earnings covered, and contributions above that threshold to a 0.041 per cent increase in benefits, the maximum monthly pension being $85. The self-employed were taxed at one and a half times the rate of workers, but at only three-quarters of the rate of total workers' and employers' contributions. Cf. Rimlinger, Viscusi. The overall redistributive effect of these and other features increasingly favored low-paid, elderly workers and those employed independently at the cost of young high-wage earners and those without a family.

159 Until the fifties more pensions were drawn from these assistance schemes than from the main contributory plan. Skocpol, 1984–5.

160 Rimlinger, p. 224. Ikenberry and Skocpol, pp. 131–2.

161 Rimlinger, p. 216. The minimum tax and benefit levels were left undefined: 'Under the pressure of competition from other states, it became extremely difficult to resist the demands for lower taxes within any given state. The result was a serious weakening of unemployment insurance all over the country because of the lack of adequate resources' (ibid. p. 225). Amenta et al. (forthcoming) find that 'a programmatic alliance between organized labor and the Democratic party did shape generous insurance in New York' and was influential in other states.

162 Ohio had enacted a scheme with 'fixed taxes and a state-wide insurance pool sufficient to provide uniform benefits for all workers thrown out of employment (regardless of their employers' previous tax payments). Another, even more influential model was developed in Wisconsin by John R. Commons and Edmund Witte, who was to play a central role in preparing federal legislation: each company was taxed in proportion to the number of workers laid off and from this 'unemployment reserve' its dismissed workers were compensated – 'but only up to the point that each company's reserve was exhausted.' Skocpol and Ikenberry, p. 118. It was this program with its overtones of 'welfare capitalism' that was finally preferred to the Ohio scheme and to more direct federal intervention. Cf. also Amenta et al.

163 All along, the program was presented as no more and no less than an enforced individual saving scheme, while its redistributive aspects among contribuants was carefully played down. Cf. Viscusi, p. 104, on this 'payroll myth'. Furniss and Tilton speak of 'administrative stealth', pp. 164ff. Derthick, p. 8, mentions 'ambiguity, inconsistency, obscurity, and paradox – qualities that go far toward explaining the overwhelming, seemingly unqualified acceptance of social security.'

164 Cf. Heidenheimer, Heclo and Adams, p. 211.

165 Furniss and Tilton, p. 173; cf. Root, pp. 106–8.
166 Cf. Price.
167 Janowitz, p. 35; cf. also Heidenheimer, 1973 and 1981.
168 Cf. Greenstone, pp. 336ff, on the unions' active support for social legislation after 1945.
169 Cf. Weir et al. p. 30: 'in each episode, the coalitions favoring new social politics were temporary, fragile, incapable of any permanent institutionalization – and very soon undone by conservative backlashes that drew on localist plus business and other resistances to enhanced state power in the United States.'
170 The Netherlands was not an all-out laggard in social security legislation, rather it occupied a middling position (fourth to ninth) among fifteen European countries with regard to the time of introduction of the four main forms of social insurance; cf. Alber, 1982, p. 28.
171 Cf. Hoefnagels, p. 91; Kossmann, p. 361.
172 Cf. P. E. de Hen.
173 Cf. Lijphart.
174 Cf. De Swaan, 1973, pp. 205–26. The one significant interruption occurred during the First World War when a government of liberal signature presided over a neutral country.
175 For a discussion of these cross-cutting lines of cleavage, cf. Stuurman, pp. 319–20: 'The opposition between bourgeois parties and Social Democrats was more important than the antithesis [this was the historical term] between confessional and anti-confessional and the antithesis was again more important than the opposition between Protestants and Catholics . . . Pillarization may then be seen as the unintended and unanticipated result of the synchronous operation of these three oppositions.'
176 The large Catholic and Social Democrat federations were amalgamated in 1976.
177 Cf. Hoefnagels, p. 119; De Vries, p. 463.
178 De Vries, p. 461; indeed, it was the government's avowed intention to enact a sickness-insurance law in connection with the accident insurance and it was widely criticized for its failure to do so.
179 This was the largest of the 'reinsuring' agencies, which handled the appeals for the employers, restituted amounts saved by safety measures, and generally operated at lower costs than the state bank; personal communication by J. Mannoury.
180 'The struggle over the Compensation Act is of interest, first because the social-political currents manifested themselves clearly in reaction to one another and to this law . . .' Van Oenen et al. II. 356.
181 Cf. Mannoury, p. 29; Witert van Hogland, p. 108.
182 Moreover, universal suffrage had been introduced a year before and union membership more than tripled between 1915 and 1920; cf. Kossmann, p. 692, Stuurman, p. 183.
183 Premiums were to be paid by the employers, the 'labor councils' would

execute the law, old-age pensions began at the age of sixty-five, the independently employed then over sixty-five might apply for free benefits, and those under that age could join voluntarily.

184 Cf. Mannoury, p. 32–3; Van Oenen (ed.), pp. 360ff, Veldkamp, I. 77.

185 Mannoury, 1985, p. 197; such medical opposition had been wholly absent when the Workmens' Compensation Act of 1901 granted the *Rijksverzekeringsbank* complete authority to provide medical services. On social legislation in the occupied Netherlands, cf. Asselberghs.

186 'While in our small country, scrupulously neutral at that time, the struggle raged on about details of implementation – hardly on substantive legislation . . .' Mannoury, p. 33.

187 According to the Central Bureau of Statistics, quoted by Pompe, p. 22, the number of 'heads of enterprises' (*bedrijfshoofden*) decreased from 26 per cent of the labor population to 21.5 per cent in 1930, 17 per cent in 1960 and 11.8 per cent in 1971. Conversely, the percentage of 'employees' ('workers' excluded) grew from 9.6 per cent in 1899 to 37.8 per cent in 1971.

188 The *Noodwet Ouderdomsvoorzieningen* of 1947, associated with the Social Democratic leader, Drees.

189 This law was complemented in 1976 by a General Disability Act, which insured all citizens. The General Act for Exceptional Costs of Disease of 1968 insured all citizens against the expense of long hospitalization and other costly medical treatment.

190 'The Dutch disability system is thus both comprehensive and generous . . . its provisions for replacement of at least 80 per cent of lost earnings, and the relatively low level of "real" disablement for which coverage is provided, have caused serious problems for the labor market, as well as the related problem of extremely rapid program growth.' And 'lack of suitable employment is generally considered to be caused by someone's handicap, unless the contrary can be proven.' Haveman et al., pp. 65, 63. As a result, 'there are therefore enough reasons to assume that the threat of unemployment from a deteriorating of the economic situation of the firm in which one works will cause wage earners to seek protection under the guise of ill health and disability.' p. 434; cf. also pp. 399–443 for an extensive description of the law's operation and effects.

191 Cf. Pompe, pp. 86ff.

192 Castles and McKinlay point out that these gas revenues hardly provide sufficient explanation: they could have been used for other purposes.

193 Wilensky, 1982, p. 354, suggests that: 'under conditions of intense Catholic and left competition, with accompanying discontinuities of left rule, social spending escalates.' These conditions seem custom-tailored for the Netherlands.

194 Cf. Wilterdink.

195 Cf. Huppes, esp. pp. 3–4; see also the comparative international figures there.

Chapter 7   Conclusion: the collectivizing process and its consequences

1 Titmuss, p. 22.
2 Heclo, 1982, pp. 390, 393.
3 Cf. Middlemas, p. 266; his comments about Britain (p. 300), are relevant to other countries as well: 'Between 1940 and 1945, the trade union movement achieved its fundamental aim of parity with the employers in the eyes of government. Against the odds, and the trend of electoral politics, the employers retained most of their pre-war political power while making shrewd accommodation to changed conditions. Neither, however, attempted to challenge the enormously swollen powers taken by government during the war and indeed both submitted themselves (as in 1916–1918) as agents, on the assumption that thereby the system of triangular cooperation would be strengthened – an assumption that proved axiomatic in the immediate post-war years.'
4 Since the mass mobilizations of the Napoleonic wars, modern warfare had necessitated the maintenance of large armies, and in its aftermath, care for veterans, war widows and orphans. With the advent of saturation bombing, civilian populations were increasingly drawn into 'total warfare', requiring government intervention on behalf of noncombatant citizens on a corresponding scale: a veritable 'demostrategy' in Cyril Falls's expression, as quoted in Titmuss, p. 82. Cf. also Marshall, pp. 82–95.
5 And maybe for the first time, the effort to prevent such domestic upheaval was made on an international scale: Marshall Aid served to counter domestic Communism in Europe and it certainly helped finance welfare policies; cf. Pinker, 1979, p. 64.
6 Albert, 1982, p. 152, has calculated that the proportion of the active population covered by social insurance in thirteen European countries went up from an average of 41 per cent in 1935, to 51 per cent in 1940, 60 per cent in 1950 and 65 per cent in 1955; it was 82 per cent by 1975. Average social security spending as a percentage of Gross National Product in those countries rose from 2.8 per cent in 1930 to 4.9 per cent in 1950, and 5.8 per cent in 1955; it was 13 per cent in 1975; cf. p. 60.
7 Heclo, 1981, p. 397, cf. p. 395: the twenty-five to thirty years before 1980 'have represented a uniquely smooth upward curve of economic growth.'
8 For a classic discussion of 'intense minorities' see Dahl, pp. 90–123. The formal conditions under which such a majority coalition may form and impose its distribution of costs and benefits – even if non-optimal in a Pareto sense – have been analyzed by Luce and Raiffa, pp. 233ff, and by Buchanan and Tullock, pp. 171–231.
9 For the US, see Patterson's account of the 'fantastic drop in the number of poor' and the 'stunning enlargement of social welfare programs' after the introduction of Medicare and Medicaid, food stamps, the extension of Aid to Families with Dependent Children and of other social-security provisions,

especially for the elderly, pp. 157ff. In the Netherlands the same years saw the enactment of the General Relief Act (*ABW* 1965), the Permanent Disability Act (*WAO* 1976), the increase in Old Age and Widows' Pensions (*AOW, AWW* 1972) and the extension of the Disability Act to all residents (*AAW* 1976); cf. *Waarborgen*, pp. 74–5. For the reform of the German insurance system during that period, cf. Hentschel, pp. 150–214; especially the tables on pp. 206–7.

10 These years coincided in the US with the war in Vietnam, which may have increased the pressure for social legislation along the same lines as the 'limited' wars of the early fifties. Gouldner's insistence on the 'organical' links between the welfare state and the 'warfare state' point to such a connection, cf. 1971, pp. 501, 508.

11 Piven and Cloward, 1982, argued that popular protest and electoral threat were the driving force behind social reform, especially in the US. Cf. p. 118: 'In brief, the framework of benefit programs created by the insurgent movements of the 1930s was elaborated and expanded by the insurgent movements of the 1960s.' Skocpol and Amenta, reviewing the available evidence, find it 'at best weakly supportive for circumscribed applications' of the thesis (p. 139). Most likely, such popular protests act much more indirectly by constituting mass-media events, which are next interpreted by intellectuals and then lead to new definitions of 'social problems'. These notions then become a mobilizing focus for coalitions of political elites in support of the social-reform policies of an activist political regime.

12 Cf. Patterson, p. 179, on the lawyers of the Office of Economic Opportunity; cf. also Katz, 1986, pp. 263–4, on legal assistance and health centers: 'the war on poverty's successful strategies for promoting institutional change and improving services for poor people.'

13 On the 'reform coalitions' between social scientists and policy makers in France, Germany and Italy, cf. Wagner.

14 In the German Federal Republic, for example, by 1980, 27 per cent of the electorate received some kind of social benefits; the majority of these were retired citizens who turned out to vote in very high proportion (85 per cent); cf. Alber, 1984, p. 232.

15 Cf. Kesselman, p. 318.

16 e.g. Weir et al. on the US: 'by the 1980s, when retrenchment of social expenditures is supposedly the order of the day, many conservative congressional representatives actually vie with the most liberal of their fellows to be seen as the staunchest defenders of social security' (p. 12).

17 Cf. Wilensky, p. 369: 'the more intense the competition between Catholic and left parties, the more left parties in power will spend.' It is not so much 'left power' as 'discontinuity' of left parties in office that tends to increase social spending. Kohl's findings in the same volume, p. 327, support this: 'The strongest tendency to increase total expenditure is found in conservative-socialist conditions where socialist inclinations to expand state activities found additional support in the necessities of coalition building.'

18 For the Netherlands, cf. *Waarborgen*, p. 27: social-transfer expenditure more

than doubled between 1975 and 1983, raising from 18.5 to 23.4 of net national income. According to Haveman et al., 1986, p. 173, expenditure for health care, social services, social security and housing rose from 31.8 to 38.5 per cent of GNP between 1970 and 1980, a figure surpassed only by Sweden (from 23.1 to 39.6 per cent). In Italy, according to Ferrera, p. 240, the 'timid measures of frugality' between 1978 and 1983 'were undone by a series of markedly expansive provisions.' (All quotations in this chapter from sources not in English have been translated by the author). In Scandinavia, there was '*a spectacular real growth of social security spending from 1970 to 1980*' under a succession of liberal and social democratic cabinets; Johansen, p. 140 (italics in orig.). The support came especially from employees in the public sector, 'constituting the single largest working constituency among the electorate'; the opposition came from the self-employed and the farmers (pp. 145–7).

19 Hasenfeld, p. 72, shows continuing, but declining growth rates for spending on health and human services in the US up to 1984. Meyer, p. 69, concludes: 'on balance, low-income beneficiaries received about the same level of benefits in 1980 as they had received about the same level of benefits in 1980 as they had received a decade earlier.' Yet specific categories, such as the working poor, were significantly worse off, cf. p. 86. Katz, 1986, pp. 285–9, comes to much the same conclusions; cf. also Hill.

In a survey article, Danziger and Smolensky find that retrenchments had measurable effects, but 'economic events had a far larger impact thus far than have programmatic changes' and 'the poor are measurably worse off than they would have been under any reasonable projection of past policies in the United Kingdom, the United States and the Netherlands. In Switzerland and Italy there have been no retrenchments; in France, programme changes were in the direction of greater social spending – until reversal of the trend' (p.261). For social-security cuts in Britain, cf. Loney, p. 87. Alber, 1982, pp. 67–8, while quoting figures for a decline in some social expenditure in Common Market Countries, considers this stagnation a sign of the almost complete penetration of the social structure by social-security systems – barely leaving room for further extensions, rather than evidence of a reversal, of the historical trend of generalization of social provisions.

20 Weir et al. pp. 14–15, point to the 'bifurcation' between American social policies aimed at the regularly employed, e.g. social security, and the more marginal programs for those who are outside the labor market, who are 'politically weakest' and therefore most vulnerable to budget cuts.

21 Weir et al. argue that 'poverty' policy was being developed by much less prestigious experts – sociologists, labor economists – than those involved in macroeconomic-policy advice, p. 6.

22 Cf. Offe, p. 152, 'the welfare state has, in a certain sense, become an irreversible structure, the abolition of which would require nothing less than the abolition of political democracy and unions, as well as fundamental changes in the party system.' Heclo, 1986, p. 56, comments on the US: 'Thus polls of general policy preferences show pervasive support for the established array of federal social programs – massive support for inclusive

programs such as Medicare and Social Security, more tempered support for programs confined to what are perceived as more narrow interest groups.' Cf. also Alber, 1984, on European welfare states: 'Structural points of action for a movement of resistance against the welfare state are therefore available to a weak degree only' (p. 223).

23 Reagan's failure to rescind disability benefits was instructive. Cf. Patterson, p. 213; Krieger, 1986, in his extensive, comparative discussion of 'Reaganism' and 'Thatcherism' arrives at a different conclusion, cf. p. 199: 'The expression "welfare state" never described the structural attributes of given nation-states or governments.' Accordingly, cf. p. 200: 'There is no welfare state, only a set of welfare provisions.' The Reagan and Thatcher regimes did put a definitive end to integrative 'Keynesian' welfare policies; cf. also Krieger, 1987.

24 Cf. Haveman et al., p. 148: 'although "retrenchment" of the welfare state in the interests of economic performance rolls off the tongues of politicians in the Netherlands, Sweden, and the United Kingdom, to date relatively little "retrenchment" can be found.'

25 See e.g., the contributions in J. L. Palmer (ed.), deploring the lack of a clear program for the future of the welfare state; cf. also Krieger on the disarray of the British and American opposition.

26 I once in jest suggested the term 'subsideologists' for those who mobilized ideological arguments to advocate government grants for their own pursuits, only to find it – spelled 'subsidiologists' – in all earnestness in corporate employment advertisements.

27 On this transformation from the 'old' to the 'new' middle class, or to the 'professional-managerial' class ('PMC'), cf. Gouldner, 1979, and B. and J. Ehrenreich, respectively.

28 Alber, 1984, pp. 244–5: the welfare state in the GFR is oriented towards *Statussicherung*, i.e. the safeguarding of status differentials, even though it does have vertical redistributive effects.

29 It is a shift from a coalition of the urban *petit bourgeoisie* and independent farmers defending private accumulation to an alliance of the new salaried middle class with the working class in support of collectivized arrangements that forms the core of the historical argument by Esping-Andersen and Korpi.

30 Cf. Gouldner, 1971, pp. 76–87, on the 'disposal and control of the useless'.

31 Baier, 1984.

32 For a brief and insightful discussion of terminology with respect to 'profession' and 'occupation', and for an inventory of recent criticisms, cf. Freidson, 1984: specialized expertise, credentials and relative autonomy are the characteristics in increasing order of specificity. For the role of the state in professionalization, cf. Freidson, 1970.

33 Alber, 1984, p. 232, points out that recipients of social-transfer incomes in the GFR have been the fastest growing category, representing 27 per cent of the electorate in 1980: the aged among them especially turn out in great numbers (85 per cent) at elections. And yet, cf. p. 245, the recipients of

benefits consider their status transitory and do not perceive their fellows as 'relevant to others'.

34 For parental backgrounds of French elementary teachers around 1900 cf. Muel-Dreyfus, p. 25: more than half came from a middle-class background, half of those from self-employed fathers (including farmers); almost a quarter of the male teachers were workers' sons. Cf. also Day.

35 Cf. Flora: by 1870 teachers made up half of all government personnel in France, and in 1975 when total personnel was ten times as numerous, still 37.8 per cent (pp. 210–11). In the Netherlands 37.7 per cent in 1889 and still 32.9 per cent in 1960 (p. 223), with government personnel six times as large.

36 Cf. Flora, for figures; cf. also Fischer and Lundgreen.

37 The preference within the Progressive Movement for 'regulatory agencies' and 'inspection' is in part explained by the career interests among the middle class; Skocpol and Ikenberry, p. 31. At about the same time, the Social Democratic cadre manned the jobs in the Bismarckian social-security establishment, Tennstedt p. 233.

38 e.g. Kelsall on Britain; cf. p. 3: 'before and after the Civil Service reforms of the nineteenth century, middle class penetration of what had previously been an aristocratic preserve revolutionized the position.'

39 Cf. 'De valse schaduw', in De Swaan, 1983, 115–18.

40 Fraud occurs mostly in the form of tax evasion or illegitimate claims. Embezzlement of social-insurance funds by administrators occurs every now and then, but the relative rarity testifies to a more effective separation of private motives and institutional interests in government administration and to the highly developed techniques of accountancy, surveillance and inspection in modern bureaucracy. Corruption scandals, however, tend to come in waves and most often in times of economic slump, when ventures which once seemed promising and daring suddenly fail, while Schumpeter's 'pushers of new combinations' are exposed as swindlers under the glare of publicity.

41 For an account of the early professionalizing process of such 'urban experts' in the US, see Katz, 1986, pp. 163ff.

42 In England the Medical Act of 1858, cf. Peterson, pp. 30ff; Waddington, pp. 53–134; in the Netherlands, the Act of 1865, cf. Jaspers, p. 10; for the US, the Medical Practice Restriction Acts (1880–93) cf. Berlant, p. 235, and his explanation in terms of state protection of local trade against the encroachment of national corporations, pp. 238–42.

43 Cf. Eckstein, p. 106. See also Gilbert, 1970, ch. 7, on the British Medical Association and the law of 1911. For the US cf. Starr, pp. 192ff, and Rozen. For France, Goguel, pp. 269–71; Hatzfeld, 1963, *passim.*

44 Cf. Peterson, pp. 200–1, 223, 243, on the relatively low prestige and income of doctors in Victorian England. Cf. Eckstein, pp. 75–8, on the distribution of incomes among general practitioners and the plight of young doctors in the years between the wars. For recent time series on medical incomes in the US, cf. Waitzkin, p. 38.

45 It was this experience that led British doctors, even when reform-minded, to oppose control by local authority or private agencies, and to prefer state management; cf. Eckstein, p. 129. It was also a matter of class contempt for health officers. For France, see Hatzfeld, 1971, pp. 291–3.

46 Cf. Eckstein's analysis of rank-and-file opinion within the British Medical Association after 1945, pp. 143–55.

47 Cf. Hatzfeld, 1963, for a brief comparison of England, France and Germany, pp. 36–45; Berlant on England and the US; an excellent account of the US situation in Starr.

48 Authors of Marxist orientation, especially in the US, consider such autonomy mostly apparent, shared at best with the dominant class: cf. B. and J. Ehrenreich; Brown; and Navarro. For a recent and extensive discussion of professional autonomy, in the US see Freidson, 1986.

49 Cf. Heidenheimer, 1973, p. 333.

50 Cf. De Swaan, 1989.

51 Cf. Peterson, pp. 244–82, on late Victorian medical entrepreneurs pandering new remedies and founding specialist clinics against the policy of the organized profession.

52 'During periods of change in the organization and composition of professions, then, it may be possible for new "missionaries" to emerge, and to stake out claims for new territories, or to re-colonize abandoned ecological niches.' P. Atkinson, p. 240.

53 On the functions of physicians as 'gatekeepers' in the social allocation of scarce resources, see Stone, 1979b; cf. also Freidson, 1986, on the role conflicts this creates for professionals within the bureaucracy.

54 D. Stone, 1979a, p. 519, writes: 'Although all of these distributive programs have had the effect of increasing the scope of physician authority, their growth does not represent a usurpation of power by physicians; at least in this sphere the opposite would seem to be true. Physicians have not often used their organized power to foster the establishment of programs that rely on medical certification . . .' Cf. also Stone, 1979b.

55 Cf. Waitzkin, p. 41: 'By defining social problems as medical, medicine becomes an instrument of social control . . . medical practitioners tend to remove these problems as potential objects of organized political action.'

56 Cf. De Swaan, 1989.

57 The 'medical imperialism' thesis, as advanced by Waitzkin and Waterman, among others esp. pp. 86–9, holds on the contrary that medical institutions are expansionist by nature. See for a critical discussion of this position Strong; also Eisenberg and Kleinman.

58 Cf. Crawford on the political implications of this medical attention to personal habits.

59 e.g. according to opinion polls, an increasing plurality of the Dutch, 52 per cent in 1986, find 'health' more important than anything else in life, including income, family, marriage, work and religion; *Sociaal en cultureel rapport*, 1986, p. 349.

60 And also: 'Making care of one's health into an ordinary routine is more

"rational" when life expectancy is high than when it is low . . . The social conditions of regular personal health care may be compared to the social conditions for thrift.' Goudsblom, 1986, p. 185.

61 This explains why most 'information lines' or 'data banks' are of so little use: what is truly useful to know is usually what others don't know or what is essentially ambiguous: e.g. it pays to know about a seaside resort where rents are low or beaches quiet, or about a job opening, only if few others are also aware of it. It is of limited interest to know what the customs regulations are for importing liquor, but it is very useful to know what the chances are of being caught. What matters is scarce, ambiguous and uncertain information.

62 Cf. 'The Psychotherapy Trade', in De Swaan, 1989; cf. also Ooesterbaan and Zeldenrust on help-seeking patterns of recent divorcees.

63 Elias, 1978a, 1982.

64 Elias, 1982, pp. 300–7.

65 Ibid. pp. 249–50; however, see also Elias and Scotson.

66 Elias writes (1982, p. 248): 'the general direction of the change in conduct, the "trend" of the movement of civilization, is everywhere the same. It always veers towards a more or less automatic self-control, to the subordination of short-term impulses to the commands of an ingrained long-term view, and to the formation of a more complex and secure "super-ego" agency. And broadly the same, too, is the manner in which this necessity to subordinate momentary affects to more distant goals is propagated; everywhere small leading groups are affected first, and then broader and broader strata of Western society.'

67 Baker called this the 'social conscience thesis' of social policy and found it to be very prevalent in textbooks used in social-administration courses in England (1976).

68 For a critique, see my 'Politics of Agoraphobia', 1981, and the discussion that follows.

69 For a critical discussion of the issues from within the social control perspective, cf. Mayer.

70 Muel-Dreyfus, p. 53, quotes the advice given by an instructor to young teachers (France, 1881): 'standing up, the body should be held straight, and the head also, the eyes slightly lowered as it would be impertinent and offending to stare at everyone. The hands may hang on the sides, or support one another at the height of the belt, or they may be crossed in front of the chest, but they should never be stuck in the pockets, put on the hips, or brought frequently to the face or the head.' And so forth.

71 When Freud discovered the traumatic meaning of the primal scene – the child's discovery of its parents' intercourse – this experience was just becoming rarer, as even lower-middle and working-class families were moving into homes with separate bedrooms for parents and children; cf. *The Wolfman* (1914).

72 Elias, 1982, p. 292.

73 Cf. Lenhardt and Offe.

74 Elias, 1982, pp. 251–6.

75 The term is Goudsblom's, cf. 1977, pp. 43ff.
76 Cf. De Swaan, 1986.
77 Haskell, p. 342, author's italics.
78 Ibid., pp. 550–1.
79 Ibid., p. 548.
80 Ibid., p. 548.
81 Ibid., p. 358, italics added.
82 Ibid., p. 555.
83 But see Goodin on the recent moral advocacy of 'self-reliance'.
84 Haskell, p. 359.

References

Abbiateci, A., 'Les Incendiaires dans la France du XVIIIe siècle; Essai de Typologie Criminelle', *Annales ESC*, 1970, pp. 229–48.

Abel, W., *Massenarmut und Hungerkrisen im Vorindustriellen Deutschland*. Göttingen: Vandenhoeck & Ruprecht, 1972.

Alber, Jens, *Vom Armenhaus zum Wohlfahrtsstaat; Analysen zur Entwicklung der Sozialversicherung in Westeuropa*. Frankfurt/New York: Campus, 1982.

Alber, Jens, 'Versorgungsklassen im Wohlfahrtsstaat; Überlegungen und Daten zur Situation in der Bundesrepublik' *Kölner Zeitschrift für Soziologie und Sozialpsychologie*, 36.1 (1984), 225–51.

Allain, E., *L'Œuvre scolaire de la Révolution, 1789–1802, études critiques et documents inédits*. Paris: 1891, repr.: Franklin, New York, 1969.

Amenta, Edwin, et al. 'The Political Origins of Unemployment Insurance in Five American States,' *Studies in American Political Development: An Annual*, vol. 2. New Haven: Yale UP, 1987.

Anderson, Eugene N., 'The Prussian *Volksschule* in the Nineteenth Century', in G. A. Ritter (ed.), *Entstehung und Wandel der modernen Gesellschaft: Festschrift für Hans Rosenberg zum 65. Geburtstag*, pp. 261–79. Berlin: De Gruyter, 1970.

Anderson, Michael, 'Urban Migration in Victorian Britain: Problems of Assimilation?', in: Étienne François (ed), *Immigration et Société Urbaine en Europe Occidentale, XVIe–XXe Siècle*, pp. 79–91. Paris: Éditions Recherche sur les Civilisations, 1985.

Anderson, Robert D., *Education in France 1848–1870*. Oxford: Clarendon Press, 1975.

Ariès, Philippe, 'Problèmes de l'Éducation', in *La France et les français, Encyclopédie de la Pléiade*, vol. 32, pp. 871–961. Paris: Gallimard, 1972.

Armstrong, Ellis L. (ed.), *History of Public Works in the United States, 1776–1976*. Chicago: American Public Works Ass., 1976.

Asselberghs, Karel, 'De sociale verzekering tijdens de bezetting', *(Amsterdams) Sociologisch Tijdschrift*, 9.1 (May 1982), 5–40.

References

Atkinson, Anthony B. (ed.), *Wealth, Income, and Inequality*. Oxford: Oxford UP (2nd edn), 1980.

Atkinson, Paul, 'The Reproduction of the Professional Community', in R. Dingwall and P. Lewis (eds), *The Sociology of the Professions: Lawyers, Doctors and Others*, pp. 224–41. London: Macmillan, 1983.

Aumüller, Ursula, 'Industrieschule und ursprüngliche Akkumulation in Deutschland: Die Qualifiziering der Arbeitskraft im Übergang von der feodalen in der kapitalistischen Produktionsweise', in: *Schule und Staat im 18. und 19. Jahrhundert: Zur Socialgeschichte der Schule in Deutschland*, pp. 9–145. Frankfurt a. M.: Suhrkamp, 1974.

Axelrod, Robert, *The Evolution of Cooperation*. New York: Basic Books, 1984.

Aydelotte, Frank, *Elisabethan Rogues and Vagabonds*. London: Frank Cass & Co. Ltd., 1967.

Bailyn, Bernard, *Education in the Forming of American Society: Needs and Opportunities for Study*. New York: Vintage Books, 1960.

Baker, John, 'Social Conscience and Social Policy', *Journal of Social Policy*, 8.2 (April 1979).

Banks, J. A., 'The Contagion of Numbers', in: H. J. Dyos and Michael Wolff (eds), *The Victorian City: Images and Realities*, 2 vols., Vol. 1., pp. 105–22. London and Boston: Routledge & Kegan Paul, 1973.

Banton, Michael, 'Voluntary Associations, 1: Anthropological Aspects', *International Encyclopaedia of the Social Sciences*, 16. 360–1. New York and London: MacMillan and Free Press, 1968.

Barker, Ernest, *The Development of Public Services in Western Europe, 1660–1930*. London and New York: Oxford UP, 1944.

Barnard, Howard Clive, *A Short History of English Education from 1760 to 1944*, London: University of London Press, 1947.

Bauer, Otto, *Kapitalismus und Sozialismus nach dem Weltkrieg*, I: *Rationalisierung–Fehlrationalisierung*. Vienna: Volksbuchhandlung, 1931.

Baumol, William J., *Welfare Economics and the Theory of the State*. London: Bell (2nd edn), 1965.

Bayley, David H., 'The Police and Political Development in Europe', in: Ch. Tilly (ed.), *The Formation of National States in Western Europe*. Princeton, NJ: Princeton UP, 1975.

Beier, A. L., 'Vagrants and the Social Order in Elizabethan England', *Past and Present*, 64 (August 1974), 3–29.

Beloff, Max, *Public Order and Popular Disturbances, 1660–1714* (1938). London: Frank Cass, 1963.

Bergmann, Klaus, 'Überleben im Abwasserkanal: Ein Sittenbild aus dem Wien der Jahrhundertwende', *Journal für Geschichte*, 4 (July/August 1985), 47–51.

Berlanstein, Lenard, R., *The Working People of Paris, 1871–1914*. Baltimore and London: Johns Hopkins UP, 1984.

Berlant, Jeffrey L., *Profession and Monopoly: A Study of Medicine in the United States and Great Britain*. Berkeley: University of California Press, 1975.

Bernstein, Basil, *Class, Codes and Control*, Vol. 1: *Theoretical Studies towards a Sociology of Language*. London: Routledge & Kegan Paul, 1974.

References

Berrol, Selma, 'Public Schools and Immigrants: the New York City Experience', in Bernard J. Weiss (ed.), *American Education and the European Immigrant: 1840–1940*, pp. 31–43. Urbana, Ill.: University of Illinois Press, 1982.

Binnie, G. M., *Early Victorian Water Engineers*. London: Telford, 1981.

Bloch, Camille, *L'Assistance et l'état en France à la veille de la Révolution (Généralités de Paris, Rouen, Alençon, Orléans, Chalons, Soissons, Amiens), 1764–1790*. Paris: Picard, 1908.

Bloch, Marc, *La Société féodale* (1939). Paris: Albin Michel, 1968.

Blockmans, W. P. and W. Prevenier, 'Armoede in de Nederlanden van de 14e tot het midden van de 16e eeuw: Bronnen en problemen', *Tijdschrift voor geschiedenis*, 88 (1975), 501–35.

Blum, Jerome, 'The Internal Structure and Polity of the European Village Comunity from the Fifteenth to the Nineteenth Century', *Journal of Modern History*, 43 (1971), 541–76.

Bonenfant, Paul, *Hôpitaux et bienfaisance publique dans les anciens Pays-Bas des origines à la fin du XVIIIe siècle*. Annales de la Société Belge d'Histoire des Hôpitaux III, 1965.

Boorman, Scott A. and Paul R. Levitt, *The Genetics of Altruism*. New York: Academic Press, 1980.

Bowles, Samuel and Herbert Gintis, *Schooling in Capitalist America: Educational Reform and the Contradictions of Economic Life*. New York: Basic Books, 1976.

Bowman, John R., 'The Logic of Capitalist Collective Action' *Social Science Information*, 21 (1982), 571–604.

Boyer, Paul, *Urban Masses and Moral Order in America, 1820–1920*. Cambridge, Mass.: Harvard UP, 1978.

Briod, Alice, *L'Assistance des pauvres au Moyen Âge dans le pays de Vaud* (1926). Lausanne: Éditions d'en Bas, 1976.

Brown, E. Richard, *Rockefeller Medicine Men: Medicine and Capitalism in America*. Berkeley: University of California Press, 1979.

Bruce, Maurice, *The Coming of the Welfare State*. London: Batsford (1961), 1968.

Bruin, Kees and Huibert Schijf, 'De Eerste Bewoners in een Deftige Straat', in: Michiel Jonker et al. (eds), *Van stadskern tot stadsgewest: Stedebouwkundige geschiedenis van Amsterdam*, pp. 133–56. Amsterdam: Verloren, 1984.

Buchanan, James M. and Gordon Tullock, *The Calculus of Consent; Logical Foundations of Constitutional Democracy*. Ann Arbor: University of Michigan Press, 1962.

Burg, B. R., *Sodomy and the Perception of Evil: English Sea Rovers in the Seventeenth-century Caribbean*. New York: New York UP, 1983.

Burnett, John, *A Social History of Housing 1815–1970*. London: David & Charles, 1978.

Busshoff, Heinrich, 'Die preussische Volksschule als Soziales Gebilde und Politischer Bildungsfaktor in der Erste Hälfte des 19. Jahrhunderts. Ein Bericht', *Geschichte in Wissenschaft und Unterricht*, 22. 7 (July 1971), 385–95.

Butler, Rémy and Patrice Noisette, *De la cité ouvrière au grand ensemble: La politique capitaliste du logement social 1815–1975*. Paris: Maspéro, 1977.

Butts, R. Freeman, *A Cultural History of Western Education: Its Social and*

References

Intellectual Foundations. New York: McGraw-Hill, 1955, 2nd edn.

Carasso, Dedalo, 'Op Weg naar het Begin; Reiniging en Stadsreiniging in de 19e Eeuw', *Ons Amsterdam* 29 (1977), 255–71.

Castles, Francis G. (ed.), *The Impact of Parties: Politics and Policies in Democratic Capitalist States.* London/Beverly Hills, Cal.: Sage, 1982.

Castles, Francis and R. D. McKinlay, 'Does Politics Matter? Public Welfare Commitment in Advanced Democratic States', *European Journal of Political Research*, 7 (1979).

Chartier, Roger, Dominique Julia and Marie-Madeleine Compère, *L'Éducation en France du xvie au xviiie siècle.* Paris: Société d'Édition d'Enseignement Supérieur, 1976.

Checkland, Olive, 'Local Government and the Health Environment', in: Olive Checkland and Margaret Lamb (eds), *Health Care as Social History: The Glasgow Case*, pp. 1–15. Aberdeen: Aberdeen UP, 1982.

Chevalier, Louis, *Classes labourieuses et classes dangereuses à Paris pendant la première moitié du XIXe siècle.* Paris: Plon, 1958.

Chisick, Harvey, *The Limits of Reform in the Enlightment: Attitudes towards the Education of the Lower Classes in Eighteenth-Century France.* Princeton NJ: Princeton UP, 1981.

Cobb, Richard, *The Police and the People: French Popular Protest 1789–1820.* Oxford: Oxford UP, 1970.

Cohen, Marcel, *Histoire d'une langue: la français.* Paris: Édition Hier et Aujour-d'Hui, 1947.

Coleman, William, *Death is a Social Disease; Public Health and Political Economy in Early Industrial France.* Madison, Wisc.: University of Wisconsin Press, 1982.

Coll, Blanche D., 'Public Assistance in the United States: Colonial Times to 1860', in E. W. Martin (ed.), *Comparative Development in Social Welfare*, pp. 128–58. London: Allen & Unwin, 1972.

Collins, Doreen, 'The Introduction of Old Age Pensions in Great Britain', *Historical Journal*, 8 (1965), 246–59.

Collins, Randall, *The Credential Society: An Historical Sociology of Education and Stratification.* New York: Academic Press, 1979.

Corbin, Alain, *Le Miasme et la jonquille: L'Odorat et l'imaginaire social, 18e–19e siècles.* Paris: Aubier, 1982.

Cotterau, Alain, 'The Distinctiveness of Working-Class Cultures in France, 1848–1900', in: I. Katznelson and A. R. Zolberg, *Working-class Formation: Nineteenth-Century Patterns in Western Europe and the United States*, Princeton, NJ,: Princeton UP, 1986, pp. 111–65.

Crawford, Robert, 'Healthism and the Medicalization of Everyday Life', *International Journal of Health Services*, 10.3 (1980), 365–88.

Cremin, Lawrence A., *American Education: The National Experience 1783–1876.* New York: Harper, 1980.

Cremin, Lawrence A., *Traditions of American Education.* New York: Basic Books, 1977.

Cressy, David, 'Levels of Illiteracy in England 1530–1730', in: Graff, Harvey J.

(ed.), *Literacy and Social Development in the West: A Reader.* pp. 105–24. Cambridge: Cambridge UP, 1981.

Crossick, Geoffrey and Heinz-Gerhard Haupt (eds), *Shopkeepers and Master Artisans in Nineteenth-Century Europe.* London: Methuen, 1984.

Crouch, C., *Trade Unions: The Logic of Collective Action.* London: Fontana, 1981.

Cruson, Cees, 'Van Elite-taal tot nationale taal', *Symposium*, Vol. 2.1: *Nationale integratie en sociale differentiatie.* 1980.

Dahl, Robert A., *A Preface to Democratic Theory.* Chicago: University of Chicago Press, 1956.

Danziger, Sheldon and Eugene Smolensky, 'Income Transfer Policies and the Poor: A Cross-National Perspective', *Journal of Social Policy*, 14.3 (1985), 257–62.

Dasberg, L. and J. W. G. Jansing, *Meer Kennis Meer Kans; Het Nederlands Onderwijs 1843–1914.* Haarlem: Fibula-Van Dishoeck, 1978.

Daunton, Martin J., *House and Home in the Victorian City: Working Class Housing, 1850–1914.* London: Arnold, 1983.

Dawkins, Richard, *The Selfish Gene.* London: Granada, 1978.

Day, C. R., 'The Rustic Man: The Rural Schoolmaster in Nineteenth-Century France', *Comparative Studies in Society and History*, 25.1 (Jan. 1983), 26–49.

De Hen, P. E., 'De Industrialisatie van Nederland', in: F. L. van Holthoon (ed.), *De Nederlandse samenleving sinds 1815: Wording en samenhang*, pp. 3–18. Assen/Maastricht: Van Gorcum, 1985.

De Regt, Ali, *Arbeidersgezinnen en beschavingsarbeid: Ontwikkelingen in Nederland 1870–1940: Een historisch-sociologische studie* (Diss. University of Amsterdam, with a summary in English). Amsterdam/Meppel: Boom, 1984.

De Rooy, Piet, *Werklozenzorg en werkloosheidsbestrijding 1917–1940: Landelijk en Amsterdams beleid* (with a summary in English). Amsterdam: Van Genep, 1979.

Derthick, Martha, *Policymaking for Social Security.* Washington, DC: Brookings Institute, 1979.

De Swaan, Abram, 'Armenzorg als collectieve actie: Naar een sociogenetisch paradigma van het collectiviseringsproces', in: P. K. Keizer and J. Soeters (eds), *Economie, sociologie en psychologie: Visies op integratie*, pp. 103–32. Assen/Maastricht: Van Gorcum, 1987a.

De Swaan, Abram, 'From Charitable Feeling to Social Consciousness', in: (A.) Guus J. M. van Weers (ed.), *L'État-providence: Un débat philosophique / The Welfare State: A Philosophical Debate*, pp. 131–46. Maastricht: Presses Interuniversitaires Européennes, 1986a.

De Swaan, Abram, *Coalition Theories and Cabinet Formations: A Study of Formal Theories of Coalition Formation Applied to Nine European Parliaments after 1918.* Amsterdam/London/New York: Elsevier Scientific/Jossey Bass, 1973.

De Swaan, Abram, 'Floral Figurations: Opportunities for Communication and Conflicting Interests in Evolving Multilanguage Systems', paper presented at the Conference on 'Minority Languages and Mass Communications', Ljubljana, October 1987b.

De Swaan, Abram, *Halverwege de Heilstaat: Essays (Halfway to the State of Salvation).* Amsterdam: Meulenhoff, 1983.

References

De Swaan, Abram, 'Jaloezie als klassenverschijnsel', *De gids*, 151.1 (1988), 39–49 (transl. and repr. in De Swaan, 1989).

De Swaan, Abram, *The Management of Normality; Critical Essays on Health and Welfare*. London/New York: Routledge & Kegan Paul, 1989.

De Swaan, Abram, 'De Mens is de Mens een Zorg' in: *De mens is de mens een zorg: Essays 1971–1981*. Amsterdam: Meulenhoff, 1982.

De Swaan, Abram, 'Nood en Deugd; Over Altruïsme en Collectieve Actie', *De gids* (Amsterdam), 147.3 (1984), 139–51.

De Swaan, Abram, 'The Politics of Agoraphobia', *Theory and Society*, 10.3 (May 1981), 359–86 (followed by a discussion with John Alt and Alvin W. Gouldner, pp. 387–418). Repr. in De Swaan, 1989.

De Swaan, Abram, 'Workers' and Clients' Mutualism Compared: Perspectives from the Past in the Development of the Welfare State', *Government and Opposition*, 21.1 (Winter 1986b), 36–55.

De Vries Wzn., Willem, *De Invloed van werkgevers en werknemers op de totstandkoming van de eerste sociale verzekeringswet in Nederland (De Ongevallenwet 1901)* (Diss. Free University, with a summary in English). Deventer: Kluwer, 1970.

De Wit, C. H. E., *De strijd tussen aristocratie en democratie in Nederland 1780–1848*. Heerlen: Winants, 1965.

Deacon, Alan and Jonathan Bradshaw, *Reserved for the Poor: The Means Test in British Social Policy*. Oxford: Robertson, 1983.

Delaporte, François, *Disease and Civilization: The Cholera in Paris 1832*. Cambridge, Mass./London: MIT Press, 1986.

Depauw, Jacques, 'Pauvres, Pauvres Mendiants, Mendiants Valides ou Vagabonds? Les Hésitations de la Législation Royale', *Revue d'histoire moderne et contemporaine*, 21 (1974), 401–18.

Deutsch, Karl, *Nationalism and Social Communication: An Inquiry into the Foundations of Nationality*. Cambridge, Mass.: MIT Press, 1953.

Digby, Anne and Peter Searby, *Children, School and Society in Nineteenth-Century England*. London: Macmillan 1981.

Dodde, N. L., *Geschiedenis van het Nederlandse schoolwezen: een historisch-onderwijskundige studie van het Nederlandse onderwijs gedurende de 19de en 20ste eeuw*. Purmerend: Muusses, 1981.

Donzelot, Jacques, *L'Intervention du social: essai sur le déclin des passions politiques*. Paris: Fayard, 1984.

Dorian, Nancy C., *Language Death: The Life Cycle of a Scottish Gaelic Dialect*. Philadelphia: University of Pennsylvania Press, 1981.

Dorwart, Reinhold A., *The Prussian Welfare State Before 1740*. Cambridge, Mass.: Harvard UP, 1971.

Doublet, Jacques, *Sécurité sociale*. Paris: Presses Universitaires de France, 5th edn, 1972 (former editions in collaboration with Georges Lavau).

Drucker, Peter F., 'The Educational Revolution', in: A. H. Halsey, J. Floud and C. A. Anderson (eds), *Education, Economy and Society: A Reader in the Sociology of Education*, pp. 15–21. New York, Free Press, 1961.

Duby, Georges, *L'Économie rurale et la vie des campagnes dans l'occident médiéval*,

References

Vol. 2: *France, Angleterre, Empire, IXe–XVe siècles.* Paris: Flammarion, 1977.

Dupeux, George, *French Society 1789–1970.* London, New York: Barnes & Nobles, 1976.

Dupuy, Gabriel and George Knaebel, 'Choix techniques et assainissement urbain en France de 1800 à 1977' (mimeo) Paris: Institut d'Urbanisme de Paris, 1979.

Dyos, H. J., *Exploring the Urban Past: Essays in Urban History.* (ed. by David Cannadine and David Reeder), Cambridge: Cambridge UP, 1982.

Eckstein, Harry, *The English Health Service: Its Origins, Structure, and Achievements.* Cambridge, Mass. Harvard UP, 1958.

Ehrenreich, Barbara and John Ehrenreich, 'The Professional-Managerial Class', *Radical America,* 11 (March–April 1977), 7–31.

Eisenberg, Leon and Arthur Kleinman, 'Clinical Social Science', in: L. Eisenberg and A. Kleinman (eds), *The Relevance of Social Science for Medicine,* pp. 1–26. Dordrecht: Reidel, 1981.

Eisenstein, Elizabeth L., 'Some Conjectures about the Impact of Printing on Western Society and Thought: A Preliminary Report', *Journal of Modern History,* 40 (1968), 7–29; repr. in: H. J. Graff (ed.), *Literacy and Social Development in the West: A Reader,* pp. 53–68. Cambridge: Cambridge UP, 1981.

Elias, Norbert, *The Civilizing Process* (1939), Vol. 1: *The History of Manners.* Oxford, New York: Blackwell/Urizen, 1978a; Vol. 2: *Power and Civility.* Blackwell/Pantheon, 1982.

Elias, Norbert and John L. Scotson, *The Established and the Outsiders: A Sociological Enquiry into Community Problems.* London: F. Cass, 1965. Also: 'Introduction' to the Dutch edn.: *De gevestigden en de buitenstaanders: Een studie van de spanningen en machtsverhoudingen tussen twee arbeidersbuurten.* Utrecht/Antwerpen: Aula/Het Spectrum, 1976.

Elias, Norbert, *What is Sociology?* London: Hutchinson, 1978b.

Elster, Jon, *Making Sense of Marx.* Cambridge: Cambridge UP, 1985.

Elster, Jon, 'Marxism, Functionalism, and Game Theory: The Case for Methodological Individualism', *Theory and Society,* 11 (1982), 453–82; 'Reply to Comments', ibid., 12 (1983), 111–20.

Elster, Jon, *Ulysses and the Sirens: Studies in Rationality and Irrationality.* New York: Cambridge UP, 1979.

Endres, Rudolf, 'Das Armenproblem im Zeitalter des Absolutismus', in: F. Kopitzsch (ed.), *Aufklärung, Absolutismus und Bürgertum in Deutschland,* pp. 220–41. Munich: Nymphenburger Verlagshandlung, 1976.

Engel, Josef, ed., *Grosser historischer Weltatlas,* Vol. II: *Mittelalter.* Munich: Bayerischer Schulbuch Verlag, 1970.

Esping-Andersen, Gösta and Walter Korpi, 'Social Policy as Class Politics in Post-War Capitalism: Scandinavia, Austria, and Germany', in: John H. Goldthorpe (ed.), *Order and Conflict in Contemporary Capitalism: Studies in the Political Economy of West European Nations,* pp. 179–208. Oxford: Oxford UP, 1984.

Esser, Hartmut, 'Figurationssoziologie und methodologischer Individualismus:

References

Zur Methodologie des Ansatzes von Norbert Elias' *Kölner Zeitschrift für Soziologie und Sozialpsychologie*, 36.4 (1984), 667–702.

Evans, Peter, Dietrich Rüschemeyer and Theda Skocpol (eds), *Bringing the State Back In*. Cambridge: Cambridge UP, 1988.

Ewald, François, *L'État providence*. Paris: Grasset, 1986.

Feldstein, Martin, 'Social Security, Induced Retirement, and Aggregate Capital Accumulation', *Journal of Political Economy*, 82.5 (Sept./Oct. 1974), 905–26.

Feldstein, Martin, 'Toward a Reform of Social Security', *Public Interest*, 40 (1975), 75–95.

Ferrera, Maurizio, *Il Welfare State in Italia: sviluppo e crisi in prospettiva comparata*. Bologna: Il Mulino, 1984.

Finer, S. E., *The Life and Times of Sir Edwin Chadwick*. New York/London: Barnes & Noble/Methuen, 1952.

Fischer, Thomas, *Städtische Armut und Armenfürsorge im 15. und 16. Jahrhundert: Sozialgeschichtliche Untersuchungen am Beispiel der Städte Basel, Freiburg i Br. und Strassburg*. Göttingen: Schwartz, 1979.

Fischer, Wolfram and Peter Lundgreen, 'The Recruitment and Training of Administrative and Technical Personnel', in: Tilly, Charles (ed.), *The Formation of National States in Europe*. Princeton, NJ: Princeton UP, 1975.

Flora, Peter and Arnold J. Heidenheimer (eds), *The Development of Welfare States in Europe and America*. New Brunswick and London: Transaction, 1981.

Flora, Peter (ed.), *State, Economy, and Society in Western Europe 1815–1975: A Data Handbook*, Vol. 1: *The Growth of Mass Democracies and Welfare States*. Frankfurt a. M.: Campus Verlag, 1983.

Foucault, M., *Histoire de la folie à l'âge classique*. Paris: Gallimard, 1972.

Foucault, M., *Surveiller et punir: naissance de la prison*. Paris: Gallimard, 1975.

Fraser, Derek, *The Evolution of the British Welfare State: A History of Social Policy since the Industrial Revolution*. London: Macmillan, 1973.

Fraser, Derek, 'The English Poor Law and the Origins of the British Welfare State', in Wolfgang J. Mommsen and W. Mock (eds), *The Emergence of the Welfare State in Britain and Germany 1850–1950*, pp. 9–31. London: Croom Helm, 1981.

Freidson, Eliot, 'Are Professions Necessary?', in: Thomas L. Haskell (ed.), *The Authority of Experts: Studies in History and Theory*, pp. 3–27. Bloomington, Ind.: Indiana UP, 1984.

Freidson, Eliot, *The Profession of Medicine: A Study of the Sociology of Applied Knowledge*. New York: Dodd, Mead, 1970.

Freidson, Eliot, *Professional Powers: A Study of the Institutionalization of Formal Knowledge*. Chicago and London: University of Chicago Press, 1986.

Freud, Sigmund, *The Wolfman* (1914), in: *Standard Edition of the Complete Psychological Works of Sigmund Freud*, Vol. 17, pp. 1–122. London: Hogarth Press, 1953–74.

Frevert, Ute, *Krankheit als politisches Problem 1770–1880: Soziale Unterschichten in Preussen zwischen medizinischer Polizei und staatlicher Sozialversicherung*. Göttingen: Vandenhoeck & Ruprecht, 1984.

References

Friedrich, Carl J., *Man and his Government: An Empirical Theory of Politics*. New York: McGraw-Hill, 1963.

Frijhoff, Willem, 'Van Onderwijs naar Opvoedend Onderwijs; Ontwikkelingslijnen van Opvoeding en Onderwijs in Noord-Nederland in de Achttiende Eeuw', in: *Onderwijs en Opvoeding in de achttiende eeuw*, pp. 3–39. Amsterdam/Maarssen: Holland University Press, 1983.

Fröhlich, Sigrid, *Die soziale Sicherung bei Zünften und Gesellenverbänden: Darstellung, Analyse, Vergleich*. Berlin: Duncker & Humblot, 1976.

Furet, François and Jacques Ozouf, *Lire et écrire; l'alphabétisation des français de Calvin à Jules Ferry*, Vol. 1: Paris: Minuit, 1977.

Furet, François, 'Pour une Définition des Classes Inférieures á l'Époque Moderne', *Annales ESC*, 18 (1963), 459–74.

Furniss, Norman and Timothy Tilton, *The Case for the Welfare State: From Social Security to Social Equality*. Bloomington, Ind.: Indiana UP, 1977.

Garraty, John A., *Unemployment in History: Economic Thought and Public Policy*. New York: Harper, 1979.

Gauldie, Enid, *Cruel Habitations: A History of Working-Class Housing 1780–1918*. London: Allen & Unwin, 1974.

Geist, Johann Friedrich and Klaus Kuervers, *Das Berliner Mietshaus, II: 1862–1945: Eine dokumentarische Geschichte*. Munich: Prestel, 1980.

Gerbod, Paul, 'De l'influence du catholicisme sur les stratégies éducatives des régimes politiques français de 1806 à 1906', in: Frijhoff, Willem (ed.), *L'Offre de l'école/The Supply of Schooling: Contributions to a Comparative Study of Educational Policies in the XIXth Century*, pp. 233–43. Paris: Sorbonne, 1983.

Geremek, Bronisław, 'Criminalité, Vagabondage, Paupérisme: La Marginalité à l'Aube des Temps Modernes', *Revue d'histoire moderne eïcontemporaine*, 21 (1974), 337–75.

Geremek, Bronisław, *Les Marginaux parisiens aux XIVe et XVe siècles*. Paris: Flammarion, 1976.

Giddens, Anthony, *The Constitution of Society: Outline of the theory of Structuration*. Oxford: Polity Press, 1984.

Gilbert, Bentley B., *British Social Policy, 1914–1939*. Ithaca, NY/London: Cornell UP/Batsford, 1970.

Gilbert, Bentley B., 'The Decay of Nineteenth-Century Provident Institutions and the Coming of Old Age Pensions in Great Britain', *Economic History Review* (2nd series), 17.3 (1965), 551–63.

Gilbert, Bentley B., *The Evolution of National Insurance in Great Britain: The Origins of the Welfare State*. London: Michael Joseph, 1966.

Gillis, John R., 'Aristocracy and Bureaucracy in Nineteenth-Century Prussia', *Past and Present*, 41 (1968), 105–15.

Glass, David V., 'Education and Social Change in Modern England', in: A. H. Halsey, J. Floud and C. A. Anderson (eds), *Education, Economy and Society: A Reader in the Sociology of Education*, pp. 391–413. New York & London: Free Press, 1961.

Gleichmann, Peter R., 'Die Verhäuslichung körperlicher Verrichtungen', in:

References

P. R. Gleichmann, J. Goudsblom and H. Korte (eds), *Materialien zu Norbert Elias' Zivilisationstheorie*, pp. 254–78. Frankfurt: Suhrkamp, 1979a.

Gleichmann, Peter R., 'Städte reinigen und geruchlos machen: Menschliche Körperentleerungen, ihre Geräte und ihre Verhaüslichung', in: Hermann Sturm (ed.), *Ästhetik und Umwelt.* Tübingen: Gunter Narr, 1979b.

Glück, Helmut, *Die preussisch-polnische Sprachenpolitik; Eine Studie zur Theorie und Methodologie der Forschung über Sprachenpolitik, Sprachbewusstsein und Sozialgeschichte am Beispiel der preussisch-deutsche Politik gegenüber der polnischen Minderheit vor 1914.* (Diss. Osnabrück). H. Buske, 1979.

Godechot, Jacques, *Les Institutions de la France sous la Révolution et l'Empire.* Paris: Presses Universitaires de France, 1951.

Goglin, Jean-Louis, *Les Misérables dans l'occident médiéval.* Paris: Éditions du Seuil, 1976.

Goguel, François, *La Politique des partis sous la IIIe République.* Paris: Éditions du Seuil, 1946.

Gontard, Maurice, *L'Enseignement primaire en France de la Révolution à la loi Guizot (1789–1833).* Paris: Les Belles Lettres, 1959.

Gonthier, Nicole, *Lyon et ses pauvres au moyen âge (1350–1500).* Lyons: Éditions l'Hermès, 1978.

Goodin, Robert E., 'Self-Reliance versus the Welfare State', *Journal of Social Policy*, 14 (1985), 25–47.

Goody, Jack, *The Logic of Writing and the Organization of Society.* Cambridge: Cambridge UP, 1986.

Gosden, P. H. J. H., *Self-Help: Voluntary Associations in the 19th Century.* London: Batsford, 1973.

Goubert, Jean-Pierre, *The Conquest of Water.* Cambridge: Polity Press, forthcoming.

Goudsblom, Johan, 'Het algemeen beschaafd Nederlands', *Sociologische gids*, 11 (1964), 106–24, repr. in: Sj. Groenman and H. de Jager (eds), *Staalkaart der Nederlandse Sociologie*, pp. 108–26. Assen: Van Gorcum, 1970.

Goudsblom, Johan, 'Public Health and the Civilizing Process', *Milbank Quarterly*, 64.2 (1986), 161–88.

Goudsblom, Johan, *Sociology in the Balance: A Critical Essay.* Oxford: Blackwell, 1977.

Gouldner, Alvin W., *The Coming Crisis of Western Sociology.* London: Heinemann, 1971.

Gouldner, Alvin W., *The Future of Intellectuals and the Rise of the New Class.* London: MacMillan, 1979.

Gouldner, Alvin W., *For Sociology; Renewal and Critique in Sociology Today.* London: Allen Lane, 1973.

Graff, Harvey J. (ed.), *Literacy and Social Development in the West: A Reader.* Cambridge: Cambridge UP, 1981.

Graus, František, 'Au Bas Moyen Âge: Pauvres des Villes et Pauvres des Campagnes', *Annales ESC*, 16.6 (Nov.–Dec. 1961), 1053–65.

Greenberg, Joseph H., 'The Measurement of Linguistic Diversity', *Language*, 32.1 (1956), 109–15.

References

Greenstone, J. David, *Labor in American Politics* (2nd edn.). Chicago: University of Chicago Press, 1977.

Guillemard, Anne-Marie (ed.), *Old Age and the Welfare State*. London/Beverly Hills, Cal.: Sage, 1983.

Gutton, Jean-Pierre, *La Société et les pauvres. L'Exemple de la généralité de Lyon (1534–1789)*. Paris: Belles Lettres, 1971.

Handlin, David P., *The American Home: Architecture and Society, 1815–1915*. Boston/Toronto: Little Brown & Co., 1979.

Handlin, Oscar, *Boston's Immigrants: A Study in Acculturation* (1941). Cambridge, Mass./London: Harvard UP (rev. and enl. edn), 1979.

Handlin, Oscar, 'Education and the European Immigrant, 1820–1920', in: Bernard J. Weiss (ed.), *American Education and the European Immigrant 1840–1940*, pp. 3–16. Urbana, Chicago, London: University of Illinois Press, 1982.

Harrigan, Patrick J., 'The Social Origins, Ambitions, and Occupations of Secondary Students in France during the Second Empire', in: Lawrence Stone (ed.), *Schooling and Society: Studies in the History of Education*, pp. 206–35. Baltimore: Johns Hopkins UP, 1976.

Harris, José, *Unemployment and Politics: A Study in English Social Policy 1886–1914*. Oxford: Oxford UP, 1972.

Hasenfeld, Yeheskel, 'The Administration of Human Services', in: Y. Hasenfeld and Mayer N. Zald (eds), *The Welfare State in America: Trends and Prospects*. Beverly Hills, Cal.: Sage. *(Annals of the American Academy of Political and Social Science)* 479 (May 1985), 67–81.

Haskell, Thomas L., 'Capitalism and the Origins of the Humanitarian Sensibility', Parts 1 and 2, *American Historical Review*, 90.2 (1985), 339–61; 90.3 (1985), 547–66.

Hatzfeld, Henri, *Du paupérisme à la sécurité sociale: essai sur les origines de la sécurité sociale en France, 1850–1940*. Paris: Colin, 1971.

Hatzfeld, Henri, *Le Grand Tournant de la médecine libérale*. Paris: Editions Ouvrières, 1963.

Haveman, Robert, Barbara Wolfe and Victor Halberstadt, 'The European Welfare State in Transition', in: John L. Palmer (ed.), *Perspectives on the Reagan Years*. Washington, DC: Urban Institute Press, 1986, pp. 147–74.

Haveman, Robert H., Victor Halberstadt and Richard V. Burkhauser, *Public Policy toward Disabled Workers: Cross-National Analyses of Economic Impacts*. Ithaca and London: Cornell UP, 1984.

Hay, Roy, 'Employers and Social Policy in Britain: The Evolution of Social Welfare Legislation, 1905–1914', *Social History*, 4 (January 1977), 435–55.

Heath, Shirley Brice and Richard Laprade, 'Castilian Colonization and Indigenous Languages: The Cases of Quechua and Aymara', in: Robert L. Cooper (ed.), *Language Spread: Studies in Diffusion and Social Change*, pp. 118–48. Bloomington: Indiana UP, 1982.

Hechter, Michael, *Internal Colonialism: The Celtic fringe in British national development, 1536–1966*. London: Routledge & Kegan Paul, 1975.

Heclo, Hugh, 'Reaganism and the Search for a Public Philosophy', in: John L.

References

Palmer (ed.), *Perspectives on the Reagan Years*, pp. 31–64. Washington, DC: Urban Institute Press, 1986.

Heclo, Hugh, 'Toward a New Welfare State?', in: Peter Flora and Arnold J. Heidenheimer (eds), *The Development of Welfare States in Europe and America*, pp. 383–406. New Brunswick and London: Transaction, 1981.

Heclo, Hugh, *Modern Social Politics in Britain and Sweden: From Relief to Income Maintenance*. New Haven: Yale UP, 1974.

Heidenheimer, Arnold J., 'Education and Social Security Entitlements in Europe and America', in: Peter Flora and Arnold J. Heidenheimer (eds), *The Development of Welfare States in Europe and America*, pp. 269–304. New Brunswick and London: Transaction, 1981.

Heidenheimer, Arnold J., 'The Politics of Public Education, Health and Welfare in the USA and Western Europe: How Growth and Reform Potentials Have Differed', *British Journal of Political Science*, 3 (1973), 313–40.

Heidenheimer, Arnold J., Hugh Heclo and Carolyn Teich Adams, *Comparative Public Policy: The Politics of Social Choice in Europe and America*. London: Macmillan (1976), 2nd edn. 1983.

Heinemann, Manfred, *Schule im Vorfeld der Verwaltung: die Entwicklung der preussischen Unterrichtsverwaltung von 1771–1800*. Göttingen: Vandenhoek & Ruprecht, 1974.

Hennock, E. Peter, 'The Origins of British National Insurance and the German precedent, 1880–1914', in: Wolfgang J. Mommsen and W. Mock (eds.), *The Emergence of the Welfare State in Britain and Germany 1850–1950*, pp. 84–106. London: Croom Helm, 1981.

Hentschel, Volker, *Geschichte der deutschen Sozialpolitik (1880–1990): Soziale Sicherung und kollektives Arbeitsrecht*. Frankfurt a. M.: Suhrkamp, 1983.

Higgins, Joan, *States of Welfare: Comparative Analysis in Social Policy*. Oxford: Blackwell & Robertson, 1981.

Hill, Martha S., 'The Changing Nature of Poverty', in: Y. Hasenfeld and Mayer N. Zald (eds), *The Welfare State in America: Trends and Prospects*, Beverly Hills, Col.: Sage (*Annals of the American Academy of Political and Social Science*), 479 (May 1985), 31–47.

Hinrichs, Karl, Claus Offe and Helmut Wiesenthal, 'The Crisis of the Welfare State and Alternative Modes of Work Redistribution', *Thesis Eleven*, 10–11 (1984–5), 37–55.

Hobsbawm, Eric J., *Labouring Men: Studies in the History of Labour*. London: Weidenfeld & Nicholson, 1964.

Hobsbawm, Eric J. and Terence Ranger (eds), *The Invention of Tradition*. Cambridge, Cambridge UP, 1983.

Hodgkinson, Ruth G., *The Origins of the National Health Service: The Medical Services of the New Poor Law*. London: Wellcome Historical Medical Library, 1967.

Hoefnagels, H., *Een eeuw sociale problematiek: De Nederlandse sociale ontwikkeling van 1850 tot 1940*. Alphen aan de Rijn: Samsom, 1977.

Hufton, Olwen H., *The Poor of Eighteenth Century France, 1750–1789*. Oxford: Clarendon, 1974.

References

Hulsink, Wim and Guido de Grefte, 'Ancient Order of Foresters' (unpubl. MA thesis, Institute of Sociology, University of Amsterdam), Amsterdam: 1986.

Huppes, T., *Inkomensverdeling en institutionele structuur; De invloed van institutionele veranderingen op de ontwikkeling van de inkomensongelijkheid*. Leiden: Stenfert Kroese, 1977.

Hurt, John S., *Education in Evolution: Church, State, Society and Popular Education 1800–1870*. London: Paladin, 1972.

Hurt, John S., *Elementary Schooling and the Working Classes 1860–1918*. London: Routledge & Kegan Paul, 1979.

Ignatieff, Michael, *A Just Measure of Pain; The Penitentiary in the Industrial Revolution, 1750–1850*. New York: Columbia UP, 1978.

Janowitz, Morris, *Social Control of the Welfare State*. New York: Elsevier, 1976.

Jaspers, J. B., *Het medische circuit; Een sociologische studie van de ontwikkeling van het netwerk van afhankelijkheid tussen cliënten, artsen, centrale overheid, ziekenfondsen en ziekenhuizen in Nederland (1865–1980)* (Diss. University of Leyden). Utrecht/Antwerpen: Bonn, Scheltema & Holkema, 1985.

Jefferson, Carter, 'Worker Education in England and France, 1800–1914', *Comparative Studies in Society and History*, 6 (1963–4), 353–66.

Johansen, Lars Nørby, 'Welfare State Regression in Scandinavia? The Development of Scandinavian Welfare States from 1970 to 1980', in: Else Øyen (ed), *Comparing Welfare States and their Futures*, pp. 129–51. Aldershot: Gower, 1986.

Johnson, Richard, 'Educational Policy and Social Control in Early Victorian England', *Past and Present*, 49 (November 1970), 96–119.

Jones, Colin, *Charity and Bienfaisance: The Treatment of the Poor in the Montpellier Region, 1740–1815*. Cambridge: Cambridge UP, 1982.

Jones, David J. V., *Crime, Protest, Community, and Police in Nineteenth-Century Britain*. London: Routledge & Kegan Paul, 1982.

Jones, Gareth Stedman, *Outcast London: A Study in the Relationship between Classes in Victorian Society*. New York/London: Pantheon, 1971.

Jordan, Wilbur K., *Philanthropy in England, 1480–1660: A Study of the Changing Pattern of English Aspirations*. London: Allen & Unwin, 1959.

Joyce, James, *Ulysses* (1922), corr. edn. New York: Vintage, 1986.

Junius, Wolfgang and Otto Neuloh, 'Soziale Innovation als Folge Sozialer Konflikte, Dargestellt am Beispiel der "Bismarck'schen Socialgesetzgebung" (Unfallversicherung)' in: Otto Neuloh (ed.), *Soziale Innovation und Soziales Konflikt*, pp. 146–81. Göttingen: Vandenhoeck & Ruprecht, 1977.

Kaestle, Carl F., ' "Between the Scylla of Brutal Ignorance and the Charybdis of a Literary Education": Elite Attitudes toward Mass Schooling in Early Industrial England and America', in: Lawrence Stone (ed.), *Schooling and Society: Studies in the History of Education*, pp. 177–91. Baltimore: Johns Hopkins UP, 1976.

Kaestle, Carl F., *The Evolution of an Urban School System: New York City, 1750–1850*. Cambridge, Mass.: Harvard UP, 1973.

Kalff, Elsbeth, 'La Sensibilisation à l'Hygiène, Paris 1850–1880: La Loi sur les logements insalubres,' *Annales de la rercherche urbaine*, 33 (Mar.–Apr. 1987), 97–104.

Kaplow, J., *The Names of Kings: The Parisian Laboring Poor in the Eighteenth Century*. New York, 1972.

Katz, Michael B., *The Irony of Early School Reform*. Cambridge: Harvard UP, 1968.

Katz, Michael B., 'The Origins of Public Education: a Reassessment', *History of Education Quarterly*, 16 (Winter 1976) 381–407.

Katz, Michael B. (ed.), *School Reform: Past and Present: Readings*. Boston: Little Brown, 1971.

Katz, Michael B., *In the Shadow of the Poorhouse: A Social History of Welfare in America*. New York: Basic Books, 1986.

Kelsall, R. K., *Higher Civil Servants in Britain from 1870 to the Present*. New York: Humanities Press, 1955.

Kesselman, Mark, 'Conclusion' in: Mark Kesselman (ed.), *The French Workers' Movement: Economic Crisis and Political Change*, pp. 311–22. London: Allen & Unwin, 1984.

Kingdon, Robert M., 'Social Welfare in Calvin's Geneva', *American Historical Review*, 76.1 (Feb. 1971), 50–69.

Kleerekoper, S., *Vergelijkend leerboek der bedrijfseconomie* (2 vols.). Groningen: Noordhoff, 1956.

Knippenberg, Hans, *Deelname aan het lager onderwijs in Nederland gedurende de negentiende eeuw: Een Analyse van de landelijke ontwikkeling en regionale verschillen* (Diss. University of Amsterdam). Amsterdam: 1986.

Koch, K., 'Staatsvorming en Conjunctuurontwikkeling', *Acta Politica*, 13 (July 1978) 331–53.

Koch, Lotte, *Wandlungen der Wohlfahrtspflege im Zeitalter der Aufklärung*. Erlangen: Palm & Enke, 1933.

Köhler, Peter A., Hans F. Zacher with Martin Parrington (eds.), *The Evolution of Social Insurance, 1881–1981: Studies of Germany, France, Great Britain, Austria and Switzerland*. New York/London: St Martin's/F. Pinter, 1982; also publ. in German.

Kohl, Jürgen, 'Trends and Problems in Postwar Public Expenditure Development in Western Europe and North America', in: Peter Flora and Arnold J. Heidenheimer (eds), *The Development of Welfare States in Europe and America*, pp. 307–44. New Brunswick and London: Transaction, 1981.

Koot, A. C. J., 'Charles T. Liernur, Oud Kapitein–Ingenieur (Amerika)' *H20*, 2.26 (1969), 682–6.

Kosselleck, Reinhart, *Preussen zwischen Reform und Revolution: Allgemeines Landrecht, Verwaltung und Soziale Bewegung von 1791 bis 1848* (Industrielle Welt, Vol. 7). Stuttgart: Ernst Klett, 1967.

Kossmann, E. H., *The Low Countries 1780–1940*. Oxford: Clarendon, 1978.

Kossmann-Putto, J. A., 'Armen- en Ziekenzorg in de Noordelijke Nederlanden', *Algemene Geschiedenis der Nederlanden*, Vol. 2, pp. 254–67. Haarlem: Fibula-Van Dishoeck, 1982.

References

Krieger, Joel, *Reagan, Thatcher, and the Politics of Decline.* Oxford/New York: Polity Press, 1986.

Krieger, Joel, 'Social Policy in the Age of Reagan and Thatcher,' in: Ralph Milliband et al (eds), *Socialist Register 1987*, pp. 177–98. London: Methuen, 1987.

Kudrle, Robert T. and Thedore R. Marmor, 'The Development of Welfare States in North America', in: Peter Flora and Arnold J. Heidenheimer (eds), *The Development of Welfare States in Europe and America*, pp. 81–121. New Brunswick and London: Transaction, 1981.

Küther, Carsten, *Räuber und Gauner in Deutschland: Das organisierte Bandenwesen im 18. und frühen 19. Jahrhundert.* Göttingen: Vandenhoeck & Ruprecht, 1976.

La Berge, A. E. Fowler, *Public Health in France and the French Public Health Movement, 1815–1848.* Diss. University of Tennesee (University microfilms) 1974.

Lampard, Eric E., 'The Urbanizing World', in: H. J. Dyos and Michael Wolff, *The Victorian City: Images and Realities*, 2 vols, vol. 1, pp. 3–57. London and Boston: Routledge & Kegan Paul, 1973.

Laqueur, Thomas W., 'English and French Education in the Nineteenth Century', *History of Education Quarterly*, 13 (1973), 53–60.

Laqueur, Thomas W., *Religion and Respectability; Sunday Schools and Working Class Culture, 1780–1850.* New Haven: Yale UP, 1976.

Laslett, Peter, *The World We Have Lost: England before the Industrial Age.* New York: Scribner, 1971.

Lavielle, Romain, *Histoire de la mutualite: sa place dans le régime français de la sécurité sociale.* Paris: Hachette, 1964.

Lawson, John and Harold Silver, *A Social History of Education in England.* London: Methuen, 1973.

Le Goff, Jacques, *La Civilisation de l'occident médiéval* (1964). Paris: Flammarion, 1982.

Lenhardt, Gero and Claus Offe, 'Staatstheorie und Sozialpolitik. Politisch-soziologische Erklärungsansätze für Funktionen und Inovationsprozesse der Socialpolitik', in: Chr. von Ferber and F.-X. Kaufmann (eds), *Sociologie und Sozialpolitik; Kölner Zeitschrift für Soziologie und Sozialpsychologie* (Sonderheft), 19 (1977), 98–127.

Leroy Ladurie, Emannuel, 'Alphabétisation et Stature: Un Tableau Comparé', *Annales ESC*, 35 (1980); repr. in: E. Leroy Ladurie, *Parmi les historiens*, pp. 156–9. Paris: Gallimard, 1983.

Lieberson, Stanley, 'An Extension of Greenberg's Linguistic Diversity Measures' (1964), in: Anwar S. Dil (ed.), *Language Diversity and Language Contact: Essays by Stanley Lieberson*, pp. 304–13. Stanford, Cal.: Stanford UP, 1981.

Lieberson, Stanley, *A Piece of the Pie; Blacks and White Immigrants Since 1880.* Berkeley etc.: University of California Press, 1980.

Light, Paul, *Artful Work: The Politics of Social Security Reform.* New York: Random House, 1985.

References

Lijphart, Arend, *The Politics of Accommodation: Pluralism and Democracy in the Netherlands.* Berkeley: University of California Press, 1968.

Lis, Catharina and Hugo Soly, *Poverty and Capitalism in Pre-industrial Europe.* Brighton: Harvester Press, 1979.

Lis, Catharina, *Social Change and the Labouring Poor; Antwerp, 1770–1860.* New Haven and London, Yale UP, 1986.

Lockridge, Kenneth A., 'Literacy in Early American 1650–1800', in: Graff, Harvey J. (ed.), *Literacy and Social Development in the West: A Reader*, pp. 183–200. Cambridge: Cambridge UP, 1981.

Lofland, Lyn H., *A World of Strangers: Order and Action in Urban Public Space.* New York: Basic Books, 1973.

Loney, Martin, *The Politics of Greed: The New Right and the Welfare State.* London: Pluto Press, 1986.

Luce, R. Duncan and Howard Raiffa, *Games and Decisions: Introduction and Critical Survey.* New York: Wiley, 1957.

Lundgreen, Peter, 'Educational Expansion and Economic Growth in Nineteenth Century Germany: A Quantitative Study', in: Lawrence Stone (ed), *Schooling and Society: Studies in the History of Education*, pp. 20–66. Baltimore: Johns Hopkins UP, 1976.

MacHugh, P., *Prostitution and Victorian Social Reform.* London: Croom Helm, 1979.

Mackay, John Patrick, *Tramways and Trolleys; The Rise of Urban Mass Transport in Europe.* Princeton, NJ: Princeton UP, 1976.

McKeown, Thomas, *The Modern Rise of Population.* London: E. Arnold, 1976.

McNeill, William H., *Plagues and Peoples.* Garden City, NY: Doubleday, 1976.

McNeill, William H., *The Pursuit of Power.* Chicago: University of Chicago Press, 1982.

Magraw, Roger, 'The Conflict in the Villages. Popular Anticlericalism in the Isère (1852–70)', in: Theodore Zeldin (ed.), *Conflicts in French Society*, pp. 169–227. London: Allen & Unwin, 1970.

Maier, Charles S., *Recasting Bourgeois Europe; Stabilization in France, Germany, and Italy in the Decade after World I.* Princeton, NJ: Princeton UP, 1975.

Mandeville, Bernard (de), *The Fable of the Bees or Private Vices, Public Benefits* (1714). London: Wishart & Co., 1934.

Mannoury, J., 'De Ontwikkeling van het sociale verzekeringsstelsel', in: F. L. van Holthoon (ed.), *De Nederlandse Samenleving sinds 1815; Wording en Samenhang*, pp. 187–202. Assen/Maastricht: Van Gorcum, 1985.

Marsden, W. F., 'Diffusion and Regional Variation in Elementary Education in England and Wales 1800–1870', *History of Education*, 11.3 (Sept. 1982), 173–94.

Marshall, T. H., *Social Policy in the Twentieth Century.* London: Hutchinson (4th rev. edn) 1975.

Martin, E. W., 'From Parish to Union: Poor Law Administration, 1601–1685', in: E. W. Martin (ed.), *Comparative Development in Social Welfare*, pp. 25–56 London: Allen & Unwin, 1972.

Marwick, Arthur, 'The Labour Party and the Welfare State in Britain, 1900–

1948', *American Historical Review*, 73 (1967), 380–403.

Mayer, John A., 'Notes Towards a Working Definition of Social Control in Historical Analysis', in: Stanley Cohen and Andrew T. Scull (eds), *Social Control and the State: Historical and Comparative Essays*, pp. 17–38. Oxford: Martin Robertson, 1983.

Mayeur, François, *L'Éducation des filles en France en XIXe siècle*. Paris: Hachette, 1979.

Maynes, Mary Jo, *Schooling in Western Europe, A Social History*. Albany, NY: State University of New York Press, 1985.

Maynes, Mary Jo, 'The Virtues of Archaism: The Political Economy of Schooling in Europe, 1750–1850', *Comparative Studies of Society and History*, 21 (1979), 611–25.

Melief, P. B. A., *De Strijd om de Armenzorg in Nederland, 1715–1854*. Groningen: Wolters, 1955.

Merton, Robert K., *Social Theory and Social Structure*. New York: Free Press, 1968.

Meyer, Jack A., 'Social Programs and Social Policy', in: John L. Palmer (ed.), *Perspectives on the Reagan Years*, pp. 65–90. Washington, DC: Urban Institute Press, 1986.

Mialaret, Gaston and Jean Vial (eds), *Histoire mondiale de l'éducation*, vol. 3. Paris: Presses Universitaires de France, 1981.

Middlemas, Keith, *Politics in Industrial Society: The Experience of the British System since 1911*. London: Deutsch, 1979.

Midwinter, E. C., 'Victorian Social Provision: Central and Local Administration', in: E. W. Martin (ed.), *Comparative Development in Social Welfare*, pp. 191–218. London: Allen & Unwin, 1972.

Miller, Wilbur R., 'Police Authority in London and New York City 1839–1870', *Journal of Social History* 8 (Winter 1975), 81–95.

Mollat, Michel, *Les Pauvres au moyen âge: étude sociale*. Paris: Hachette, 1978.

Mommsen, Wolfgang J. and W. Mock (eds), *The Emergence of the Welfare State in Britain and Germany 1850–1950*. London: Croom Helm, 1981; also publ. in German.

Monroe, Paul, *Founding of the American School System; A History of Education in the United States*, Vol. I: *From the Early Settlements to the Close of the Civil War Period*. New York: MacMillan, 1940.

Morgan, Prys, 'From a Death to a View: The Hunt for a Welsh Past in the Romantic Period', in: E. Hobsbawm and T. Ranger (eds), *The Invention of Tradition*, pp. 43–100. Cambridge, Cambridge UP, 1983.

Morgan, Kenneth O., *Rebirth of a Nation: Wales 1880–1980*. Oxford: Clarendon, 1981.

Morris, Robert J., *Cholera, 1832: The Social Response to an Epidemic*. London: Croom Helm, 1976.

Muel-Dreyfus, Francine, *Le métier d'éducateur: les instituteurs de 1900, les éducateurs specialisés de 1968*. Paris: Éditions de Minuit, 1983.

Müller, Detlef K., *Sozialstruktur und Schulsystem: Aspekte zum Strukturwandel des Schulwesens im 19. Jahrhundert*. Göttingen: Vandenhoeck & Ruprecht, 1977.

Murard, Lion and Patrick Zylberman, 'La Raison de l'expert, ou l'hygiène comme science sociale appliquée', *Archives européennes de sociologie*, 26.1 (1985), 58–89.

Musgrave, P. W., *Society and Education in England since 1800*. London: Methuen, 1968.

Musgrove, Frank, 'Middle-Class Families and Schools 1780–1880: Interaction and Exchange of Function Between Institutions', in: P. W. Musgrave (ed.), *Sociology, History and Education: A Reader*, pp. 117–25. London: Methuen, 1968.

Navarro, Vincente, *Crisis, Health, and Medicine; A Social Critique*. London/New York: Tavistock, 1986.

Nota 2000. Tweede Kamer der Staten Generaal, 1985–6, 19500, 1–2.

O'Connor, James, *The Fiscal Crisis of the State*. New York: St Martin's Press, 1973.

Offe, Claus, *Contradictions of the Welfare State*. London: Hutchinson, 1984.

Oldewelt, W. F. H., 'De Zelfkant van de Amsterdamse samenleving en de groei der bevolking (1578–1795)', *Tijdschrift voor Geschiedenis*, 77.1 (1964), 39–56.

Olsen, Donald J., *The City as a Work of Art: London, Paris, Vienna*. New Haven and London: Yale UP, 1986.

Olson, Mancur, *The Logic of Collective Action: Public Goods and the Theory of Groups*. Cambridge, Mass., and London: Harvard UP, 1965.

Oosterbaan, Henny and Winkie Zeldenrust, *Gescheiden wegen; Sociale netwerken, protoprofessionalisering, psychische problemen en hulpzoekend gedrag bij gescheiden mensen* (Help-Seeking Behavior among Divorcees), with a Preface by A. de Swaan. Utrecht: Nederlands Centrum voor Geestelijke Volksgezondheid, 1985.

Orloff, Ann Shola and Theda Skocpol, 'Why not Equal Protection? Explaining the Politics of Public Social Spending in Britain, 1900–1911, and the United States, 1880s–1920', *American Sociological Review*, 49 (December 1984), 726–50.

Orwell, George, *The Road to Wigan Pier* (1937). Harmondsworth/New York: Penguin, 1962.

Oxley, Geoffrey W., *Poor Relief in England and Wales, 1601–1834*. Newton Abbot: David & Charles, 1974.

Palmer, John L. (ed.), *Perspectives on the Reagan Years*. Washington, DC: Urban Institute Press, 1986.

Palmer, R. R., 'Much in Little: the Dutch Revolution of 1795', *Journal of Modern History*, 26.1 (March 1954) 15–35.

Palmer, Roy, *The Water Closet: A New History*. Newton Abbot: David & Charles, 1973.

Parker, Samuel Chester, *The History of Modern Elementary Education* (1912). Totowna, NJ: Littlefield Adams, 1970.

Parsons, Talcott, 'The School Class as a Social System: Some of its Functions in American Society', *Harvard Educational Review*, 29; repr. in: A. H. Halsey, J. Floud and C. A. Anderson (eds), *Education, Economy and Society; A Reader in the Sociology of Education*, pp. 434–55. New York: Free Press, 1961.

Patterson, James T., *America's Struggle against Poverty 1900–1985*. Cambridge, Mass.: Harvard UP, 1961.

Pelling, Margaret, *Cholera, Fever and English Medicine, 1825–1865*. Oxford: Oxford UP, 1978.

Peterson, M. Jeanne, *The Medical Profession in Mid-Victorian London*. Berkeley, Cal.: University of California Press, 1978.

Pinker, Robert, *The Idea of Welfare*. London: Heinemann, 1979.

Piven, Frances Fox and Richard A. Cloward, *The New Class War; Reagan's Attack on the Welfare State and its Consequences*. New York: Pantheon, 1982.

Piven, Frances Fox and Richard A. Cloward, *Regulating the Poor: The Functions of Public Welfare*. London: Tavistock, 1972.

Pompe, Johannes H., 'De kleine middenstand in Nederland: Een vergelijkende studie over de oude en de nieuwe middenstand'. Diss. University of Groningen with a summary in English, 1980.

Popkin, Samuel L., *The Rational Peasant: The Political Economy of Rural Society in Vietnam*. Berkeley: University of California Press, 1979.

Poutet, Yves, 'L'Enseignement des Pauvres dans la France du XVIIe Siècle', *XXVIIe siècle*, 90–1 (1971), 87–110.

Price, Daniel N., 'Cash Benefits for Short-Term Sickness: Thirty-Five Years of Data, 1948–83', *Social Security Bulletin*, 49.5 (May 1986), 5–19.

Prost, Antoine, *Histoire de l'enseignement en France, 1800–1967*. Paris: Armand Colin, 1968.

Raeff, Marc, 'The Well-Ordered Police State and the Development of Modernity in Seventeenth- and Eighteenth-Century Europe: An Attempt at a Comparative Approach', *American Historical Review*, 80 (1975), 1221–43.

Rapoport, Anatol, *N-Person Game Theory: Concepts and Applications*. Ann Arbor: University of Michigan Press, 1970.

Richter, Donald C., *Riotous Victorians*. Athens and London: Ohio UP, 1981.

Rijksverzekeringsbank 1901–1941 (Gedenkboek opgedragen aan Dr. H. L. van Duyl). Haarlem: Tjeenk Willink, 1941.

Rimlinger, Gaston V., *Welfare Policy and Industrialization in Europe, America and Russia*. New York: Wiley, 1971.

Ritter, Gerhard A., *Sozialversicherung in Deutschland und England: Entstehung und Grundzüge im Vergleich*. Munich: Beck, 1983.

Roberts, David, *Victorian Origins of the British Welfare State*. New Haven: Yale UP, 1969.

Roessler, Wilhelm, *Die Entstehung des modernen Erziehungswesens in Deutschland*. Stuttgart: Kohlhammer, 1961.

Rogin, Michael, 'Voluntarism: The Political Functions of an Antipolitical Doctrine', *Industrial and Labor Relations Review*, 15 (1962), 521–35.

Röling, H. Q., 'Onderwijs in Nederland', in: B. Kruithof, J. Noordman and P. de Rooy (eds), *Geschiedenis van Opvoeding en Onderwijs; Inleiding, Bronnen, Onderzoek*, pp. 66–87. Nijmegen: SUN, 1982.

Root, Lawrence S., 'Employee Benefits and Social Welfare: Complement and Conflict', in: Y. Hasenfeld and Mayer N. Zald (eds), *The Welfare State in*

America: Trends and Prospects. Beverly Hills, Cal.: Sage. (*Annals of the American Academy of Political and Social Science*), 479 (May 1985), 101–18.

Rosanvallon, Pierre, *La crise de l'état-providence.* Paris: Éditions du Seuil, 1981.

Rosen, George, *From Medical Police to Social Medicine: Essays on the History of Health Care.* New York: Science History Publs., 1974.

Rosenberg, Charles E., *The Cholera Years: The United States in 1832, 1849, and 1866.* Chicago and London: University of Chicago Press, 1962.

Rosenkrantz, Barbara Gutmann, *Public Health and the State: Changing Views in Massachussets, 1842–1936.* Cambridge, Harvard UP, 1972.

Rothfels, Hans, 'Bismarck's Social Policy and the Problem of State Socialism in Germany', *Sociological Review*, 30 (1938), 81–94; 288–302.

Rothfels, Hans, 'Prinzipienfragen der Bismarckschen Sozialpolitik' (1927), repr. in: Hans Rothfels, *Bismarck, der Osten und das Reich*, pp. 165–81. Darmstadt: 1962.

Rothman, David J., *The Discovery of the Asylum: Social Order and Disorder in the New Republic.* Boston: Little, Brown & Co., 1971.

Rusche, Georg and Otto Kirchheimer, *Punishment and Social Structure.* New York: Columbia UP, 1939.

Sachsse, Christoph and Florian Tennstedt, *Geschichte der Armenfürsorge in Deutschland vom Spätmittelalter bis zum 1. Weltkrieg.* Stuttgart: Kohlhammer, 1980.

Sahlins, Marshall, *Stone Age Economics.* London: Tavistock, 1974.

Saint-Jours, Y., 'France', in: Peter A. Köhler and Hans F. Zacher with Martin Parrington (eds), *The Evolution of Social Insurance 1881–1981: Studies of Germany, France, Great Britain, Austria and Switzerland*, pp. 93–149 (also publ. in German). London/New York: Pinter/St Martin's Press, 1982.

Salgado, Gamini, *The Elizabethan Underworld.* London: Dent & Sons, 1977.

Schama, Simon, *Patriots and Liberators: Revolution in the Netherlands 1780–1813.* London: Collins, 1977.

Schama, Simon, 'Schools and Politics in the Netherlands 1796–1814', *Historical Journal*, 13.4 (1970), 589–610.

Schelling, Thomas C., *The Strategy of Conflict.* New York: Oxford UP, 1963.

Schmal, H. (ed.), *Patterns of European Urbanisation since 1500.* London: Croom Helm, 1981.

Schmidt, Alvin J., *Fraternal Organizations* (The Greenwood Encyclopedia of American Institutions). Westport, Conn.: Greenwood, 1980.

Schoenwald, Richard L., 'Training Urban Man: A Hypothesis about the Sanitary Movement', in: H. J. Dyos and M. Wolff, *The Victorian City: Images and Realities*, 2 vols, vol. 2, pp. 669–92. London and Boston: Routledge & Kegan Paul, 1973.

Schofield, R. S., 'Dimensions of Illiteracy, 1750–1850', *Explorations in Economic History*, 10 (1973), 437–54; repr. in: Graff, Harvey J. (ed.), *Literacy and Social Development in the West: A Reader*, pp. 201–13. Cambridge: Cambridge UP, 1981.

Schönhoven, Klaus, 'Selbsthilfe als Form von Solidarität: Das gewerkschaftliche

Unterstützungswesen im Deutschen Kaiserreich bis 1914', *Archiv für Sozialgeschichte*, 20 (1980), 147–93.

Sennett, Richard, *Families against the City: Middle Class Homes of Industrial Chicago, 1872–1890.* Cambridge, Mass.: Harvard UP, 1970.

Sewell, William H., 'Property, Labor, and the Emergence of Socialism in France, 1789–1848', in: J. M. Merriman, ed., *Consciousness and Class-Experience in Nineteenth-Century Europe*, pp. 45–64. New York and London: Holmes & Meier, 1979.

Shefter, Martin, 'Trade Unions and Political Machines: The Organization and Disorganization of the American Working Class in the Late Nineteenth-Century', in: I. Katznelson and A. R. Zolberg, *Working-class Formation: Nineteenth-Century Patterns in Western Europe and the United States*, pp. 197–278. Princeton, NJ,: Princeton UP, 1986.

Siguan, Miquel, 'Language and Education and Catalonia', *Quarterly Review of Education* (UNESCO), 14.1 (1984), 107–119.

Silver, Allan, 'The Demand for Order in Civil Society: A Review of some Themes in the History of Urban Crime, Police and Riot', in: David J. Bordua (ed.), *The Police: Six Sociological Essays*, pp. 1–24. New York: Wiley, 1967.

Silver, Harold, *The Concept of Popular Education: A Study of Ideas and Social Movements in the Early Nineteenth Century.* London: Methuen, 1977.

Silver, Harold, *English Education and the Radicals, 1780–1850.* London: Routledge & Kegan Paul, 1975.

Simon, Brian, *The Two Nations and the Educational Structure 1780–1870.* London: Lawrence & Wishart, 1960.

Skocpol, Theda, 'Social Security without the State: The Politics of Public Social Provision in the United States' (unpubl. mimeo). Russell Sage Foundation, 1984–5.

Skocpol, Theda and Edwin Amenta, 'States and Social Policies', *American Review of Sociology*, 12 (1986), 131–57.

Skocpol, Theda and John Ikenberry, 'The Political Formation of the American Welfare State in Historical and Comparative Perspective', *Comparative Social Research*, 6 (1983), 87–148.

Skocpol, Theda and Margaret Weir, 'State Structures and the Possibilities for "Keynesian" Responses to the Great Depression in Sweden, Britain, and the United States', in: Peter Evans, Dietrich Rüschemeyer and Theda Skocpol (eds), *Bringing the State Back In.* Cambridge: Cambridge UP, 1988.

Smelser, Neil J., *Social Change in the Industrial Revolution: An Application of Theory to the Lancashire Cotton Industry, 1770–1840.* London: Routledge & Kegan Paul, 1959.

Smith, Adam, *The Wealth of Nations* (1776). Harmondsworth: Penguin, 1970.

Smith, Phillip Thurmond, *Policing Victorian London: Political Policing, Public Order, and the London Metropolitan Police.* Westport Conn., and London: Greenwood Press, 1984.

Sociaal en cultureel rapport, 1986 (Sociaal en Cultureel Planbureau). 's-Gravenhage: Staatsuitgeverij, 1986.

References

Soltow, Lee and Edward Stevens, *The Rise of Literacy and the Common School in the United States: A Socio-Economic Analysis to 1870*. Chicago: University of Chicago Press, 1981.

Spree, Reinhard, *Sociale Ungleichheit vor Krankheit und Tod: Zur Sozialgeschichte des Gesundheitsbereichs im deutschen Kaiserreich*. Göttingen: Vandenhoeck & Ruprecht, 1981.

Starr, Paul, *The Social Transformation of American Medicine*. New York: Basic Books, 1982.

Statistical Yearbook 1984. Unesco, Paris, 1984.

Stearns, Peter N., *Old Age in European Society: The Case of France*. London: Croom Helm, 1977.

Stekl, Hannes, *Österreichs Zucht- und Arbeitshäuser 1671–1920*. Munich: Oldenbourg, 1978.

Stephens, Meic, *Linguistic Minorities in Western Europe*. Llandysul: Gomer Press, 1976.

Stone, Deborah A., 'Diagnosis and the Dole: The Function of Illness in American Distributive Politics', *Journal of Health Politics, Policy and Law*, 4.3 (Fall 1979a), 507–521.

Stone, Deborah A., 'Physicians as Gatekeepers: Illness Certification as a Rationing Device', *Public Policy*, 27.2 (Spring 1979b), 227–54.

Stone, Lawrence S., 'Literacy and Education in England, 1640–1900', *Past and Present*, 42 (1969), 69–139.

Storch, R. D., 'The Policeman as Domestic Missionary: Urban Discipline and Popular Culture in Northern England, 1850–1880', *Journal of Social History*, 9 (1975–6).

Strasser, Johanno, *Grenzen des Sozialstaats? Soziale Sicherung in der Wachstumskrise*. Cologne/Frankfurt a. M.: Europäische Verlagsanstalt, 1979.

Strauss, Gerald, 'Techniques of Indoctrination: the German Reformation', in: J. Harvey Graff (ed.), *Literacy and Social Development in the West: A Reader*, pp. 96–105. Cambridge: Cambridge UP, 1981.

Strong, P. M., 'Sociological Imperialism and the Profession of Medicine: A Critical Examination of the Thesis of Medical Imperialism', *Social Science and Medicine* 13A (1979), 199–215.

Stuurman, Siep, *Verzuiling, kapitalisme en patriarchaat: aspecten van de ontwikkelng van de moderne staat in Nederland*. Nijmegen: Sun, 1983.

Supple, Barry, 'Legislation and Virtue: An Essay on Working-Class Self-Help and the State in the Early Nineteenth Century', in: N. McKendrick, ed., *Historical Perspectives: Studies in English Thought and Society in Honour of J. H. Plumb*, pp. 210–54. London: Europa publ., 1974.

Sutherland, Gillian, *Elementary Education in the Nineteenth Century*. London: The Historical Association, 1971.

Tampke, Jürgen, 'Bismarck's Social Legislation: A Genuine Breakthrough?', in: Wolfgang J. Mommsen and W. Mock (eds), *The Emergence of the Welfare State in Britain and Germany, 1850–1950*, pp. 71–83. London: Croom Helm, 1981.

Tate, W. E., *The English Village Community and the Enclosure Movements*. London: Gollancz, 1967.

Taylor, James S., 'The Unreformed Workhouse, 1776–1834', in: E. W. Martin (ed.), *Comparative Development in Social Welfare*, pp. 57–84. London: Allen & Unwin, 1972.

Taylor, Michael, *Anarchy and Cooperation*. New York: Wiley, 1976.

Tennstedt, Florian, *Sozialgeschichte der Sozialpolitik in Deutschland: Vom 18. Jahrhundert bis zum Ersten Weltkrieg*. Göttingen: Vandenhoeck & Ruprecht, 1981.

Thane, Pat, *Foundations of the Welfare State*. London and New York: Longman, 1982.

Thernstrom, Stephen (ed.), *Harvard Encyclopedia of American Ethnic Groups*. Cambridge, Mass.: Harvard UP, 1980.

Thompson, E. P., *The Making of the English Working Class*. Harmondsworth: Penguin, 1980.

Tilly, Charles, 'Food Supply and Public Order in Modern Europe', in: C. Tilly (ed.), *The Formation of National States in Western Europe*, pp. 380–455. Princeton, NJ: Princeton UP, 1975.

Tilly, Charles, Louise and Richard Tilly, *The Rebellious Century, 1830–1930*. Cambridge, Mass.: Harvard UP, 1975.

Tilly, Louise A. and Charles Tilly (eds), *Class Conflict and Collective Action*. Beverly Hills and London: Sage, 1981.

Timmer, E. M. A., *Knechtsgilden en knechtsbossen in Nederland: Arbeidersverzekering in vroeger tijden* (Diss. University of Amsterdam). Haarlem: Kleynenberg, 1913.

Titmuss, Richard M., *Essays on 'The Welfare State'*. London: Unwin, 1958, 2nd edn 1963.

Trattner, Walter I., *From Poor Law to Welfare State; A History of Social Welfare in America*. New York/London: Free Press, 1974.

Treble, James H., 'The Attitudes of Friendly Societies Towards the Movement in Great Britain for State Pensions, 1878–1908', *International Review of Social History*, 15 (1970), 266–99.

Trempé, Rolande, 'The Struggle of the French Miners for the Creation of Retirement Funds in the 19th Century' in: A.-M. Guillemard (ed.), *Old Age and the Welfare State*, pp. 101–13. London/Beverly Hills, Cal.: Sage, 1983.

Troeltsch, Ernst, *Die Soziallehren der christlichen Kirchen und Gruppen*. Tübingen: Mohr, 1912.

Tyack, David B., *The One Best System: a History of American Urban Education*. Cambridge, Mass.: Harvard UP, 1974.

Ullmann, Hans-Peter, 'German Industry and Bismarck's Social Security System', in: Wolfgang J. Mommsen and W. Mock (eds), *The Emergence of the Welfare State in Britain and Germany, 1850–1950*, pp. 133–49. London: Croom Helm, 1981.

Van Daalen, Rineke, *Klaagbrievem en gemeentelijk ingrijpen: Amsterdam, 1865–1920* (Diss. University of Amsterdam, with a summary in English). Amsterdam: 1987.

Van den Eerenbeemt, H. F. J. M., *Armoede en arbeidsdwang: Werkinrichtingen voor 'Onnutte' Nederlanders in de republiek 1760–1795: Een mentaliteitsgeschiedenis*. 's-Gravenhage: Nijhoff, 1977.

References

Van den Eerenbeemt, H. F. J. M., *In het spanningsveld der armoede: agressief pauperisme en reactie in Staats-Brabant.* Tilburg: Zuidelijk Historisch Contact, 1968.

Van der Giezen, A. M., *De eerste fase van de schoolstrijd in Nederland (1795–1806).* Assen, 1937.

Van der Plank, Pieter H., *Taalassimilatie van Europese taalminderheden: Een inventariserende en hypothesevormende studie naar assimilatieverschijnselen onder Europese taalgroepen* (Assimilation of European Linguistic Minorities: Ph. D. Diss. Utrecht). Rotterdam, 1971.

Van Loo, Frank *'Den arme gegeven . . .': Eeen beschrijving van armoede, armenzorg en sociale zekerheid in Nederland, 1784–1965.* Meppel, Amsterdam: Boon, 1981.

Van Oenen, G. J. (ed.), *Staat en klassen in het interbellum: De arbeidersbeweging in een periode van aanpassing en ordening in Nederland 1918–1940*, 2 vols. (Mededelingen van de FSWa, 28). Amsterdam: University of Amsterdam, 1982.

Van Stolk, Bram and Cas Wouters, *Vrouwen in tweestrijd: Tussen thuis en tehuis: Relatieproblemen in de verzorgingsstat, opgetekend in een crisiscentrum.* Deventer: Van Loghum Slaterus, 1983.

Vanthemsche, Guy, 'De Oorsprong van de werkloosheidsverzekering in België: Vakbondskassen en gemeentelijke fondsen (1890–1914)', *Tijdschrift voor sociale geschiedenis*, 11.2 (May 1985), 130–64.

Van Tijn, Th., *Schoolstrijd en partijvorming in Nederland.* Amsterdam: Meulenhoff, 1967.

Van Zon, Henk, *Een zeer onfrisse geschiedenis: Studies over niet-industriële vervuiling in Nederland, 1850–1920* (A Very Dirty Affair – Studies in Non-Industrial Pollution in the Netherlands, with a summary in English). Diss. University of Groningen. Groningen, 1986.

Vaughan, Michalina and Margaret Scotford Archer, *Social Conflict and Educational Change in England and France 1789–1848.* Cambridge: Cambridge UP, 1971.

Veldkamp, G. M. J., *Inleiding tot de sociale zekerheid en de toepassing ervan in Nederland en België*, Vol. I: *Karakter en geschiedenis.* Deventer: Kluwer, 1978.

Verberne, L. G. J., *Geschiedenis van Nederland*, Vol. 7: *Nieuwste geschiedenis.* Amsterdam: Uitgeverij Joost van den Vondel 1938.

Verdoorn, J. A., *Het gezondheidswezen te Amsterdam in de 19e eeuw.* Nijmegen: SUN, 1981.

Viscusi, W. Kip, *Welfare of the Elderly: An Economic Analysis and Policy Prescription.* New York: Wiley Interscience, 1979.

Vossler, Otto, 'Bismarcks Sozialpolitik', in: *Geist und Geschichte: Von der Reformation bis zur Gegenwart. Gesammelte Aufsätze*, pp. 215–34. Munich: Piper, 1964.

Waarborgen voor zekerheid: Een nieuw stelsel van sociale zekerheid in hoofdlijnen. 's-Gravenhage: Wetenschappelijke Raad voor het Regeringsbeleid, Staatsuitgeverij, 1985.

Waddington, Ivan, *The Medical Profession in the Industrial Revolution.* Dublin: Gill & MacMillan/Humanities Press, 1984.

Wagenaar, Michiel, 'Van "gemegde" naar "gelede" wijken: Amsterdamse stadsuitbreidingen in het laatste kwart van de negentiende eeuw', in: M. Jonker et al. (eds), *Van stadskern naar stadsgewest: Stedebouwkundige geschiedenis van Amsterdam*, pp. 157–82. Amsterdam: Verloren, 1984.

Wagner, Peter, 'Social Sciences and Political Projects: Reform Coalitions between Social Scientists and Policy-Makers in France, Italy, and West Germany', in: S. Blume et al (eds), *The Social Direction of the Public Sciences: Sociology of the Sciences – A Yearbook*, Vol. 11, pp. 277–307. Dordrecht: Reidel, 1987.

Waitzkin, Howard B., *The Second Sickness; Contradictions of Capitalist Health Care*. London/New York: Free Press/Macmillan, 1983.

Waitzkin, Howard B. and Barbara Waterman, *The Exploitation of Illness in Capitalist Society*. Indianapolis/New York: Bobbs-Merrill, 1974.

Waldeyer, Hans, 'Zur Entstehung der Realschulen in Preussen im 18. Jahrhundert bis zu den dreissiger Jahren des 19. Jahrhunderts, in: *Schule und Staat im 18. und 19. Jahrhundert; Zur Socialgeschichte der Schule in Deutschland*. pp. 146–71. Frankfurt a. M.: Suhrkamp, 1974.

Walker, Alan, 'Social Policy and Elderly People in Great Britain: The Construction of Dependent Social and Economic Status in Old Age', in: Anne-Marie Guillemard (ed.), *Old Age and the Welfare State*, pp. 143–67. London/Beverly Hills, Cal.: Sage, 1983.

Wallerstein, Immanuel, *The Modern World-System: Capitalist Agriculture and the Origins of the European World-Economy in the Sixteenth Century*. New York: Academic Press, 1974.

Wardle, David, *English Popular Education, 1780–1975*. Cambridge: Cambridge UP, 1970.

Weber, Anatole, *A Travers la mutualité: Étude critique sur les sociétés de secours mutuels*. Paris: Rivière, 1908.

Weber, Eugen, *Peasants into Frenchmen: The Modernization of Rural France 1870–1914*. Stanford, Cal.: Stanford UP, 1976.

Wehler, Hans-Ulrich, *Das Deutsche Kaiserreich, 1871–1918*. Göttingen: Vandenhoeck & Ruprecht, 1973.

Weir, Margaret, Ann Shola Orloff and Theda Skocpol, 'The Future of Social Policy in the United States: Political Constraints and Possibilities', in: Margaret Weir, Ann Shola Orloff and Theda Skocpol (eds), *The Politics of Social Policy in the United States*. Princeton, NJ: Princeton UP, 1988.

Weiss, Bernard, J., *American Education and the European Immigrant: 1840–1940*. Urbana, Ill.: University of Illinois Press, 1982.

Wiebe, Robert H., *The Search for Order, 1877–1920*. New York: Hill & Wang, 1967.

Wilensky, Harold L., 'Leftism, Catholicism, and Democratic Corporatism: The Role of Political Parties in Recent Welfare State Development', in: Peter Flora and Arnold J. Heidenheimer (eds), *The Development of Welfare States in Europe and America*, pp. 345–82. New Brunswick and London: Transaction, 1981.

Wilson, Edward O., *Sociobiology: The New Synthesis*. Cambridge, Mass., and London: Belknap/Harvard UP, 1975.

Wilterdink, Nico, *Vermogensverhoudingen in Nederland: Ontwikkelingen sinds de negentiende eeuw* (Diss. University of Amsterdam, with a summary in English). Amsterdam: de Arbeiderspers, 1984.

Withrington, Donald J., 'Scots in Education: A Historical Retrospect', in: D. J. Withrington et al. (eds), *The Scots Language in Education* (Association for Scottish Literary Studies, Occasional Papers, no. 3), pp. 9–16. Aberdeen: Aberdeen College of Education, 1974.

Wittert van Hoogland, E. B. F. F., *De parlementaire geschiedenis der sociale verzekering*. Haarlem: Tjeenk Willink, 1930.

Wohl, Anthony S., *Endangered Lives: Public Health in Victorian Britain*. London: Dent, 1983.

Wohl, Anthony S., *The Eternal Slum: Housing and Social Policy in Victorian London*. London: Edward Arnold, 1977.

Wouters, Cas, 'Onderhandelen met De Swaan', *De gids*, 142 (1979), 510–21. ('Negotiating with De Swaan', paper British Sociological Ass. Conf. on 'The Civilizing Process and Figurational Sociology', Oxford, 5–6 January 1980).

Wright, Lawrence, *Clean and Decent: The Fascinating History of the Bathroom and the Water Closet etc.* London: Routledge & Kegan Paul, 1960.

Wrightson, Keith and David Levine, *Poverty and Piety in an English Village: Terling, 1525–1700*. New York: Academic Press, 1979.

Yeo, Stephen, 'Working-Class Association, Private Capital, Welfare and the State in the Late Nineteenth and Twentieth Centuries', in: Noel Parry, Michael Rustin and Carole Satyamurti (eds), *Social Work, Welfare and the State*, pp. 48–71. London: E. Arnold, 1979.

Zeldin, Theodore (ed.), *Conflicts in French Society: Anticlericalism, Education and Morals in the Nineteenth Century: Essays*. London: Allen & Unwin, 1970.

Zöllner, Detlev, 'Germany', in Peter A. Köhler, Hans F. Zacher with Martin Parrington (eds), *The Evolution of Social Insurance, 1881–1981: Studies of Germany, France, Great Britain, Austria and Switzerland*, pp. 1–92. New York/London: St Martin's / F. Pinter, 1982; also publ. in German.

Index

welfare capitalism, 206
welfare economics, 1–4
welfare regime, 11, 237, 244; *see also* relief regime
witchcraft, 19m 259n.18

workhouse, 42–4, 46–9, 51, 114, 184, 193, 220
equilibrium, 42–9
illusion of the, 7, 42–9, 220
working class strength, hypothesis of, 169, 189